WORLD YEARBOOK
OF EDUCATION 2001

VALUES, CULTURE AND EDUCATION

Edited by
Jo Cairns, Denis Lawton and Roy Gardner

Series Editors:
David Coulby and Crispin Jones

KOGAN
PAGE

First published in 2001

Kogan Page Limited
120 Pentonville Road
London N1 9JN
UK

Stylus Publishing Inc.
22883 Quicksilver Drive
Sterling
VA 20166-2012
USA

British Library Cataloguing in Publication Data

A CIP record for this book is available from the British Library.

ISBN 0 7494 3472 4

Typeset by Kogan Page
Printed and bound by Creative Print and Design Wales, Ebbw Vale

Contents

Contributors

Meesuk Ahn, Post Doctoral Research Associate, Curriculum Studies, Institute of Education, University of London, UK

David Aspin, Professor of Education, Monash University, Australia

Jo Cairns, Senior Lecturer, Curriculum Studies, Institute of Education, University of London, UK

Clélia de Freitas Capanema, Professor of Education, Catholic University of Brasilia, Brazil

Judith Chapman, Dean of Education, Australian Catholic University, Australia

Kai-ming Cheng, Professor of Education and Pro-Vice Chancellor, University of Hong Kong

Pam Christie, Associate Professor, Graduate School of Education, University of Queensland, formerly, University of the Witwatersrand, Republic of South Africa

Rebecca Priegert Coulter, Associate Dean, Faculty of Education, University of Western Ontario, Canada

Olivier Cousin, Chargé de recherche, CADIS-CNRS, Université Victor Segalen, Bordeaux, France

Robert Cowen, Reader in Comparative Education, Institute of Education, University of London, London, UK

Brian Davies, Professor, School of Social Sciences, University of Cardiff, Wales

John Evans, Professor, Department of Physical Education, Sports Science and Institutional Management, University of Loughborough, UK

Susan Douglas Franzosa, Professor of Education, University of New Hampshire, USA

Roy Gardner, Senior Lecturer, Institute of Education, University of London, UK

Candido Alberto Gomes, Professor of Education, Catholic University of Brasilia, Brazil

Andreas Kazamias, Professor of Comparative Education and Policy Studies, University of Wisconsin, Madison, USA and Emeritus Professor, University of Athens, Greece

Val Klenowski, Senior Lecturer, Institute of Education, University of London, UK

Manfred Kwiran, Professor, Faculty of Theology, University of Berne, Switzerland and Director, Institute of Religious Education and Audio-Visuals, Wolfenbüttel, Germany

Denis Lawton, Professor of Education, Institute of Education, University of London, UK

Wing On Lee, Dean of Education and Co-Head of the Centre for Citizenship Education, School of Foundations in Education, Institute of Education, Hong Kong

John Mace, Senior Lecturer, Policy Studies, Institute of Education, University of London, UK

Geoffrey Milburn, Emeritus Professor, Faculty of Education, University of Western Ontario, Canada

Yoshiko Nomura, Director General, Nomura Center for Lifelong Integrated Education, Tokyo, Japan

Audrey Osler, Professor, Director, Centre for Citizenship Studies in Education, University of Leicester, UK

Hugh Starkey, Staff Tutor, Faculty of Education and Language Studies, Open University, UK

Janusz Tomiak, formerly Senior Lecturer, School of Slavonic Studies and the Institute of Education, University of London, UK

Paddy Walsh, Head of Curriculum Studies Group, Institute of Education, University of London, UK

Thyge Winther-Jensen, Professor in Education, Institute of Education, Philosophy and Rhetoric, University of Copenhagen, Denmark

Series editors' introduction

The World Yearbook of Education is probably the longest-running publication of its kind, the first volume being published as far back as 1933. In 1981, Dr Bob Cowen, one of the contributors to this volume, estimated that the volumes published by that date marked a significant monument to scholarship, not least in their sheer volume, as he estimated they totalled more than 3 million words. Twenty years and many volumes later, the total would be much greater.

The first editor of the *Yearbook* was Lord Eustace Percy but Sir Percy Nunn, the then Director of the Institute of Education, London University, was closely involved, an involvement that other directors of the Institute maintained until 1974. Indeed, one of the editors of this volume, Professor Denis Lawton, was also a director of the Institute. As the *Yearbook*'s coverage became less Euro-focused and more international, a close relationship was built up with staff at Teachers' College, Columbia, a fruitful collaboration that lasted until the early 1970s. In 1974, the *Yearbook* ceased to be published by Evans Brothers; the series resumed in 1979, at this point being published by Kogan Page, still the current publisher.

The aim of the *Yearbook* since its inception has been to treat current educational concerns in as thorough and current a manner as is possible. More recently, the globalization of educational concern has made these international surveys a fascinating and valuable comparative resource for educationists around the world.

This current volume on values and culture in education complements last year's *Yearbook*, the concern of which was the analysis of education systems in transition, attempting to delineate the massive changes that had taken place in education systems in the latter part of the last century. This current volume explores some of the key issues that influenced (or failed to influence) those changes. A distinguished group of scholars from around the world offer us a fascinating insight into the range of issues encompassed by the broad themes of values and culture in education. Ably pulled together by the volume's editors, Jo Cairns, Roy Gardner and Denis Lawton, it makes an important contribution to our understanding of some key issues that underlie current educational debates and practices.

David Coulby and Crispin Jones
Series editors

General introduction: Globalization and educational cultures in late modernity: the Agamemnon syndrome

Andreas M Kazamias

Prologue – the myth of Agamemnon

In the Greek tragedy *Iphigenia en Aulis*, the classical dramatic poet Euripides uses the myth of Agamemnon of the House of Atreus to 'theorize' and critically interpret the politico-social conditions and problems of the democratic city of Athens during a turbulent period of its history, ie towards the waning years of the 5th century BC. According to the myth as dramatized by Euripides, Agamemnon the commander-in-chief of the Greek expedition to Troy was enjoined by the gods to sacrifice his beloved daughter Iphigenia so that favourable winds would blow and the huge armada, anchored at the port of Aulis, could set sail for Troy. The expedition to destroy Troy was ostensibly for the purpose of avenging the insult to the Achaians (the Greeks) and the House of Atreus that was perpetrated by the abduction of Helen, Agamemnon's sister-in-law, by the Trojan prince Paris. But there was more to the expedition than mere retribution for an insult. More importantly, perhaps, it was sparked by the Greek arrogance of power as personified in the Argive King Agamemnon, by imperialism and the desire for conquest and domination.

Thus, the myth of Agamemnon is used for a twofold purpose: 1) as a device/tool, to dramatize a particular human condition/problem – this being the emotionally stirring element; and 2) as a way of thinking, to 'theorize' or look critically at a problem, the significance of which could only be revealed through an imaginary, without the dramatist being able to offer a solution. As the classical scholar C M Bowra, referring specifically to Euripides' mythical way of thinking, explains: 'A myth is no less useful when the dramatist is unable to see any solution to a problem and wishes to present it for its own sake, as something which troubles him and of which others should be at least aware' (Bowra, 1957: 127–28).

Like Euripides, but without his dramaturgical artistry, I shall use the myth of Agamemnon and the sacrifice of Iphigenia as a methodological and epistemological device/tool to make a comparative and critical interpretation of a politico-economic and socio-cultural phenomenon that is in the forefront of contemporary social discourse and social policy worldwide. This, simply stated, is the problem of education in the contemporary epoch of 'late modernity', particularly as the problem of education pertains to 'values' and what I would call 'educational cultures'. Reading and reflecting on contemporary trends in this socio-cultural area, both at the secondary level of schooling and at the post-secondary university level, I shall try to dramatize the following saga.

In order for contemporary nation-states to participate effectively and competitively in the world economic system, modern systems of education, as state-steering mechanisms, are called upon to emphasize certain types of educational knowledge and culture at the expense of conventional others. In order to accommodate themselves or adjust to the new societal demands and expectations, secondary schools and, more so, universities, as socio-cultural institutions and significations in modern democratic societies, are being transformed in their identity and role. From socio-cultural enclaves, one of whose main functions has been the construction of persons and citizens with cultivated 'minds and souls', they are being metamorphosed into sites for the production of instrumental knowledge and the acquisition of marketable skills. In such transformation, their mission becomes mainly the construction of knowledgeable, efficient and skilled workers in the competitive world economic markets. To use the ancient Greek word *paideia*, which connoted both education, in the rather narrow sense of instruction, and, more broadly, culture, ie the holistic notion of the formation of both 'minds' and 'souls', schools and universities are being transformed from human enclaves for the cultivation of *paideia* to places for what a contemporary US educational philosopher has called 'education for productive purposes' (Martin, 1995: 78). Especially in the case of the modern European and to a large degree the North American university, the 'idea of the university' is being transformed. University education is changing in orientation and function. It is changing from one whose main ingredient has been the English and US concept of 'liberal education/culture', the German *Bildung*, the French *culture* or the Greek *paideia* to one where the main ingredients are 'instrumental rationality' and what the postmodernist French thinker Lyotard has called 'performativity' (1984). To use Robert Cowen's apt terminology (2000), the modern university is being transformed to 'the market-framed university'.

Globalization in late modernity – blessing or curse?

Writing in 1995, Malcolm Waters in his book *Globalization* reflected: 'By now, just as postmodernism was *the* concept of the 1980s, *globalization* may be *the* concept of the 1990s, a key idea by which we understand the transition of human society into the third millennium.' Indeed, more so perhaps than postmodernism, globalization has become *the* word slogan of the socio-political and economic discourse in the epoch of late modernity. A polymorphous concept, globalization is used to refer to a historical process of social change or modernization as well as to institutions and significations that increasingly characterize the world order. Like other all-encompassing theoretical constructions, however, globalization is a contested and controversial concept. Indeed, some recent European social theorists have questioned its very authenticity, calling it a 'chimera' (Vergopoulos, 2000) or, in equally fanciful language, a 'mythology' (Tombazos, 1999). To such sceptics, globalization has deep historical roots. It has always been there, at least since the advent of modernity in the 18th century or even earlier. So why all the current fuss? Others, however, perhaps the majority of scholars, social theorists or informed observers, to a degree more or less, have been more accepting of globalization as an expansive social and cultural historical reality, whose nature and scope are quite recent. One such intellectual is the well-known and influential English sociologist Anthony Giddens. In his recent political manifesto *The Third Way*, Giddens has written:

> Economic globalization therefore is a reality, and is not just a continuation of, or a reversion to, the trends of previous years. While much trade remains regionalized, there is a 'fully global economy' on the level of financial markets. However, the idea of globalization is misunderstood if it is only applied to connections that are literally world-wide and if it is treated as only, or even primarily, economic. Globalization... is not only, or even primarily, about economic interdependence, but about the transformation of time and space in our lives. Distant events, whether economic or not, affect us more directly and immediately than ever before. Conversely, decisions we take as individuals are often global in their implications. (Giddens, 1998: 30–31)

In the same discursive vein as Giddens, Anthony McGrew understands the concept of globalization as referring to 'the multiplicity of linkages and interconnections that transcend the nation-states (and by implication the societies which make up the modern world system)'. To McGrew, globalization is an all-encompassing social, economic and cultural reality. He elaborates: 'Nowadays, goods, capital, people, knowledge, images, communications, crime, culture, pollutants, drugs, fashions and beliefs all readily flow across territorial boundaries. Transnational networks, social movements and relationships are extensive in virtually all areas of human activity from the academic to the sexual' (McGrew, 1992: 65–66).

Still others have gone as far as to describe the new world order as a 'global village'. Within the space of the 'global village', some social analysts have seen pressures 'toward increased uniformity across traditional national boundaries' and 'homogenization', on the one hand, 'and localized differentiation, on the other'. Ka Ho Mok's recent observation appears to command wide acceptance:

> While there is not a single, consensual definition of globalization, it is evi-
> dent that the whole world is undergoing 'a set of processes which in various
> ways – economic, cultural, and political – make supranational connections'.
> In addition, the impact of globalization has not only been felt in the eco-
> nomic realm but, indeed, has also caused significant changes in the ideologi-
> cal-cultural realm and in the transformation of time and space. Even though
> no country is immune from the impact of globalization, heated debates have
> been held about the positive and negative consequences of globalization.
> (Mok, 2000: 148–49)

We tend to concur with the aforementioned views about the 'empirical reality'
of globalization. In any case, whether it exists in reality or not, globalization
has become a legitimization concept in contemporary discourses and policies
relating to national economies and to national-state management of public
services, in general. It has also become a legitimization concept in the restructuring and reform of educational systems, in particular. In this sense, therefore, ie as part of the rationale that is often used to justify reforms in education,
globalization may be said to have indeed acquired an ontological existence.
Apropos of this, in a recent study on educational reforms in 'Anglo-American
democracies', Davies and Guppy noted:

> In these Anglo-American democracies [Canada, the United States, Australia,
> the United Kingdom and New Zealand], education policy debates are in-
> fused with the imagery of 'globalization'. Whether debating assessment and
> evaluation, curricular content, or school governance, and regardless of who
> is party to the debate (e.g. parents, union leaders, politicians, business advo-
> cates), phrases like 'increasing global competition', 'international trade', and
> 'transnational exchange' dominate. (Davies and Guppy, 1997: 435)

Globalization, whether real or imaginary, is quite germane to our saga regarding changes in values and what we have called 'educational cultures'. Globalization, as a concatenation of social processes, institutions and significations
that transcend national borders, constitutes the context/matrix of the transformation of values and 'educational cultures'. But from our perspective here of a
mythical way of thinking – the Agamemnon syndrome – globalization, *particularly its 'economistic' and rationalistic aspects*, is viewed as more than the historical context of change in values and cultures. Globalization in the sense of
'economic globalization' and 'global rationalization', to use Davies and
Guppy's apt terminology, is also viewed as a 'curse' or, less strongly, as an
anomia (anomie) that propels into action certain choices at the sacrifice of
long-cherished others. Such choices may indeed bring about glory and benefits. In the Greek myth, Agamemnon's choice resulted in the conquest and pil-
laging of Troy. But, in addition to impelling the sacrifice of Iphigenia,
Agamemnon's course of action had other tragic consequences: the complete
destruction of the city of Troy, the rape and enslavement of the Trojan
women, the slaughter of noble men and women and, after Troy, the murder of

Agamemnon himself by Clytaimnestra, his wife, and then Clytaimnestra's murder by her son Orestes. In our story, educational policies, as impelled by globalization, could also have dire consequences.

The Agamemnon syndrome – gaining the world, sacrificing social justice, citizenship and the *paideia* of the 'soul'?

As indicated in recent surveys and more detailed studies, including some of ours, as well as in some important texts by international organizations such as the European Union, OECD, the World Bank and UNESCO, the dominant educational reform discourse, as rhetoric (*logos*) and as framework for *praxis* at the macro-level of public policy and the micro-level of schooling, is pervaded by a predominantly economistic 'ethos', instrumental rationality, 'neo-liberal' values and a business ethic. These ideas and values can be said to inhere in such terms as efficiency, competition, output, yield, markets, liberal individualism, destatization/deregulation, privatization and the like. Below we refer to only a few such narratives.

1 Narratives – gaining the world

(a) In his recent international survey of 'new educational proposals for the global economy', indicatively titled *Education and the Rise of the Global Economy*, Joel Spring documents the contemporary dominant discourse on the interdependent relationship between education and the global economy, with special reference to the geo-cultural regions/rims of North America (the United States), Europe (the United Kingdom and the European Community) and East Asia (Japan and Singapore). He also refers to international organizations such as the OECD, the World Bank and UNESCO. In his words:

> Education and the global economy are envisioned as having an interdependent relationship. Competition in the global economy is dependent on the quality of education, whereas the goals of education are dependent on the economy. Under these circumstances, education changes as the requirements of the economy change. As a result, human capital theory now dominates discussions of education for the global economy. Under human capital theory, education is a social investment that, in the most efficient manner, prepares human resources (students) to contribute to economic growth. (Spring, 1998: 6)

Referring to educational reform discourses and policies (eg school or parental choice, national curricula, national and world-class academic standards, national achievement tests) during the heyday of neo-liberal ideas and virtues, in the United States and the United Kingdom in the 1980s and early 1990s, Spring writes: 'The free market ideas of Friedrich von Hayek provided the

underpinnings for discussions of school choice, national standards and curricula, eliminating the welfare state, and lifelong learning in the United States
and the United Kingdom' (1998: 123). Equally significant for our purposes, the
promulgation of 'free market ideas' was bolstered by neo-conservative capitalist ideas and virtues, and even the 'Protestant ethic'. Thus, the blending of
'religion, capitalism, and nationalism provided a justification for British hegemony over the global economy in the 19th century and American hegemony
in the 20th century'. And reflecting the traditional virtues of the Protestant
ethic, the British Conservative prime minister Margaret Thatcher moralized:
'Capitalism encourages important virtues, like diligence, industriousness,
prudence, reliability, fidelity, conscientiousness, and a tendency to save in order to invest in the future. It is not material goods but *all of these great virtues, exhibited by individuals working together, that constitute what we call the marketplace*
(quoted in Spring, 1998: 128).

The crisis and reform discourse in British and US education continued in
pretty much the same vein as adumbrated above after Thatcher and Reagan,
and has been evident in the rhetoric and policy statements during the current
administrations of the so-called 'third way' political gurus Tony Blair and Bill
Clinton. Core socio-educational ideas, principles, values and reform policies
in the ongoing crisis and reform drama performed on the educational/school
stage in the UK and the United States include, *inter alia*, the following: global-
ization/global economy, and education and training as 'objects of economic
policy'; enterprise culture, competitive free markets and competitive free
market approach to education; standards (national, world-class) and educational achievement, particularly in techno-science and mathematics; lifelong
learning; school/parental or consumer choice; and vouchers.

(b) Similar ideas, principles and education reform policies are reflected in texts
on the larger European scene. For example, Simon Gunn examines the political significance of the 'New Conservatives' and the 'New Right' in the Europe
of the 1980s, and comments on such New Right thrusts as: 1) *modernization,*
'which is closely identified with the *"liberalization"* of the economy and the creation of an *"enterprise culture"*,' and 'a crusading commitment to *free market economics*'; 2) *authoritarianism* 'associated with a concentration of state power in
selective areas and a strong emphasis on *social and cultural traditionalism*'; and
3) *rolling back the state, privatization* and *deregulation* (Gunn, 1989: 20–31).

(c) More pertinently for our purposes, however, is the widely quoted and influential White Paper entitled *Teaching and Learning – Towards the learning society*, issued by the Commission of the European Communities in 1995. This
important paper pays homage to globalization, viz the 'internalization of
trade, the global context of technology and, above all, the arrival of the [global]
information society'. In the global 'learning society' of the future, as predicted
by the authors of *Teaching and Learning*, knowledge and cognitive skills will be
of pivotal importance, especially knowledge and skills in techno-science and

mathematics, particularly for purposes of economic growth and prosperity. The White Paper urged that education and training in the 'learning society' should not be narrowly instrumental, but multi-purpose. It should: 1) focus on '*a broad knowledge base*' and emphasize *breadth* and *flexibility* rather than narrowness; 2) build bridges between schools and 'the business sector'; 3) combat '*social exclusion*'; 4) develop proficiency in 'at least two foreign languages', ie in 'three Community languages'; and 5) 'treat capital investment and investment in training on an equal basis'. The White Paper, further, talked about the importance of 'personal development', the 'passing of cultural heritage' and 'the teaching of self reliance'. Finally, it referred to the development of '*human values*' and '*citizenship*', which according to it '*is essential if European society is to be open, multicultural and democratic*' (Commission of the European Communities, 1995: 5–30).

Nevertheless, from a careful reading of this text it is patently clear that in the imagined global 'learning society' greater emphasis and space were given to the acquisition of certain types of knowledge and the development of cognitive skills that would be instrumental for the productive employability of the worker, for economic growth and the accumulation of wealth, and for national and global prosperity. In this connection, John Field's critical observations of the Paper's reformist orientation are well taken: 'although the White Paper paid due lip-service to the need for personal development and social learning, and even active citizenship, as well as training, there was no sign that the Commission had any concrete proposals in these areas. In fact, the White Paper simply replicated the established boundary between vocational training and general education' (Field, 1998: 75). And so are those of others. In fact, according to Spring, even subjects such as literature and philosophy, not to mention science and mathematics, are viewed not for 'their intrinsic beauty or personal satisfaction', but 'for their instrumental value in improving Europe's position in the global economy' (Spring, 1998: 105; also see Grollios, 1999: 43–51). Field adds that the Commission's White Paper was criticized by the education ministers 'for its vocational emphasis and instrumental approach, indicating that the Commission had fallen victim to an Enlightenment view of social change, in which excessive hopes are placed in knowledge as an end in itself' (Field, 1998: 76).

The core ideas and values, or what we have called the 'educational cultures', as adumbrated in the White Paper on Education and Training (1995), are embodied, to a degree more or less, in other EC texts (reports/papers and programmes). Among the reports, the following are especially worthy of citation: *Growth, Competitiveness, Employment: The challenges and ways forward into the 21st century* (1994); *Education, Training and Research* (1996); *Study Group on Education and Training Report: Accomplishing Europe through education and training* (1997). In addition, one should mention the education and action programmes such as COMMETT, ERASMUS, EUROTECHNET, SOCRATES, COMENIUS and LEONARDO.

(d) Several of the aforementioned core ideas and values are to be found in texts and pronouncements by other international organizations such as the OECD and, as one would expect, the World Bank. The OECD, for example, has unequivocally accepted globalization 'as the dominant trend in the world economy' and the creation of 'a borderless global market system'. More than that, the OECD sees nothing but good accruing from the evolving global economy and the concomitant global marketplace: economic growth, material progress, increased prosperity and human welfare, political stability and greater equality. OECD's educational discourse and policies are connected to what we have previously referred to as the 'economistic' and 'rationalistic' aspects of globalization. These are well summarized as follows: 'Education plays a dual role in OECD's plans. First, education is to aid the development of market economies through human resource development and lifelong learning. Second, education is to remedy problems resulting from globalization such as unemployment, increasing economic inequality, and fears of social and economic change. This dual role is similar to the function of education in European Union policies' (Spring, 1998: 160).

(e) Educational reform discourses and policies that put a high premium on efficiency, performativity, instrumental rationality and knowledge production, marketable schooling and values can also be seen in such differing countries as Japan, Singapore, Hong Kong, Greece, Cyprus and Turkey. In Greece, a member of the European Union, studies by the present writer show that recent efforts at restructuring the educational system and modernizing the curriculum are being made in response to the 'challenges' posed by 'neo-European modernization' and globalization. Specifically, emphasis is being placed on raising national standards, the development of vocationalism in secondary schools and marketable knowledge in post-secondary and tertiary institutions, and generally, as the reform manifesto *Education 2000 – Toward an education/paideia of open horizons* put it, 'the development of competencies and the acquisition of new and flexible skills' (Kazamias, 1997). Furthermore, an Open University has been established and there is a growing private sector of non-accredited post-secondary institutions, the so-called 'Centres of Free Studies' (*Kentra Eleutheron Spoudon*). At the same time, there is considerable pressure to change the constitution to allow for the establishment of private universities. The Open University and the Centres of Free Studies are providing knowledge and training to meet market needs, ie mostly instrumental rationality. This will also most assuredly be the case with anticipated private universities. Even the newly legislated general 'Unified Lyceum' (*Eniaio Lykeio*), a sort of comprehensive upper secondary school considered by some to be the linchpin of the new reform architecture, is perceived less as a cultural enclave for the promotion of *paideia, culture generale* or *Bildung*, and more as a propaedeutic institution preparing youth for post-secondary educational establishments and universities or for the world of work (Kazamias and

Roussakis, 1998). The bias towards schooling for economic efficiency, performativity and a market-oriented restructuring and modernization of the entire educational system, particularly at the post-secondary level, is also noticeable in Cyprus and Turkey, both aspirants to European Union membership. In Cyprus, which listens carefully to developments in Greece, there is talk about 'educational standards', quality control and educational efficiency; new areas of specialization in technical and vocational education have been established; and, most pertinently here, the government is encouraging the marketization of post-secondary education by recognizing and accrediting a host of 'market-framed', consumer-oriented, privately owned and for-profit educational establishments (Kazamias, 1994, 1999).

The case of Turkey presents its own idiosyncratic elements. As a modern state, Turkey in the closing decades of the 20th century was still engaged in nation building along the modernist lines and the ethno-nationalist principles (eg secularism, republicanism, nationalism) as originally laid out by Mustafa Kemal Ataturk and the Kemalists after the establishment of the Turkish Republic in 1923. However, since 1980 its economy 'has been gradually opened to international competition' and the government 'has decided to rely increasingly on market forces by encouraging entrepreneurship, promotion of private investment... and the deregulation of markets'. Also, given a revival of Islam, an attempt has been made to bring about what has been called a 'Turkish–Islamic' synthesis. In the educational arena, the 'principles, objectives, goals and priorities' of national education continue to include such Kemalist ideas as secularism, equality of opportunity and 'Ataturk's nationalism'. Article 42 of the Turkish Constitution states that 'training and education shall be conducted along the lines of the principles and reforms of Ataturk'. At the same time, however, in the basic texts on the reorganization and restructuring of the Turkish national education system, one also notes the following ideas and policy statements:

1. compulsory instruction 'in religious culture and moral education in the curricula of primary and secondary schools';
2. education as 'the most effective instrument of both the democratic and [socio-economic] development processes'; and
3. education to be planned 'in order to meet the socio-economic needs of the individuals and society'.

(OECD, 1989: 93–99)

The OECD study *Reviews of National Policies for Education – Turkey* (1989) reiterates Turkey's policy emphasis on 'economic modernization, privatization, financial stabilization and opening to foreign markets', on education and training for purposes of 'economic and social modernization' and on 'vocational education and training' (pp12–14).

The case of Japan also presents its own idiosyncrasies. These are brought out in a paper by Andy Green, entitled 'Education and globalization in Europe and East Asia: convergent and divergent trends' (1999). Based on a blend of traditional Confucian and modern values, Japan's school system, according to Spring, 'was created by and for the global economy'. The image of the ideal Japanese seems to be that of the moral worker for the global economy, work being the defining element of an individual's citizenship in the new corporate state. In Japanese schools the five subjects of importance, ie Japanese, mathematics, science, social studies and English, 'are considered essential for economic development and Japanese participation in the global economy' (Spring, 1998: 37, 57 and 62). Andy Green also points out that in Japan the 'specific form of articulation' between the formal school system and the labour market is 'not found elsewhere' (Green, 1999).

In Hong Kong, the impact of globalization on education, particularly on higher education, appears to be quite salient. According to a recent study, 'educational practitioners and academics in Hong Kong found themselves caught in an "iron cage of rationality", as Weber suggested' and 'Hong Kong's higher education is going through a process of "McDonaldization"'. Specifically, 'more emphasis has been given to efficiency, calculability, predictability, [non-human technology], and control', which 'has changed the lifestyle of universities'. The impact of globalization on education in Singapore appears to be less salient. But, as in other East Asian countries, 'economic instrumentalism is a cornerstone of educational provision' (Mok, 2000: 172). Singapore's 1997 plan for national education, according to Spring, 'transforms the study of social studies, civics, history, geography, and moral education into methods for promoting self-sacrifice for the economic good of the nation' (Spring, 1998: 86).

(f) The cases of these two East Asian countries gives us the opportunity to add to what was said or implied above with respect to what is happening *in the educational cultures of higher education* in the contemporary period of globalization and late modernity. Commenting on changes in tertiary education, a recent OECD study noted: 'Tertiary education is changing to address client and stakeholder expectations, to respond more actively to social and economic change, to provide for more flexible forms of teaching and learning, to focus more strongly on competencies and skills across the curriculum' (OECD, 1998: 49). Mok's recent study highlights the transformation of university education, in response to the 'economistic' and 'rationalistic' aspects of globalization, in terms of the following phraseology: 'efficiency', 'competitiveness', 'managerialism', 'accountability', 'output based schemes', 'commodification of knowledge', 'the ideology of "market knows best"', 'performance indicators' and the like. The same author adds: 'Students are no longer students but rather clients or customers; admission to the university is about access instead of selection; the curriculum is market driven, and it encompasses practical courses and options which students as customers can choose' (Mok, 2000:

150–51). To these characteristics of contemporary higher education we could add related ideas such as Cowen's 'market-framed university', Lyotard's 'performativity' and others, such as the 'entrepreneurial university' and the 'commercialization of university education'. Cowen has described the market-based university as follows:

> Epistemologically, the market-framed university must deliver marketable, saleable, pragmatically useful knowledge. The market-framed university exists within a knowledge-market, and it must respond to the demands of its clients and customers (e.g., students; research funders). The knowledge production of the university must also be measurable – otherwise performance cannot be judged. Thus managerial decisions must be taken about the differential worth of knowledge products, against rules and criteria which are externally mandated. (Cowen, 2000: 4)

Elsewhere we have argued as follows: in the gradually evolving 'post-Fordist' global economy and the concomitant commercial competition, contemporary societies such as the United States, Germany, the UK and Japan, which depend more and more on scientific and technological knowledge, in order to survive and participate effectively in the global *kosmos*, are called upon to put all their 'knowledge eggs' in the 'techno-scientific basket'. As a consequence, they put pressure on those institutions traditionally responsible for the production of such knowledge, namely the universities, to put a heavier premium on 'techno-scientific' know-how and instrumental rationality. In turn, the university becomes hitched on to the wagon of the economy, its traditional autonomy is eroded and so is the modern *liberal-cultural idea of the university*. In short, we observe the transformation of the modern university from a *studium generale* to a *studium speciale*, where narrow scientific specialism and instrumental rationality have supplanted and overshadowed what in English has been known as 'liberal education' or the 'liberal humanistic canon', in German as *Bildung und Wissenschaft* and in Greek as *paideia* (Kazamias, 1997: 39–42).

2 The sacrifices: social justice, citizenship and the paideia of the 'soul'?

The 'crisis and reform' discourse (*logos*) in education and the concomitant reform policies (*praxeis*) presented above provide us with an excellent modern scenario to use the ancient myth of Agamemnon to dramatize and critically interpret a contemporary socio-cultural phenomenon. In the ancient myth, Agamemnon was 'cursed' because of a family 'hybris' that, as dramatized by Euripides, meant he had to follow a course of action that necessitated the sacrifice of his daughter with ultimately tragic consequences. In our drama, we look at globalization as the 'curse' or the '*anomia*' that enjoins the construction of a certain form of 'crisis and reform' discourse in education as well as certain educational policies. The dominance of this discourse and the attendant educational policies, which were presented in the 'narratives' as staged above, have had as consequences: 1) the 'sacrifice' of what we have referred to as the *cultural* and *liberal humanistic* aspects of schooling and university education, encapsulated in such terms as *culture generale, Bildung* or *paideia*; and 2) a 'shift in values and social ethic', whereby, according to Neave, education is 'increasingly viewed as a sub-sector of economic policy' and less as 'part of social policy' (Neave, 1988: 274). Essentially the same moral (*epimythion*) is implied in judgement statements made by others. For example:

- Stephen Ball has argued that 'problems of globalization frame and produce the contemporary problems of education' and 'new orthodoxies', one of which, according to him, is 'the increasing colonization of education policy by economic policy imperatives' (Ball, 1999).
- John Field has commented that the 'EU's action programmes are relentlessly vocational, utilitarian and instrumental in their emphasis', a 'technological option' that has created a tension between 'instrumentalism' and the European 'attachment to the humanistic tradition of education' (Field, 1998: 8).
- On 'schooling and the free market' in the US and UK, Spring has exclaimed in obvious despair: 'The bean counters are taking over! Accountants and economists are replacing Confucius, Buddha, Plato, John Newman, Robert Hutchins, and the many others who have discussed the meaning of a good education and the good life' (Spring, 1998: 149).
- Robert Cowen has written: 'The contemporary crisis – globalization and the relative increase in powerlessness of the "nation-State" – is not merely an economic crisis. It is a cultural one, which requires historical, sociological, anthropological, cultural and philosophical analysis. If the social and human sciences are impoverished by technicization – by performativity, by pragmatism, by an excessive concern for the immediate and the useful – then one of the defences of nations to understand what is happening to them will be dramatically weakened' (Cowen, 2000: 4).

Epilogue

In Euripides' play *Iphigenia en Aulis*, when Agamemnon's daughter Iphigenia is brought to the altar to be sacrificed, she is snatched by the goddess Artemis and taken to join the gods as a high priestess. Agamemnon is elated and hastens to comfort his distraught wife Clytaimnestra that they should feel happy because their daughter is alive among the company of the gods. He then bids her farewell, telling her that he looks forward to seeing her again when he returns from Troy. Clytaimnestra, however, remains ominously silent. And the curtain falls after these rather sibyllic stanzas by the chorus:

Farewell, son of Atreus, I wish you good voyage to Phrygia
and a good return, bringing with you beautiful spoils from Troy!

Of course, the Athenian audience knew the myth and what these words portended: triumph and spoils, but also tragic consequences. In our 'mythical way of thinking', we have argued that discursive statements and practices in education (*logos* and *praxis*) that are constructed and legitimatized in response and through the prism of globalization and its imperatives may indeed bring wealth, blessings and Trojan spoils. But, as the myth of Agamemnon presaged, they will also necessitate 'humanistic' sacrifices, the loss of social justice, liberal culture and what we would call the *paideia* of the 'soul', with ultimate dire consequences.

References

Ball, S (1999) Global citizenship, consumption and education policy, Unpublished paper

Bowra, C M (1957) *The Greek Experience*, Mentor Books, London

Commission of the European Communities (1994) *Growth, Competitiveness, Employment: The challenges and ways forward into the 21st century*, Luxembourg

Commission of the European Communities (1995) *White Paper on Eduaction and Training: Teaching and Learning – Towards the learning society*, Brussels

Commission of the European Communities (1996) *Education, Training and Research: Elementary obstacles to transnational mobility*, Luxembourg

Commission of the European Communities (1997) *Study Group on Education and Training Report: Accomplishing Europe through education and training*, Luxembourg

Cowen, R (1999) The market-framed university: the new ethics of the game, Unpublished paper, *The Third Way: The renewal of social democracy*

Davies, S and Guppy, N (1997) Globalization and educational reforms in Anglo-American democracies, *Comparative Education Review*, **41** (4), November, pp 435–59

Field, J (1998) *European Dimensions: Education, training and the european union*, Jessica Kingsley Publishers, London

Giddens, A (1998) *The Third Way: The renewal of social democracy*, Polity Press, Cambridge

Green, A (1999) Education and globalization in Europe and East Asia: convergent and divergent trends, Unpublished paper

Grollios, G D (1999) *Ideology, Pedagogy and Educational Policy*, Gutenburg, Athens

Gunn, S (1989) *Revolution of the Right: Europe's New Conservatives*, Pluto, London

Kazamias, A M (1994) *Not for Techne but for Paideia*: Tertiary Education for the 'Good of the City', in the newspaper *Phileleftheros*, Nicosia, Cyprus, February 22/23 (in Greek)

Kazamias, A M (1997) Comparative analysis of the international experience in post-graduate studies and the case of Greece, in *Education 2000, Post-graduate Studies and Research in Greek Institutions of Higher Learning*, pp 26–43, Kallithea, Athens (in Greek)

Kazamias, A M (2000) Crisis and reform in US education: *A Nation at Risk*, 1983 and all that, in *World Yearbook of Education 2000: Education in times of transition*, ed D Coulby, R Cowen and C Jones, pp 214–31, Kogan Page, London

Kazamias, A M and Roussakis, Y (1998) Crisis and reform in Greek education: the modern Greek Sisyphus, in *National Cases: Educational systems and recent reforms*, ed S Lindblad and T Popkewitz, pp 68–115, Department of Education, University of Uppsala, Uppsala

Lyotard, J-F (1984) *The Postmodern Condition: A report on knowledge*, Manchester University Press, Manchester

Martin, J R (1985) Becoming educated: a journey of alienation or integration?, *Journal of Education*, **167** (3), pp 71–84

McGrew, A (1992) A global society, in *Modernity and its Futures*, ed S Hall, D Held and A McGrew, Polity Press, Cambridge

Mok, Ka Ho (2000) Impact of globalization: a study of quality assurance systems of higher education in Hong Kong and Singapore, *Comparative Education Review*, **44** (2), May, pp 148–74

Neave, Guy (1988) Education and social policy: demise of an ethic or change of values?, *Oxford Review of Education*, **14** (3), pp 273–83

Organization for Economic Cooperation and Development (OECD) (1989) *Reviews of National Policies for Education – Turkey*, OECD, Paris

OECD (1995) *Government in Transition: Public management reforms in OECD countries*, OECD, Paris

OECD (1998) Education at a glance: OECD, *OECD Indicators*, OECD, Paris

Spring, J (1998) *Education and the Rise of the Global Economy*, Lawrence Erlbaum Publishers, New Jersey

Tombazos, S (1999) *Globalization and European Union: Introduction to the criticism of globalization and neo-liberalism*, Hellinika Grammata, Athens (in Greek)

Vergopoulos, C (2000) *The Chimera of Globalization*, Nea Sinora–Livanis, Athens (in Greek)

Waters, M (1995) *Globalization*, Routledge, London and New York

Section I

Perspectives on values, culture and education

1. Values, culture and education: an overview

Denis Lawton and Robert Cowen

We are now accustomed to the discourse that stresses the relationship between educational systems and economics. Indeed we are accustomed to the ways in which some educational discourses have absorbed the vocabulary of the market.[1] Policy statements in many countries speak of consumers and choice and diversity and even of the market itself. This is an interesting shift. For 2,000 or even 3,000 years educational discourse used the language of philosophy and religions and not of economics. Defining how to live wisely in the world (and not how to live well off it) has been the oldest educational question.

This has been the case in East Asia, with its Confucian tradition, and within Asia more generally – with its mixture of Buddhist and Confucian traditions. It has also been true of 'the West' whose discourse about values drew on the Greek and Roman civilizations and on the Hebrew and Christian religious traditions. It has also been true of the Middle East and of much of Africa, where educational traditions were also affected by the rise of Islam.

Everywhere the questions have been about the relationships between 'heaven' and society, education and the good person. All of the classic writings in the history of educational thought have drawn on traditions defining the good, the virtuous and the pure before specifying what should properly be defined as educational.

However, within all such traditions, there has typically been a distinction between the virtuous and the very virtuous. Thus within Confucianism, the search for harmony and virtue should be followed by all – but it is especially the virtue of the ruler that is of importance to society. Similarly, virtues were gendered: the correct Confucian virtues should be displayed by women but within a hierarchical pattern. Within the Greek tradition, virtue was not merely gendered but some men were potentially wiser than others and could be most fully wise through education. Plato's philosopher kings were the most virtuous and were kings because they were philosophers. The virtue of others was also linked to their abilities and, as a consequence, to their social position. In the later Western educational tradition the education of the courtier attracted more attention than the education of the son (and finally the daughter) of a peasant.

Overall, then, much of the thinking that has guided definitions of a good education in many cultures has been about the relationship of education to the acquisition of virtue. Discussion of education has been a discussion of the nature of virtue. Discussion about education has been an extension of philosophizing about the metaphysical into the social world. For many civilizations, virtue was not merely metaphysical and personal but also social: it positioned. It was differentially distributed in local patterns: by hereditary inheritance (by caste in India; by race in the southern United States); by social position (the courtier and prince; the labouring classes; and in Mao's inversion, the peasants); by gender and by age (Confucianism).

The educational problem has thus been to decide what virtue is – often by logical deduction from a religious tradition or a world view – and then to define its proper distribution, which frequently meant its differential distribution; the remaining problem was to decide how virtue might be correctly transmitted by education.

Thus for many centuries it is possible to interpret education as being strongly influenced by religion or world views. Later in the 19th century we see the emergence of educational systems that shift their *Gestalt* from being guided and influenced by a church or institutionalized world view to a different principle: nationalism, whether in the expanded form of nationalism known as colonialism and the construction of empire, or through the 'domestic' agenda of nationalism itself – the construction of the nation. Here the definition of virtue in educational systems alters. For example, in Germany, to be virtuous is to be German and a citizen of Prussia. In France in a revolutionary period this might involve interpreting the world as rational and secular, rather than in religious terms. But across Europe and in North America there was a tendency for educational systems to be influenced by the secular ideology of nationalism – although often with some accommodation to the interests of the organized value systems of religion (the churches).

Now – or at least for the moment – after several thousands of years of educational discussion that has addressed the relationship of 'man' to 'heaven' and to 'virtue', we are increasingly accustomed to a discourse in education that uses economic terms as the vocabulary of valuation: it is in economic terms that education itself is to be understood. That which is economic has become that which is virtuous. Virtue is efficiency and effectiveness – values that have been identified in surprising places. For example, Confucianism has been interpreted as carrying values such as caution, thrift or deferred gratification and other variants on the 'Protestant' ethic. However, it should be recalled that the Confucian question was about stability and virtue and the way of heaven, just as the old Puritan question was about the soul and the way of God and therefore virtue. The current Confucian–Protestant equation identifies some fashionable similarities and ignores historic differences. Even the most messianic moments of efficiency and effectiveness (the market and its invisible hand) do not directly pose a metaphysical question.

We note that new virtues have been aggressively defined – how may people and educational systems become effective and efficient? This is a dramatic shift away from the metaphysical. It is such a historical break within a number of traditions that we can ask: how did that happen? How did we get this shift – for many countries – into a value system that trivializes even the rationalized world of Max Weber? How did we get the shift from the religious into the secular?

One way was by defining the secular as if it were religious. That is, the moment that secular social systems are defined as being indicative of relations with God or the devil, the possibilities exist for the worship of the secular. If nations are divisible not merely into the civilized and the barbaric (as in Greece before the Roman Empire, or in the 19th-century Eurocentric world views) but also into 'God' and 'devil' nations, then the secular becomes metaphysical. Thus, if a capitalist social and economic organization is contrasted with a state-socialist system *in these terms*, then this simple mythic reading of the world is a complex cause of the contemporary situation.

In such a populist world view, there were two forms of the social organization of industrial production and there were two main forms of the social organization of political life. The very wealthiest countries produced wealth from corporate industrial capitalism and those very wealthy nations had forms of government that they called 'democratic', sometimes 'liberal democratic'. Other rather wealthy countries produced wealth through industrial production in which the state planned and commanded the economy, and those forms of government were called 'state-socialist', sometimes 'communist'. This of course is a socio-political and a socio-economic classification, which can be extended.

Also in such a populist world view, there were other kinds of countries, which were mainly agricultural, and these were called 'underdeveloped'. These were traditional in their social structure and values and even in their forms of political organization. And there were other kinds of – more promising – countries, which were newly industrializing and these were called 'modernizing'. They had to have social formations that were non-traditional and values that put individualism and hard work first and they were often experimenting with 'democratic' forms of government. In the 'happy ending' of the populist world view, all four groups of nations traded – though the socialist countries traded mainly with each other – until the richest countries became so rich that everyone else gave up and joined them in trading across the world and that was the end of history and socialism. In this pastiche of history, we then reach the absurd point where judgements are entered that this was 'a good thing' and values and cultures and schools are expected to become the same everywhere. History has ended – except for those nations that rejected modernity.

That way of reading the world was mythical: that is, it was a powerful belief system that informed a way of acting upon the world. It was a myth that sustained policy and a myth that sustained research and a myth that sustained much of the activity of the international agencies.

A much more cautious and tentative reading of the world may be advisable, given that it is possible to say that many, but not all, parts of the world have continued to move away from a religious and spiritual world view to one that is more secular and materialistic. In the West, other grand narratives have also been lost: not only religion, but also progress, patriotism and even science. But the values behind the grand narratives seem to have survived in some form. In all cases values are, by definition, embedded in social formations and culture. However, these shifts are not simple and even in a small range of countries need very cautious and qualified illustration. It is useful to work, for a moment or two, on a smaller canvas, such as the shifting balances of individualism and collectivism.

In the move from modernism to late modernity or even postmodernity, one of the changes in culture and values that has received a good deal of attention is the shifting balance between individual and society (or individualism and collectivism).

This has moral, economic, political and educational implications. From Tawney (1926) onwards it was accepted that the Renaissance and the Reformation in Europe encouraged the growth of individualism – the Protestant was encouraged to relate to God as an individual rather than through the mediation of a priest representing the collective Catholic Church – and this swing away from the community and collectivism continued in a different way into the 18th century when Adam Smith's philosophy offered a secular version of individualism. (And we should remember that Adam Smith was a moral philosopher first and an economist second.) This kind of individualism developed into the *laissez-faire* capitalism of the 19th century, and only in the 20th century was there a limited collectivist revival in the form of socialism, social democracy, various versions of the welfare society and a search for values to contest some of the excesses of capitalism. The result in many countries was a 'mixed economy' – an uneasy balance between individualism and collectivism – which continued until, as we shall see later in this chapter, there was a revival of individualism in the 1970s. The two sets of values associated with individualism and collectivism are crucial to an understanding of education in the 20th and 21st centuries.

David Marquand (1996) has offered an interesting and interestingly complex analysis. That paper, which has been curiously neglected by writers on late-20th-century Western culture, began with an expression of dissatisfaction with the polarization of the two key concepts of modernist cultural discourse – individualism and collectivism. Marquand's main point is that, especially since the end of the cold war, the simple contrast between individualism and collectivism is misleading:

However, despite its distinguished lineage, the distinction between individualism and collectivism is too crude to catch the full meaning of the story… Individualism, but for what kind of individuals? Collectivism, but for which collective goals? The abstinent, energetic, self-improving, God-fearing puritans whom Max Weber pictured as the ancestors of modern capitalism were individualists. So were (and are) the rationally calculating utility-maximizers of Jeremy Bentham, of neo-classical economics and of the public-choice theorists of the Virginia School. But the moral and emotional meanings of these two kinds of individualism are far apart: so far, in fact, that it hinders understanding to use the same term for both. The same is true of 'collectivism'. Joseph Stalin and R.H. Tawney both held 'collectivist' values, but their conceptions of the purposes and modalities of collective action were diametrically opposed. (Marquand, 1996: 20)

Marquand neatly solved his self-imposed problem by introducing two additional concepts, covering contrasting notions of the self, the good life and of human possibilities and purposes: Marquand's contrast is between hedonists and moralists. Hedonists see the self as a static bundle of preferences, and the good life as being able to pursue those preferences without interference. On the other hand, moralists see the self as a developing entity, and the good life as progress from lower preferences to higher ones. Hedonists stress satisfaction, moralists engagement and activity. Hedonists reject the idea that some satisfactions can be morally superior; moralists believe 'that it is better to be Socrates unsatisfied than a pig satisfied'. Hedonists are passive; moralists are active.

Instead of a simple contrast between individualism and collectivism, Marquand proposes a fourfold classification: collectivists can be moralist and active or hedonist-passive; so can individualists, valuing liberty either because it promotes pleasure or because it encourages a more powerful form of life. Having established his four categories, Marquand then proceeds to trace the 'ebbs and flows in the struggle for moral and intellectual hegemony' in post-war Britain. Five periods are described, which we summarize as follows:

- *Stage 1. Mid-1940s to mid-1950s: active and moralistic collectivism.* Keynesian social democrats dominated post-war optimistic social thinking. Rights and duties, security and activity were seen as part of the just society. The vision was of a moral society not only because it aimed at the equitable distribution of goods but also because members of that society led good lives, actively participating in a just society.
- *Stage 2. The 1950s to the mid-1970s: hedonist-passive collectivism.* According to Marquand, economists at this time began to see themselves as technicians rather than as Keynesian moralists. The emphasis was now on equality for its own sake rather than as a means to a better (more moral) life. Marquand points out that hedonistic collectivism contains a serious flaw: redistribution makes some better off and some worse off; unless there is

some clear moral purpose in this collectivism, and if rights are not accompanied by duties, why should the rich accept this model? The main failure of the period was not articulating explanations in terms of moral values. This failure was, of course, not confined to the UK or even to Europe.

- *Stage 3. Late 1970s to 1980s: moralistic individualism.* After the 1979 election Mrs Thatcher and others began to express a desire for a return to 19th-century individualistic values: the arguments employed were moral ('Victorian morality') as well as economic. But, according to Marquand, the New Right's moral vision was at odds with its economic values. Market forces do not in themselves possess moral values. The tension between morality and the market was too great: one of them would eventually have to go. Once again the problem of market forces was not a local one – it rapidly became worldwide.

- *Stage 4. Mid-1980s to mid-1990s: hedonistic individualism.* The moralistic individualist vision gradually collapsed and was replaced by hedonistic individualism – selfish consumerism. At this stage the Conservative Party seemed to lose its sense of direction. Late Thatcherism was less attractive than the early moralistic individualism.

- *Stage 5. Mid-1990s onwards: a new version of moral collectivism?* The paper by Marquand was published in 1996, and had presumably been written a year or so earlier. Marquand suggested that by then Stage 4 was giving way to a Stage 5. Marquand suggested that despite talk of moral relativism and other passive tendencies there is still a strong element of moral-activist collectivism in Western political culture. This seemed to be confirmed by the 1997 election in the UK.

A surprising feature of Marquand's analysis was that there was no mention of education. This is a sad omission because the five-stage analysis of the whole post-war period would appear to be extremely relevant to the recent history of educational thought and practice – not only in Europe. Marquand himself was careful to say that his analysis was incomplete and oversimplified. This may be an appropriate time to attempt to fill in one of the gaps by discussing educational change in the United Kingdom in those same five stages:

- *Stage 1. 1940s–1950s: active and moralistic collectivism.* This was an optimistic period for education in which secondary education for all was implemented (without much care about what it might mean – more education was simply taken for granted to be a good thing, which young people would enjoy as a right and participate in for the benefit of society as a whole). Much educational progress was made during this stage of post-war optimism when it was assumed that the world would be a better place for all, but – curiously – insufficient educational planning took place. The moral collectivism was there but not enough active replanning.

- *Stage 2. 1950s–1970s: hedonist-passive collectivism.* The post-war school building programme continued and large numbers of teachers were recruited and trained in most countries on the assumption that expansion was good in itself. There was still plenty of optimism in the educational world despite the findings of official reports, which showed that many young people were happy to leave school as soon at it was legally permitted – or even before. Another feature of hedonism was the view of primary education that stressed the importance of play for young children rather than routine work. Even in secondary schools there was a vision of happy young people rather than anxiety about higher levels of achievement. The value of equal opportunity for a while took precedence over established standards: all political parties moved happily towards comprehensive secondary education, many seeing this as an inevitable long-term trend or as the kind of fairness that parents wanted. Selection was seen not only as unjust but as socially divisive.
- *Stage 3. 1970s to 1980s: moralistic individualism.* By the end of the 1960s the education tide was turning in England and elsewhere. Critics focused on three main targets: the progressive methods (including the play way) in primary schools; the destruction of good grammar schools in the policy of uniform, mediocre comprehensive secondary education; the expansion of higher education and therefore the lowering of standards in universities ('more means worse'). In the United Kingdom, in 1976, James Callaghan, a Labour Party prime minister, demonstrated that the concern about educational standards and purposes was shared by many on the left. Parents and employers were also critical of the educational scene. Criticisms were often expressed in terms of value for money in education, but the malaise went much deeper.

In 1979 there was a famous change of government in the UK. During the Thatcher years there was a clear relation between education policies and political, social and economic developments, which set a trend for many other parts of the world. Consumerism in the form of parental choice became a major theme. All of this was part of an attack on the collectivist state: individual parents knew what was best for their children and those who made efforts on behalf of their offspring should be encouraged to do so, and must be protected from bureaucratic waste and the kind of uniform provision that favoured the producer rather than the consumer. A moralistic element in education policy was ensured by Keith Joseph[2] who not only strongly supported parental choice in education but disapproved of the principle of a state education system.

The moral confusion of the Thatcher years was symbolized by a privatizer being put in charge of an enormous collectivist system. Meanwhile, other legislation along the lines of parental choice consumerism continued during the 1980s. In 1988 a major piece of legislation was masterminded by Kenneth Baker:[3] the Education Reform Act. Baker's moralistic fervour was, however, different from Joseph's. He also disliked uniformity of provision, and encouraged schools to take more individual responsibility, but he also believed in a national curriculum. This was an issue that divided the Conservative Party. More confusion of values: how can a system based on choice also prescribe a national curriculum for all?

- *Stage 4. Mid-1980s to 1990s: hedonistic individualism.* The process of consumerism in education continued to develop in most parts of the world. It was reinforced by what some have referred to as the vocationalization of education, which was characterized by an increased tendency to see the benefits of education purely in terms of improving industrial and commercial efficiency and a desire to measure educational efficiency in terms of pupil performance on a range of arbitrary targets or benchmarks. From time to time the poverty of this one-dimensional approach seemed to be acknowledged and once again discussions about values were raised.

- *Stage 5. Mid-1990s onwards: the return of moral collectivism?* There has been much talk of 'a third way' in politics, but also much scepticism about its distinctive features or even its existence. The only fact that emerges unambiguously is that any third way will be values-saturated. More specifically, such terms as 'inclusiveness', 'pluralism' and 'greater equality of opportunity' become priorities. To what extent might Marquand's distinctions help in the analysis of education and values in the 21st century? In the new millennium what might be the link between education and a new vision of the good life?

One feature of education today that might not have been predicted is the swing back – in many parts of the world – to a view of education that includes a basis in values, together with the explicit inclusion of values education as part of the curriculum. This is, as Wing On Lee points out in his chapter in this volume, sometimes the result of seeking further means of socialization and social control. But there are also examples, as in England, of the curriculum being used consciously to foster democratic values and practices. If the 21st-century view of the good life is capitalist-liberal democracy or social democracy then democratic values of a kind will tend to appear as part of the curriculum: if the desired product of education is a person who is a participating citizen, then the school will take on the task of 'forming' the good citizen – not simply someone who knows what good democratic behaviour is but one who acts accordingly. A very tall order! It may well be, however, that a major shift in terms of educational aims will be away from the moral person to the active citizen and, of course, the hard worker.

Later – perhaps a couple of decades from now – it will be interesting to look back and to compare. Would it be the case that between 1790 and 1970 we saw the construction of 'modern' education systems? That is, patterns of educational institutions that were organized by state agencies to provide mass schooling for more and more people, around value considerations that stressed cohesive and centralist national identities? (Thus, in France, Spain or the UK, regional identities such as those of the Breton, the Catalan or the Welsh were undervalued by those making policy in Paris or Madrid or London.) With hindsight, it may be possible to argue that modern educational systems in their value configurations stressed not merely the acquisition of the literacies required of labour, and the confidence in science and technology required of very skilled labour but also the cohesions demanded in the long processes of social construction of nations. Thus modern educational systems combined the traditional values of a religious identity (or its explicit cancellation) *and* embracement of the values of technical efficiency *and* socialization into principles of social cohesion – of which official nationalism was the major project (of Prussia, of the United States, of France, of Italy, of Greece and of Spain – for example).

In contrast, is it likely to be the case that we saw the beginnings between 1970 and 2020 of the construction of a range of late-modern educational systems? In such an argument, a late-modern educational system in its patterns of pedagogic process, knowledge acquisition and public evaluation locates (a) the moral as the concern of the family, (b) the national principle as the concern of a homogenizing regional agency (NAFTA, MERCOSUR, the EU) and (c) defines the 'values' of the education system as those of effectiveness and efficiency. Thus in the late-modern educational system the values embedded in curricular evaluation, curriculum content and pedagogic process become those of performance and surveillance – to the point where these cease to be techniques and become the main values that educational processes signify and institutionalize.

Perhaps 30 years from now (or sooner?) it may be possible to write of the embracement, in late-modern educational processes, of values and political and economic aspirations that extended 'upwards' beyond 'national' boundaries in an empathetic search for a range of cultural understandings; of values and aspirations that penetrated 'downwards' into democratic and local forms of community participation; and of values and aspirations based on new meta-propositions about relations between homeland and the cosmos. In other words, it would be pleasing to report that two or three thousand years of reflection on the human condition and how to educate the young was no longer being reduced to the proposition that education was an extension of the dismal science of economics and the utilization of all that we knew (from all of the other social sciences) about control and surveillance.

Finally, we note that before the end of the 20th century some church leaders were beginning to criticize the kind of secularism that results in statism. In Ireland Bishop Donal Murray (1995) allied himself with the Chief Rabbi of the Commonwealth in condemning 'a tenacious modern fallacy; the omnipotence of politics, in the narrow sense of governments, policies and parties. Roughly speaking, this amounts to the view that the political system is the only significant vehicle of change in societies as secular as our own' (Sacks, 1991: 11–12). It will be interesting to look back on those statements to see whether they were significant turning-points or whistling in the wind.

Notes

1. John Mace's chapter in this volume includes a criticism of the notion of a market in education.
2. Secretary of State for Education 1981–86.
3. Secretary of State for Education 1986–89.

References

Marquand, D (1996) Moralists and hedonists, in *The Ideas That Shaped Post-War Britain*, ed D Marquand and A Sheldon, Fontana, London
Murray, D (1995) The role of the Catholic school, *Studies in Education*, **11** (1), p 1
Sacks, J (1991) *The Persistence of Faith*, Weidenfeld and Nicolson, London
Tawney, R H (1926) *Religion and the Rise of Capitalism*, Penguin, Harmondsworth

2. Moral perspectives on values, culture and education

Wing On Lee

Values and culture

Value-free social and cultural changes

There was a time, particularly in the mid-20th century, when the notion of value-free culture and education was quite popular. This was a time dominated by positivist beliefs that scientific discovery and technological development are based on rational, empirical and objective criteria not attached to any specific social value systems. As Pacey (1983: 78) put it: 'Technology is value-free. People have come to feel that technological development proceeds independently of human purpose. They see it as the working out of a rational pattern based on impersonal logic.'

This trend of thought was extended to the understanding of socio-cultural change and education. According to Chilton (1989: 135–36), at the time when the value-free belief was prominent, theories accounting for social change tended to ignore the moral or normative causes. These theories can be classified into two major groups, namely the change/i (impersonal) theories and the change/e (empirical) theories of social change. The former group of theories simply ignores the importance of moral factors. Social change does not result from the moral choices of social actors, but instead through technology's impact on them. The latter group admits that social change is affected to some extent by normative choices of social actors, but alleges that these choices basically rest on non-moral factors or principles, such as 'survival for the fittest'. Hence the determining factors for social change are again basically non-normative.

Moral factors in social and cultural changes

However, the above views have increasingly been challenged. It has been refuted that the emphasis on rationality, empiricism and objectivity itself actually reflects a kind of value orientation. Moreover, the increasing concern about environmental problems created by science and technology development has triggered the thought that unless we can develop proper values, sci-

27

ence and technology development may continue to ruin our own planet. Instead of being value-free, science and technology have become perceived as not only value-bound, but even culture-bound (Vente, 1981; Hutchinson and Waddell, 1986: 9).

Translating this argument to society and culture, people also argue that social development is value-bound. Chilton (1989: 139) alleges that 'any complete theory of social change inevitably incorporates a normatively grounded theory of moral choice'. It is because the formation of social institutions mainly depends on 'ways of learning'. In other words, meaningful social intercourse is based upon the participants in a certain society adopting an agreed way of relating or a common framework for interaction. Theories of social dynamics thereby require an embedded empirical theory of how people choose among ways of relating. Although the choice among alternative ways of relating is affected by both normative and practical factors, the normative emphasis is significant. Chilton thus argues that the choice among ways of relating involves both ethical choice and practical choice: a moral decision as to what ways of relating are right, and a practical decision as to what ways of relating the participants can establish as normative.

In discussing the relationship between values and culture, Kluckhohn (1951: 86) points out that the essential core of culture consists of traditional ideas and their attached values. The view is supported by Hofstede (1984: 19–23), who has identified many historical cases showing the persistence of cultural patterns despite sweeping changes to the various cultural groups such as loss of independence, deportation or even loss of language, eg Jews, Gypsies and Basques. From his analysis of cultural patterns in 40 modern nations, Hofstede observes that at the core of the cultural patterns lie societal norms comprising value systems of major groups of population. Social institutions may be changed, such as family, education systems, politics, legislation, but the societal norms, comprising value systems, hardly change. When these social norms remain unchanged, the persistent influence of a majority value system will patiently smoothen the new institutions until their structure and functioning are adapted to the societal norms. To Hofstede, values are an attribute of individuals as well as collectivities, and culture presupposes a collectivity. However, the two interact with each another. On the one hand, culture determines the identity of a human group in the same way as personality determines the identity of an individual. On the other hand, cultural traits can sometimes be measured by personality tests.

Culture and education

Notions of context-free and culture-bound education

The positivists possess a context-free ontology as well as a value-free episte-mology. Within this tradition, the knower and the known are independent of each other, as the known is to be objective and of a distant nature. Applying this view to education, enquiry is both culture-free and value-free. Enquiry is a process of learning to know what is 'out there', and what is known as a result of the cause–effect generalization. Accordingly, the methodology of enquiry is to be characterized by experimental and empirical approaches (Zeera, 1993: 50). However, the critics of the positivists, while rejecting a value-free culture, also reject culture-free education. Instead of holding a deterministic perspec-tive of knowledge, the post-positivists hold probabilistic and speculative per-spectives. Their ontology acknowledges limitation in fully comprehending what is 'out there', and their epistemology is revised to emphasize the need for external guardians, such as the critical tradition and the critical commu-nity, ie the culture, to approximate objectivity. The critical theorists go further to suggest that what counts as truths and procedure is tied to institutional his-tory and social struggles, and values exist at all layers of science. Holding simi-lar ontological perspectives as the post-positivists in acknowledging limitations of full comprehension of the objectivity, the critical theorists de-velop an epistemology that takes into account subjectivist values in the pro-cess of enquiry. As Guba says: 'If values do enter into every enquiry... [and] if the findings of studies can vary depending on the values chosen, the choice of a particular value system tends to empower and enfranchise certain persons' (cited by Zeera, 1993: 53).

Educational attainments as cultural attainments

If values and culture are interactive and intertwined with each other, so is the relationship between values, culture and education. The immanent relation-ship between culture and education is often expressed in national educational documents. For example, in China, the term 'education' is expressed in terms of culture. The term 'cultural attainments or levels' is often used in yearbooks and statistics documents to refer to educational attainments (eg Minister of National Population Statistics, 1993: 124, 132). The term 'educational culture' in the *Statistical Yearbook of Guangdong* (Guangdong Statistics Department, 1992: 9) refers to the educational attainments of the population as well as the educational facilities in the province. In Britain, the measurement of attain-ments in general education is sometimes expressed in terms of cultural attain-ments (Richmond, 1963: 14–15). In the United States, the term 'cultural literacy' emerged in 1983 in *The American Scholar*, a US periodical. Hirsch, in his book *Cultural Literacy* (1988: xi), alleges that cultural literacy is a body of knowledge

that every literate American is expected to possess. This is a basic requirement
of functional literacy, as a minimum attainment of education. The requirement of cultural literacy in education reinforces the view that knowledge,
which is the essential content of education, is always culture-bound. By definition, knowledge is a collective organization, reorganization and interpretation of human experiences; and different collectivities, ie cultures, would have
different ways of organizing and interpreting their collective experiences.

Education as socialization and enculturation

For a long time, education has been seen as a mechanism and process of transmitting culture and values. Such notions as socialization and enculturation ex-
emplify the intricate relationships between education and culture. Chelser and
Cave (1981: 4) concede that the meaning of education is in many ways similar to
that of socialization, a process whereby persons are enculturated into the cultural characteristics of the particular society. This will involve learning to appreciate the shared meanings and values that exist in the culture at large, and that
they internalize these beliefs and values as guides for the conduct of their lives.
According to Hansen (1979: 27–28), enculturation entails acquisition of behavioural skills, knowledge of cultural standards and symbolic codes such as language and art, culturally sanctioned motivations and perceptual habits,
ideologies and attitudes. Enculturation cannot be understood without education, as education denotes a subset of enculturation, which is a deliberate and
systematic attempt to transmit skills and understandings, habits of thought and
behaviour required by the group of which the learner is a novice member.

Durkheim's (1956: 70–71) definition of education is in fact a cultural definition: 'Education is the influence exercised by adult generations on those that
are not yet ready for social life. Its object is to arouse and to develop in the child
a certain number of physical, intellectual and moral states that are demanded
of him by both the political society as a whole and the special milieu for which
he is specifically destined.'

For Durkheim, each society sets up a certain ideal for humans, of what they
should be, not only in intellectual terms, but also in physical and moral. This
ideal is, to a degree, the same for all the citizens, and becomes the foundation
of the social structure. Moreover, Durkheim stresses that society can survive
only if there exists among its members a sufficient degree of homogeneity,
and education plays the role of ensuring the persistence of such homogeneity.
In sum, for Durkheim, the function of education is a kind of socialization.
While Hofstede argues that culture is value-bound, Durkheim (1956: 64, 76)
argues that personal values are culture-bound: 'It is society that has taught us
to control our passions, our instincts, to prescribe law for them, to retrain ourselves, to deprive ourselves, to sacrifice ourselves, to subordinate our personal
ends.' To an extreme, education trains individuals to subordinate themselves
to the collectivity and to become the creatures of the society.

Values and education

No values, no education

If culture is immanent to education, so are values. If education functions as cultural transmission, so does education as value transmission. This is very well put in a British educational document entitled *Choice and Diversity* (HMSO, 1992, para 8.3):

> Education cannot and must not be value-free. Recognizing this, the Education Reform Act 1988 requires the school curriculum to promote the spiritual, moral and cultural, as well as the mental and physical, development of pupils and society. At the heart of every school's educational and pastoral policy and practice should lie a set of shared values which is promoted through the curriculum, through expectations governing the behaviour of pupils and staff and through day to day contact between them. Every attempt should be made to ensure that these values are endorsed by parents and the local community.

Many philosophers of education have viewed the relationship between education and values as both immanent and intricate. For example, Kneller (1971: 26) says: 'Values abound everywhere in education; they are involved in every aspect of school practice; they are basic to all matters. Using values, teachers evaluate students and students evaluate teachers. Society evaluates course of study, school programmes, and teacher competence; and society itself is evaluated by educators.'

Ward's delineation (1971: 428) is even stronger: 'Education is turning towards values. It is for values – it has to be. As soon as we delete values, we delete education. No values, no education; and where there is real education, there are genuine human values.'

Education as a value

According to Ward, there are three types of values: intrinsic values, extrinsic values and contributory values. An intrinsic value is an end-state of value, beyond which there are no higher-order values. An extrinsic value is a means to attain the end-states, or the 'good' that helps people to be. The former is sometimes termed terminal value, and the latter instrumental value. The distinction between terminal and instrumental values is supported by many value analysts, such as Rokeach (1968) and Allport, Vernon and Lindzey (1960). Examples of terminal values are comfortable life, a world at peace and family security, and examples of instrumental values are ambition, responsiveness and self-control.

Ward's major contribution is his insight in identifying the existence of contributory values. He points out that there is a kind of value that is both a means and an end. Health is an example. Health is an intrinsic value itself because health is a terminally good value itself. However, health is at the same time instrumental for achieving other kinds of values. Another example of contributory value is education. Ward argues that education is an inner development. It is something that humans want and something that nature wants. Education is a value and a very human value. However, education is not only a being, ie an end itself, but also an interior becoming, a growth in values, a relative leaving of our primeval stage and a development within us of a relative fullness of humanhood.

Education for values

Butler (1970: 58–61) outlines four types of relationship between education and values. First is the necessity for human subjects to participate in the realization of values in order to achieve and enjoy them, and value realization is an educative process and necessarily involves people in growth and development that is educational at its heart. Second is the nature of school as a value-realization institution. Individually, education begins with the individual pupil as he/she is at any given stage in his/her growth and nurture and seeks to convey him/her into a stage of development and value achievement that is not now actual. Socially, education begins with its society or culture as it is at a given point in history. The school not only conserves what is good in the culture, but its vision reaches quite beyond this objective to conveying the society into a new orbit of value possession, in which that which is desired, but is not now actual fact, becomes more than an ideal or an objective, namely, a present realized possession of the culture.

Third is the necessary relationship between educational objectives and value theory. Any objectives that can be conceived for any phase of life are an expression of value judgements. And when objectives are proposed for education, whether general or specific, whether by teachers or administrators for individual classes or schools, or by national bodies, some answers to value problems are implicit in these objectives. And those objectives cannot be adequately conceived without being formulated in the light of a value theory. Fourth is the significance for children and youth of their value problems and decisions. Value problems are the first reflective steps of maturing youth. They provide the first occasion for reflective decisions; therefore value concerns in education are of unique importance with all children, but especially with adolescents because in their struggles and tensions are the early occasions for genuinely reflective decision. Every child must come eventually to live his/her own life with some measure of responsibility. The closer he/she can approach a theory of value within which his/her value judgements can make some real sense, the more adequate and responsible he/she can be in facing the demands of life. It is for this purpose that his/her value experiences can be made educational.

Competing approaches to values education: descriptive and prescriptive

Butler's discussion has touched upon the major controversies and dilemmas in the relationship between values and education. This relates to the questions of whether school plays a role of attaining individual value judgements and value realization that are important to the pupils as individuals, or whether school plays a role of transmitting societal values that perpetuate the culture of the society. Butler has presented these two perspectives from a complementary perspective, ie both for individual and societal purposes. But for many value theorists, the two can be competing concepts. In his opening chapter of a recent book on education and values, Halstead (1996b: 5) asks a list of questions pertaining to the competing functions of education in teaching values:

- Do the values that are currently taught in schools necessarily reinforce (intentionally or otherwise) the privileged position of certain social classes or religious or cultural groups?
- Are there any absolute values?
- Should schools reflect *traditional* values or seek to transform these?
- Should schools instil values in pupils or teach them to explore or develop their own values?
- Should teachers aim for a neutral (or value-free) approach to their subject matter?

The way these questions are answered will more or less determine the approaches to values education in school. Two major approaches to the education of values in school can be identified in the literature, namely prescriptive and descriptive. The prescriptive approach to the education of values is variously described as a value transmission approach, focusing on moral content, and sometimes loosely called 'moral education'. The primary concern of this approach, in the process of values education, is to distinguish between what is moral and immoral. It has an emphasis on shared or approved values of society, and has a tendency to assign a particular sort of values and standards to persons, actions, intentions, policies and decisions. It aims to produce behaviour and attitude in children that are seen as morally good. It also considers the achievement of this behaviour and attitude as one of the goals of educating values, and one of the indications of its effectiveness.

The descriptive approach to education of values would define the role of education as mainly describing what we refer to as 'the moral area', ie a particular category of issues, concerns and activities distinguishable from other categories such as the scientific, or the artistic, or the political, or the religious area. 'Moral' in its descriptive sense merely defines the limits within which 'operations in the moral area' can take place. People considering what is morally good will distinguish between what is moral and non-moral. This approach is seen as holding a procedural, rather than the moral content, with emphasis on certain ways of thinking and reasoning that children will need to acquire if they are to become 'morally educated' (eg values clarification and the development of moral reasoning) (Straughan, 1988: 27–42; Frankena, 1975: 23–24).

The complicated relationships between descriptive and prescriptive approaches

The two approaches, however, may not be at all easy to entirely separate from each another. Kohlberg's moral reasoning and Raths's values clarification approaches can be classified as descriptive approaches to the education of values. However, to some extent, they become prescriptive. For instance, Kohlberg's notion of justice as the highest order of value is prescriptive; so is his belief in Stage 7, defining the highest order of values from religious origins (Kohlberg, 1981). Concerning values clarification, even though the value judgement process can be rationally descriptive, when pupils have to act upon values, they are bound to face the dilemma of choosing between socially acceptable norms and personal values, and this cannot be dissociated from prescriptive concerns. Moreover, the guide for teachers to help pupils with value clarification has strong emphasis on feeling or emotional aspects, and because of this the process of value judgements is not at all 'descriptive' (see Raths, Harmin and Simon, 1966). Jarrett's (1991: 15) discussion of Socrates' philosophy is very revealing. According to Jarrett, Socrates' philosophy has two major concerns: morality and logic. But for Socrates, logic and morality were much closer to each other than might be supposed. On the one hand, Socrates practised his logic on the definition of such terms as piety, friendship, courage, moderation. On the other hand, Socrates took the position that immoral conduct is invariably a matter of mistaken thinking. 'Famously, Socrates professed himself to be ignorant of the answers to the questions he propounded, with perhaps only one exception: the dependence of virtue upon logical reasoning,' says Jarrett (1991: 15).

Moral perspectives of values and culture

Moral values as the core of values and culture

Values can be defined and categorized differently according to the different frameworks of the value theorists. Ormell (1980: 78–79) classifies values into moral values, aesthetic values, social values, spiritual values, intellectual values and educational values. Obviously, morality is only one kind of values in Ormell's framework. Moral values refer to the judgement of the worth of actions and products; aesthetic values refer to the judgement of the worth of actions and products that affects the impact of a situation on the senses; social values refer to the judgement that affects the manner of life in communities; spiritual values refer to the judgement that helps people see a purpose or meaning in life; intellectual values refer to the judgement that helps people achieve a coherent mental picture of the natural and human worlds; and education values refer to the judgement conducive to the education of the child.

There are three types of values, according to Blachford (1972), namely behavioural, procedural and substantive. Behavioural values are those related to a mode of conduct that underlies our behaviour towards other people. Procedural values involve the valuing of the various ways of thinking. Substantive values are those values that guide people in judging controversial issues in society and the world.

Other kinds of classifications and definitions include: health and comfort, ambition, love and friendship, ethical or moral, knowledge, and technology (efficiency) (DeWitt H Parker, cited by Jarrett, 1991: 13); moral, aesthetic, intellectual, religious, economic, political and legal (Paul Taylor, cited by Jarrett, 1991: 13); desirable end-state or behaviour, transcendent situations, and guide selection of behaviour (Schwartz and Bilsky, 1990: 878); moral, religious, cultural, aesthetic, civic, democratic, national, personal and social, and pastoral (Taylor, 1994: 11–12), etc. However, as Jarrett observes (1991: 13), despite the variation in typologies, they overlap with moral values. Moral value lies at the heart of the various types of values. Particularly, in Ormell's classification, meanings of the various kinds of values develop from moral values.

Some value theorists look at values mainly from a moral perspective. Scott (Scott and Scott, 1965: 1, 3) defines values as moral ideals, or the bases of moral judgements. Rokeach (1968: 159–60) defines values as mode of conduct:

> To say that a person has a value is to say that he has enduring belief that a specific mode of conduct or end-state of existence is personally or socially preferable to an opposite and converse mode of conduct or end-state of existence. Once a value is internalized it becomes, consciously and unconsciously, a standard or criterion of guiding action, for developing and maintaining attributes towards relevant objects and situations, for justifying one's own and others' actions and attitudes for morally judging self and others and for comparing oneself with the others.

Moral perspectives of education

Values education as the core objectives of education

It is important to note that values education is seen as important across countries. In the Values in Education in Europe survey conducted by the Consortium of Institutions for Development and Research in Education in Europe in the early 1990s, over three-fifths of the 26 participating countries clearly dem-

onstrated that certain values are explicit in the general goals of education issued by the ministries of education in the respective countries. Some of these
examples are:

- Malta: The National Minimum Curriculum stipulates that 'good
  behaviour' ought to result from values education as well as a respect for
  God and fellow citizens.
- Romania: The general aim of [Romanian education] is embodied in various
  educational objectives focusing on the peculiar teaching – learning process
  of intellectual, moral, aesthetic, social and other values, during specific
  school stages.
- Hungary: According to the proposed 'law of education', values education
  should get more attention, first of all mediating traditional, national and
  general human values, individualism, values of national identity and
  ethnic tolerance.
- Sweden: The Curriculum Guides stress the teaching of values in their
  overriding aims.
- Slovenia: Values education is… integrated in the principle of education as
  a whole by an argument that the choice of teaching content, the structure
  of the curriculum plan already present a kind of value orientation. This
  document includes a range of moral principles or principles related to
  values education.

(Taylor, 1994: 25–26)

Values education as moral education

Values education covers a wide range of areas, including religious values,
character building, cultural heritage, societal norms, political values, mode of
behaviour, attitudes, affection towards the nation and the community, ideologies etc. However, like morality that overlaps with the various typologies of
values, moral education overlaps with the various definitions of values education. This does not only apply to the Asia-Pacific countries, but also to the
Western countries. In the Values in Education in Europe survey project conducted in the early 1990s, when asked to define values education, several
countries defined values education in terms of moral education, such as:

- Austria: Conveying specific attitudes and moral viewpoints.
- Belgium: Education in moral values.
- Finland: Supporting pupils' ethical growth.
- Germany: The terms 'moral/ethical education'… and 'values education'
  are used almost synonymously. The moral dimension of education is
  discussed in connection with social, political and religious education.
- Russia: Speaking about values education usually means moral and
  political values.

(Taylor, 1994: 11)

Obviously, there are education theorists who see values education in terms of moral education. As Beck (1981: 210) says: 'Indeed, in large measures values education and ethical [moral] inquiry are the same thing, no matter how elementary the level, and accordingly have methodologies and contents in common.' In China, the definition of moral education, values education and political education is far from clear-cut, and the terms are officially used interchangeably. Moral education is referred to as ideo-political education or ideo-moral education, and is seen as a means of transmitting ideological and political values (Lee, 1996: 106).

The definitions of values education and moral education do overlap with each other. In a cross-country affective education study conducted by UNESCO that involves basically the Asia-Pacific countries of the Education for Humanistic, Ethical/Values and Culture project, the definitions of values education and moral education overlap. For example, in referring to the meaning of moral education, the report quotes:

- In the countries where moral education is taught as a distinct subject, it is defined as a sequence of experiences and activities aimed at preserving, developing and promoting good behaviour, values, attitudes and characteristics of the individual societies. Belief in God is highlighted. Moral education is also designed to promote national ideologies and philosophies.
- Objectives of moral education were reported as: inculcate desirable habits, values and attitudes; educate pupils to become good citizens who believe in Almighty God; foster national integration and national identity; control and be responsible for one's own actions; understand basic manners and moral rules needed in everyday life; acquire knowledge needed for living in village communities and social organizations; believe in the state ideology; and train children in revolutionary ideas.

In referring to values education, the report mentions:

- To ensure that social, civic and scientific values are taken care of, without focusing on a particular religion. Furthermore it is easy to integrate such values in existing areas and avoid the possibility of exercising one's religious bias under the name of moral education.
- Objectives of values education were reported as: the teaching of human values and moral ideas concerning cleanliness, truth, kindness, obedience, patriotism, justice, dignity of labour and the teaching of scientific values, which are similar to those in moral education.

(UNESCO, 1992: 21–22)

As mentioned above, debates on moral or values education can be largely categorized into the descriptive or prescriptive approaches. Moreover, the former is seen as more associated with Western educationists and the latter with Eastern educationists. However, as also mentioned, the two approaches are sometimes difficult to entirely dissociate from each another. When looking into recent developments in moral education across countries, it is interesting to find that prescriptive emphasis becomes increasingly prominent in countries in which descriptive approaches have been emphasized and vice versa.

Recent emphases on moral education in Britain

Values clarification and positivist approaches have been very prominent in the West for several decades since their introduction in the 1960s. However, despite their merits, these approaches have increasingly been criticized as individualistic and relativistic, without being able to provide any guidance to the younger population for appreciating and adhering to social and cultural traditions and norms. The moral reasoning approach also received criticism. There were reports of difficulties in handling discussions of moral dilemmas in the classroom (Leming, 1997; Mortier, 1995). The increase in youth moral problems, like drug and alcoholic addiction and juvenile delinquency, have made people question more and more to what extent young people should make their own value judgements without adult intervention, and how neutral the adults should be in the process (eg Warnock, 1996: 50–51). On the other hand, directive approaches have been very prominent in the East, but with increased exchanges with the West, as well as economic liberalization, especially in the case of China, there are more and more emphases on allowing for individualization in values education.

For example, in Britain, the descriptive approaches to values education have been rather prominent. This is represented by an emphasis on meaning clarification in the tradition of logical positivism, an emphasis on rationality and personal autonomy in values education and an emphasis on the process rather than 'ends' in education in general. However, these assumptions have recently been challenged. Liberal values are challenged by the need to define limitations to personal freedom and draw attention to utilitarian values that suit the upcoming enterprising economy (Dunlop, 1996: 84; Halstead, 1996a: 27–28; Pring, 1996: 109–11). While the value of personal choice has been maintained, there has been increased emphasis on 'shared values' in the values education literature in the 1990s (Warnock, 1996: 48–49; Taylor, 1996: 125–26; Talbot and Tate, 1997). Moreover, there are emphases that teachers and parents should steer children in the directions of development, so that they can possess certain moral qualities, eg pleasure-loving, altruistic, commitment and the pursuit of shared values, which are prerequisites for an autonomous person (White, 1990: 76–77). The National Curriculum Council's discussion paper on spiritual and moral development published in 1993 has made a clear departure from the neutral stance of the school and teacher. First, it has stated clearly the moral expectations on children:

- Children need to know the difference between right and wrong.
- Personal morality combines the beliefs and values of individuals, those of the social, cultural and religious groups to which they belong, and the laws and customs of the wider society.
- Morally educated school-leavers should be able to distinguish between right and wrong, articulate their own attitudes and values, take responsibility for their own actions, recognize the moral dimension to situations, understand the long- and short-term consequences of their actions for themselves and others, develop for themselves a set of socially acceptable values and principles, and set guidelines to govern their own behaviour, recognize that their values and attitudes may have to change over time, and behave consistently in accordance with their principles.

Second, schools should uphold and reject certain values:

- Schools should be expected to uphold those values that contain moral absolutes, including telling the truth, keeping promises, respecting the rights and property of others, acting considerately towards others, helping those less fortunate and weaker than ourselves, taking personal responsibility for one's actions, and self-discipline.
- Schools should reject such values as bullying, cheating, deceit, cruelty, irresponsibility and dishonesty.
- It is important that a school establishes those values that determine behaviour throughout the school and particularly in the classroom.
- Values lie at the heart of the school's vision of itself as a community.
- The most important point about a statement of values is that it should be implemented.

Third, teachers should realize that they have a responsibility in moral education:

- Values are inherent in teaching.
- Teachers are by the nature of their profession 'moral agents' who imply values by the way they address pupils and one another, the way they dress, the language they use and the effort they put into their work.

While prescriptive approaches are being built upon the descriptive traditions in Britain, an opposite direction can be identified in the East. For example, the Korean report in the Asian study on education for humanistic, ethical/moral and cultural values says:

> The approach to moral education in the sixties had emphasized conformity and practices of existing moral principles. However, from the late seventies, this approach has been changed into an approach that has focused on rational moral judgement and underlying principles of moral values. (NIER, 1991: 30)

Recent emphases on values education in Asia

Moreover, the affective development project, mainly comprising Asian countries, has actually adopted a descriptive approach to values education. In defining the project, the report says what it is not:

- It is not prescriptive: values cannot be imposed.
- It is not exhaustive: it does not purport to be a complete list of human values.
- It makes no statement on regional, local and institutional needs and priorities.

And what it is:

- It is descriptive: it is an attempt at an orderly description of a desirable value system on the basis of an understanding of the human person.
- It is conceptual: it lists ideals that have to be internalized in the educational process.
- It is broad and flexible enough for adaptation to specific contexts.
- It is desirable that regions, localities and institutions construct their own values map, with clearly defined priorities, suited to their peculiar context and needs.

(UNESCO, 1992: 61–62)

Recent emphases on moral education in China

In China, where moral education is always ideologically and politically defined, significant adaptations can be identified since the adoption of the open policy and the Four Modernizations in 1979. In 1985, a 'Notice on reforming the teaching of the ideological, moral and political theory curriculum in schools' was issued by the government, with clear stipulations on the adoption of a descriptive-orientated approach. Some of the points made in the Notice are:

- Avoid indoctrination, but use eliciting/heuristic methods of teaching, guiding students to raise their knowledge level, and seek answers to questions by self-learning and independent thinking.
- Teaching should be supported with evidence and facts, instead of simply indoctrinating concepts.
- Encourage students to organize free class discussions, field practice and surveys, in order to nurture capacity of discovery, questioning and answering theoretical and practical questions.
- Introduce to students a variety of perspectives, and encourage them to be engaged in free and interesting discussions, on the basis of the Four Upholds, in order to help them get hold of Marxist methods and theorizing principles.

(Lee, 1996: 113–14)

In 1990, the government issued another document, namely 'Opinions on further strengthening of moral education work in primary and secondary schools'. While reiterating the need for education for patriotism and collectivism, the document also stressed the need for cultivating students' capacities of self-management and self-education, as well as integration between collectivism and individualism, and called for the expression of individual characters in the collectivity. In fact, emphases on self-management, independent learning and autonomy abound in the literature on moral education in China since the 1980s. For example, Li (1992) proposes self-education in moral education, and argues that unless pupils know how to establish their values, they cannot counter bad influences in the society. Li and Zhong (1997: 108–09) write in a text on moral education:

> The pursuit of values in life requires one to rationally ensure one's value goals… As experience proves, the more such pursuit fits one's personal needs (including the choice of starting point, content, methods, process), the more there is an awareness of choice, the more effective is the pursuit of values, and the more possible it is to apply the values to practice. From the point of view of life establishment, life is a matter of choice.

According to content analyses of Chinese language textbooks in Hong Kong, it is found that there is significant emphasis on self-orientated values. However, interpreters of this self-orientation suggest that self-orientation in the Chinese context actually refers to self-cultivation, which is actually a kind of character building essential for attainment of shared values at the societal level (Lee, 1997: 125).

Conclusions

The review in this chapter delineates the immanent relationships between culture, value, morality and education. Culture represents a set of values adopted by a society, accumulated over time, which provides society's continuity. Culture is thus always defined in terms of values. According to this understanding, values are also culture-bound. However, values, at the same time, are a determinant for culture, as cultural differences across societies and communities are always reflected or measured by differences in value systems. Further, values, despite being loosely, and thus always variously, defined into typologies, also have very strong moral connotations. Values form the bases of moral judgement, as well as the determinant of the mode of conduct. At one extreme, values are perceived as moral values. Education plays a role of transmitting values, preserving culture and sustaining both personal and social morality.

However, the role of education is not confined to preservation and transmission. It also plays a role of development. It is the discussion on this dual role that characterized educational debates in relation to culture, value and morality. From a cultural perspective, the conservative role of education is reflected in its functions as socialization and enculturation. However, for human and societal development, there is a need to emphasize acculturation that focuses on adaptation of culture to social changes, as well as critical enculturation that requires critical judgement in determining what kinds of cultural traditions to maintain, and what new cultures to develop.

From the perspectives of value and moral education, the conservative role of education, being seen as prescriptive, is reflected in value transmission and inculcation of moral judgements. Both the value and the moral dimensions are so vast that nearly any value-related areas can be covered including religious, political, ideological and behavioural. It is this vast coverage that makes values education and moral education difficult to define, difficult to determine where it is to be taught and how it is to be taught. Moreover, educationists never agree upon the conservative role of education on values and morality. Their struggle for a descriptive role focuses on individual and rational judgements, with open option for choices. However, how far, and how early, the individual choices can be exercised is always a struggle. To societies where the descriptive approaches are prominent, there are worries about the lack of directions provided for the individual, and also the lack of adherence to social norms. To societies where the prescriptive approaches are prominent, there are also concerns for the lack of personal autonomy, and thus personal initiatives. Evidence suggests that every society is struggling between the conservative and liberalizing roles of education. The dissatisfaction towards one of the roles being dominant seems to be pervasive in all societies in all times, as well as the struggle for a balance towards the two contrasting roles. However, the review above also suggests that the two contrasting roles are contradictory on the surface, but there can also be some overlap between the two. That is where the complications reside.

References

Allport, G W, Vernon, P E and Lindzey, G (1960) *Study of Values: Manual and test booklet*, Houghton Mifflin, Boston

Beck, C M (1981) The reflective approach to values education, in *Philosophy and Education*, ed J F Soltis, The University of Chicago Press, Chicago

Blachford, K R (1972) Values and geographical education, *Geographical Education*, (1), pp 319–30

Butler, J D (1970) The role of value theory in education, in *Theories of Value and Problems of Education*, ed P G Smith, pp 58–64, University of Illinois Press, Urbana

Chelser, M and Cave, W (1981) *A Sociology of Education: Access to power and privilege*, Macmillan, New York

Chilton, S (1989) Any complete theory of social change inevitably incorporates a normatively grounded theory of moral choice, *Journal of Developing Societies*, **IV**, July–October

Dunlop, F (1996) Democratic values and the foundations of political education, in *Values in Education and Education in Values*, ed J M Halstead and M J Taylor, pp 68–78, The Falmer Press, London

Durkheim, E (1956) *Education and Sociology*, tr S Fox, The Free Press, New York

Frankena, W K (1975) Morality and moral philosophy, in *Moral Education*, ed B Charzan and J F Soltis, pp 19–29, Teachers College Press, Columbia University, New York

Guangdong Statistics Department (1992) *Statistical Yearbook of Guangdong*, China Statistics Press, Jiangxi

Halstead, J M (1996a) Liberal values and liberal education, in *Values in Education and Education in Values*, ed J M Halstead and M J Taylor, pp 17–32, The Falmer Press, London

Halstead, J M (1996b) Values and values education in schools, in *Values in Education and Education in Values*, ed J M Halstead and M J Taylor, pp 3–14, The Falmer Press, London

Hansen, J (1979) *Sociocultural Perspectives on Human Learning: An introduction to educational anthropology*, Prentice Hall, Englewood Cliffs, NJ

HMSO (1992) *Choice and Diversity: A new framework for schools*, Presented to Parliament by the Secretaries of State for Education and Wales, HMSO, London

Hirsch, E, jun (1988) *Cultural Literacy: What every American needs to know*, Vantage Books, New York

Hofstede, G (1984) *Culture's Consequences: International differences in work-related values*, abridged edn, Sage Publications, Newbury Park

Hutchinson, F and Waddell, L (1986) *People, Problems and Planet Earth*, Macmillan, Melbourne

Jarrett, J L (1991) *The Teaching of Values: Caring and appreciation*, Routledge, London

Kluckhohn, C (1951) The study of culture, in *The Policy Sciences*, ed D Lerner and H Lasswell, pp 86–101, Stanford University Press, Stanford, CA

Kneller, G (1971) *Introduction to the Philosophy of Education*, John Wiley & Sons, New York

Kohlberg, L (1981) *Essays on Moral Development*, vol 1: *The Philosophy of Moral Development*, New York, Harper & Row

Lee, W O (1996) Changing ideo-political emphases in moral education in China: an analysis of the CCP Central Committee Documents, *Asia-Pacific Journal of Education*, **16** (1), pp 106–24

Lee, W O (1997) Measuring impact of social value and change, in *Values in Education: Social capital formation in Asia and the Pacific*, ed J D Montgomery, pp 113–33, Hollis Publishing Co, Hollis, New Hampshire

Leming, J S (1997) Whither goes character education? Objectives, pedagogy, and research in education programmes, *Journal of Education*, **179** (2), pp 11–35

Li, P (1992) A preliminary study on cultivating the self-education abilities of pupils, *Curriculum, Teaching Materials and Teaching*, (7), pp 29–31 (in Chinese)

Li, P and Zhong, M H (1997) *Introduction to the Cultivation of Life*, Zhongshan University Press, Guangzhou (in Chinese)

Minister of National Population Statistics, ed (1993) *China Population Statistics Yearbook 1992*, China Statistics Press, Beijing

Mortier, F (1995) Separate values education and moral development in Flemish secondary schools, *Journal of Moral Education*, **24** (4), pp 409–27

National Curriculum Council, UK (1993) *Spiritual and Moral Development: A discussion paper*, National Curriculum Council, York

NIER (1991) *Education for Humanistic, Ethical/Moral and Cultural Values: Final report of a regional meeting*, National Institute for Educational Research, Tokyo

Ormell, Christopher (1980) Values in education, in *Values and Evaluation in Education*, ed R Straughan and J Wrigley, pp 71–95, Harper & Row, London

Pacey, Arnold (1983) *The Culture of Technology*, The MIT Press, Cambridge, Mass

Pring, R (1996) Values and education policy, in *Values in Education and Education in Values*, ed J M Halstead and M J Taylor, pp 104–17, The Falmer Press, London

Raths, L E, Harmin, M and Simon, S B (1966) *Values and Teaching: Working with values in the classroom*, Merrill, Columbus, Ohio

Richmond, W K (1963) *Culture and General Education*, Methuen, London

Rokeach, M J (1968) *Beliefs, Attitudes and Values*, Jossey-Bass, San Francisco

Schwartz, S H and Bilsky, W (1990) Toward a theory of the universal content and structure of values: extensions and cross-cultural replications, *Journal of Personality and Social Psychology*, **18** (5), pp 878–91

Scott, W A and Scott, R (1965) *Values and Organizations: A study of fraternities and sororities*, Rand McNally & Co, Chicago

Straughan, R (1988) *Can We Teach Children to be Good? Basic issues in moral, personal and social education*, new edn, Open University Press, Milton Keynes

Talbot, M and Tate, N (1997) Shared values in a pluralist society? in *Teaching Right and Wrong: Moral education in the balance*, ed R Smith and P Standish, pp 1–14, The Cromwell Press Ltd, Wiltshire

Taylor, M, comp and ed (1994) *Values Education in Europe: A comparative overview of a survey of 26 countries in 1993*, The Consortium of Institutions for Development and Research in Education in Europe, Dundee, UNESCO, New York

Taylor, M (1996) Voicing their values: pupils' moral and cultural experience in *Values in Education and Education in Values*, ed J M Halstead and M J Taylor, pp 121–42, The Falmer Press, London

UNESCO (1992) *Education for Affective Development: A guidebook on programmes and practices*, UNESCO Principal Regional Office, Bangkok

Vente, E (1981) Reconciling technical learning with cultural learning, in *Cultural Heritage versus Technological Development: Challenges to education*, ed E Vente, R Bhathal and R Nakooda, pp 8–14, Maruzen Asia, Singapore

Ward, L (1971) Education and values, in *Modern Philosophies of Education*, ed J P Strain, pp 428–38, Random House, New York

Warnock, M (1996) Moral values, in *Values in Education and Education in Values*, ed J M Halstead and M J Taylor, pp 45–53, The Falmer Press, London

White, J (1990) *Education and the Good Life: Beyond the national curriculum*, Kogan Page, London

Zeera, Zahra Al (1993) Paradigm shift in the social sciences in the East and the West, in *Knowledge Across Cultures: Universities East and West*, ed R Hayhoe, pp 49–74, Hubei Education Press, Hubei/OISE Press, Toronto

3. Religious perspectives on values, culture and education

Jo Cairns

Introduction

> A careful look at the struggles over religion and public education in the United States for the last many decades, and an examination of the climate of the country on the eve of the new millennium, leads this historian to conclude that many issues about the proper relationship between religion and the schools are likely to be lively ones for a long time to come. (Fraser, 1999: 217)

Modernity as the context of religious perspectives on values, culture and education

Writing about religion and education at the turn of the century has a curious edge. The reflection and analysis from which it comes seem unable to ignore the curious symmetry of the figures involved in the Western calendar of this time. Yet the spirit of modernity challenges such unreasonableness. Modernity itself was the key to understanding the Western world as it turned the last century. In turn science, technology, industry and democracy have been named the 'dominant powers of modernity' by the theologian, Hans Kung (Küng and Kuschel, 1993: 72). In this modern age, Kuschel reminds us, religion becomes only a partial sphere of reality as a result of 'the modern process of differentiation of reality into autonomous spheres (beginning with autonomous science and philosophy and the autonomous understanding of the state and politics)' (p 79). Yet the modern age has its source in religion seeking to take account of modern cultural conditions. Processes of adjustment to new conditions, changing bases of power, rapid expansion of our knowledge base and the opening up of alternative lifestyle possibilities to growing numbers have all marked this modern age. Thus in a century that began so triumphantly with modernity as its watchword, modern and postmodern have grappled with the nature of experience and means of knowing about it.

As the 20th century progressed, the impact of 'the dominant powers of modernity' on the social, political, philosophic, economic and cultural lives of individuals and their communities grew. Commentators were thus able to name many societies as pluralist and multicultural, post-Christian and secular. The ease with which a new language was developed the better to describe hugely changing patterns of migration, dramatic redistributions of wealth, status and gender patterns, complex reforms in legal structures and changes in working patterns was not, however, matched by an equivalent facility either by individuals or their communities to adjust with ease personally, socially or culturally. This must in part be related to two central characteristics of a century dominated by the powers of modernity: a greatly increased individual and collective consciousness of cultural and religious diversity, alongside an awareness that individual and collective beliefs, values and institutions are open to contest. Communities, individuals within them and their cultures were fractured. Disjuncture in tradition, and traditional values, culture, history and identity became an overriding characteristic of personal, communal and national lives. Against this complex and challenging background new directions were sought; little wonder that they sometimes went in many and often opposing directions.

The new mapping of experience came to be known as postmodernism. The condition of postmodernism has been characterized by Judith Squires in the following way (1993: 2):

> ... as involving three key features: the death of Man, History and Metaphysics. This involves the rejection of all essentialist and transcendental conceptions of human nature; the rejection of the pursuit of the real and the true. In the place of these illusory ideals we find assertions that man is a social, historical or linguistic artefact; the celebration of fragmentation, particularity and difference; the acceptance of the contingent and apparent.

Modernity and human values

Charles Taylor (1989: 499) has written an excellent summary of 'the disengaged instrumental mode of life' so troubling to our modern times:

> Modern identity is peculiarly differentiated. Because of the plurality of social worlds in modern society the structures of each particular world are experienced as relatively unstable and unreliable. The individual in pre-modern societies lives in a world that is much more coherent. It therefore appears to him as firm and possibly inevitable. By contrast, the modern individual's experience of a plurality of social worlds relativizes every one of them... Therefore, the individual seeks to find his foothold in reality in himself rather than outside himself.

The proposed solution favoured from the 1970s onwards of the world 'shrinking' through technology and increasing knowledge, thus enabling all its citizens to form one global village, has not materialized. As individuals are faced with making choices in a world alienated from them, they see other consequences of living in the shadow of the 'dominant powers of the modern age', all of which demand ethical responses: poverty, famine, inequality, women.

Science and industry too have posed as many challenges as solutions. They have spawned a culture that not only has been responsible in part for some of these dominant concerns of our age but also does not easily recognize the total sum and possibilities of being human. In particular, the industrial, mechanistic age gives little import to the affective side of human life. With our powers to reason we might expect to be glad when our freezers are full and our pressured work environment is secure, regardless of the consequences for our fellow human beings. But that is not the case. Perhaps the greatest expectations for providing solutions to human problems have resided in technology. It has most noticeably been expected to create the conditions for reconnecting the individual human being to powerful centres of knowledge and provide continuous opportunities to engage with other individuals. For example, Paul Virilio (1991: 70), in reflecting on the Gulf War, was able to write: 'Curiously, telecommunications sets in motion in civil society the properties of divinity: ubiquity, instantaneousness, immediacy, omnivision, omnipresence. Every-one of us is metamorphosed into a divine being here and there at the same time.'

Our difficulty lies in the fact that such powers coupled with our ready access to knowledge do provide us with a fascinating set of windows on our world and the knowledge it is capable of achieving but it does not provide any clues as to how or why we should use them either for good or not, for ourselves or for others. At a personal level, with mobile telephones we experience greater alienation from our fellow humans as they consciously disengage from their immediate surroundings and choose instead to speak with others some distance away. The exaggerated pace of change brought about by telecommunications in the workplace and in social and personal relationships highlights the difficulties experienced in modern societies by human beings where reality is differentiated into autonomous spheres. As the individuals are left in this wasteland vacuum to chart their individual journey with no authoritative map to guide them, it is little wonder they seek refuge and authority from within themselves and grow wary of others.

Perhaps the major difficulty for individuals and their communities is that to live in modern times means to live with a set of paradoxes and 'cultural contradictions', if we might borrow Daniel Bell's phrase, which he generated in 1976.

Identity, value and culture in a new century

While the sense of cultural disjuncture and personal alienation persists, at the beginning of the new century a new theme is emerging within cultural and personal agenda in the Western world. The interplay of modern and postmodern has yielded interesting developments within the field of religion. In his introduction to *Postmodernity, Sociology and Religion* (1996: 1), Kieran Flanagan writes of his experience in organizing a conference in 1993 on the impact of postmodernity on traditional religions, the New Age, the self, aesthetics and the sociology of religion. The response was great. As a result of the conference and its contributors, he wrote:

> As an issue religion seems disconnected from society, a corpse of modernity buried with a tombstone called secularisation. But now comes a resurrection, the seeds of which can be denoted in the issues which have come to signify postmodernity. A searching, an escaping, a rootlessness of image and affiliation, the effects of technology and globalization, mark an unsecured self, now forced to ask questions of metaphysical identity inconceivable on the agenda of a radical sociology of critical concern two decades ago.

May we therefore conclude that our deliberation about religious perspectives on values, culture and education should be frameworked within a modern rather than a postmodern context? We will take our lead from a sensible and robust comment made by Paul Heelas (1998: 9): 'Could it be the case that modernity is too complex and variegated, with too many strands and cultural trajectories, for religion to become "post"?' Heelas then goes on to introduce the contributors to this collected volume (1998: 10): 'Contributors have had free rein in deciding whether to conceive, portray, construct or theorise religion in terms of "modernity" or in terms of "postmodernity". It might be noted that the majority have opted for the former... Steve Bruce comes to an uncompromising conclusion: "postmodernity"... is unnecessary, when it comes to the study of religious change... and best avoided.'

What this chapter will not do is to ignore some of the hermeneutical processes that characterize much of postmodernism and have become an almost innate part of the human condition, when we set out the possibilities and challenges for cultural and educational development in the new century. These particular conditions have been set out clearly by Robert Beckford (1992: 14):

- refusal to regard positivistic, rationalistic, instrumental criteria as the sole or exclusive standard of worthwhile knowledge;
- willingness to combine symbols from disparate codes or frameworks of meaning, even at the cost of disjunctions and eclecticism;
- celebration of spontaneity, fragmentation, superficiality, irony and playfulness;
- willingness to abandon the search for overarching or triumphalist myths, narratives or frameworks of knowledge.

Thus in late modern society at the start of a new century it is the individual who must find and identify ways of thinking and behaving that are appropriate in a world of constant flux. Anthony Giddens (1991) has identified social disembeddedness as a significant feature of our times. He argues that individuals must reconstruct their identities rather than automatically accept the traits and aspirations of traditional persons and groups. This need for self-development and identity is particularly acute in a pluralist and largely secular society like that in the UK. For in the UK the different values and mores of the many groups need to be understood and accommodation reached if frameworks and patterns for social harmony are to be successfully established.

The continuing place of modernity and democracy in our times

Against this background of personal, social and communal restlessness and concerns with current lifestyles and work patterns, the pervasive influence and attraction of democracy, the fourth 'dominant power' of modernity, continues. The democratic values have been the driving force behind the collapse of Communism in Eastern Europe, the international movement towards democratization and the demand for human rights. They are also evident in campaigns against aspects of traditional religions throughout the north and south. Richard Peters (1981: 37–41) distinguishes three groups of values implicit in a democratic way of life:

- values and procedural consensus;
- values and the pursuit of truth and the settling of matters through reason;
- values and the quest for a personal good.

From this we can conclude that the task for formal education within any liberal democracy at this present time is to engage all participants alike in a common learning culture, the aims and pedagogy of which take seriously the predicament of the individual and the myriad communities that make up our society, whilst ensuring ongoing and critical encounters with democratic values and experiences: and we take our cue from S Ranson (1994) where he argues: 'In periods of social transition education becomes central to our future well-being. Only if learning is placed at the centre of our experience can individuals continue to develop their capacities, institutions be enabled to respond openly and imaginatively to periods of change and the different communities become a source of reflective understanding.'

That very real human predicament, for which our particular period of social and cultural transition is responsible and with which this chapter is concerned, has been succinctly stated by Charles Taylor (1991: 14): 'The principle [of individualism] goes something like this: everyone has a right to develop their own form of life, grounded on their own sense of what is really important or of value. No one can or should try to dictate its content.'

In turn, an 'ethic of self-fulfilment' now lies at the heart of a democratic society; and its effects on policy makers, politicians and educators can be crippling, in relation to both the vision that they offer and the methods they adopt. In the UK, the government's attempt to respond to this predicament through a 'third way' has ensured that the charge of a 'nanny state' is frequently heard. Our challenge is to take the opportunity that the benefits of living in a peaceful democracy offer to a formal education system and present a possible ground-plan for the restructuring of that system.

Taylor goes on to argue that this preoccupation with self leads to the inability of human beings to reach out to and connect with others in communities of shared values and memory. The real predicament is the difficulty of discerning the nature of human and individual identity. In turn we find it problematic to describe, or rather justify, the nature of human relationships as they connect personally, socially, morally. Indeed at present the only well-defined relationships are those that seek to explore ways of working with and protecting natural earth resources, excluding the human.

Modernity and the culture of education

The tensions that have so far been highlighted, which arose as a result of modernity becoming involved in all the increasingly complex political, social and personal relationships upon which modern liberal democracies are built, led to a concentration on education for individual autonomy. This led in values education to the introduction of the individual to the norms of society as they were perceived by the educator, as opposed to the former mode of education exemplified in the statement found in the 'Syllabus for religious instruction for Cambridgeshire' in 1939, which stated that 'all education rightly conceived is religious education'. In that former model of values education was an inherently holistic view of the purpose and content of education whose main purpose was to initiate the young of a relatively stable society into its values and mores. The emphasis is now greatly changed. Sutherland (1997) wrote: 'The relentless march of technology will require more radical responses than before, particularly if we are not only to equip our citizens for employment but also for personal fulfilment and participation in the processes of democratic action and social change. We need an effective balance between economic concerns and the empowerment of individual citizens.'

The educational agenda has changed. Not only have the 'powers of modernity' generally made education effectively autonomous, cutting it off from the other modes of knowing and being, but the need to support individuals in their personal search for fulfilment is now widely found to be a requirement of state education. For example, in the UK, in the introduction to the *Review of the National Curriculum* (DfEE, 1999), we find:

> We have set a challenging agenda to raise standards. We aim to raise the level of achievement of all young people, enabling them to fulfil their potential and to make a full contribution to their communities. We wish to help young people develop morally, spiritually, culturally, mentally and physically. And we want them to become healthy, lively and enquiring individuals capable of rational thought and discussion and positive participation in our ethnically diverse and technologically complex society.

These aims for state education are reflected too in Australia's Common and Agreed National Goals for Schooling (Ministry of Education, 1998: 10):

> Australians in the 21st Century will be active and informed citizens of complex and rapidly changing local and global communities. They will be enterprising, adaptable, and socially responsible contributors to our democratic, cohesive, culturally rich and diverse Australian society. In particular, when they leave school they should have qualities of self-confidence, optimism, high self-esteem and a commitment to personal excellence as a basis for their potential life roles as family, community and workforce members.

The Australian and UK statements of aims at the turn of the century highlight a subtle shift that is occurring in the articulated educational missions of liberal democracies at this time. If we contrast them with a statement published 20 years earlier, in 1980, by the Ministry of Education in Ontario, we see a firm move now at the turn of the century towards focusing on the involvement of the individual in the learning process. Ontario's 13 fundamental principles involved in the learning process included:

- esteem for the customs, cultures and beliefs of a wide variety of societal groups;
- respect for the environment and a commitment to the wise use of resources;
- values related to personal ethical or religious beliefs and to the common welfare of society.

In this example we see that as modernity and postmodernity battled for the high ground of cultural perspectives in the 1970s and 1980s, education sought to offer knowledge in an 'at a distance mode'. The way to survive the perils of diversity, plurality and personal searches for fulfilment lay in being initiated not into the cultural orthodoxy of the early part of the century but into highly specialist autonomous 'forms of knowledge'. The pursuit of knowledge for its own sake and the processes involved in acquiring different 'forms of knowledge' were argued to be worth while not only in themselves but also as a means of developing young people adequately for the challenges of living in a complex, pluralist democracy. A battle then ensued between those who championed an education whose intrinsic value lay in the initiation it offered into hard knowledge of technical know-how with no personal reference to the individual learner and those instead who rather more wisely promoted a middle way by which people encountering new knowledge should be given the tools to accommodate it and make it personal.

Those educators who were involved in the thinking of the exponents of these two approaches, namely Richard Peters and Michael Polanyi, were sometimes able to tailor aims and pedagogies to the contexts for which they taught. Nevertheless the characterization that is described here was noticeable in the classrooms of the 1960s and 1970s.

Within the changing agenda for education at the beginning of the new century, it is not always clear at this stage which movements and ideologies have interacted and become interwoven with formal educational processes towards the end of the last century. For example, it is not yet clear how greatly the communitarian movement has impacted on the self-consciousness of liberal democracies. Nevertheless the movement, which is now so marked in education, of attempting to engage young people with formal education through socially related themes such as citizenship and ecology, does indeed resonate with the concerns of communitarians, namely that we can only make sense of the individual self in the context of a communal vision of the good (Green, 1999).

What is important at this time of diversity and plurality in interpreting the cultures that sustain liberal democracies is that we are able to clarify and articulate the culture specific to the educational endeavour on which we are newly engaged. There has been much written of late about the culture of individual schools, but the task of clarifying the culture of education in which different local and national communities operate has not been widely addressed. In that much-used and valued statement by Hargreaves (1994: 58), 'one of the greatest educational crises of the post-modern age is the collapse of the common school; a school tied to its community and having a clear sense of the social and moral values it should instil', we are given clues about both the problems and the possibilities that such a task may involve. The outcome of such an enterprise would be to set out the dimensions and ethos of such an educational culture in terms coherent with and supportive of the assumptions and values inherent to the tasks of education in a late-modern democracy. Stewart Sutherland (Sacks and Sutherland, 1996: 48–49) has set out the problem that failure to articulate a coherent culture of education can cause: 'but may I remind you that the problem facing teachers is a very serious one. Unless the society in which they live and work gives some coherent account of what it considers important in human life then teachers have no real framework in which to operate.' Denis Lawton (1996: 33) too has warned us: 'England is a democratic society with a high rate of social mobility, but schools tend to divide the young socially, academically and culturally, rather than to encourage co-operation, social harmony and a common culture.'

In proposing the development of a ground-plan for a common culture in which education can effectively operate, two definitions of culture will be used. The first is taken from the school effectiveness literature and written by Louise Stoll: 'Culture describes how things are... in essence, it defines reality for those within a social organization, gives them support and identity and creates a framework for occupational learning. Each school has a different reality or mindset of school life' (Stoll and Fink, 1996: 82–83).

The definition of culture here is helpful for our purpose of attempting to set out the basis for a common educational culture. Its difficulty and helpfulness lie in the final sentence that ties culture to shaping the individual school's mindset. Our recent concentration on effective outcomes for each child delivered by individual schools has in part robbed us of the imperative to discern the overall mindset in which educators work. Assumptions are made and the greatly significant implicit values that shape and define individual cultures are frequently overlooked. Defining reality will need to take account of the overriding values and assumptions pertaining to education both within and outside the school. So we might begin the process of defining an overall approach to the development of an educational culture by seeing schools as 'structures which are intimately and irrevocably woven into others, all of which serve political, economic, cultural, religious and social aims. The interrelated nature of such institutions makes it almost impossible to plan and implement change in one without affecting the others' (Rigsby, Reynolds and Wang, 1995: 7).

Part of the process involved in modernism that we have noted is the growing self-consciousness of individuals; individual cultures and communities are increasingly conscious of others, sometimes to the extent that without a sense of existing within a strong central structure, each person and community can feel isolation and alienation. As the movement grows within education to engage individual learners with their own growth in knowledge and development by recognizing that they are part of a wider group and shared experience, the time is right to evaluate the potential for defining an educational culture that is conscious of its positive role in a wider community development. As Chodorkoff (1990: 71) argues:

> True community development, from the perspective of social ecology, must be a holistic process, which integrates all facets of a community's life. Social, political, economic, artistic, ethical and spiritual dimensions must all be seen as part of the whole. They must be made to work together and to reinforce one another. For this reason, the development process must proceed from a self-conscious understanding of their relationships.

The learner and the teacher in our schools spend much time involved in separate aspects of the formal curriculum, while at the same time engaging in social and personal relationships and development. At stake in our present systems is the ability to relate these differentiated aspects of school life to a whole perspective. In observing individual school cultures it is not always possible to clarify the integrating factor at work, either in the explicit or in the hidden or implicit curriculum. The question is whether at the beginning of the new century we have the will to put the recently articulated overarching aims that we have found for education in a wide number of education systems into practice. Those who recognize the urgency of the present situation urge 'a new paradigm' and frequently one that demands the use of 'emotional intelligence' (for example, Goleman 1996: 20). The five domains of emotional intelligence are: knowing one's emotions, managing emotions, motivating oneself, recognizing emotions in others and handling relationships.

A new paradigm that can do justice to the concept of emotional intelligence and at the same time work within the parameters of a knowledge-based curriculum will support the development of the educational culture for which we are calling. On the one hand it will satisfy Gardner's (1991: 198) important dictum that 'organised subject matter represents the ripe fruitages of experiences... it does not represent perfection or infallible vision; but it is the best at command to further new experiences', while taking seriously the now consciously articulated wish in education to make connections between separated aspects of knowledge, the development of the whole person and communal self-fulfilment. In other words, knowledge might then be personal but acquired within the social context of the school, which in turn is part of a complex web of relationships within the wider society. Potentially giving further impetus to this movement is the present ongoing thinking related to the 'intelligent school'. In seeking to describe the corporate intelligence of the intelligent school, MacGilchrist, Myers and Reed (1997: 112) include four strands of intelligence particularly pertinent to our theme: contextual intelligence, emotional intelligence, spiritual intelligence and ethical intelligence.

In other words, the effective school in the new paradigm will both reflect and articulate the primary sources of epistemology appropriate to education in late-modern times and construct and uphold meta-processes for learning, teaching and living together in a school community that do justice to the late-modern ethic, an ethic that can be characterized by its concerns with pluralism and consensus, individual fulfilment and global prosperity, reasoned commitments and collective ideals. In seeking to root its mission in the wider communal, national and global context, the intelligent school will equally strive to develop itself and its individual members through a combining of the rational and affective in human learning, valuing and action.

To take forward the development of the ground-plan, we require, however, an even greater articulation of the innate processes and emerging knowledge that characterize our liberal democratic communities at the turn of the century. What we must do is to take into account some of the meanings that we have recently and not so recently constructed about ourselves as human beings in a modern age, as well as the processes in which we currently engage as we bind ourselves together into cultures appropriate to our times. We have seen a demand for a more holistic view of education, an increased relationship between knowledge and social and community development. What is not clear is how consciously and clearly we are engaging all partners in the learning and teaching enterprise in that vision.

In order to have half a chance to succeed, the vision with its underlying values and assumptions must be clothed into a form capable of being described, recognized and shared. Thus a further definition of culture is needed, which might encourage and support us in our task. For this purpose I propose that we put alongside Stoll's definition an earlier one by Leslie White (1949: 464):

Culture is the name of a distinct order, or class, of phenomena, namely those
things and events that are dependent upon the exercise of a mental ability
peculiar to the human species, that we have termed 'symbolling' (that is the
invention and use of symbols). It is an elaborate mechanism, an organization
of ways and means employed by a particular animal, man, in the struggle for
existence and survival.

Here we are seeking an end to the often rough-and-ready 'outcomes' model
of education, where the purpose of engaging young people with education
is seen as ensuring they develop specific characteristics and skills appropriate to an age that sees its survival in almost wholly economic terms. At a time
when our late-modern culture can be mainly defined by its characteristics
and not by any common authorities or consensual values, it is inappropriate
not to involve communities whose main business is learning in the task of
seeking means of describing, communicating, evaluating and testing the
sources of values, cultural norms and powerful narratives that inform our
present lives. In earlier times after the passing of the 1944 Education Act,
when religious education was required to foster the personal and spiritual
values of the English nation, it was noticeable that the curriculum diet fed to
the young was devoid of two major ingredients. The first was the absence of
teaching specific to Christian denominations; thus the pupil was deprived of
the nuances of religious belief and action that underpinned genuine Christian practice. The second was the failure to introduce pupils in the UK until
the sixth-form to the lively and very current debates surrounding biblical
hermeneutics that were raging around this time. Pupils came to perceive religion as a tale of strange facts and larger-than-life figures and they frequently ultimately rejected it because its language and means of making
sense of experience were alien.

It is vitally important for the nature of cultural development and ultimately
the effectiveness of education in late-modern times that we learn from the in-
eptness with which religion was handled in education in the UK. A subject
that is made compulsory in the curriculum should not be introduced in half
measures and with a deliberate intent of shielding the young from the real en-
gagements with human and cultural experience that it promotes. The danger
for our present time is that the overriding need to transform the educational
achievements for all citizens for the economic good will lead to a lack of serious engagement in formal education with the cultural disjunctures that are
experienced by all living in late-modern democracies. The new national curriculum in the UK speaks of 'entitlement' for all and much energy is expended
in discussing access and equality of opportunity in higher education. A democracy should ensure that all education involves its citizens in learning
about and reflecting in community on the major questions that the business of
living raises. Thus the definition of culture set out by White challenges us to
ensure that all pupils have the opportunity to become familiar with the problems and opportunities of living at a time when lack of cultural definition and

its consequences are possibly the greatest threat to the stability of late-modern democratic processes.

Recognizing and working with religion in the new century

We are now able to return to Flanagan's assertion that there has been a resurrection of religion and to reflect on the role in the ground-plan of the culture of education. He argued that this has come about as a result of the effects of technology and globalization on the individual. The individual now without a satisfactory identity is forced to ask questions about his or her metaphysical identity. In setting out the conditions for developing a ground-plan for an educational culture we should therefore take seriously this aspect of human enquiry and engagement at the present time. We might begin, then, by reference to R M Hare (1992):

> For myself, I have found it impossible to discuss education for long without bringing in religion. One's attitude to religion will impinge powerfully on one's approach to education. This is because the irrational side of our nature, from which none of us can escape, needs to be educated, and religion, interpreted broadly to include humanistic beliefs, is the only way of doing this.

In earlier writings, Hare had helpfully attempted to speak about religion in ways that might do justice to it within a modern age in which the logical positivist position, put forward most clearly by A J Ayer (1946), attempted to insist that only those statements that can be tested by sense reference have any meaning. Hare responded by pointing out that religious language is of another kind, namely that religious language was not talk about the world but about our attitude to it, our evaluation of it and our opinion about how we ought to react to it. For Hare (1955: 99–103), this was our 'blik' to the world. Clearly it is a struggle to know how to say meaningful things about religion in a world in which modern thought seeks to assert essential differences from among the many varieties of religious traditions and establish hierarchies of value and discrimination upon them.

In earlier times William James (1961: 39) asserted that 'the very fact that [the definitions of religion] are so many and so different from one another is enough to prove that the word "religion" cannot stand for any single principle or essence, but is rather a collective name'. The anthropologist Robin Horton (1960) is helpful here, for he sets out a definition of religion that takes account of his assertion that 'we can point to no single ontological and epistemological category which accommodates all religious entities. Secondly we find that every major ontological and epistemological category we can devise contains religious as well as secular entities (p 205).'

Horton (1960: 205) therefore proposes the following definition:

In every situation commonly labelled religious we are dealing with action directed towards objects which are believed to respond in terms of certain categories – in our own culture those of purpose, intelligence and emotion – which are also the distinctive categories for the description of human action... The relationship between human beings and religious objects can be further defined as governed by certain ideas of patterning such as categorize relationships among human beings... In short religion can be looked upon as an extension of the field of people's social relationships beyond the confines of purely human society.

Religion and the individual in the new century

Perhaps it is an often unarticulated recognition by many of their lives as 'patterned desperation' that leads to a strong and continuing interest in the matter of religion? Turner (1990: note 6, pp 6–7), in commenting on Weber, has spoken of the burden that modernity imposes: 'Modernisation brings with it the erosion of meaning, the endless conflict of polytheistic values and the threat of the iron cage of bureaucracy. Rationalization makes the world orderly but it cannot make the world meaningful.' Clifford Geertz (1966: 4) recognized the human need to see the world as meaningful and ordered. Three aspects of human experience, however, threaten to lead individuals to see the world as meaningless: bafflement, suffering and evil. He therefore offers the following definition of religion: 'a system of symbols which acts to establish powerful, persuasive and long-lasting moods and motivations in men by formulating conceptions of a general order of existence and clothing these conceptions with such an aura of factuality that the moods and motivations seem uniquely realistic'.

The individual's struggle to come to terms with a new century, which exhibits in communities worldwide characteristic elements of the traditional, the modern, the postmodern and the late modern, may well be met in Western societies by a restatement of the need to promote the moral and intellectual autonomy of the individual. Such thinking has underpinned the philosophies of education and the programmes of moral and values education since the second half of the 20th century. It has been considered essential for the well-being of an industrial and modern people to develop an ability in each of its citizens to think critically and independently. This is a central view propounded by Joseph Raz (1986: 369–70) and he goes on to argue: 'For those of us who live in an autonomy supporting environment there is no choice but to be autonomous: there is no other way to prosper in such a society' (Raz, 1986: 163).

At this stage we should heed the clear warning given by Hanan Alexander (2000: 301) to take care not to be seen to follow the 'pragmatic descendants of Mill, such as William James, who claimed that religious faith should be embraced because it leads to the consequence of more meaningful, purposeful lives'. In seeking a working definition for religion that can assist our thinking about religious perspectives on values, culture and education, we must resist any such thing. It will be more coherent with the overarching themes of this chapter to propose the adoption of a more sensitive understanding of the way religion and religious belief are born, 'not of a collection of statements about God, Providence, heaven and hell' (Kolakowski, 1982: 194). Instead Leszek Kolakowski argues that 'religion is indeed the awareness of human insufficiency, it is lived in the admission of weakness'.

Religion in education at the present time

In the UK alone there are over 50 institutions of higher education that provide programmes in theology and religious studies (QAAHE, 2000: 1). The authors of that report comment on 'the vitality and richness of the subject which reflects its significance in the context of a world coming to terms with its cultural and religious diversity'. We know too that almost every country in Europe, except France, has some form of religious education. New religious education provisions have appeared in England, Norway and several other countries, and in almost every country there is a resurgence of religious education curriculum development. Such movements are also to be found in Australia and New Zealand, in post-apartheid South Africa, and in many other countries of Africa and Asia. In the UK, in the 1998 public examinations more than 190,000 young people enrolled for religious education examinations, almost a third of the entire cohort of the year.

Yet the fact of the decline in formal beliefs and commitments in organized religions by large sectors of the population must not be overlooked. In the UK today only one in four people hold any belief in God. Decline in attendance at formal worship is noticeable. Thus the young people in many education systems are far from prepared, even hostile to, an introduction to the study of modes of thought and practice that is outside of their experience. Pluralism has permitted them to grow up in a permanent state of choosing, rather than commitment. For those who may be religiously committed, the ideals of pluralism and the study of a number of traditions may be hostile to their personal identities and searches for meaning.

In the UK there is specific attention paid in the Education Reform Act 1988 to the 'spiritual, moral and cultural development of pupils and of society'. The whole curriculum is to prepare pupils for 'the opportunities, responsibilities and experiences of adult life' (Great Britain, 1988). The legislation in 1998 surrounding religious education was also hardened but no specific guidance was given on social, moral and political development for pupils. Certainly the legislators seem to have thought that the way to a moral society was through a more effective religious education. As John Hull (1999) asserts: 'Insofar as it is a legitimate heir to the Enlightenment, offering an image of a social and cultural life lived in peace and justice, religious education may be described as the Utopian Whisper in the ear of modern society.' Within higher education a group of specialists in the field was recently asked by the Quality Assurance Agency for Higher Education (QAAHE) to develop a 'subject benchmark statement' as a means by which the academic community might describe the nature and characteristics of programmes in theology and religious studies. The authors of the QAAHE statement on theology and religious studies described the current situation in the UK, regarding appropriate definitions of the subject for use in education, thus (2000: 1):

> Theology and Religious Studies in the higher education sector is a dynamic subject area marked both by expansion and diversification. Given that constant new development has been the characteristic of the field since the latter half of the twentieth century, both in the UK and elsewhere, it is vital that any definition of the subject does not constrain future innovation, whether in response to global trends and issues or new intellectual climates.

The overview they offer of the diverse kinds of programmes available in different institutional contexts, where reflective engagement takes place with religion in order better to understand human culture, suggests a higher education system that has taken the differing place of religion in culture and identity in modern times very seriously indeed. 'Some providers aim to study and analyse religion(s) as a significant dimension of human culture, especially to enhance understanding of its importance in shaping societies, history and peoples, and in turn of their influence in shaping religions; while others focus on key bodies of literature (eg the Bible) and particular religious traditions within a general humanities framework.' The authors go on to state that 'some providers would argue in principle that at least two religions should be studied in depth, some because students may go on to train as teachers in multicultural and pluralist Britain' (p 1).

In discussing the nature and extent of the subject, the idea is developed of a subject characterized as 'a family of methods, disciplines and fields of study, clustered around the investigation both of the phenomena of religions and belief systems in general and of particular religious traditions, texts, practices, societies, art and archaeology'. The report goes on to describe what it sees as the unifying principle of addressing questions raised about, within or between religions. 'Some would affirm as a core the intention of raising questions of meaning and truth, beauty and value' (p 3).

Finally, academics describe the nature of engagement with the subject undertaken by students in this field. Students will explore the religious thought of one or more traditions, and analyse the historical, social, cultural and artistic role of religion or belief systems.

At its heart is the commitment both to developing knowledge and information about religion, and to learning from it. In both contexts students explore both an 'inside' and an 'outside' perspective. Each of these may be achieved in a variety of different ways, for example through the study of the extant works of a major religious thinker, prophet or leader, or through the generation of a hermeneutic of suspicion by taking seriously a Marxist or feminist analysis.

It is of interest within the parameters of this present chapter that the academics argue that the field of theology and religious studies has developed in dialogue with modernity. They note it is now also responding to postmodernity. They conclude (p 4):

> Once the European Enlightenment set an agenda that profoundly shaped Biblical Studies and Modern Theology. Increasingly hermeneutics, critical theory and post-modern agendas have informed all aspects of the subject. Global perspectives, interfaith and ecumenical issues, issues of gender, race and culture, as well as fundamental debates about methods and study, figure large in discussions about the nature and parameters of Theology and Religious Studies.

All teaching of the study of religion, however, is made more complex by the business of ensuring that students are aware and initiated into the values surrounding what has come to be known as 'an ethics of belief'. For Hobson and Edwards (1999: 85): 'Principles and values from an ethics of belief complement democratic values to provide ethical and epistemological norms which should inform the teaching of religion and act as a guide to how religious differences should be handled in the curriculum.'

Standards and coherence within the evidence chosen and presented to enable students to come to terms with the discipline's specialist knowledge should be maintained. We are, though, yet again brought face to face with the challenge presented by modernity to make effective use of autonomous areas of knowledge in our search to make these bit parts of knowledge relevant to our selves and our experience. Does all our personal knowledge flow from sustained reasoning from evidence gathered?

In short, the current field of theology and religious studies is well placed to contribute to the content and processes of a developing culture of education, not least through its commitment to exposing the ways in which human culture has sought to identify the sources of its authority and open up knowledge of the diversity of values and beliefs to a very wide audience and through a variety of methods.

Values and culture in education: the contribution of religion

In 1943 the UK government published the White Paper that preceded the 1944 Education Act. Concern for traditional and religious values was considered to be the fundamental purpose for religious education: 'There has been a general wish not confined to representatives of the churches, that religious education should be given a more definite place in the life and work of schools, springing from the desire to revive the spiritual and personal values in our society and in our national tradition' (Board of Education, 1943: 36).

Today in a consciously plurally diverse modern society it is no longer appropriate for religion in general or one religion in particular to form the hub of cultural and educational endeavour. In particular, it is possible to argue alongside Bryan Wilson writing in 1985 that the dominant effect of religion becoming accommodated with modernity has been the increased growth of secularization. The place of organized religion in the public arena therefore becomes increasingly tenuous (p 19): 'The secularisation thesis implies the privatisation of religion; its continuing operation in the public domain becomes confined to a lingering rhetorical invocation in support of conventional morality and human decency and dignity – as a cry of despair in the face of moral panic.'

Yet at this time of cultural disjuncture so oppressive both for individuals and for their wider communities alike, when there is evidence of a search for a metaphysical identity, eclectic or otherwise, to what extent should religion influence institutions and corporate actions?

With Martha Nussbaum (1997: 294) we share a vision of liberal education that involves drawing 'citizens to one another by a complex mutual understanding and individual self-scrutiny, building a democratic culture that is truly deliberative and reflective'. On a wider world stage, the failure of modernity to sustain a worthwhile belief in the value of seeking consensus, thereby engaging globally in a shared 'grand project', nevertheless does not diminish the will to seek common features in the religious changes that have taken place in the modern age and in the lives of citizens throughout the world.

Here the thesis of Robert Hefner becomes important, offering as it does a strong rebuttal to the notion that the rise of modernity must imply a diminishing of the role of organized religion in the modern state. Indeed he makes a convincing case for modernity to create conditions in which the religion of Islam can both flourish and resist the potential perils of secularization. At the same time he charts the onward progress of pluralism in the thoughts and state systems of Indonesia (Hefner, 1998: 162–65). He cites Indonesia as a particular locus of encounter between tradition and the modern world.

Hefner describes two camps in the construction of the modern Indonesian state. 'Some rivals in this contest reject religious disestablishment and insist on a direct and literal application of Islamic law to all aspects of government and social life. Others insist that such a view distorts the true meaning of Islam, attributing a fixed and closed quality to what is supposed to be a universal and thus open ethical system.' Thus there have been powerful pressures against the creation in Indonesia of an Islamic state. Yet, rather than being 'privatized', Hefner argues, Islam has grown increasingly dominant in public life. Yet even as public piety has come to conform to Muslim norms, Muslim politics has remained decidedly pluricentric.

Hefner concludes his article, 'Secularisation and citizenship in Muslim Indonesia', with a major concern that this chapter has noted throughout a number of education systems. It is that concern shared by governments, their citizens and often those concerned with the study of religion in democracies that conditions in society in general and in education specifically must be organized effectively within the challenges of pluralism and multiculturalism, to ensure that human beings can live cooperatively to good purpose: 'In an era when certain Western and Muslim leaders speak of an inevitable "clash of civilizations", it is useful to remind ourselves of these shared challenges, and the fact that on all sides there are people of good will struggling to devise and defend a modern civility' (p 165).

This brief survey and evaluation of current trends within the study of religion in education with its concerns for the reflective understanding of religion both in human cultures and in the lives of individuals, be they committed religiously or not, might best be summarized through reference to the description of the aims of religious education in the UK offered by Robert Jackson (1997: 129):

> One basic aim for RE [is] to develop an understanding of the grammar – the language and wider symbolic patterns – of religions and the interpretive skills necessary to gain that understanding... RE also needs to develop critical skills in order to achieve the goal of developing a knowledge of the language and wider symbolic patterns of religions... Thus the debates about the nature of religions and cultures become part of religious education: preconceived definitions are no longer taken as received wisdom.

Conclusion

The poet Seamus Heaney has drawn our attention to the need for 'a search for images and symbols adequate to our predicament' (quoted in Richard Pine, 1990). Kolakowski drew our attention to defining religion around the core idea of human insufficiency. The task for education must surely be to work towards the cultural development of pupils and of society in a way that does justice to the cultural predicaments of our time. In respect of the place of religion in our educational and cultural processes, it is clear that we cannot afford to deny the religious dimensions of developments in our secular cultures or indeed to overstate them. We all need the information that helps us contextualize the values and approaches advocated by the cultures and education of which we are a part.

In elaborating our ground-plan for the development of an educational culture we must ensure that it will permit all learners, of whatever age, creed or ethnic origin, to participate in the development, promotion and acquisition of the values implicit in a democratic way of life (Peters, 1981). In order to ensure the participation that holistic and connective learning demands, recognition, understanding and agreed sharing of those values can only follow if a culture is developed that permits the learner to be fully cognizant and participatory in our current knowledge about experience, both material and spiritual, and the processes by which we deem some knowledge and some processes to be more important than others. At its heart the education culture must take responsibility for individuals and their developing sense of identity at a time when the wider culture offers such a bewildering set of directions and evaluation of none.

The place of religion in culture is both diffuse and specific. Specifically there are movements towards greater and harder religious commitment and identification, as some citizens seek reassuringly positive frameworks by which to live in these plurally unsettling times. Equally there are signs of trends away from organized belief systems towards more generalized spiritually aware modes of life, sometimes culminating in what has been called New Age religion. For others the characteristics of secular thought and patterns of identity remain agreeable. To serve this developing culture best, with its particular metaphysical and social concerns, it will be helpful for religion in all its varieties to be integrated into a knowledge-based curriculum by reference to the classifications set out by Woodhead and Heelas (2000: 2–3). Their typologies, namely religions of difference, religions of humanity and spiritualities of life, have been succinctly developed as 'three points on a spectrum of understandings of the relationship between the divine, the human and the natural order'.

Such typologies will usefully inform the curricula of schools, which themselves will increasingly articulate their identities and purposes as constitutive communities. A 'constitutive community' is one that is identity-building; it is fundamental to our self-description (Golby, referred to by Sullivan, 1999). Thus the school shares too in the development of a coherent account of what it considers important in human life and Sutherland's proposed framework for teachers to operate in also begins to take shape.

If the essence of the ground-plan for an articulated and widely understood culture of education were to be the quest for a personal and common good through experiences and processes involving 'symbolling', then we would be closer to achieving a match between the real needs relating to autonomy that individuals and their community have in order to come to terms with living in these particular times. Not only that; the exploration of culture and its possibilities in our modern age would be an integral part of the identity of human beings and all human beings would have shared in its creation.

References

Alexander, H (2000) In Search of a Vision of the Good: Values, education and the postmodern condition, in *Education for Values, Morals, Ethics and Citzenship in Contemporary Education*, eds R Gardner, J Cairns and D Lawton, Kogan Page, London

Ayer, A J (1946) *Language, Truth and Logic*, Gollancz, London

Beckford, J (1992) Religion, Modernity and Postmodernity, in *Religion: Contemporary Islam*, ed B R Wilson, Bellew, London

Bell, D (1976) *The Cultural Contradictions of Capitalism*, Heinemann, London

Board of Education (1943) *Educational Reconstruction*, HMSO, London

Chodorkoff, D (1990) Social ecology and community development, in *Reviewing the Faith: The province of social ecology*, ed J Clark, Greenprint, London

Department for Education and Employment (DfEE) (1999) *Review of the National Curriculum: The Secretary of State's proposals*, DfEE, London

Flanagan, K and Jupp, P (1996) *Postmodernity, Sociology and Religion*, Macmillan, Basingstoke

Fraser J W (1999) *Between Church and State: Religion and public education in a multicultural America*, Macmillan Press, Basingstoke

Gardner, H (1991) *The Unschooled Mind*, Basic Books, New York

Geertz, C (1966) Religion as a cultural system, in *Anthropological Approaches to the Study of Religion*, ASA Monographs No. 3, ed M Banton, Tavistock, London

Giddens, A (1991) *Modernity and Self Identity*, Polity, Oxford

Goleman, D (1996) *Emotional Intelligence: Why it sometimes matters more than IQ*, Bloomsbury, London

Great Britain (1988) *Education Reform Act in Statutes*, HMSO, London

Green, T (1999) *Voices: The educational formation of conscience*, Notre Dame Press, University of Notre Dame, NJ

Hare, R M (1955) Theology and Falsification (i) The University Discussion, in *New Essays in Philosophical Theology*, eds A Flew and A McIntyre, SCM Press, London

Hare, R M (1998) *Essays on Religion & Education*, Clarendon Press, Oxford

Hargreaves, A (1994) *Changing Teaching, Changing Times*, Cassell, London

Heelas, P (1998) *Religion, Modernity and Postmodernity*, Blackwell, Oxford

Hefner, R (1998) Secularisation and citizenship in Muslim Indonesia, in *Religion, Modernity & Postmodernity*, ed P Heelas, Blackwell, Oxford

Hobson, P R and Edwards, J S (1999) *Religious Education in a Pluralist Society*, Woburn Press, London

Horton, R (1960) A definition of religion and its uses, *Journal of the Anthropological Institute*, **90**, pp 201–26

Hull, J (1999) Preface, *Religious Education in a Pluralist Society*, P R Hobson and J S Edwards, Woburn Press, London

Jackson, R (1997) *Religious Education: An interpretative approach*, Hodder & Stoughton, London

James, W (1961) *The Varieties of Religious Experience*, Collier-Macmillan, New York

Küng, H and Kuschel, K J (ed) (1993) *A Global Ethic: The declaration of the Parliament of the World's Religions*, SCM Press, London

Kolakowski, L (1982) *Religion: If there is no God... On God, the devil, sin and other worries of the so-called philosophy of religion*, Fontana, London

Lawton, D (1996) *Beyond the National Curriculum*, Hodder & Stoughton, London

MacGilchrist, B, Myers, K and Reed, J (1997) *The Intelligent School*, Paul Chapman, London

Ministry of Education (1998) *The Social Education Framework*, Ministry of Education (Schools Division), Victoria

Nussbaum, M C (1997) *Cultivating Humanity: A classical defense of reform in liberal education*, Harvard, Cambridge, Mass

Peters, R S (1981) *Essays on Education*, Allen & Unwin, London

Pine, R (1990) *Brian Friel and Ireland's Drama*, Routledge, London

Quality Assurance Agency for Higher Education (QAAHE) (2000) *Theology and Religious Studies*, QAA, Gloucester

Ranson, S (1994) *Towards the Learning Society*, Cassell, London

Raz, J (1986) *The Morality of Freedom*, Clarendon Press, Oxford

Rigsby, L, Reynolds, M G and Wang, M C (ed) (1995) *School – Community Connection: Exploring issues in research practice*, Jossey-Bass, San Francisco

Squires, J (1993) *Principled Positions: Postmodernism and the rediscovery of value*, Lawrence & Wishart, London

Stoll, L and Fink, D (1996) *Changing our Schools: Linking school effectiveness with school improvement*, Open University, Buckingham

Sullivan, J (1999) in *Values and the Curriculum: The school context*, ed D Lawton, J Cairns and R Gardner, Curriculum Studies Group, Institute of Education, London

Sutherland, S (1996) Education, Values and Religion, in *Education, Values and Religion*, Sacks J and Sutherland S, Victor Cook Memorial Lecture, Centre of Philosophy, University of St Andrew's

Sutherland, S (1997) Introduction, in *Imagining Tomorrow*, ed V Mayo, NIACE, Leicester

Taylor, C (1989) *Sources of the Self: The making of modern identity*, Cambridge University Press, Cambridge

Taylor, C (1991) *The Ethics of Authenticity*, Harvard, Cambridge, Mass

Turner, B S (ed) (1990) *Theories of Modernity and Postmodernity*, Sage, London

Virilio, P (1991) *L'écran du desert*, Galilee, Paris

White, L (1949) *The Science of Culture*, cited in *Ritual & Religion in the Making of Humanity*, R Pappaport, Cambridge University Press, Cambridge

Wilson, B (1985) Secularisation: the inherited model, in *The Sacred in the Secular Age*, ed P E Hammond, University of California Press, Berkeley

Woodhead, L and Heelas, P (2000) *Religion in Modern Times*, Blackwell, Oxford

4. Economic perspectives on values, culture and education: markets in education – a cautionary note

John Mace

Introduction

The role and value of markets as an efficient, if not the most efficient, mechanism for providing goods and services was described over two centuries ago by Adam Smith in his book *The Wealth of Nations* (Smith, 1776). Since then economics books continue to describe the wonders of the market and bemoan the malignant influence of monopolies, cartels, monopsonists and government policies on the 'free' operation of this mechanism for promoting the greatest happiness for the greatest number. As Hayek has succinctly put it: 'The market is the only guarantee of progress and civilisation' (Hayek, 1960: 156). Admittedly, some economists expressed some concerns about the issue of how markets might affect the distribution of goods and services between people, *exchange efficiency* in economic parlance, and the degree to which this might not contribute to the satisfaction, sometimes called utility, of individuals and society. However, since there were difficulties in agreeing unambiguous ways of measuring utility and how it should be changed so as to increase the level of society's overall utility (this being impossible to operationalize), economists have instead tended to focus on production efficiency. Here the issue of efficiency is not concerned with the utility it yields to society but whether a given quantity of goods and services can be produced more cheaply or not. Any reduction in the volume of inputs, or costs, needed to produce a given output is deemed to be an increase in production efficiency.

Within the field of the economics of education, efficiency questions, when they were addressed, tended to focus on the macro-level. In particular, questions that were addressed concerned the way in which education contributed to economic growth and how education could be reallocated to raise economic growth rates (Schultz, 1963; Blaug, 1970; Psacharopoulos, 1973). However, by the middle of the 1980s new policy priorities had begun to appear, which by the end of the decade were generating as much interest as had the economics of human capital a quarter of a century earlier. The driving force was market-based ideologies, which were claiming to provide the basis for more successful economies than the social democratic welfare and Marxist models that had been dominant since the end of the Second World War. These ideas were given a strong boost by the collapse of the Soviet Union at the beginning of the 1990s and the demise of centralized planning in the whole of Eastern Europe.

The economics of education followed this new pattern, and what began to emerge in the mid-1980s was a subject much more concerned with microeconomics issues, with the interactions of individual student consumers with one another and with individual school or university providers of education. The interest of economists in educational issues is an integral part of the ideology of market and quasi-market approaches to the provision of public services generally, which in the United Kingdom has been associated with the name of Margaret Thatcher and her colleagues, but appears also to be an article of faith of the left-of-centre government under Tony Blair that came to power in 1997. In the wider world the message of greater consumer power and the development of market-supporting policies were closely associated with the policies of the World Bank and the International Monetary Fund, particularly through their structural adjustment programmes. Associated with these developments were the debates about student fees, cost recovery and finance of higher education by loans. The overarching theme in these developments was the increased introduction of market forces into national economies; with respect to education it was through the device of giving greater 'power' to the consumers that greater efficiency in education provision would be promoted. Although there had been some work in this area in the post-war period, it was really only in the mid-1980s that market forces entered the mainstream of economic thinking about public sector services such as education.

The ideas of the market are being introduced into the provision of public services in a number of different ways, one example of which is the development of the New Public Management Paradigm (NPMP). With NPMP it was claimed there would be a clearer focus on efficiency, effectiveness and quality as a result of the following:

- the introduction of decentralized management structures;
- more emphasis on indirect public provision to provide more cost-effective outcomes;
- more accountability at all levels;
- the strengthening of strategic policy at the centre so that government can influence policy quickly, flexibly and cheaply;
- the greater application of mechanisms such as contracting-out, performance-related pay and the like to introduce market and quasi-market forces, both internally, within institutions, and externally, between institutions.

(derived from Pollitt, 1995)

Pollitt was not alone in perceiving these developments. Power, Halpin and Whitty (1997) reviewed research findings in five Western countries and detected similar tendencies taking place. They also emphasized the growing gap between 'managers' and 'managed': 'school managers are becoming increasingly isolated from colleagues and classrooms' (p 342).

Policies to promote 'marketization' of education are now high on the political agenda in many European countries, especially in the former centrally planned economies of Central and Eastern Europe. Marketization takes two main forms: one is 'privatization', where the main aim is to attract additional private sector resources into schools and universities; the other is decentralization and devolution downwards of financial decision making with the main purpose of increasing the efficiency of resource use, at least at the local level (Williams, 1997).

An example of proposed privatization was the acrimonious debate in Greece in 1998 about the private provision of parts of the university system. Although the debate raised important constitutional issues, the main purpose of the proposed reform was to bring in resources from the private sector and thus permit the creation of more university places to meet the 'excess student demand' for university places without increasing the demands on the public sector education budget. At present much of this excess demand is met by Greek students seeking their qualifications in other countries. A similar debate is taking place in Germany where several private quasi-universities are being established, often under the tutelage of established state universities. A second reason for such proposals is the belief that the introduction of market forces and competition will put pressure on public universities to adapt to changing technological, social, economic and political circumstances and to provide their academic services more efficiently.

Decentralization often means the creation of what are often called quasi-markets in which the state continues to provide much of the funding, usually by means of output-oriented formulae, but as many decisions as possible are devolved to local or institutional levels. The 'evaluative state' 'steers' the system (Neave and van Vught, 1991) rather than administers it.

Nowhere in Europe have the rhetoric, and the reality, of the 'market' been stronger than in Great Britain. In Britain most education legislation from the Education Reform Act of 1988 onwards has been concerned with releasing and regulating market forces at primary, secondary and tertiary levels of education. In order to make the 'market' work better, a plethora of performance indicators (PIs) have been developed so that the government can make judgements about the effectiveness and efficiency of schools and local authorities, and consumers (students) and their families are enabled to make better-informed choices in deciding where they should obtain their educational services. Other European countries are either moving, or thinking of developments, along similar lines and there have also been significant developments of the 'market' idea on the other side of the Atlantic.

The idea of the market

This chapter is about the role and possible effects of markets in education, but before discussing this it will be useful to make some distinctions clear. These distinctions need to be made because of the frequent confusion/obfuscation/ignorance so often demonstrated in the use of these terms by politicians, the media and, often it has to be conceded, the teaching profession.

Privatization is the handing over of the whole or some part of the provision, funding or control of education to the private sector. There is obviously the private school sector, but more recently some schools and LEAs have been taken over by non-public-sector bodies. The recent growth of Private Finance Initiatives and Private/Public Partnerships are also examples of the encroachment into education provision of the private sector. However, as will become clear, merely because control has changed hands does not mean that markets or market forces have been introduced. To illustrate the point: the fact that British Rail has been sold (given) to the private sector may merely mean that a public sector monopoly has been replaced by a private sector monopoly and *not* that markets or even market forces have been introduced.

Marketization is the setting up of practices/bodies that attempt to *sell*, though not necessarily for cash, the services of education providers to consumers. Hence, the development of glossy brochures, marketing managers and local or national advertising are examples of the marketization of education. However, although this suggests some of the characteristics of competition in education, this is not the same as the establishment of 'markets' or even 'quasi-markets'.

Markets have a very specific meaning in economics, the essential features of which are that there are large numbers of buyers and sellers competing with one another through some sort of 'pricing' system to buy and sell a product or service. As Brighouse points out, in the *Independent* Education section, where demand exceeds supply, as for many schools because of accidents of geography, prestige etc, then you get what is termed 'producer control', ie monopoly power, hence no market (Brighouse, 2000).

Both in the United States and in Britain there have been many evaluations of the idea and practice of markets and these analyses need to be carefully considered before countries wholeheartedly embrace the idea as a panacea for the actual and imagined flaws in their existing educational provision. Before examining some of the empirical evidence of the effects of 'marketization', the concept of a 'market' itself needs to be explored so as to understand its appropriateness or inappropriateness as a system for providing education.

The idea of the market and its potential benefits in ensuring efficient resource allocation have been around for more than two centuries. As stated earlier, Adam Smith was arguing for the benefits accruing from the 'invisible hand' of the market. The operation of the market, it was claimed, would secure the greatest benefit for the greatest number, because the individual pursuit of self-interest would result in an efficient ordering of production and distribution of society's goods and services. The result of the market process would be that 'exchange efficiency' would result in that it will be impossible to make anyone better off without making someone else worse off. At the same time the markets would ensure that goods and services are produced in the most efficient way, that is, the cost per unit of output would be minimized. This is called 'production efficiency'.

To the classical and neo-classical economists of the 19th and early 20th centuries, the ideal market is embodied in the model of perfect competition. Such a market rarely if ever exists, but it is used as a benchmark of how competitive a market really is. For a market to be 'perfect' many assumptions need to be met, of which the following are particularly important:

- There are many buyers and sellers, all of whom act independently and have little power to affect the market by their individual behaviour.
- Producers produce homogeneous products.
- There is freedom of entry to, and exit from, the market.
- All buyers and all sellers have full knowledge of what all others in the market are doing.
- Prices (and hence income of sellers and costs to buyers) are determined by unrestricted transactions between individual buyers and individual sellers.
- Sellers are concerned to maximize their incomes and buyers to minimize their costs.
- There is unrestricted mobility of 'factors of production', particularly homogeneous labour and homogeneous capital.
- There are no economies of scale, for if they exist monopolies are likely to develop.
- There are no externalities, ie consumption of a good or service does not confer costs or benefits on third parties.

A legitimate question is the extent to which these assumptions are satisfied in the 'real world' where there are monopolies, monopsonies (both very often government departments), multinationals, cartels and restricted access to information about the quality and price of products and services. A recent example of the way in which sellers can 'segment' markets and earn excess profits is to be found in the car market in the UK where identical cars to those available in Continental Europe earn a 'premium' of up to 35 per cent. It has recently been argued that this segmentation of markets takes place in other goods and services, such as clothing and food where prices are lower in the United States and Continental Europe.

Markets and education

If the above conditions existed there would be a 'perfect market' and it would result in an optimal allocation of resources in the economy in the sense that with available resources output would be maximized and outputs would be shared equally among all purchasers. If applied in education the same would be true of that set of activities. In practice, of course, there is little chance of education resembling perfect competition since the major assumptions do not hold. There is certainly not perfect knowledge of the potential benefits among buyers, nor of the efficiency of different production processes among sellers. It is usually bought by governments on behalf of the ultimate consumers. The product is a differentiated one; students' knowledge about the choices available to them is very dependent on the amount and type of information the schools and colleges, or the government, choose to publish. In many areas where the choice of school or educational institution is limited, usually by geography, sometimes by law, if any economic model fits it is that most closely associated with monopoly rather than competitive markets. In a monopoly there may be many buyers but there is only one dominant supplier. Obviously this gives great power to the seller. Many primary and secondary schools do in practice effectively have a local monopoly.

As far as the concept of the market is concerned, the major issue for examination is how exactly it is expected to work and what the intended benefits are. This we will consider in the first part of this section. In the second, problems associated with education markets will be discussed. This will be followed by a brief conclusion.

The key concepts used by its advocates to justify a market approach to the provision of public education are competition and choice. This, proponents of markets claim, is in marked contrast to the effects of state-controlled education in which competition and consumer choice are either non-existent or severely inhibited by the rigidities and inertia of government bureaucracy. The so-called 'new right' believes that government, by its very nature, is doomed to fail as internal dynamics cause it to grow too big, which drains resources and has damaging effects on efficiency and liberty (Le Grand and Robinson, 1989: 269). Friedman (Friedman and Friedman, 1960) and Tooley (1996) make very much this point, though the most extreme proponents of this view are Chubb and Moe (1990). For Chubb and Moe, the decline in US student achievement is attributable to state control, which has allowed a bureaucratic system to evolve in which the interests of administrators and professionals have become paramount, to the detriment of consumers (parents) who are not sufficiently organized to withstand the 'myriad associations of principals, school boards, superintendents, administrators and professionals' (Chubb and Moe, 1990: 32). It is interesting to note that some commentators on the effect of educational reform in England assert that it has given *more* power to the government and 'administrators' of education and largely disempowered the professional (Ball, 1993). The whole market process has been characterized by Le Grand and Robinson in the following way (1989: 24): 'There is no need for a complex administrative system to make decisions about changes in the composition of output. This is achieved by the supposedly uncoordinated, individual actions of a vast number of consumers and producers, each acting in response to "price signals".'

The perceived benefits of markets were behind the British reforms of 1988. Competition was introduced by the simple expedient of schools receiving funding related to the numbers of students they enrolled, and students and their families were given considerable freedom to choose which school they wished to attend through 'open' enrolment. In order to enable consumers to make an informed and rational choice, essential for a market to function effectively, they would be provided with a range of information about schools, hence the development of performance indicators (PIs). They are thus put in a position to make choices and take their custom to whichever school they consider to be most appropriate for them.

Schools in the United Kingdom are now competing for pupils. They are becoming more consumer-oriented: they must attract 'customers' into the school if they are to continue to receive income. The British government of the early 1980s was convinced that the 1944 Education Act that had provided the framework for the education system for 40 years enabled it to be far too 'producer dominated'. Consumer sovereignty is now the dominant philosophy in education as in many other public services. 'Their [schools'] survival should depend on their ability to satisfy their customers. And their principal customers are parents who should therefore be free to place their custom where they wish, in order that educational institutions should be shaped, controlled and nourished by their demand' (Hillgate Group, 1987: 7).

'Poor' schools face falling pupil numbers and falling resources. The market provides an incentive for 'poor' schools to improve. 'Good', or popular, schools will gain resources that they can use to invest to improve further the services they provide. They are motivated by the desire to succeed and stay ahead of the rest. The market is motivating them to do better and improve standards. Indeed this is the key: poor schools will improve because of fear of closure, good schools will improve because of fear of failure and consequently standards for everyone will improve. This is the way the market works according to its advocates.

Another issue here is the management of individual schools (in England this is called the local management of schools, in Scotland devolved school management). If schools are to be more reactive to 'customers' they should be able to adjust their resource allocations, within their budgets, to take account of their local 'markets'. If, for example, it is clear that local parents want better sports facilities, a school should be able to react to that. Consequently, the market approach calls for expenditure to be decided as near to the customer as possible, at school level. Centralized decision making by local or national education authorities is too rigid and slow.

The market approach makes great claims for efficiency. Education has for too long been producer-led and inefficient with little incentive to be efficient. The introduction of simulated market practices in which surpluses can be spent in accordance with the priorities of the individual school introduces a quasi 'profit motive' into its management. If schools can notionally be directed at 'profit maximization' this would, in terms of market models, lead to a drive for greater cost efficiency and better value for money. The target now becomes student numbers. Now the emphasis is clear: the education system, under such an approach, would shift from a supply-oriented system to a demand-based system. This establishes the pre-eminence of the consumer who is the basis for any market-led model. However, one consequence is that the state takes a much more direct interest in the quality of education services being provided. It is no coincidence that, at the same time as there has been a marked move towards devolved responsibilities, particularly in tertiary education, elaborate quality assurance mechanisms have been established. Otherwise there is a clear temptation for market-oriented schools and colleges to cut corners on quality in order to maximize their disposable income.

Technical efficiency improvements result from a fear of failure and a desire to succeed. Successful schools will wish to innovate to keep ahead of competitors, thus driving education forward in a positive way. Schools that are unattractive to students will attempt to emulate their more successful counterparts thus improving standards as they take on board 'good practice' from their more successful counterparts.

If, across the system as a whole, resources are allocated in accordance with the wishes of student consumers, this ensures that the maximum amount of consumer 'benefit' is achieved, at least as expressed by their revealed individual preferences, and within a given budget the 'right' amount of resources are allocated to each school. The Pareto optimum is achieved whereby any change in the distribution of the available resources would result in less educational benefit than is achieved by the existing distribution. 'Allocative efficiency' as well as technical efficiency is achieved.

Other benefits claimed for a market model include greater choice and a rational and neutral decision-making process for the allocation of resources and the fact that the market makes no subjective allocative decisions. The market is simply a mechanism and performs its allocative functions without subjectivity – an 'invisible hand' in Adam Smith's famous 18th-century phrase. This is more efficient than the value-driven judgements of local or central government officials and less self-interested than those of the teachers and managers who are the direct providers of education.

In brief, the market model is simple to understand and the benefits from its introduction into education are increased efficiency and accountability to consumers, which include the state. Consequently, it is no accident that it has political appeal as the best way to organize educational provision. Ordinary parents can see what it is trying to achieve, they understand its most basic force, self-interest, and they live and work in a market world anyway. For many the surprise is that it has not been tried before, especially since it claims to bring such benefits in terms of efficiency, motivation, responsiveness, accountability and freedom.

The market model: a critique

The market for education can never meet the conditions of perfect competition. As already mentioned, many schools and colleges bear more resemblance to local monopolies since there is only one or at best a very small number of establishments for students to choose from. Those who are not convinced by the claims of market advocates are also extremely doubtful whether education ought to be organized along strictly market lines even if it could be. The nature of educational transactions means that there is always some submission of the learner to the knowledge and expertise of the teacher. The issue is how these transactions are to be organized in a way that is efficient and fair to both.

The first issue is the nature of the education market itself. There is no such thing as a free market in education. To illustrate the point, in the United Kingdom, after more than a decade of marketization, the education system is still closely controlled and regulated by the state. Indeed, the irony is that without a huge degree of regulation and legislation from the government to underpin the present arrangements the quasi-market arrangements that do exist could not actually work. This point is very forcibly made by the staunch advocate of education markets, James Tooley (1996), who argues that the failure of reforms to bring the promised benefits of markets is that there are actually no real markets in education; the state shackles the system through its interventions in carrying out inspections and controlling the curriculum. There is little basis for confidence in a market model that needs government intervention to survive. The market is in practice a 'quasi market' organized on market principles, but underpinned by government finance and government regulation. The state controls the supply of and, to a considerable degree, the demand for education and it is important to note that it does so. This undermines the concept of free economic agents exchanging resources in a market system.

There are, of course, many questions about whether there are competitive markets in any part of modern economies. 'Real' economies consist of monopolists, monopsonists, cartels, ill-informed consumers, rigidities, laws, regulations and, above all, economies of scale and technological change, which have never been seriously allowed for by free-market theorists. The area where global markets come, perhaps, nearest to being free is the worldwide money markets. But these are not propitious. First they are, in fact, hemmed in by regulations of all kinds, by governments and through self-regulation to protect various vested interests. Second, a major consequence of markets constantly seeking equilibrium can be wild fluctuations as buyers and sellers adjust to external pressures. The financial crisis in the Asian-Pacific area of the late 1990s is only the most recent of a long line of booms and slumps ever since markets in their modern form began to appear in the 18th century.

Initial examination of the education market needs to focus on what product is being traded. What *do* schools and universities produce? Can it be clearly identified? Can it be measured meaningfully? Is it places for students to study and learn, examination results, future job opportunities, better attitudes, a fairer society, something else or some combination of these? It is difficult to know and this raises doubts about how to organize a state-regulated market for something that cannot be clearly identified and quantified. It seems that at this level education and schooling are used to mean one and the same thing, but it is doubtful if they really are. If we do not know the product and how to measure it, we are left with no means of putting a price on it. The core feature of markets is the operation of a pricing mechanism to which consumers and producers respond. But no such mechanism exists in state-provided education.

The second set of questions is about who the 'buyers' are in this market. Are they the students who actually experience the process of education and emerge as its products?[1] Is it parents, or is it local business or the economy as a whole? Could it be that the true buyer is society as a whole? But what can *this* mean in practice? Once again the answer is ambivalent, rendering unclear the concept of the customer, a key concept in the ideology of the market.

Who are the producers of education? Initially it seems easy to identify schools as the producers of education. However, they often produce a product, a curriculum perhaps, which is actually designed by government agencies. In some respects, schools, even those to which considerable authority has been devolved, are no more than individual franchisees selling the same branded product in a particular geographical area. Are they then the real producers? Once again the answer is unclear and it is this lack of clarity in all of these areas that calls into question the relevance of the market metaphor, quasi or otherwise, to education.

In some respects the core problem with the concept of selling education in a market lies in the 'commodification' of education. Education is in many respects a unique product. It is not like motor cars or compact discs. The purchase of a car or a compact disc does not affect other individuals' purchases or consumption of similar products. However, the education market has what Ranson (1993) calls 'chameleon'-like qualities. The decision by an individual to purchase education at a particular school brings about changes in the characteristics of that school. For example, decisions made by parents to send their children to School X will result in School X expanding in size. With increasing numbers might come a change in the way the school is organized, the culture of the school or the relationship between staff and pupils. This is particularly likely to be the case if the new students are from a particular social background. In general, individual education choices affect other consumers.

Moreover, individual consumption decisions also impact upon society because education carries with it positive externalities.

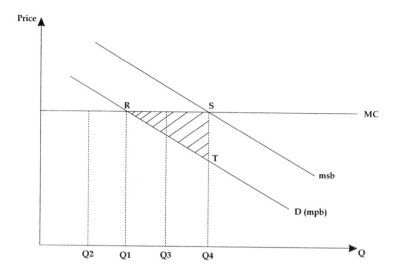

Figure 4.1 The effect on individual consumption decisions on society

The way this may occur is conceptualized in Figure 4.1. In Figure 4.1, line D(mpb) represents the 'marginal private benefit' accruing to an individual consuming education. This is the amount of extra benefit that is obtained if an additional 'unit' of education is provided. It assumes, of course, that such benefit can be meaningfully measured. Line MC represents the marginal cost to the individual of education – that is the cost of each additional unit. If an individual pursues a rational course s/he will consume an amount of education denoted by Q1. This is the point of allocative efficiency for this individual. At Q2, for example, the marginal benefit gained from the next unit of education would be greater than the marginal cost; the individual would gain from consumption of this unit. Therefore Q2 represents an underconsumption of education. Q3, on the other hand, shows that units of education have been consumed where the marginal cost is higher than the marginal benefit. There has been an overconsumption of education. Consequently, Q1 represents the optimum consumption of education for this individual. However, education carries with it a positive externality. That is, others in society benefit from the individual's purchase of education. A so-called third-party effect arises from the consumption of a good or service. In this case society and the economy stand to gain from a more educated population.

In a free-market system, with the onus on self-interest, the consumer will consume only Q1 of education. However, if we now include the value of the external benefit to society of education, the total benefit of education is now measured by line msb (marginal social benefit). Allocative efficiency now occurs at Q4 since it would be in the interests of society for the consumer to consume each unit where the marginal social benefit is higher than the marginal cost (MC). Q1 now represents an underconsumption from society's point of view and area RST the potential welfare loss if the consumer is not forced, or encouraged, to consume the extra units of education.

This is why the concept of leaving education to the free market organized solely around self-interest is not acceptable. Indeed, the way education exists today reflects this. In a true free market the consumer is free to choose how much to consume of a product, even none of it. In education this is not allowed. The government, realizing the external benefits from education and the potential welfare loss if education is not undertaken, does not allow consumers the choice of zero consumption. The market for education cannot allow the most basic choice available to any consumer in a market.

Once again the concept of choice in the market comes under pressure. Consumers now have no choice about the basic level of consumption and, if there is a national curriculum and nationally imposed testing system, little choice about the nature of their consumption. Indeed, choice seems to be restricted in this sense to the packaging of education rather than its content. Furthermore, the choice seems to have drifted from consumers to producers. With education now being marketed as what Hirsch (1977) called a 'positional good', the element of choice has swung toward the producer. The demand for places at so-called 'successful' schools far outstrips the supply. Consequently, the schools can now choose. In a market the price of such a product would have risen. Since there is no effective price, although top-up fees are beginning to emerge, the price in terms of entry requirements is rising. Schools are choosing pupils. Producer sovereignty rather than consumer sovereignty appears to be the pattern.

For markets to operate efficiently, consumers and producers need information about the qualities of the product and its price. As we have already pointed out, there is no price and there is also a problem as to what the educational 'product' is, let alone its quality. One way around this problem is to develop reliable indicators of performance (PIs) to which consumers can respond. This inevitably means some state involvement to ensure that there is no cheating. In the UK there has been an avalanche of PIs at all levels of the education system: every year there are school league tables comparing examination results, test scores, truancy rates and so on; every four years the university system is subjected to a research assessment exercise, which determines funding council support for individual universities' research for the next four years.

There are two major problems with PIs as currently constructed. The first is that unless there is agreement as to what the outputs of education are and on how to measure them, PIs indicate nothing other than performance with respect to the narrowly defined outputs that have been chosen by the government, usually because the data needed is readily available, rather than because they are the most appropriate indicator of educational effectiveness. In many respects an even more serious criticism is that PIs do not, or do not adequately, relate the output indicator to inputs. School A may be much more successful than School B in terms of student academic achievement, but this 'success' may be because the school has better teachers, resources and, perhaps most important, 'abler' students. School effectiveness needs to be related to the 'value added' by the school and this requires measures of *both* inputs and outputs of schools.

A further problem with information flows is how they are used by the consumers of education. Sophisticated PIs may be developed, but unless consumers respond *rationally* to them they will not have the effect desired by the proponents of markets, that is, consumers should go to those schools performing well and leave those not performing well. But parents may be more concerned with sending their child to the nearest school or to one where the child will be mixing with children with similar social, cultural or academic characteristics. Evidence suggests that the groups least likely to respond to PIs are the most disadvantaged in society and so their disadvantage by remaining in the least effective schools may be exacerbated.

A different sort of problem in market-oriented education provision is the *principal–agent* problem. How does the principal, the government, get the agents, the schools and colleges, to carry out its wishes? Put another way, how does he who pays the piper ensure that the tune he wants is played? However, it appears to us that simple payer–piper relationships are even less valid for education than they are for the skilled mechanic who services our modern motor vehicles. We can legitimately expect him to ensure that it works as it is supposed to work at a reasonable price. Beyond that we must trust his judgement and perhaps sue him if his servicing proves to have been incompetent. The technical competence of the schoolteacher or the university professor is of an even higher order and should be subject to correspondingly greater respect. It is perhaps relevant to note that the old adage refers to the simple craftsman-piper, not the symphony orchestra, even less Mozart or Beethoven.

But the principal–agent problem in education goes beyond matters of technical competence. It is also an ethical issue and a political problem of a fundamental kind. The central issue is the validity of a government's claims to consider itself the principal/payer, with the right to insist that all agent/pipers play tunes of its choosing. When the tunes concern the socialization and skilling of the next generation and the creation and analysis of the fundamental knowledge and thinking of a society, it may be claimed with some justification that the line between legitimate political practice and totalitarianism is a thin one. It was certainly not just by whim that the dictatorships of the mid-20th century took a close interest in the music and the higher education they authorized.

Of course, the governments of Western European countries would claim that this is dramatic nonsense on two counts. One is that they are reflecting the will of the majority as reflected in democratic elections. The other is that they are not imposing a monolithic will on higher education but merely reinforcing the claims of consumers.

The implications of the first of these claims go far beyond a paper on the economics of education. However, in a world that is beginning to see the rise of local nationalism and religious fundamentalism, it is legitimate to pose the question of the extent to which success in an election gives governments the right to impose the will of the majority on any recalcitrant minority.

More specific to schools and colleges and universities, however, is the question of the extent to which it is appropriate for it to be consumer-oriented. Certainly any publicly funded education system must be responsive to national needs as interpreted by a democratically elected government: certainly privately funded education has to respond to what its consumers are willing to buy. But educational institutions have other responsibilities as well: to truth, to professional integrity and to longer-term cultural traditions. They should not be subject to every whim of political or social fashion. We have the mass media and other organizations in the knowledge society for that.

To return to more strictly economic concerns, sociological research suggests in fact that where information about what actually takes place in classrooms can be concealed the government's intentions can be 'subverted', to use Ball's terminology (Ball, 1993). The central concern with situations where there may be principal–agent problems is that objectives desired by the principal may not be provided by the agent. If the outcomes are not those desired by the principal then there may be inefficiency in provision, in so far as efficiency is about providing the principal's desired outcomes at lowest cost.

The claims by proponents of market thinking that a quasi-market approach to the provision of education will lead to efficiency gains is hard to uphold as other than an empirical truth in some circumstances. Initially the problem lies in a sensible definition of efficiency. Secondly, efficiency cannot be divorced from effectiveness. A school could be made more cost-efficient in terms of annual recurrent expenditure per student. A 'pile 'em high, teach 'em cheap' policy would be financially more cost-effective, and more students could be housed for the same money, reducing average costs per pupil, but is this really more efficient? Efficiency relates output to input. If the output in terms of quantity increases but the quality of what is provided were to fall, would this be an increase in efficiency? For example, a school could replace its older, experienced staff with younger, less experienced and cheaper teachers. It could therefore teach the same pupils for less money, claiming an increase in efficiency in the process. However, can this claim be justified? We do not know until we have some measure of the quality of education provided by the older staff and their younger replacements.

Government-regulated quasi-markets are usually little more than an improvement in 'cost-effectiveness', which is a shallow and meaningless measure in terms of education unless considerable attention is paid to the question, 'Effectiveness in doing what?' In fact, the output is hard to measure and the output consists of both immediate outcomes and longer-term impact. An increase in pupil/teacher ratios can *appear* to improve cost-effectiveness. But it is not necessarily more efficient or more effective. The proponents of markets in education have not really come to grips with these concepts in a convincing way.

The external benefits of education, described above, also highlight the problem that allocative efficiency is not a guaranteed outcome in a market for education. If a consumer chooses a school and gains a place, it follows that another cannot take that place. For every winner in the market there must be a loser. In terms of Pareto criteria, a welfare improvement can take place only if one person can be made better off without making someone else worse off. In the example given above this does not happen. For every expanding school there will be a contracting school. For every graduate who obtains a good employment post there is another who did not get it.

This then highlights the market's impact on equity. A market has losers as well as winners. Whatever their virtues no one claims that markets in themselves promote equity. If some schools close, some students will suffer as a result. And yet a lack of equity is seen as the driving force behind the market; the idea that losing will force everyone to be winners may not be the case. A market for education results in some winners and some losers since it is organized on the basis of effective demand and self-interest. However, those who believe in the efficacy of the market do not try to argue the case. In one sense they appear to rejoice in the lack of equity that may result from a market approach. Milton Friedman, for example, is concerned that people have equality of opportunity: 'No arbitrary obstacles should prevent people from achieving those positions for which their talents fit them and which their values lead them to seek' (Friedman and Friedman, 1960: 132). Friedman is not concerned with another definition of equity that is concerned with equity of outcomes, since this is seen as reducing the choices that people can make and, as such, is an infringement on personal liberty. Indeed, the reduction in liberty may lead to undesirable social outcomes. 'Hard as it is to believe, the growth of crude criminality in Britain in recent decades may well be one consequence of the drive for equality,' claims Friedman (Friedman and Friedman, 1960: 145).

James Tooley (1996), after exploring the meaning of the term 'equality', asserts that 'equal outcomes' are undesirable and that, even if there were equal access to educational opportunity and resources, outcomes would be different because of 'natural differences' between students and other external factors over which education authorities have no control (p 58): 'it [the argument for reducing inequities in schooling to overcome social disadvantage] vastly over-estimates the potential of schooling in any social engineering project... If middle class families cannot buy into better schools, we can be sure that they would buy into more opportunities outside schools, and use the full weight of their influence...'.

This may be seen as a rather simplistic misrepresentation of the anti-market position since none has argued that schooling can ever totally 'compensate' for disadvantage, however defined. The argument and the emphases within the argument may differ, but the overriding concern is that any 'market' within education is almost certainly going to work in favour of those already advantaged in society. Markets in education will work as markets do elsewhere in the society, with those who have information, use the information and can support their choices with money being in a better position than those without information or resources.

The whole question of choice is central to the critique of markets by Ball. Choice is possible only if a surplus of places is available. However, to have a substantial surplus of places represents inefficient resource use. As certain schools become more popular they are able to use some other form of selection and become, in Ball's words, 'in a position, in one way or another, of choosing students, not the other way round' (Ball, 1994: 11). In an earlier article, Ball makes the point even more forcibly when he claims: 'The education market reasserts, reinforces and celebrates in a major way the opportunity advantages of middle class parents' (Ball, 1993: 11). A somewhat more measured conclusion of the effects of the 'marketization' of education is provided in Whitty, Power and Halpin (1998). This book draws on research findings from England and Wales, Australia, New Zealand, Sweden and the United States. The book's conclusion with respect to marketization and its effects on equal opportunity and equity in education provides a note of caution for countries embarking on the market route to the provision of education (p 14):

> Although it is early days, recent research suggests that the fragmentation of bureaucratic systems of education is leading to a polarization of provision, with 'good' schools being rewarded and able to choose their students – usually those that are academically and socially advantaged – while 'failing' schools are thrown into a cycle of decline from which they and their students – usually the least socially advantaged – find it difficult to recover.

This result may be acceptable to policy makers promoting markets in which there will necessarily be losers and winners. But if this is their intention they should be prepared to make it public, rather than argue that the introduction of markets, or quasi-markets, into education will benefit all.

Conclusion

The case for markets in education can be seen as ultimately a case for a particular conception of society. Economic concepts are used but that does not make it an economists' solution to the problem of deciding how much public funds to devote to education nor how to distribute them. Proponents of an education market-place appear ready to accept and indeed to reinforce the existing distribution of income and power within society, however unequal this may be. As Ball has presented it, a market implicitly assumes 'that the skill and predisposition to choice, and cultural capital which may be invested in choice, are generalised' (Ball, 1994: 118). The evidence from a number of countries around the world provides some support for the claim that 'markets' are more likely to reinforce existing inequities (Whitty, Power and Halpin, 1998). There is a *prima-facie* case, given above, for contending that markets will result in a sub-optimal, inefficient provision of education. Recognition of the possible inequitable and inefficient results of introducing markets is apparent when even its most ardent advocates suggest that a 'safety net' should be available for the most disadvantaged in society (Tooley, 1996: 28–29).

However, although the case for markets appears to flounder on both theoretical and empirical grounds, this by no means implies that the existing education systems in Europe are efficient or equitable. The evidence that is available suggests that in many countries the present systems, based on bureaucratic funding methods, with financing being increased on an incremental basis year on year, show too little concern with the inefficiency and inequity already in the system. What is needed, and it will need to be analysed at the national and probably local level, is what these inefficiencies and inequities are and what solutions might be called for. The panacea is not the universal introduction of 'markets', or for that matter any universal model of education provision; it is the careful economic and social analysis of what the objectives of society are for education and the policies that need to be applied at the local level in order to achieve them.

Note

1. Indeed those who treat education as an economic production process are rarely clear about whether students are an input into the schooling process or an output of it. Policies to increase participation in higher levels of education or in lifelong learning or which treat reductions in expenditure per student as an increase in efficiency are implicitly treating the student as the *output*. On the other hand, exponents of school-effectiveness policies usually treat students and their personal and social attributes as one of the inputs into the teaching process (along with teaching and managerial competence of the schools), which contribute to the production of examination results and, more rarely, other measurable outcomes of the process.

References

Ball, S (1990) *Markets, Morality and Equality in Education*, Hillgate Group Paper 5, Tufnell Press, London

Ball, S (1993) Market forces in education, *Educational Review*, 7 (1)

Ball, S (1994) *Education Reform: A critical and post-structural approach*, Open University Press, Buckingham

Blaug, M (1970) *Introduction to the Economics of Education*, Penguin, Harmondsworth

Brighouse, T (2000) *Independent*, Education section, 10 February 2000

Chubb, J and Moe, T (1990) *Politics, Markets and American Schools*, Brookings Institution, Washington

Friedman, M and Friedman, R (1960) *Free to Choose*, Harcourt, New York

Hayek, F (1960) *The Constitution of Liberty*, Routledge & Kegan Paul, London

Hillgate Group (1987) *The Reform of British Education: From principles to practice. A sequel to Whose schools? A radical manifesto*, Claridge Press, London

Hirsch, F (1977) *The Social Limits of Growth*, Routledge & Kegan Paul, London

Le Grand, J and Robinson, R (1989) *The Economics of Social Problems*, 2nd edn, Macmillan, London

Neave, G and van Vught, F A (1991) *Prometheus Bound: The changing relationship between government and higher education*, Pergamon Press, Oxford

Pollitt, C (1995) Justification by works or faith? Evaluating the new public management, *Evaluation*, 1 (2), pp 133–54

Power, S, Halpin, D and Whitty, G (1997) Managing the state and the market: 'new' education management in five countries, *British Journal of Educational Studies*, 45 (4), pp 342–62

Psacharopoulos, G (1973) *Returns to Education: An international comparison*, Elsevier, Amsterdam

Ranson, S (1993) Markets or democracy for education, *British Journal of Education Studies*, 41 (4)

Schultz, T W (1963) *The Economic Value of Education*, University Press, Columbia, New York

Smith, A (1776) *The Wealth of Nations*, Whitestone, Dublin

Tooley, J (1996) *Education without the State*, Institute of Economic Affairs, London

Whitty, G, Power, S and Halpin, D (1998) *Devolution and Choice in Education: The school, the state and the market*, OUP, Buckingham

Williams, G L (1997) Principals, agents, producers and consumers in higher education, in *Educational Dilemmas: Debate and diversity*, vol 2, *Reforms in Higher Education*, ed K Watson, C Mogdil and S Mogdil, Cassell, London

5. Legal perspectives on values, culture and education: human rights, responsibilities and values in education [1]

Audrey Osler and Hugh Starkey

Introduction

The transmission of values and culture is a primary purpose of education, and schools provide a key institutional context in which these processes take place. At a time of unprecedented economic, social and political change, a culture of values that can maintain social cohesion and provide a common sense of direction is essential. The United Nations is the world body entrusted with giving such a lead and its values are expressed in the Universal Declaration of Human Rights. Many of these rights are supported by guarantees in law, most powerfully in Europe by the European Convention on Human Rights. Thus law, values and culture interact with education and with schooling on a reciprocal basis, each element affecting and, in principle, supporting the others.

In the United Kingdom, 2000 saw the coming into force of the Human Rights Act, which incorporates the European Convention on Human Rights into British law. The implications of this legislation for education have been considered and a number of areas identified that may take on significance (Teasdale, 2000). The beginning of the new century was also the point at which England brought itself into line with other European countries by introducing citizenship as a foundation subject of the national curriculum in secondary schools. These two developments illustrate a national education system aligning itself quite explicitly with international norms that are founded on a notion of universal values and standards.

The promotion of human rights education, as a means of promoting understanding of and respect for these universal values, is a core goal of international organizations working with and through national and regional education authorities. The United Nations has declared 1995–2004 to be the decade for human rights education, and the Council of Europe has recognized such education as a priority since 1978. The results of the work of these organizations and of non-governmental organizations (NGOs) working in this field have been widely disseminated internationally and have had an impact in Britain on the programmes of study and the guidance for citizenship (Starkey,

1991; Osler and Starkey, 1996; Osler, 1998, 2000). In many respects the content and pedagogy associated with human rights education are well developed and supported by policy statements and internationally agreed texts. However, the notion of human responsibilities, which is commonly collocated with human rights, is less obviously agreed and defined. This paper discusses the concept of internationally agreed rights and responsibilities and considers their implications for education.

Legal steps towards a human rights culture

Within Western European democracies, the term human rights is often linked in the media and thus in the public mind to violations of civic and political rights such as those exposed by Amnesty International or Human Rights Watch. In reality, a recognition of human rights is a prerequisite for any social interaction that is not subject to the pressures of abusive or arbitrary force. This understanding of human rights, namely that human relationships should be conducted on the basis of equality of respect and dignity, is universally accepted, in principle at least. Any negotiation with respect to business or to daily life depends on an acceptance of the rule of law and the renouncing of violence and coercion as means to an end. Behaviour not in conformity to these principles is likely to be stigmatized as unacceptable or indeed criminal.

At the World Conference on Human Rights in Vienna in 1993, 171 states, representing 98 per cent of the world's population, signed a Declaration and Programme of Action, which reaffirmed in Article 1: 'the solemn commitment of all States to fulfil their obligations to promote universal respect for, and observance and protection of, all human rights and fundamental freedoms for all in accordance with the Charter of the United Nations, other instruments relating to human rights, and international law. The universal nature of these rights and freedoms is beyond question' (UNHCR, 1994).

The United Nations is thus able to claim legitimately that the rights embedded in the Universal Declaration of Human Rights:

> have gained prominence as a universally recognized set of norms and standards that increasingly inform all aspects of our relations as individuals and as collective members of groups, within communities and among nations. There is now near-universal recognition that respect for human rights – the rights of political choice and association, of opinion and expression, and of culture; the freedom from fear and from all forms of discrimination and prejudice; freedom from want and the right to employment and well-being and, collectively, to development – is essential to the sustainable achievement of the three agreed global priorities of peace, development and democracy. (United Nations, 1998)

The above quotation defines the scope of human rights to include culture and, by implication, education. It also sets out the three global priorities of *peace, development* and *democracy*. These three global priorities reflect a gradual evolution of the international agenda since the formation of the United Nations in 1945. The goals of the UN as set out in its Charter are: *peace*, or at least saving 'succeeding generations from the scourge of war'; justice and respect for international law; 'social progress and better standards of life in larger freedom'. In 1969 the UN General Assembly proclaimed a Declaration on Social Progress and Development.

By 1986, with the adoption of the Declaration on the Right to Development, there was full recognition within the UN community that *development* was the term to describe this third element relating to 'social progress and better standards of life in larger freedom'. Such development was now explicitly defined as a right. At the Vienna conference of 1993 this was reaffirmed and linked to *democracy* as the expression of the concept most likely to ensure the second goal of the UN Charter, namely justice and respect for international law. Thus peace, development and democracy, which require a commitment to human rights by states and an understanding of human rights by individuals, are the current expression of universal goals. This is well expressed in the Vienna Declaration:

> The efforts of the United Nations system towards the universal respect for, and observance of, human rights and fundamental freedoms for all, contribute to the stability and well-being necessary for peaceful and friendly relations among nations, and to improved conditions for peace and security as well as social and economic development, in conformity with the Charter of the United Nations (Article 6).
>
> Democracy, development and respect for human rights and fundamental freedoms are interdependent and mutually reinforcing. Democracy is based on the freely expressed will of the people to determine their own political, economic, social and cultural systems and their full participation in all aspects of their lives. In the context of the above, the promotion and protection of human rights and fundamental freedoms at the national and international levels should be universal and conducted without conditions attached. The international community should support the strengthening and promoting of democracy, development and respect for human rights and fundamental freedoms in the entire world (Article 8).

For the achievement of peace, development and democracy, a culture of human rights is necessary. This was expressed by one of the architects of the Universal Declaration, René Cassin, in an address to teachers:

> When [teachers] teach about human rights, when they convey to their pupils the notion of their rights, their dignity and their duties as citizens and human beings, then they are carrying out a task that complements wonderfully the work that we have achieved at the highest level...

> Legal force of itself is only a secondary safety valve: it is the education of young people and even of adults that constitutes the primary and real guarantee for minority groups faced with racial hatred that leads so easily to violence and murder (Alliance Israélite Universelle, 1961: 123, our translation)

Cassin's argument is twofold. First, rights are only meaningful when people know about them and understand them. Secondly, it is the culture of a society more than the law itself that creates the conditions for democracy and for social peace. The law, of course, contributes in its turn to the creation of such a culture. For example, in Britain, anti-discriminatory legislation, notably the 1976 Race Relations Act, which outlawed both direct and indirect racial discrimination and gave powers to a new Commission for Racial Equality, have contributed to a social climate of improved race relations (Parekh, 1991; Blackstone, Parekh and Sanders, 1998). Despite limitations and flaws, the law has enabled a climate to develop over the past 25 years in which direct discrimination and overt manifestations of racism are no longer a regular feature of daily life.

Education and a global culture of human rights

Education and development

The crucial role of education with respect to economic and social development was the theme of the World Education Forum meeting in Dakar, Senegal in April 2000. This meeting of governments, UN agencies, the World Bank, NGOs and academics was convened to determine the direction education is to take in the new millennium, both in individual countries and on a global basis. The Forum is committed to education for all (EFA), in other words the implementation of commitments already entered into by states, but not fulfilled. Indeed, none of the targets set 10 years previously at the 1990 World Conference on Education for All in Jomtien, Thailand for achieving EFA by 2000, halving adult literacy and ending male/female disparities have been realized.

A number of NGOs, including Oxfam, formed a Global Campaign for Education to encourage all parties to the Forum to work against illiteracy and for education in the spirit of Article 26 of the Universal Declaration, which states:

> Everyone has the right to education. Education shall be free, at least in the elementary and fundamental stages. Elementary education shall be compulsory. Technical and professional education shall be made generally available and higher education shall be equally accessible to all on the basis of merit.
>
> Education shall be directed to the full development of the human personality and to the strengthening of respect for human rights and fundamental freedoms. It shall promote understanding, tolerance and friendship among all nations, racial or religious groups, and shall further the activities of the United Nations for the maintenance of peace.

Some states have been slow to implement this commitment, pleading poverty or other priorities. A survey by UNESCO of 100 developing countries found that two-thirds saw a decline in expenditure per pupil during the 1980s and half saw a decline in the proportion of pupils enrolled in primary school. The cause in most cases was the cut in public spending forced on many countries by the debt crisis (UNICEF, 1992). At the 1990 World Education Conference, while it was recognized there is a close connection between the burden of debt and whether children go to school or not, it was also acknowledged that school enrolment and literacy rates could still be improved within existing budgets. This nevertheless required an adjustment of priorities that favoured mass primary schooling rather than higher education for the few.

Following the World Education Forum in 2000, renewed efforts to ensure EFA are likely to depend on the quality of education. This is particularly the case for girls. Sometimes the reason for lack of progress in ensuring EFA is ideological and political. Some governments, such as the Taliban in Afghanistan, deny the equality of women. In many regions, however, initial enrolment in primary school is high, but high drop-out rates mean that substantial numbers of poor children, and in particular girls, fail to complete their primary education. Both the 1989 Convention on the Rights of the Child and the 1979 Convention on the Elimination of All Forms of Discrimination against Women stress girls' human right to education. However, to improve general access to schooling and, in particular, girls' access, experience has shown that, amongst other things, attention needs to be paid to:

- Parental and community involvement – families and communities must be important partners with schools in developing the curriculum and managing children's education.
- Low cost and flexible timetables – basic education should cost very little or be free. For example, when school uniforms and school fees were abolished in Malawi, attendance rates improved (DfID, 2000). School hours should be flexible so as to allow children to help at home and still attend school.
- Schools should be close to home – many parents are anxious about girls travelling long distances.
- Relevant curricula: learning materials should be relevant to the cultural background and be in the local language. Texts should also avoid gender stereotyping.

(UNICEF, 1996)

A global culture of human rights

The Director-General of UNESCO, Koichiro Matsuura (2000), points out the dual potential of education:

We have to note that, unfortunately, education has not always and in all circumstances served to liberate people from the barriers of ignorance. It hasn't always helped them to affirm their dignity nor to map their own destiny freely. It has also served, and continues to do so, to bolster ruling elites, to exclude and even, it has to be said, to ferment conflicts. And this is precisely because education is not just a means of acquiring knowledge, but also a vehicle for moral and ideological training available to any social organization.

Matsuura poses the question as to whether education in the spirit of the United Nations is compatible with equally powerful claims to the freedom for communities to determine their own culture. It is often women and girls whose human rights are denied when claims to cultural specificity outside the frame of reference provided by international standards are pursued. They may be denied access to education or to the best-quality education available, particularly when resources are limited. Other discriminatory practices operating within schools, such as low expectations of female students and the use of textbooks that reinforce gender stereotyping, are sometimes justified as being in keeping with community norms and cultural practices. In such contexts the universality of human rights is called into question. Matsuura responds by reaffirming this universality (2000): 'In spite of the vast number of systems of values, surely a common corpus of values is acknowledged in the Universal Declaration of Human Rights? The respect of this text by all human communities will in any case determine whether humanity can control its own destiny. And this is precisely the crusade being undertaken by UNESCO.'

The creation of a global culture of human rights appears to be the only means by which the universal goals of peace, development and democracy can be achieved. Other radical solutions, such as state socialism, have been tried but have failed to deliver both development and freedoms. Education has a crucial role in promoting such a culture. In turn, a culture of human rights has profound implications for educational structures and priorities.

The concern to promote a global culture of human rights is international, but it is equally relevant and applicable at national and at local level. For example, within the UK, the government has promoted a discourse of a 'culture of rights', based on a 'shared understanding'. Within this discourse, rights are 'balanced' by the responsibilities and duties of citizens:

> The Human Rights Act is fundamentally about modernising our society and building a new culture of rights balanced by responsibilities within UK law. Rights and responsibilities go together. They are two sides of the same coin. The new culture that we want to build is one in which the Human Rights Act gives us a shared understanding of what is fundamentally right and wrong, a culture where people recognise the duties that citizens owe to each other and the wider community and are willing to fulfil them – and one in which public authorities understand that the Human Rights Act defines what the basic rights are. It will sometimes require us to be robust about an individ-

ual's rights if we are to maintain the rights of others. That is the culture that we want to build. That is what the Human Rights Act is all about. (Lord Bassam, Home Office minister, in *Hansard*, 2000a)

While the building of such a culture at national level can be the responsibility of both government and NGOs, the building of such a culture in microcosm, at school level, is a legitimate goal for headteachers and school governing bodies. We explore below ways in which this culture can be promoted and the benefits to schools of adopting such an approach. However, first we note a particular threat to this culture.

Racism: threatening the culture of human rights

In May 2000, as part of the United Nations programme in its Third Decade to Combat Racism and Racial Discrimination, a preparatory conference was held in advance of the World Conference Against Racism, South Africa, 2001. The focus of the Third Decade is based on the recognition that every society in the world is affected and hindered by discrimination. Prevention through education, particularly human rights education, is seen as pivotal in order to look at the roots of racism and make institutional changes in order to prevent its eruption.

Looking ahead to the conference and the preparatory meetings in her message on International Human Rights Day in 1999, the UN High Commissioner for Human Rights, Mary Robinson, stressed the threat of racism to a global culture of human rights (United Nations, 1999): 'Racism and xenophobia are powerful causes of conflict; in fact, if you look closely at the roots of history's most violent confrontations, you will see their malign influence at work. And they are found everywhere. No society is free from at least some people who are intolerant of difference, whether ethnic or religious, and whose intolerance finds violent expression.'

The crucial importance of education as a means to tackle the roots of racism is also stressed by Matsuura. He notes the tension between the unifying forces of globalization and the need for communities to assert their rights to cultural diversity. Such assertions, when they are coupled with a refusal to respect the rights of others, are the basis of the most serious conflicts currently preoccupying the world community: 'Individuals and communities need to harness the potential of culture to ensure that globalisation and the consequent homogenisation of knowledge is counterbalanced by the preservation of cultural diversity and individual identities... Each society and each citizen needs the values and skills to counter intolerance and conflict at the root.'

The contribution of citizenship education

The role of education for citizenship in helping young people to acquire 'the values and skills to counter intolerance' is seen as crucial in most democratic societies. In France, for instance, the programmes of study for the lower secondary school define the purpose of this stage of schooling as to provide an education: 'for human rights and citizenship, through the acquisition of the principles and the values which underpin and organize democracy and the Republic, through knowledge of institutions and laws, through an understanding of the rules of social and political life' (Ministère de l'Éducation Nationale, 1998: 36, our translation).

The equivalent statement in a British context is the second aim of the revised national curriculum for England. While this statement can be interpreted as supporting education for human rights, it avoids any direct or explicit reference to human rights or human rights education. Indeed the term rights is used in a restricted sense to refer to consumer rights:

> It should develop [pupils'] knowledge, understanding and appreciation of their own and different beliefs and cultures, and how these influence individuals and societies. The school curriculum should pass on enduring values, develop pupils' integrity and autonomy and help them to be responsible and caring citizens capable of contributing to the development of a just society. It should promote equal opportunities and enable pupils to challenge discrimination and stereotyping. It should develop their awareness and understanding of, and respect for, the environments in which they live, and secure their commitment to sustainable development at a personal, local, national and global level. It should also equip pupils as consumers to make informed judgements and independent decisions and to understand their responsibilities and rights. (QCA, 1999)

Certainly there is a commitment to promoting an 'appreciation of their own and different beliefs and cultures', to 'the development of a just society', to equal opportunities and challenging 'discrimination and stereotyping' and to 'sustainable development'. This might be summarized as an education for the three UN priorities of peace, development and democracy, although only one of these three terms is actually used.

Other government departments in Britain are more robust in promoting a culture of human rights, which is, by definition, a culture of anti-racism. As a Home Office minister put it:

> Anti-racism is not about helping black and Asian people; it is about our future – white and black. We all live in a multicultural society and we all have a choice: either we make a success of multicultural Britain or we do not. If we fail to address those issues, our children – white and black – will pay the price of that failure. That is why all of us, white and black, have a vested interest in the Race Relations (Amendment) Bill and in anti-racism. We must make Britain a success as a multicultural society. (Mike O'Brien, in *Hansard*, 2000b)

Racism operates to deny equality and to limit or exclude some citizens from full participation in society. One of the stated purposes of the citizenship education programme within the national curriculum for England is to strengthen democracy, and one of the means by which it expects to achieve this is by developing the political literacy of young people. Since racism poses a threat to democracy, a politically literate citizen needs the skills to challenge racism (Osler, 2000).

Initiatives to promote equality in schools also need an anti-racist dimension. Schools and the education service, like other institutions in a former colonial power such as Britain, are likely to suffer from institutional racism. Recent studies that highlight the disproportionate numbers of black and ethnic minority children among those excluded from school (for example, Osler and Hill, 1999; Wright, Weekes and McGlaughlin, 2000) suggest strongly that this is, in fact, the case. Education programmes and initiatives that address prejudiced attitudes among pupils, but neglect to review structures and consider staff training, are therefore unlikely to be adequate in addressing racism and promoting a culture of human rights.

Creating a culture of human rights in schools is a project that will contribute to peace and justice globally. The introduction of citizenship to the national curriculum in England in 2000 provides an opportunity to include knowledge of human rights in the programme of study of all children, in accordance with Article 26 of the Universal Declaration. However, the inclusion of human rights in a programme of study is no guarantee that such teaching will be well received. The culture of the school needs itself to be based on a culture of human rights for such education to be credible and effective.

Evaluating the culture of human rights in schools

Inspection is one means by which standards in schools are assessed. In England the inspection agency, OFSTED, is required to report on how well the school cares for its pupils, the quality of the curriculum opportunities offered and the extent to which equal opportunities and inclusion prevail in a school. However, such inspections provide a snapshot view at a particular moment in a school's development and they rely to a considerable extent on what can be seen and measured. Schools need also to engage in a continuous process of self-evaluation, and a number of instruments have been developed to help schools in this respect.

Given the importance of the United Nations Convention on the Rights of the Child (1989), which is by far the most widely ratified human rights convention, and given its particular relevance for schools, we have developed an instrument entitled 'Does your school environment give everyone a chance to enjoy their rights?' (Osler and Starkey, 1998). Pupils, teachers, heads, parents and governors are provided with 23 statements and invited to respond by 'always', 'sometimes' or 'never'. These are arranged in three sections according to their relevance to the three broad themes of the Convention, namely provision, protection and participation. Each statement is followed by a list of the main articles of the Convention to which it relates. For example:

- (Provision) In the teaching of national history, due weight is given to women and minorities and to their versions of history (Articles 2, 13, 28, 29.1c & d, 30).
- (Protection) A student accused of breaking the rules is presumed innocent until proven guilty and carries on with classes (Article 28.2, 40).
- (Participation) Students and adults (including parents, teachers and administrative staff) are consulted about the quality of the teaching in the school (Article 5, 12, 18).

The questionnaire also draws on descriptions of pedagogic principles derived from the Convention (Osler and Starkey, 1996: 153–56). A similar instrument, but based on the Universal Declaration of Human Rights, can be found in Shiman (1999). Both these questionnaires are draft instruments that can be adapted by schools for their own use. They are indicative of an approach to school self-evaluation within a human rights framework. We see them as contributing to the development of a culture of self-evaluation for human rights rather than as providing definitive measures. Since it is often also difficult for inspectors to assess the human rights culture of a school, it is important that teachers feel confident in developing their own methods of self-evaluation, which may form the basis of a discussion of such issues with external assessors such as school inspectors.

Identifying responsibilities

Article 29 of the Universal Declaration states that: 'Everyone has duties to the community in which alone the free and full development of his personality is possible'. This explicit reference to duties, or what are now more usually referred to as responsibilities, as an essential element of a human rights framework, has received relatively little attention in liberal democracies. Whereas it took three years, between the signing of the United Nations Charter and the final adoption of the Universal Declaration, to define human rights to the satisfaction of all parties, no such attempt was made to define human responsibilities.

René Cassin attempted, in 1947, to include a formulation of duties in the Universal Declaration. However, Eleanor Roosevelt argued that the principles of individual liberty, which had driven the war against Nazism and Fascism, were overriding. It was agreed to leave the formulation of duties until after the completion of the formulation of rights, but no commission was ever convened to undertake this task (Cassin, 1969).

As we have noted above, much current discourse of human rights brackets responsibilities with rights. The prime architect of the 'third way' goes so far as to propose the maxim 'no rights without responsibilities' (Giddens, 1998: 66).

It is possible to derive responsibilities from rights, but in attempting to arrive at a definition in this way, it becomes clear that there is not a straightforward one-to-one equivalence between rights and responsibilities. It is therefore most important to be able to obtain agreement on a definition of the concept, as has been achieved for the concept of rights. Indeed the Committee of Ministers of Education of the Council of Europe adopted, in May 1999, a 'Declaration and programme on education for democratic citizenship, based on the rights and responsibilities of citizens' (Council of Europe, 1999a), which will attempt to define this relationship in the context of education. The key issues to be pursued under this programme include: 'the relationships between rights and responsibilities as well as common responsibilities in combating social exclusion, marginalisation, civic apathy, intolerance and violence'. We might expect that they will review existing definitions of responsibilities in current human rights instruments and explore their meaning.

The first attempt to define responsibilities in a human rights instrument is contained in the African Charter of Human and People's Rights, adopted in 1981 by the member states of the Organisation of African Unity. The Charter includes defined duties and responsibilities. Article 25 places an obligation on states to promote education for the rights in the Charter and to: 'see to it that these freedoms and rights as well as corresponding obligations and duties are understood'. There follows a section (Articles 27–29) that defines the duties and responsibilities of individuals, as opposed to those of states and of parents.

Article 27
1. Every individual shall have duties towards his family and society, the State and other legally recognized communities and the international community.
2. The rights and freedoms of each individual shall be exercised with due regard to the rights of others, collective security, morality and common interest.

Article 28
Every individual shall have the duty to respect and consider his fellow beings without discrimination, and to maintain relations aimed at promoting, safeguarding and reinforcing mutual respect and tolerance.

Article 29
The individual shall also have the duty:

1. to preserve the harmonious development of the family and to work for the cohesion and respect of the family; to respect his parents at all times; to maintain them in case of need;

2. to serve his national community by placing his physical and intellectual abilities at its service;
3. not to compromise the security of the State whose national or resident he is;
4. to preserve and strengthen social and national solidarity, particularly when the latter is threatened;
5. to preserve and strengthen the national independence and the territorial integrity of his country and to contribute to its defence in accordance with the law;
6. to work to the best of his abilities and competence, and to pay taxes imposed by law in the interest of the society;
7. to preserve and strengthen positive African cultural values in his relation with other members of the society, in the spirit of tolerance, dialogue and consultation and, in general, to contribute to the promotion of the moral well-being of society;
8. to contribute to the best of his abilities, at all times and at all levels, to the promotion and achievement of African unity.

While the above definitions have a distinctively African flavour, an attempt to define a list of universal responsibilities was made by the Commission for Global Governance in its report published at the time of the 50th anniversary of the United Nations (Commission on Global Governance, 1995). The impetus for setting up the Commission came from Willy Brandt soon after the fall of the Berlin Wall in 1989. It was subsequently endorsed by the then Secretary-General of the United Nations, Boutros Boutros-Ghali. The Commission, chaired by Shridath Ramphal of Guyana and Ingvar Carlsson of Sweden, included members from nearly 30 countries, broadly representative of the world community.

The Commission distilled from all the human rights instruments available a list of eight fundamental universal rights and seven universal responsibilities. The list of responsibilities is as follows:

- Contribute to the common good.
- Consider the impact of one's actions on the security and welfare of others.
- Promote equity, including gender equity.
- Protect the interests of future generations by pursuing sustainable development and safeguarding the global commons.
- Preserve humanity's cultural and intellectual heritage.
- Be active participants in governance.
- Work to eliminate corruption.

Although the form in which these responsibilities are expressed varies from the African Charter, it broadly echoes its intentions, while attempting to provide explicit but concise formulations. The seventh responsibility, the elimination of corruption, is innovative in human rights discourse. It is not hard to justify, however, as corruption is corrosive of democracy, which is the main guarantee of justice, equality and sustainable development.

A third document that goes some way to defining responsibilities is another regional instrument, this time developed by the Council of Europe. In 1999 the Parliamentary Assembly adopted a Recommendation (1401), 'Education in the responsibilities of the individual' (Council of Europe, 1999b). Drawing on expressions of fundamental values, particularly as expressed in the European Convention on Human Rights, the Universal Declaration of Human Rights, the European Social Charter and the Framework Convention for the Protection of National Minorities, the Assembly concludes:

> Everyone should, *inter alia*:
> a. fully respect the dignity, value and freedom of other people, without distinction of race, religion, sex, nationality, ethnic origin, social status, political opinion, language or age; everyone must act towards others in a spirit of fellowship and tolerance;
> b. act peacefully without recourse to physical violence or mental pressure;
> c. respect the opinions, privacy and personal and family life of other people;
> d. show solidarity and stand up for the rights of others;
> e. in practising his or her own religion, respect other religions, without fomenting hatred or advocating fanaticism, but rather promoting general mutual tolerance;
> f. respect the environment and use energy resources with moderation, giving thought to the well-being of future generations.

It would appear that the European formulation was produced in ignorance of the seven responsibilities identified by the Commission for Global Governance. Given the cultural mandate of the Council of Europe, a reference to the preservation of cultural heritage would be logical. Similarly, given its mission to promote democracy, the failure to highlight active participation appears an oversight.

An audit of responsibilities

Both the African Charter and the Parliamentary Assembly of the Council of Europe identify responsibilities that are not found in the report of the Commission on Global Governance. However, the clarity of the Commission's conclusions and its claim to universality lead us to focus on these rather than on the regional instruments. We suggest that the seven responsibilities have implications for schools, and we see them as forming a minimal requirement. In particular, young people should learn about their responsibilities and the implications of these for their behaviour and lifestyle. The provenance of this formulation of universal responsibilities should ensure the possibility of acknowledgement of its legitimacy in multi-faith and multi-ethnic communi-

ties. In the context of education for citizenship, and in addressing personal, social and health education, schools should provide opportunities for pupils
and teaching staff and other stakeholders to consider the following as both individual and shared responsibilities.

Contribute to the common good

This active obligation to work to further the aims of the community supposes
that the aims are made known and that they are shared, that is that each member of the community feels ownership of the goals of the institution. The aims
will need to be revisited periodically to take into account changing circumstances and changing cohorts of students and to enable new members of the
community to contribute to the process of reformulation. There are many ways
in which institutions can initiate their members and retain their loyalty to the
common purpose. In some cases this will include an identification of common
goals in some form of shared acknowledgement of symbols. These may take
many different forms, but might include school assemblies, a school song, celebration or prize-giving or perhaps the wearing of a uniform or badge. Provided
that the ceremonies or rituals are based on human rights principles and inclusive of all, it can be expected that all members of the school will be able to support the aims expressed. All activity in the school should then be directed to
achieving the aims and thus contribute to the common good. However, cere-
monial expression of common loyalties needs to be matched by real opportunities for sharing in the benefits provided by the institution.

Consider the impact of one's actions on the security and welfare of others

This obligation follows from the previous one. When many people interact in
close physical proximity, as in schools, these considerations are particularly
important. Although individuals have the responsibility to be considerate, the
institution is greatly helped when approved practices and procedures are for-
malized. For instance, something as simple as keeping to the left on stairs or
not running in corridors will contribute greatly to security and welfare.

Promote equity, including gender equity

In view of the right to equitable treatment, the institution is obligated to have
policies that help to ensure equity. At the same time, individuals have the responsibility to do their best to promote the policies. At a minimum that implies
that both staff and students are familiar with equal opportunities issues and
the policies that derive from them. Ideally, both staff and students should be
involved in the formulation of such policies and all parties or their representatives should be involved in the design and monitoring of such policies. They
should cover the curriculum as well as the informal provisions of the school

and its ethos. Gender equity should not be divorced from other equality issues such as those relating to race and disability.

Protect the interests of future generations by pursuing sustainable development and safeguarding the global commons

All members of the institution will be committed to preserving its assets and protecting communal facilities. They will also have an education that helps them acquire a global perspective and an understanding of the concept of sustainable development. Schools will provide opportunities for pupils to become familiar with local Agenda 21 initiatives. The publication *A Curriculum for Global Citizenship* (Oxfam, 1997) provides detailed guidance and resources across the whole age-range.

Preserve humanity's cultural and intellectual heritage

Traditionally this has been a major function of schools and universities. The reference is to the heritage of humanity rather than of single nations or regions. This implies a broadly based curriculum, again with a global perspective. For example, in the teaching of history no one national or religious perspective should be adopted. Students should be encouraged to understand that historical events are interpreted from a variety of perspectives in different times and places.

Be active participants in governance

Institutions are obligated to provide structures for participation. Individuals have a responsibility to be involved. Involvement can take many forms, and at its most basic may simply imply voting for a representative. The school has a responsibility to establish participative structures, such as school or class councils, and students should be encouraged to consider issues and decisions that affect them. Such structures might share responsibility for the allocation of resources.

Work to eliminate corruption

Most schools are financed with public funds and those ultimately responsible for the institution must be accountable for the use of those funds. Democracy implies transparency in the use of resources and any use of the funds for purposes incompatible with the goals of the institution may be considered corrupt. All members of the institution, staff and students, should be aware of the possibility of corruption and know what steps are open to them if corruption is suspected. As with issues of security, measures of prevention should be in place. It is likely that work to eliminate corruption will be collective, perhaps involving unions or associations of parents, for example.

Children's own understandings of rights, responsibilities and participation

It is sometimes argued that, if informed about their rights, young people will begin to demand rights without acknowledging their responsibilities. Moreover, it is sometimes asserted that young people do not want responsibilities, and that they see these as the preserve of adults. Not only is this a fundamental misunderstanding of the nature of children's human rights, which are based on the principle of reciprocity, that is to say respecting and upholding the rights of others (see, for example, Osler and Starkey, 1996 and 1998; Flekkøy and Kaufman, 1997) but it is also, perhaps, to underestimate young people's capacity and willingness to acknowledge their responsibilities.

In a research project conducted on behalf of the UK Commission for Racial Equality into exclusion from school (Osler, 1997), young people were invited to give their opinions on improving school discipline. They acknowledged that they shared a responsibility with teachers for ensuring that the school was an orderly place where everyone had an opportunity to learn, and were eager to develop their own skills and capacities to resolve conflicts and to participate more fully in decision-making processes. Their consultation and involvement in our research, which set out to identify good practice in managing school discipline and minimizing school exclusions, produced a wealth of creative ideas, which complemented those of their teachers and gave us new insights. In particular, pupils highlight that if schools are to ensure the greater participation of young people in decision making in line with the provisions of the Convention on the Rights of the Child, schools must not only provide structures for participation (school councils, class councils etc) but also equip children with the skills to participate (eg advocacy, counselling and listening skills, conflict resolution). Pupils saw structured opportunities for exercising their participation rights as a fundamental part of a well-disciplined school.

Conclusion

The 21st-century world is a global village within which diverse traditions and cultures coexist and interact. This is a source of rich creativity, but also potentially a source of tensions and conflicts. Schools, particularly those in cities, are often microcosms, reflecting the global diversity of populations. Even when schools are more homogenous in their composition, they have to prepare their pupils to live and work in a heterogeneous world. For all these reasons education is crucially about helping young citizens to develop those values and skills that will help them contribute to the global priorities of peace, sustainable development and the means to achieve these, namely democracy and respect for human rights.

Institutions and individuals have rights and responsibilities. In the case of education, those involved as students, teachers or in support roles are expected to be aware of the key principles and guidelines set out in Article 26.2 of the Universal Declaration of Human Rights. The study of this and the full text of the Universal Declaration can inspire local statements of values, such as those contained in school mission statements and policy documents.

Much work has been done on the application of human rights values to education. There is a developing rhetoric stressing the essential reciprocity of rights and responsibilities. It is relatively easy to convince individuals that they have rights, for these are strong claims that they can make in the expectation that they will receive benefits, such as protection and the provision of services. Responsibilities, on the other hand, imply not receiving, but giving, not individualism but a sense of the communal and the collective. This has been and continues to be a feature of many religious traditions and values. In an increasingly secular context, there is a continuing pedagogical challenge, namely to promote responsibilities linked to rights for the achievement of global priorities.

Note

1   This chapter draws upon an earlier version in Osler A (ed) (2000) *Citizenship and Democracy in Schools: Diversity, identity, equality*, Trentham, Stoke-on-Trent. Osler (*et al*) have the copyright of the orginal

References

Alliance Israélite Universelle (1961) *Les Droits de l'Homme et L'Éducation*, Presses Universitaires de France, Paris

Blackstone, T, Parekh, B and Sanders, P (ed) (1998) *Race Relations in Britain: A developing agenda*, Routledge, London

Cassin, R (1969) *From the Ten Commandments to the Rights of Man* (original source unknown), published at www.udhr50/org/history/tencomms.htm

Commission on Global Governance (1995) *Our Global Neighbourhood*, OUP, Oxford

Council of Europe (1999a) Declaration and programme on education for democratic citizenship, based on the rights and responsibilities of citizens, CM (99) 76, Committee of Ministers of Education, Council of Europe, Strasbourg, www.coe.int

Council of Europe (1999b) Education in the responsibilities of the individual, Recommendation 1401 of the Parliamentary Assembly, Council of Europe, Strasbourg, www.coe.int

Department for International Development (DfID) (2000) *Strategies for Achieving the International Development Targets: Education for all – the challenge of universal primary education,* March consultation document, DfID, London

Flekkøy, M and Kaufman, N (1997) *The Participation Rights of the Child: Rights and responsibilities in family and society,* Jessica Kingsley, London

Giddens, A (1998) *The Third Way,* Polity Press, Cambridge

Hansard (2000a) 10 January, columns 481–82

Hansard (2000b) 9 March, column 1281

Matsuura, K (2000) in UNESCO press release, 15 February, www.unesco.org

Matsuura, K (2000) in *Le Monde,* 20 April (authors' translation)

Ministère de l'Éducation Nationale (1998) *Histoire, Géographie, Éducation Civique: Programmes et accompagnement,* Centre National de la Documentation Pédagogique, Paris

Osler, A (1997) *Exclusion from School and Racial Equality,* Commission for Racial Equality, London

Osler, A (1998) Human rights, education and racial justice in Britain: rhetoric and reality, in *Voices for Democracy: A North-South dialogue on education for sustainable democracy,* ed C Harber, Education Now, Ticknell

Osler, A (2000) The Crick Report: difference, equality and racial justice, *Curriculum Journal,* **11** (1), pp 25–37

Osler, A and Hill, J (1999) Exclusion from school and racial equality: an examination of government proposals in the light of recent research evidence, *Cambridge Journal of Education,* **29** (1), pp 33–62

Osler, A and Starkey, H (1996) *Teacher Education and Human Rights,* Fulton, London

Osler, A and Starkey, H (1998) Children's rights and citizenship: some implications for the management of schools, *The International Journal of Children's Rights,* **6,** pp 313–33

Oxfam (1997) *A Curriculum for Global Citizenship,* Oxfam, Oxford, http://www.oxfam.org.uk/coolplanet/teachers/cat2000/

Parekh, B (1991) Law torn, *New Statesman and Society,* 14 June

Qualifications and Curriculum Authority (QCA) (1999) *The National Curriculum 2000,* QCA, London

Shiman, D (1999) *Teaching Human Rights,* Center for Teaching International Relations, University of Denver, Denver (also available at: www.hrea.org)

Starkey, H (ed) (1991) *The Challenge of Human Rights Education,* Cassell, London

Teasdale, J (2000) *European Convention Rights in Education,* Briefing Paper 4 on the Human Rights Act 1998, Local Government Information Unit, London

UNICEF (1992) *The State of the World's Children,* Oxford University Press, Oxford

UNICEF (1996) *The State of the World's Children,* Oxford University Press, Oxford

United Nations (1998) *Human Rights Today, A United Nations Priority,* UN briefing papers, www.un.org/rights/HRToday/

United Nations (1999) Press release HR/99/115, 10 December, www.unhchr.ch

United Nations High Commission for Refugees (UNHCR) (1994) *Human Rights: The new consensus*, Regency Press (Humanity), London

Wright, C, Weekes, D and McGlaughlin, A (2000) *'Race', Class and Gender in Exclusion from School*, Falmer, London

Section II

Changing values and cultures in education: national case studies

6. Mapping patterns of change in cultures and schools

Roy Gardner

Introduction

This section of the book provides a number of country case studies, each of which gives an insight into the history of educational development in relation to the major events that have influenced the course of growth and change. Each chapter also points to the specific factors integral to each context, which have conditioned the dimensions and directions of the changes in the organization and control of societies, their spiritual and social identities and the impact these have had on cultures and schools; and also the impact the schools and educational provision have had on societies and subsequent movements for change. The framework in which the authors have contributed in-depth studies of individual national perspectives on values, culture and education was necessarily broadly based and flexible. The underpinning was provided by the dynamic relationship between all three. In this chapter an attempt will be made both to examine some of the individual cases (the bricks) and to analyse whether the dynamic mix between culture, values and education (the mortar) might contain some constant ingredients (the global) as well as some case-specific ingredients (the national).

No review of change in cultures and schools could confine itself to the study of individual countries or just to comparisons. A viable review needs to take account of pressures and trends on a regional, continental and global scale that affect the perceptions that planners and politicians have of both the standing that their systems have in profiles of educational provision worldwide and also those signposts and directions being counselled by international organizations. Such bodies have considerable impact, either through political influences they are able to exert or perhaps with greater importance through the provision of finance and other support, which many countries need to expand and refocus the education provided to maximize the potential benefits likely to be derived from it.

The role of education

Education has a Janus role with responsibilities both to look to the past and to anticipate the future. Perhaps a Janus analogy may not be quite correct because education has a further role, which is to interpret and reflect current cultures and society. In more cynical moments it might be appropriate to compare education to a Hydra since each facet of the education system and its transference into education activities reflects a differing aspect of educational thought. As one phase becomes less popular, eg competitive selection for secondary schools, it is replaced by another, eg the comprehensivization of school provision. However, the changing scene in education may be represented by Janus provided the head turns back and forth to provide insights into the ebb and flow of emphasis and fashion in education.

Davies and Evans (below) seek to capture the essence of the continuing effect of the past on present educational practice and the need to anticipate change: 'Education systems contain and resist change but also are expected to initiate it.' Similarly, Halstead (1996) notes: 'Schools reflect and embody the values of society, indeed they owe their existence to the fact that society values education and seeks to exert influence over its own future development' (p 3). Within this quotation lies the dilemma for education systems of how far they should preserve or even promulgate the cultural heritage of a society while at the same time reflecting upon or encouraging current thought on mores and behaviours, which may lead to change in society. The long-established but still unanswered question is how far the education provided should reflect society or should be a vehicle to change it. Discussions about the content of history and English in the revised *National Curriculum 2000* of England and Wales illustrate this dilemma since the choice of periods and persons in history and literature in English is clearly significant in the degree of ethnocentralism that might be engendered in the schools. The abandonment of British history calls forth cries of a disowning of cultural heritage and the focusing on British history calls forth equally strident calls of nationalism and attitudes of supremacy. Other cries of the need to inculcate a sense of identity tend to be marginalized.

Cheng (below) provides an important insight into changing cultures and schools in China where education was seen as a means of social mobility open to all with a very real possibility for the very few from poor backgrounds to achieve high office. Schools were not conceived first for the elite, and attending school was and still is part of the culture (Cheng, 1996). Scholarship was treasured. At the same time, Chinese culture stressed the role of the individual in society, which was to contribute to society as a whole. The individual was a small self as part of the family, the community and the nation (Hubei Department of Education, 1958) and Cheng stresses the importance of this societal view in the successful introduction of the Cultural Revolution. The collapse of the Cultural Revolution in 1976 led to a reappraisal of the role of education and the need for change as radical as that of the Cultural Revolution. Education again became a means to achieve social mobility but this time on a broader basis with individuals being able to change their status from 'rural' to 'urban' and being able to move into the cities in search of a better life. This change introduced a greater focus on the person as an individual and has also reflected a change in role of central government towards a liberalization of the organization of education and a reduction of state influence and control.

Nomura (below) offers a cogent perspective on education in Japan, which has a long tradition of being widespread with a holistic objective based on a moral framework of training the individual to be a good citizen. Nomura reminds us that education is appropriate to the period in which it is provided but at the same time helps to form the period itself. Nomura argues that Japanese indigenous spirituality underpins thinking in the early 21st century and supports a consciousness of being an intrinsic and symbiotic part of the natural world. This enables Japan to accept foreign and heterogeneous cultures into the national bloodstream, creating a multi-layered culture. This spirit underpins and pervades the foundation of Japan's history, culture and education. However, Nomura goes on to assess the profound impact of the collapse of spirituality after World War II and the loss of the holistic approach based on morality and ethics. This was followed after the San Francisco Peace Treaty with the Fundamentals of Education Act, which was dedicated to the fostering of personal development and dignity to contribute to peace and the welfare of society, the country and the world. Nomura sees that there is a long way to go to recapture the lost tradition of spirituality but argues that, despite very many Western and global influences, the need for a return to traditional orthodoxies is pivotal to ensure the survival of the unique cultural heritage of Japan.

This foray into the underlying spiritual basis of Japanese society provides parallels for other countries represented in case studies below where spiritual factors have been vital to sustain the viability of national identities during periods of great stress and strain. Tomiak (below) has described the all-pervading impact of the periods of Nazi and Russian occupation and subjugation of Poland. He has stressed the spiritual and mental trauma accompanying the upheaval, which resulted from that subjugation with the related crisis of confidence in the established religious or political authority (Tomiak, 1994: 415–30, 1999: 83–92). Such a long period of external control can lead to deep changes in politics, religious values and society as a whole, challenging persistent values, leading to a confused state of affairs. With the collapse of the Eastern Bloc it might have been expected for Poland to emerge rudderless and without social forces to guide its future direction. This was certainly not the Polish case for, although the economy suffered greatly from the need to reform its activities and to accept vast changes in the economic framework in which it worked, the country and the people found within its traditions a power to lead and direct the cultural forces that had in earlier times provided the mainstay for Polish culture and society. That power was the Catholic

Church, which had survived both Nazi and Russian oppression and emerged again as a stable and enduring force to support Poland.

A fourth case study illustrates further the persistence of cultural values at times of stress and change and the struggle that has to take place to reconcile varying influences in a society. In analysing the cultural context of Denmark in the late 20th century, Winther-Jensen (below) has clearly identified the dilemma that exists between attempting to define what is the indigenous culture of Denmark and the need to understand new cultures. Winther-Jensen calls these two approaches on the one hand empathetic with a need to have sympathy and commitment to Danish cultural heritage and on the other analytic with a need to become familiar with and responsive to the customs, mores, behaviours of non-indigenous communities. In attempts to stimulate greater respect and support for foreign cultures, Danish policy has been to strengthen aspects of Danish culture, especially in the arts. This, Winther-Jensen claims, is a paradoxical approach since, while it may provide a secure base for the maintenance of Danish culture and thereby offer a strong framework to which migrant cultures could relate, its very security provides a front that other cultures have found obstructs their easy integration into one national entity:

> Cultural changes have in the Danish context caused unpleasantness on the analytical as well as the pedagogic front. It is apparently not easy to understand foreign cultures nor what is particularly Danish. The two attitudes to culture have not yet manifested themselves in a concrete and assimilative practice. The solution could be a concentration on academic standards, less anxiety from the state and more confidence in the different cultures being able, on their own, to move towards a common new culture.

These four illustrations of societies undergoing change have placed emphasis on the respect for inherited culture and the need to hark back to earlier times to find meaning in the current-day world in which we live. China, Japan, Poland and Denmark have looked to cultural roots upon which to graft responses in cultural terms to modern-day pressures. This search for certainty is based on culture as an artefact strongly rooted in the past, and while this may provide a bedrock during periods of upheaval and massive disruption, it cannot provide the only basis for the future. Winther-Jensen succinctly summarizes the dilemma with: 'Culture is, like other ideas, not static in its contents'. Other influences are at work, which guide educational development change, and it is to these we must now turn.

Universalizing education

One of the most enduring and persistent movements in educational provision has been toward the universalization of education. Long historical precedents have been presented in the case studies (eg Davies and Evans; Franzosa; Aspin, Chapman and Klenowski) of the growth of education at, first, primary, secondary and, in the closing decades of the 20th century, tertiary levels. Legislation in the 19th century led to the provision of universal primary education in many Western countries but the very limited provision in low-income countries led in the 1960s to UNESCO conferences calling for primary education for all by 1980. This has been followed by the World Conference on Education for All (EFA) in 1990 and its follow-up conferences up to 2000. Very many countries have made great strides towards the objective of universal primary education and some, like Indonesia, achieved enrolments in primary education of percentages in the upper 90s early in the 1980s. Others would have achieved full participation but for rapid increases in population growth and totals and the positive effect of improved health programmes. The goal of full primary education leading to automatic progression to secondary is yet to be achieved but it does represent an overwhelming desire of all nations. This desire is based on the United Nations Charter of Human Rights and of the Education of the Child and at the secondary level it will eventually see the eradication of selection and entrance examinations. In time, the school may be seen as an accepted part of the culture with full-time universal attendances being the norm. As we have seen above, this has been the case in China and Japan for a substantial period of time.

At the same time as the increasingly rapid spread of educational provision, there has been a move towards increased democratization in terms of direct participation both in education and in the management of educational systems and its provision. This is part of a wider movement towards democracy as the only acceptable basis for government, which strongly underpins the approach international and bilateral donors adopt to fund aid programmes for social improvement and change. What exactly is meant by 'democracy' has to be related to the specific contexts but minimally it could be taken to mean greater participation at all levels in the organization and conduct of the business of government. This may be reviewed in the light of two countries not included in the case studies below. In India, which is a union of semi-autonomous states, the focus of activity has been to devolve decision making to districts within the states to encourage greater involvement of local people in affairs that affect their lives. The same movement can be seen in the increased number of states in Nigeria and in the devolving of the Ministry of Education and Culture responsibilities to the 30 provinces in Indonesia, signalling perhaps a move towards a more federal management of that vast country. Similarly, 1999 saw the establishment of national assemblies in Scotland and Wales and earnest discussions about the need and desirability of regional assemblies with devolved powers in England. Canada, the United States and Australia have, of course, a long history of devolved powers within an agreed national framework.

This pattern of change in both state control and education reflects a need for self-actualization in both the political and educational spheres. The devolution of management to schools in the United Kingdom, and the May 2000 declaration by David Blunkett, Secretary of State for Education and Employment, to pass government financial support direct to schools and not through local education authorities, represent a recognition of the capability of school managements to carry out their responsibilities and the need for them to be given the chance to do so. Further, the School Management Initiative of Hong Kong is but one of a number of examples worldwide where increased responsibility is being placed on individual schools and management bodies.

This increased responsibility placed on the schools is underpinned by debates about the virtue or otherwise of the centralization or decentralization on government activities. The assumption by the schools of these broader tasks is of course not without difficulties. The same applies to the move towards greater inclusiveness in schools ensuring not only that all who are able to attend school are provided with an opportunity to do so but also that what is provided is of value to the consumer (or, dare we say it, the customer). This is because in the modern world what the school provides is open to question not only because of culture heritage, the making of the whole person and the inculcation of all forms of personal development but also about its value in society at large. This applies equally to differing cultural groups whose needs may not be easily recognized or provided for in an overall curriculum provision that meets the aspirations and requirements of the majority. Indeed, Cousin (below), in reviewing provision in France, points to the difficulty of providing for the specific needs of migrant groups where special organizational frameworks and curricular programmes might easily lead to claims of implied discrimination. Such well-meant provision might be misinterpreted to suggest racial, cultural or religious bias.

Questions over the values of educational provision are also aptly reviewed by Cousin in his repetition of the need of education systems to respect the specific requirements of the individual. In this respect school programmes can become customer-driven and the difficulty of devising, implementing and sustaining broad programmes of education becomes exacerbated when the programmes themselves may not reflect the culture of the adolescent world in which the students spend most of their time. Educational programmes are designed around a core of aims and goals that seek to express the conception of a worthwhile set of experiences. Where these do not meet the needs of the adolescents as they perceive them then the possibility exists of the development of patterns of rejection, truancy, boredom, anomie, violence and other unacceptable forms of behaviour. Where students do not see the purpose of education there is a recipe for problems for which the only solution may be the design and provision of individual-based programmes of study selected by students according to their desires and perceived needs. This moves the debate in education away from compulsory education (since why should attendance be obligatory if what is offered is not useful?); away from centrally devised (or perhaps even school-based) curricula towards individually constructed learning experiences (a sort of Open Plan School approach at all levels); away from institutional control of the education provided to autonomy of the individual. If democracy is the goal with active participation being the target then perhaps this should be encouraged in practice in the school, with the individual being able to select from a range of options and accepting the responsibility for the selection made. This is the adult world to which the student will belong: when the student should be allowed, encouraged or coerced into performing as an adult is the question behind who should decide what should be learnt by whom and at what stages in the education system. This has to be coupled with a question: what is the responsibility of the school during a movement towards greater individual autonomy?

The content of education

The gradual spread of mass education has brought with it questions of the management of education and returns to investment made in it. The move to increased participation at the local level has brought new voices into the discussion of the management of education and has encouraged the growth in power of local bodies that provide schools and actively support them. Cheng (below) has reminded us of the need for the mobilization of local resources to establish and maintain schools. Schools have tended to become community schools with a diminution of state control. Parents and pupils have not escaped the desire to spread costs and the provision of material resources has been passed on to parents. This is especially true of textbooks, which can become a heavy burden even where one child attends school. Where more than one or several children attend from the same family, the total cost can be restrictive even when the price of books is heavily subsidized as in South Asia. Add to textbooks the cost of pencils and other stationery, school uniforms and contributions to school funds, and the total call on family incomes can be daunting.

The increase in financial commitments placed on parents has led to the development of a market economy with decisions about schooling being taken on a critical analysis on the potential returns to education. This review of education has become significant with the spreading of attendance by girls. Traditionally, in low-income situations when choices have had to be made in the past about who should attend school or for how long, favour has been given to the elder boys, and attendance by girls has been given a low priority. The constraints on girls attending school in many cultures and economies are well documented. However, international pressures have led to the acceptance of the right of girls to equal participation in education and the percentage of girls of school-going age in school is taken as an indication of the degree of progress a country is making towards equal opportunities for all.

This assessment of the worth of education is also important in higher levels of education and Cheng (below) also notes the relative attractiveness of teacher training in China where there are no fees as opposed to other tertiary provision where entrance fees as well as tuition fees are levied. The need for students to raise loans to cover university expenses leaves completers with potentially substantial debts, which may take a long period after employment to pay off. The impact of this approach to the funding of tertiary education may be seen in high drop-out rates. England and Wales provides a perspective on the dual effects on university education of increased provision leading to over 30 per cent of the age group participating and of the indebtedness of the student population. The overall standard of university education has had to be matched to the broader profile of participation placing heavy demands on the students in their modularized courses with frequent assessment points. At the same time many students have been less able to spend time in study because of the need to earn funds with which to support themselves.

Where economics play such an important part in educational provision and participation the culture of choice comes to the forefront of all minds, be those of the members of the family, the institution or the government. For the family, the choice is between differing worthwhile options, and the assessment of the value of a course of study will rest for the majority of the population on the likely benefit in economic terms, ie in employment. Cousin (below) has drawn attention to the level of unemployment generally in France and particularly among the young. This leads inevitably to the questioning of the value of schooling and how that value may be maximized. With this may also follow questions of the responsiveness of institutions to the provision of courses and structures that are seen by the customers to be appropriate. The need for flexibility in staffing will be marked where new and more utilitarian courses are demanded to replace well-established but less well-supported ones. Again, Cheng (below) remarks on the adoption of a 'hire and fire' culture in Chinese universities to replace the all-embracing lifelong employment culture that existed before.

If education today is seen as an investment for the individual and the community for rewards in the future, it should be to the future we should look to prepare and provide those courses, skills and competencies that will be needed in the world beyond the immediate. This is crystal-ball gazing and perhaps few had a clear enough vision in their crystal ball of the overwhelming impact of the computer and telecommunications, which brought the revolution in communication of the last decade of the 20th century. However, Robert Reich (1991) has offered a future employment scenario that deserves serious consideration. Reich forecasts that in the 21st century only three groups of workers will be required. These he describes as routine workers (who are short-term trained and compete on a worldwide scale), service workers (whose main focus is on face-to-face contact) and symbolic analysts (who are highly skilled with specific knowledge such as engineers, economists and lawyers). Reich associates each category with a level of demand for their services, a range of tasks and a level of remuneration. Such a stark forecast raises very many questions about how education should be organized and for what purposes. How would the process of sifting people into the three categories take place – by a systematic or natural selection? How will the individual and the family prepare for and relate to the emergence of these categories? Will the categories be accepted by society or will their emergence lead to conflict and unrest because of the obvious inequalities that will be manifest? And how will governments deal with the questions of participation, equity and equality of opportunity? The education provided could lead to an outcomes-based model where the process of education becomes far less important. The values placed on education in this scenario recall's Dewey's argument that vocational education should try to bring about a more equitable social order and never subject learners to the demands and standards of the current system: 'it would train the power of readaptation to changing conditions so that future workers would not become blindly subject to a fate imposed upon them' (Dewey, 1986: 319).

The way education would be organized would have to reflect not only the needs of society but also the values, attitudes and beliefs that people hold. In designing the provision to be made, hard questions might have to be asked and answered. Trant (Trant et al, 1999: 93) in seeking a reconciliation between liberal and vocational education, asked: 'Are some students deemed to be more valuable than others because of the courses they follow and the kinds of schools they attend? Are some types of learning considered to be more important than others? Are some forms of knowledge and ways in which they are assessed thought to be more prestigious than others?'

Perhaps Reich, in looking for appropriate education for his categories of workers, may have to respond positively to these questions. Yet that would leave open the problem of reconciling equal educational provision for all and education's role in economic development as well as in providing for social harmony. To what extent could such targeted education and training lead to the necessary skills demanded by the modern world of team building, problem solving and information technology? Where would be the time and space in the education to provide for adaptability and for lifelong formal education to match human potential?

Education in a global context

Cowen (1996) has noted the gradual emergence of a sense of crisis, which has stimulated educational reform movements in a wide range of countries including Australia, Canada, New Zealand, the United Kingdom and the United States. The strands of this reform have been drawn upon above and include diversification of who provides and pays for education; education

closely articulated to the needs of the economy with the state controlling qualifications, structures and learning; and with an emphasis on the acquisition of
targeted pieces of knowledge and skills, which are frequently assessed. This
analysis is seen as part of globalization where 'the international economy becomes a crucial definer of the purposes, efficiency and the effectiveness of the
education system and its structures and even some of its pedagogic modes'
(Cowen, 1996:161).

International trends have long contributed to education development. The
early transference of Western education models to other countries in the 19th
and 20th centuries primarily but not wholly through missionary activity led to
the replacement of older educational forms. While traditional education has
become less significant in recent times, it persists and forms an important part
of the inculcation of the young, and participation in established rituals still
marks an important *rite de passage*. However, Western strategies and structures of education have a dominant place in education systems worldwide.
Supported and sustained by educational research that has illustrated both
strengths and weaknesses within systems and their provision, Western education remains a very powerful force for the continuous spread of influence
internationally. Christie (below) has outlined the role of international experience and best practice in guiding plans for education reconstruction after the
end of the apartheid period in the Republic of South Africa (RSA). Guided by
international standards for the elimination of inequalities between groups
and districts, by the need for new standards for school governance, the RSA
government adopted norms and standards for school funding and a new national qualification framework for an outcome-based curriculum. In addition,
new frameworks were adopted for teacher deployment. Understandably in
the aftermath of apartheid the government wanted to adopt radical solutions
to the provision of education because these were seen as the only way forward
to establish a country based on equity. Christie, however, reminds us that
making changes is difficult any time: 'Changing schools is not simply a matter
of developing the right policies and planning more accurately for their implementation. Policies are mediated by social, economic and political influences
including powerful global trends... Far from being rational and predictable,
as legal frameworks may suggest, changing cultures and schools is a complex,
contradictory and often contestational process.'

This view of education change by Christie offers us a salutary and cautious
guide to approaches to change in societies and in the schools that are provided. Cultural globalization may well be with us. In time it may lead us all in
the very near future to recognize that all the human beings of the world have a
common heritage in the world we live in and we must all act upon the need to
adapt and accept the many aspects of life and culture we share. The requirement that we adopt a global commitment to the preservation of the world's climate through the control of emissions has been generally accepted at least in
international agreement even if not entirely in the action taken. The require-

ment that we also adopt a range of humanitarian commitments such as the eradication of persecution with the stress on human rights represents a move towards a more mature world in which people may live without fear of harm. Cultures of peace, harmony and goodwill are offered as a prospect if the adoption of these aspects of a global ethic becomes a reality. In the international world of finance there are also strong movements to eradicate barriers to trade to stimulate growth in all countries as well as the desire to replace financial structures that were designed in the mid-20th century, which in the early 21st century appear to be archaic and unable to ensure stable financial relationships between countries. Within this complex ferment in world activities and institutions, the culture of each country has an important part to play.

Conclusion

The framework in which our contributors have presented their accounts of individual countries' educational histories and policies has supported the emergence of some dominant themes and counter-themes. In particular the following have emerged:

– globalization;	increasing national consciousness
– centralization in educational reform;	trends to localization
– vocational educational purposes;	liberal educational principles
– generalized inputs of identity, cultural understanding, ecological awareness;	narrow educational outputs of IT skills and communications competences
– autonomy;	citizenship

The question therefore arises whether it is sanguine and useful to develop and employ a common tool to analyse individual models of education in order to promote some common data. That data might then be used to construct and support worthwhile conversations across national boundaries about the purposes of formal education at primary, secondary and tertiary levels and within lifelong learning models. Presently, the recurring theme in educational discourse and among these case studies is the strong interrelationship between economic activity and education. The framework of the case studies in this volume added explicit dimensions of values and culture. This both captures the often silent unease with the current apparently global emphasis on the economic benefits of education and takes us a stage nearer to eliciting purposes for education at the time of the millennium from sources other than economic competitiveness and success.

At present, forecasts for education in the new millennium have concentrated on the possibilities of instant global communications, cultural interdependence and of human connectedness to previously improbable databases of knowledge and technical competence. Yet Reich's stark presentation of the kinds of individuals who are needed for these new times demands the following questions to be raised. By what means and by what authority are educational values derived, articulated and agreed? Which models of being human prevail in our present and medium-term education systems and cultures?

We can benefit greatly from the case studies because they provide data to respond to these questions. To those of us outside the particular country under study they provide 'extensive sources of information, templates for the organisation of social and psychological processes', those very elements by which Geertz (1985) defined the role of culture. Even more so we might compare the benefits of the knowledge we have gained from them with Geertz's thinking about ideology: 'they come most crucially into play in situations where the particular kind of information they contain is lacking, where institutional guides for behaviour, thought or feeling are weak or absent. It is in country unfamiliar emotionally and typographically that one needs poems and road maps. So too with ideology' (Bocock and Thompson, 1985: 81).

There is a sense present in our case studies that there are challenges and opportunities presented by living at the time of the new millennium, which sometimes dictate changes in education before they are sifted, analysed and digested. With these case studies we find some pointers to how to define and articulate the values and purposes of education in our very complex, fast-changing and ever-challenging worlds. Yet the studies have shown a grappling with common themes in very diverse contexts. In common the global and economic challenges and opportunities seem to give rise to a determination to respond civilly, through teaching citizenship, and humanly, by looking to personal development. The case studies written 70 years on from Freud provide means of answering his question about being human:

> The fateful question for the human species... is whether and to what extent their cultural development will succeed in mastering the disturbance of their communal life by the human instinct of aggression and self-destruction. It may be that in this respect precisely the present time deserves a special interest. Men have gained control over the forces of nature to such an extent that with their help they would have no difficulty in exterminating one another. They know this and hence comes a large part of their current unrest, their unhappiness and their mood of anxiety. (Bocock and Thompson, 1985: 61)

The unease is apparent throughout the case studies. Together with the effect of pluralism, we can agree with Charles Taylor that 'modern man has suffered from a deepening condition of homelessness'. Taylor continues: 'human beings are not capable of tolerating the continuous uncertainty of existing without institutional support' (1989: 502).

The case studies' analysis gives evidence that we rely heavily on institutional education to provide purpose. Often, however, explicit purpose is defined as economic and technical competence, without an underpinning of some identified form of specific human values. They appear to argue for our present times to demand an articulation and clarification of the values underpinning education systems. This would therefore form a precondition for worthwhile conversations about the purpose of education now, an *explicit statement* about the values and models of being human with each education system. There are two useful prompts already about how to set about this. In England, for example, the Education Reform Act 1988 set out the purpose of education as being the promotion of the 'spiritual, moral, and cultural development of pupils... and of society'.

Building on this, Monica Taylor (1998) then went on to analyse specific categories of values found in school systems and organizations in England. She delineates six: moral, social, spiritual, cultural, personal and educational values. In this volume Nomura is able to identify a model of 'the ideal Japanese' 'created by and for the global economy'. The image of the ideal Japanese seems to be that of the moral worker for the global economy, work being the defining element of the individual's citizenship in the new corporate state. Kazamias refers to Mok (2000: 148–49): 'While there is not a single, consensual definition of globalization, it is evident that the whole world is undergoing "a set of processes which in various ways – economic, cultural, and political – make supranational connections"'. By linking Taylor's method with Mok's articulation of a 'set of processes' we can define aspects of education systems that are susceptible to forms of values analyses. The countries of our case studies (the bricks) can thus be connected. It was important that we asked in our framework for specific descriptions of the dynamics (the mortar) in each country between culture, values and education. We need to look at the 'processes at work' in the studies, both vertically through the specific countries as well as horizontally across the studies. At each intersection we might ask: What are the challenges to our perceptions of culture, human values and education? How might we, the global partners in the education process, ask these questions together?

We have made a start; and we might go on to apply Tipton's (1984: 282–84) fourfold analysis of culture to each of the case studies: 'authoritative', 'regular', 'consequential' and 'expressive'. For example, in this taxonomy he seeks a means to analyse the 'cardinal virtue' that underpins the particular form or exercise of authority. Thus:

1. Authoritative: obedience to moral authority makes a person most worthy of praise.
2. Regular: rationality in discerning and enacting moral principles makes a person most worthy of praise.
3. Consequential: efficiency in maximizing the satisfaction of his/her wants makes a person most worthy of praise.

4. Expressive: sensitivity of feeling and situational response makes a person most worthy of praise.

From Tipton's methodology we can develop means of systematically analysing the values that underpin and permeate each educational system. At the same time, a similar schema might be devised within each system to enable students and teachers to recognize and reflect on the values among which they live and by which they define themselves.

Until we can satisfactorily answer the questions we must continue to develop studies of the education systems with which we engage with explicit reference to their inherent values and culture. We may wish to ensure that the systems that we are now supporting enable individuals to raise the question by what values they are being educated. We should most particularly ensure that movements towards lifelong education do not blind us to the problems and possibilities in that many-headed concept. For, on the one hand, lifelong education could mean an uncritical response to the changing conditions of our existence: thus governments will ensure levels of economic and social competence as and when the need arises through lifelong education. Lifelong education could also mean an acceptance of the need for all individuals in these uneasy, homeless times to share through education their perceptions, values and questions about how best to live as human beings in an increasingly complex and challenging context. These national and global views will interconnect at personal, communal and international levels. The latter would demand an honest articulation of both individual human and global value bases; the former, a quick-fix imposition of whatever values seem to match the need to stay ahead and win the global 'race'. Will Janus the god survive or will the many-headed monster, Hydra, overwhelm us?

References

Bocock, B and Thompson, K (1985) *Religion and Modernity*, Manchester University Press, Manchester

Cheng, K M (1996) *Duality of Basic Education in China: A case study of the provision of Zhe yang*, IIEP, Paris

Cowen, R (1996) Last past the post: comparative education, modernity and perhaps post-modernity, *Comparative Education*, **3.2** (2), pp 151–70

Dewey, J (1986) *Education and Democracy*, Free Press, London

Freud, S (1985) Civilization and discontents, in *Religion and Modernity*, ed B Bocock and K Thompson, Manchester University Press, Manchester

Geertz, C (1985) Ideology as a cultural system, in *Religion and Modernity*, ed B Bocock and K Thompson, Manchester University Press, Manchester

Halstead, M (1996) Values and values education in schools, in *Values in Education and Education in Values*, ed M Halstead and M J Taylor, Falmer, London

Hubei Department of Education (1958) *Qingshaonian Xiujang (Self-cultivation for Youth)*, vol 1, Hubei People's Press, Wuhan

Mok, K H (2000) Impact of globalization: a study of quality assurance systems of higher education in Hong Kong and Singapore, *Comparative Education Review*, **44** (2), May, pp 148–74

Reich, R (1991) *The Work of Nations: A blueprint for the future*, Vintage, New York

Taylor, C (1989) *Sources of the Self: The making of modern identity*, Cambridge University Press, Cambridge

Taylor, M J (1998) *Values Education and Education in Values*, NFER, Slough

Tipton, S (1984) *Getting Saved in the Sixties: Moral meaning in conversion and cultural change*, University of California Press, Berkeley

Tomiak, J (1994) Culture, national identity and schooling in Eastern Europe, in *International Perspectives on Culture and Schooling: A symposium proceedings*, ed E Thomas, Institute of Education, London

Tomiak, J (1999) Bildung and Erziehung in Osteuropa: Die Lage in der Mitte der 90er Jahre, in *'Bildungseinheit' und 'Systemstransformation': Beitrage zur bildungspolitischen Entwicklung in den neuen Bundeslandern und im ostlichen Europa*, ed W Horner, F Keubart and D Schulz, pp 83–92, Band 41, Arno Spitz, Osteuropaforschung, Schriftenreihe der deutschen Gellschaft fur Osteuropakunde, Berlin

Trant, A *et al* (1999) *Reconciling Liberal and Vocational Education*, Curriculum Development Unit, Dublin

7. Changing cultures and schools in Australia

David Aspin, Judith Chapman and Val Klenowski

Introduction

Education was made widely accessible to the Australian population by the 'free, compulsory and secular' Education Acts of the 1870s. The provision of these Acts has had wide-ranging implications for the approach to culture and values in Australian education throughout the course of the 19th and 20th centuries.

Today, Australia is a highly urbanized, multicultural country with a middle-sized economy that is strongly influenced by and subject to international economic, cultural and social trends. The nation has a political system that has its antecedents in English political and legal traditions. While its population and culture are predominantly European in origin, in recent years the migration of peoples from the nations of Asia, the South Pacific and Indian Ocean has considerably altered the ethnic composition of the population and diversified its culture.

Of an Australian population of approximately 19 million people, about 3 million are involved in school education. Some hundreds of thousands are also involved in various schemes of post-secondary further and higher education. In each state the government school system must provide educational opportunity for all children regardless of physical or intellectual ability, social and economic circumstances, cultural background and religious beliefs. State and territory ministers of education have responsibility for all government school education in their respective states and territories. However, parents do have the right to choose to send their children to non-government schools for religious or other reasons. Within the non-government sector in each state there is usually a Catholic school system, other non-government systems (eg Lutheran schools, Seventh-day Adventist schools) and independent schools. Parents electing to send their children to the non-government sector are usually called upon to provide additional financial input to the school of their choice.

Constitutionally, responsibility for education resides with the states and territories. However, there is a federal/commonwealth minister for education and a commonwealth Department of Employment, Education, Training and Youth Affairs (DEETYA). The commonwealth has considerable powers of advice and direction, and exercises a considerable degree of policy control through the supplementary funding it provides to the states for their various budget obligations and requirements each year. The commonwealth government plays an important role in considering the broad purposes and structures of schooling in accord with national priorities and in promoting national consistency and coherence in the provision of schooling. In cooperation with the individual states, the commonwealth addresses resource equity and quality issues through its recurrent capital and specific-purpose programmes. Through the agency of the Ministerial Council on Education, Employment, Training and Youth Affairs (MCEETYA) the commonwealth government also contributes to the articulation of national goals for schooling.

Ten years of schooling are compulsory for all children, roughly between the ages of five and fifteen (years 1 to 10); and there is strong encouragement to students to stay on at school for a further two years (years 11 and 12). Currently, a declining number of students (about 74 per cent) continue to participate in education in these latter years. Of students attending school on a compulsory basis, a little over 70 per cent receive their education in government schools, the rest taking it in non-government schools. Of these latter, the largest proportion attend schools provided or supported by a range of religious denominations – the greatest number of these being Catholic schools – though there are also some establishments run on lines advocated by Steiner, Montessori and the like. There is also a small but increasing number of 'Christian' schools. Such schools receive substantial income from government sources for both capital and recurrent expenditure. Government school education is 'free' in Australia, although increasingly government schools in Australia are asking parents to subsidize their expenditures by the payment of voluntary 'fees'. In some schools the amount of such assistance *requested* of parents is relatively small (about $300 each year would be a typical figure); in the case of the independent denominational day and boarding schools, by contrast, the fees *required* of parents can amount to over $30,000 per annum.

In recent times education in Australia has been the subject of an enormous range of changes. Considerations arising from Australia's economic position, the changing nature of its society and its geopolitical situation have all been among the major factors driving educational reform during the course of the 1990s. Particularly strong have been the influences on education of changes emanating from its economic condition, including increasing globalization, the revolution of communication technology, major restructurings of the labour market, a shift from reliance on raw materials export towards more value-added exports and a greater emphasis on developing a highly skilled, flexible and productive workforce. Changes in society have also impacted on education: changes in family structures, the increasing emancipation of women, the increasing number of multi-ethnic communities, people's awareness of the presence of minorities of all kinds, the growing gap between the

'haves' and the 'have-nots' in society – all these factors have exerted considerable pressure on government to bring about change in education and training
(see also Ling, Burman and Cooper, 1998).

Such pressures have been seen in the changes within the education service
that they have precipitated: a move to an acceptance of nationally agreed-
upon aims and goals of schooling; large-scale movements in the development
of curricula and the various curriculum frameworks meet to deliver them;
new approaches to student teaching and learning and the assessment of student learning outcomes both during schooling and at the end of their time in
school; changes in funding arrangements with responsibility and accountability for detailed decision making and the management of budgets devolved to local school level, along with an increase in the centralization of
control and direction; new forms of arrangement in the structure and pattern
of the relationships schools are to enjoy with one another, with their local
communities and with their employing authorities; and new awards of terms
and conditions of service for school staffs. In all the above, values issues feature largely – in the manner in which education policy is decided, in what
those decisions consist and for what purposes, and in the ways in which those
decisions are carried down and implemented at local level in the community
and its schools.

In this chapter we will consider the part played by growing awareness of
the need for considerations of 'values' and the need for an education in values
of all kinds – economic, political, social, moral – in the reform effort in education and training in Australia. We shall point to some developments that suggest that matters pertaining to values and culture are now beginning to be
taken more seriously and find overt expression in policy pronouncements, institutional planning, and curriculum developments and initiatives across
Australia. These include: the move towards the establishment of national
goals; encouraging attention to values concerns in teacher preparation and
professional development; and the increasing attention to the concerns of a
wide range of community stakeholders in the education process widely across
the education service and community bodies in Australia. Advances in all of
these areas and others having a bearing upon a growing appreciation of the
cardinal importance of values in educating institutions have been growing
and implemented in Australia in recent years.

The past and the attempted silence about values

The nature and cultural composition of Australian society

The broad-scale provision of schooling that was made possible in the 1870s
through state Education Acts instituting the provision of a public system of
schooling that was required to be 'free, compulsory and secular' had

wide-ranging effects and implications for the development of education in Australia, particularly as it pertains to issues associated with culture and values.

In the past the reason for the stipulation that education be 'secular' was closely associated with the nature of Australian society at the time. Nineteenth-century Australian society was deeply divided along religious lines: on the one hand there was an English and Scottish Protestant colonial population, which was particularly powerful in the legal, administrative and cultural establishment; on the other hand there was a large population of Irish Catholics with strong adherence to the Catholic Church, its traditions and values. In this cultural milieu tensions arose and continued to subsist between Protestantism in its Anglican and Nonconformist versions, and Catholicism.

The passing of the 1870s Education Acts did little to reduce religious, social and cultural tensions. After the passing of the 'secular' Education Acts, the Catholic community became increasingly concerned to ensure that its younger generation was familiar with the teaching of the particular beliefs, values and attitudes characteristic of and espoused by the Catholic Church. After the passing of the 1870s Acts there was a growth in numbers of Catholic schools and an influx of members of religious orders from Ireland coming to Australia to serve as teachers. An increase in the number of Anglican, Presbyterian, Methodist and other denominational schools also occurred at this time.

In more recent times the specification that government schools be 'secular' in their approach to education and the notion in many quarters that government school education should be 'value-free' perhaps explains why, in studies of parental choice for non-government schools, an overwhelming proportion of parents consider adherence to values as a major factor in securing a non-government education for their children. In recent decades this has found substantial expression in the growth of more fundamentalist 'Christian' schools and, in response to a more multicultural society, in the growth of schools associated with non-Christian religion, eg Muslim schools. An important point to make about this development is the realization that, while enrolments in government schools are declining, there has been in fact a considerable increase in the number of alternative, independent schools and in the number of students attending them. This is considered by many to be a reflection of the desire of many parents that their children have a strong and clear values base to their education.

Philosophical concerns

In the late 19th century, emphasis upon a secular 'value-free' education in state-provided government schools was also supported and encouraged by developments in thinking coming from another quarter – the philosophical. In the late 19th century there were fierce debates in the media and the public press of Australia about the character and the very possibility of relationships between such diverse domains as science, religion and ethics. Evidence of this may be found in the public correspondence in the newspapers between such eminent persons as the Chief Justice of Victoria, Sir George Hetherington, and the leaders of both Protestant and Catholic communities of that time. Hetherington, a committed humanist and atheist, was insistent about the priority of the status to be given to such matters of fact as those to be found in the realms of science, mathematics and history, as opposed to the matters of belief and opinion to be found in the realms of belief and opinion, faith and morals.

This tendency was given added impetus in the first half of the 20th century by the rise of the philosophy of empiricism, which was then being worked into an all-encompassing programme by thinkers of or associated with the philosophical movement known as the Vienna Circle. The view of such people was that the only intellectually respectable academic pursuit was that of the sciences (either analytic or empirical), in which the methods of the sciences laid down paradigms of intellectual operation to which all subjects claiming any kind of academic acceptability were supposed to conform. It was only the analytic operations of logic or mathematics, and the empirical procedures of the natural sciences, that had any claim to acceptability as meaningful and sensible bodies of theory and sets of statements. The utterances of ethics and aesthetics and the metaphysical speculations of religion were, to such people, quite literally, senseless – meaningless.

The insistence of this movement on the primacy of science, and the rejection of other forms of discourse, set up a standard of inclusion and exclusion for curriculum subjects and fields of study that many educating institutions embraced and promulgated. This tendency – which became known as logical positivism – exercised enormous importance in the English-speaking world and became the dominant philosophy in Australian educating institutions with the appointment of the philosopher John Anderson to Sydney University. The influence of Anderson spread widely throughout the life and culture of Australian university institutions for many years and it was inevitable that the influence of logical positivism should rapidly percolate throughout the rest of Australia's education service and in its schools.

From the 1950s to around the early 1980s, positivistic approaches and logical requirements dominated epistemological and curriculum concerns. During these years government direction, emphases and support tended to be given much more to the area of mathematics, the sciences and technology, which were seen as the 'hard' and 'objective' subjects – paradigms of intellectually acceptable enquiry – as against the 'soft' subjects such as literary studies, work in the arts and religious studies. As a consequence they were given a privileged status with respect to the selection and range of the 'really respectable' curriculum subjects to be taught in educational institutions. As one leading thinker of the time was alleged to have put it (in a comment attributed, probably apocryphally, to Gilbert Ryle (see Ryle, 1949)): 'There is only one philosophy worthy of the name – logic. This is followed by the philosophy of mind and psychology. Ethics is gravely suspect; aesthetics is incoherent.' That kind of attitude was still to be found in the ways in which any curriculum subjects other than mathematics, the sciences and technology were regarded, by many students, parents and employers, well into the 1980s, as 'Mickey Mouse' or 'soft' subjects.

Gradually, however, the dominance of empiricism and positivism as the leading philosophies in Australian educating institutions has come under increasing challenge. Subjected to the powerful critique advanced against them by non- or anti-empiricist philosophers, they have begun slowly to lose their sway and to be replaced by new and different styles of thinking about matters of value and the domains of science and mathematics and of their relationships to other realms of human thought and culture. The works of such thinkers as Quine (1951), Popper (1970) and Rorty (1979) have brought about a sea change in people's understanding of the complexity, diversity and intelligibility of a wide range of human realms of discourse: education has begun to be seen as being concerned with the understanding and extension of human interests and the main concerns of people's lives and cultural activities.

Now we may say that the influence of positivism has lost its dominion as the 'reputable' approach to science, applied science and, perhaps above all, the education of the professions. At the same time, the stress on the primacy of 'the secular' has begun to diminish as people have realized that education in schools is – whether related to those of religious believers or not – still imbued with values concerns and is about such vital matters as the preparation of people for life in the worlds of work, relationships and society, and the worlds of culture and the imagination. With these realizations, values considerations can no longer be kept so fiercely to one side. Thus the claims to intellectual acceptability of fields of study, such as the arts, morality and religion, that had previously been dismissed by thinkers, legislators and educators of the positivist persuasion, have begun to be taken very seriously and to find an equal place in the curricula and work of scholars and teachers in Australian educating institutions (see Hill, 1991). Talk of values, and of metaphysics for that matter, has come back in.

It should be pointed out, however, that most recently matters to do with the consideration of values in Australian education have taken what many consider to be a most controversial direction. The positivist demand for the unification of all sciences under empiricist rubrics has been challenged by post-positivist notions, in which a variety of theories and ideologies have found expression – neo-Marxism, pragmatism, postmodernism and post-structuralism. Such theories have begun to find themselves seriously entertained, accepted and in some institutions given pride of place; such philosophies are being now disseminated, practised and promoted in tertiary institutions very widely across Australia. In such approaches the view that there is no such thing as a 'truth' (in the positivist sense) and that all values are subjective to individuals and relative only to the cultural milieux in which they live has begun to dominate educational discourse in many tertiary institutions.

This influence has percolated down quite rapidly from universities to classrooms in schools, where graduates of such universities have begun to teach subjects in which such philosophies are embodied and exemplified. This kind of talk can be found in classrooms, teaching and curriculum activities such as languages and literary studies, human sciences such as anthropology and sociology, studies of society and the environment, and even the realm of the sciences, where a particular understanding of 'constructivism' has come to predominate. In many government schools and some schemes of curriculum, 'values' are now back in, but are widely taught under relativist rubrics. For the view is very widespread that Australian commitment to such virtues as tolerance and equality should make its citizens ready to accept the equal status of considerable differences in the culture and values of different individuals' and groups' lives. The approach of 'cultural relativism', according to which the validity of all values, sets and systems of values is relative only to the norms and conventions of the cultural, ethnic or religious group holding them, and only objectified and validated in procedures endemic and endogenous to that group, has ensured that there is a reluctance to see any value or set of values as superior to any other and to engage in value discourse that might go so far as to describe some social and cultural practices as mistaken or even wrong. For many people in Australia, and for many teachers in Australian schools, it is the case that 'all values are equal'.

That view, in its turn, notwithstanding its widespread tenure among very many professionals in the education service in Australia, is not without its critics. Many now, and particularly the leaders of some religious denominations, are arguing strongly that some beliefs and practices are mistaken, wrong and not to be tolerated at all. For this reason it might with some justice be said that a fight against relativism has now begun, still continues, and is one of the most contentious issues in the realm of values in Australia's educating institutions at the present time.

The nature of values

It might therefore perhaps be thought useful and important for us at this point to say something initially about what we take to be the nature of values. What, we might ask, is the nature of 'values' in educational discourse? It might be noted that, in general, when people speak about 'values' at all, they do so in the sense that values are the stuff of ethics and morality, as opposed to monetary value or the values of efficiency and effectiveness in delivering a particular product or reaching a particular desired end (cf Taylor, 1961). In ethics a value can be seen as something that is worthy of esteem for its own sake, which has intrinsic worth (see also Aspin, 2000b). It signifies the 'excellent' status of a thing, object, situation, person, performance, achievement etc, or the estimate in which it is held, according to its real or supposed worth, usefulness or importance, as 'excelling' (standing out from, being above, other things) *in a particular class of comparison with other objects of a similar kind*. Thus to assess the value of something is to consider a thing as being of some worth, importance or usefulness, in a class of comparison in which, by the application of criteria, we rate it highly, esteem it or set store by it. It also relates to the particular principles or standards of conduct by which a person seeks or chooses to live.

Values are to do with matters that take place in the public realm and that we perceive and judge to be matters of importance. We make judgements, which commend or condemn, on matters of importance that take place in the world: values relate to our praise or blame of styles of behaviour, the productions and performances of artists, verdicts of judges, the conduct of politicians, the activities of schools, the policies of economists, interpersonal relationships, occurrences that we experience as a result of the forces of nature, states of affairs in the community, decisions of churches, questions as to people's culture. Such things are part of our thinking and talking on matters of value, our value judgements, and our decisions and actions as to our own and other people's 'good'.

Thus conduct, performances, situations, occurrences, states of affairs, productions, all these are associated with the ways in which we perceive, appraise and are inclined towards or away from such objects, productions, states of affairs, performances, manifestations of conduct. We desire them, we wish to be like them or to possess them, to replicate or emulate them. And we are willing to approve, praise and commend those objects, performances and manifestations of conduct, to other people. We propose to other people that such objects or states of affairs, styles of behaviour, are targets that provide us with standards of excellence that all should aim at, that they are models that can function as guides for our conduct or for our judgement, in ways that all of us could make our own, and commend to other people. Such states of affairs, objects, performances, that we are inclined towards and commend to other people as worthy of emulation, function as norms and criteria of excellence that are interpersonal; they are prescriptive for the generality of the population who we hold can and should experience similar regard for, give similar approval and commendation to, the objects, conduct, performances etc to which they are applied. These things give us principles to guide our conduct and by which we can all regulate our lives and strongly commend to other people to follow.

We would also wish to argue that values are neither private, nor subjective. Values are public: they are such as we can all discuss, decide upon, reject or approve. Value judgements constitute bridges between us as to the ways in which we ought to act, or the things that we ought to admire. Also, values are objective. They are in quite a decided sense 'hard'. They are arrived at and get their life from their status as inter-subjective agreements in our community as to what things shall count as 'important'. Such agreements are constituted in the institutions that make up our social and communal life (see Wringe, 1998a, 1998b). For example, without the institution of banking, monetary exchange and fiduciary trust, a dollar coin is just a brute piece of metal. It is such institutions that give our values their intelligibility and their objectivity. The act of writing a cheque is quite as objective as the action of looking down an electron microscope, because it has meaning, intelligibility that we value, but not only value: it is something upon which we base our subsequent actions. Values are 'hard' in that they are fundamental parts of the fabric of our social relationships. It is in the warp and weft of those social relationships that our judgements of value are articulated, developed, agreed, settled and acted upon. And these objectivities of value are the result of discussion, negotiation and agreement, and are settled at the level of the culture of a community.

Initiatives addressing changes in values and culture in Australian schools education

In the last decade of the 20th century we saw a number of initiatives that give evidence of the increasing importance attached to matters associated with values and culture in Australian schools.

National goals for schooling

In 1989 the federal minister, meeting with the Australian Educational Council at Hobart, issued a statement on what they regarded as the desirable national goals for Australian schools. In that statement there was relatively little explicit discussion about values, the concerns being more to do with the promotion of skills and competencies in particular areas of curriculum endeavour. More recently, however, an emphasis on values has become much more overt. In 1999 the commonwealth government's MCEETYA taskforce released a document, *Australia's Common and Agreed National Goals for Schooling in the Twenty-first Century*. This document constitutes a major step towards the conceptualization and articulation of the goals of Australian schooling framed from a lifelong perspective.

This document, known as The Adelaide Declaration of National Goals is worth quoting from at length:

> **Preamble**: Australia's future depends upon each citizen having the necessary knowledge, understanding, skills and values for a productive and rewarding life in an educated, just and open society. High quality schooling is central to achieving this vision... Schooling provides a foundation for young Australians' intellectual, physical, social, moral, spiritual and aesthetic development... Governments set the public policies that... Uphold the contribution of schooling to a socially cohesive and culturally rich society... The achievement of the national goals for

schooling will assist young people to contribute to Australia's social, cultural and economic development in local and global contexts. Their achievement will also assist young people to develop a disposition towards learning throughout their lives so that they can exercise their rights and responsibilities as citizens of Australia.

Goal: 1 ...When students leave schools they should... 1.3 have the capacity to exercise judgment in matters of morality, ethics and social justice... to make rational and informed decisions about their own lives and to accept responsibility for their actions... 1.4 be active and informed citizens... 1.7 have an understanding of and concern for the stewardship of the natural environment, and the knowledge and skills to contribute to ecologically sustainable development... 1.8 have the knowledge and skills to establish and maintain a healthy lifestyle and for the creative and satisfying use of leisure time...

Goal: 3 Schooling should be socially just, so that: 3.1 students' outcomes from schooling are free from the effects of negative forms of discrimination based on sex, language, culture and ethnicity, religion or disability, and of differences arising from students' socio-economic background or geographic location... Aboriginal and Torres Strait Islander students have equitable access to, and opportunities in schooling... all students understand and acknowledge the value of Aboriginal and Torres Strait Islander cultures in Australian society and possess the knowledge, skills and understanding to contribute to and benefit from, reconciliation between indigenous and non-indigenous Australians(3.5 all students understand and acknowledge the value of cultural and linguistic diversity and possess the knowledge, skills and understanding to contribute to and benefit from, such diversity in the Australian community and internationally...

This statement was published in April 1999 and has now been established, accepted and promulgated as an important element in all policies and initiatives devoted to the advancement and enhancement of education – one that is valued because of its emphasis on quality, equity and other values (see Winch, 1996) – being developed widely in and through all education systems in Australia. It will be interesting to see how its aims, objectives and aspirations are realized, implemented and evaluated in those systems over the coming years. But what cannot be doubted is that, from the publication of that statement, values have been publicly acknowledged to form a critical part of Australian education undertakings in the years of compulsory schooling.

Programmes in citizenship and civics education

The same may be said with respect to the area in which values interests and concerns have been most widely addressed in Australian education – that of citizenship and civics education. Under the Labour government of Prime Minister Keating, a civics expert group was formed and its report, *Whereas the People*, supported with a grant of $25 million of funding for citizenship education programmes to be instituted in schools and more broadly across the community (see Pascoe, 1996). The then leader of the opposition, John Howard, agreed broadly with the need for an education in citizenship and civics and, on the Howard government's coming into power in 1996, an expanded citizenship and civics education group, under the chairmanship of Dr John Hirst, was established in May 1997 by Minister Kemp and given a mandate to develop work in citizenship and civics education, under the title 'Discovering democracy'. As opposed to the previous location of this curriculum development in that area known as SOSE (studies of society and the environment) the curriculum area selected for this educational initiative was declared to be more properly that of history – a government *fiat* that met with surprisingly little resistance (see Pascoe and Ferguson, 1999). The group set to work under these new rubrics; papers were commissioned and outside contributions invited. The group's conclusions were eventually published and evaluated and materials arising from it came out in December 1998.

Although *Discovering Democracy* (DEETYA Curriculum Corporation, 1997) is an important document, there has been to date only a limited take-up of this scheme by schools. Yet there is much in this work that is of cardinal importance to the work of values education in Australian schools. New 'developing democracy' curriculum documents are providing a most useful context for the teaching of values and helping teachers and educators generally tackle the question of how to teach values in a context of the emphasis placed upon the need for secular provision of education. This comes out strongly in many parts of the main curriculum document. As one of the aims of civics and citizenship education, for example, we read that the scheme will provide opportunities to: 'Develop personal character traits, such as respecting individual worth and human dignity, empathy, respect for the law, being informed about public issues, critical-mindedness and willingness to express points of view, listen, negotiate and compromise(Understand the rights and responsibilities of citizens. And the opportunities for exercising them.'

Under 'intended learning outcomes' we read that the experiences are intended to:

- identify values implicit in Australian democracy;
- compare and contrast features of various democratic and non-democratic states from today and the past;
- evaluate aspects of Australian democracy from a range of perspectives including those of women and indigenous people;
- evaluate the impact on civic life of changes in Australia's population and economy.

And under 'values and attitudes' we read:

> Recognising that Australian society is both cohesive and pluralistic, demo-
> cratic values will be supported through the project materials. Students will
> learn about the importance of principles such as:
>
> Democratic decision making and popular sovereignty
> Government accountability
> Civility, truth telling and respect for the law
> The value of individual and collective initiative and effort
> Concern for the welfare, rights and dignity of all people.
>
> The materials will support values such as tolerance, acceptance of cultural
> diversity, respect for others and freedom of speech, religion and association.

The broad aim here is to 'present opportunities for students to make informed
decisions about issues of importance to themselves and others'. Such knowledge, dispositions and values as the materials promote are meant to help students develop 'citizenship skills necessary for effective participation in a
democracy'. These social values form the core and provide the impetus for this
government-sponsored and supported essay into the field of values education writ large (see also Lovat and Schofield, 1998). Indeed, and as Aristotle
presented it in his *Politics* (see Kenny, 1978), active engagement in the political
process is the institutionalization of ethics in the practical situations of people's lives as citizens in a democracy.

This move for education in civics and citizenship has overtaken the previous attention addressed to the issue of Australia as a multicultural society and
the concomitant need for multicultural education – an approach that was
found in or implemented at schools across Australia in the 1980s. Under the
present Liberal government there has been a movement away from multiculturalism and multicultural education and turning towards an emphasis of students in all Australian schools to develop the dispositions and competencies,
attitudes and values necessary for them to be active citizens in the
participative democracy of the 21st century. Along with this will go an awareness of the importance of investigating, analysing and coming to some conclusions on where we are as a society, the nature of Australian identity, and how
we may best be governed in the global knowledge economy and learning society of the 21st century.

State initiatives: the values review project

One of the early developments signalling the increasing importance of values
in Australian education was the award of a National Professional Development Project (NPDP) to a team in the state of Western Australia. A 'values review' project was set up in the early 1990s and located in the offices of the
Association of Independent Schools of Western Australia (AISWA). The aim
was to undertake a comparative review of values, values in the curriculum

and schemes of values education in Western Australia, with a view to articulating and publishing a joint agreed statement of core minimum values shared by all schools participating in the project and then to publishing a scheme of 'values in education' for the use of such schools. The documents and curriculum materials were published and the project ended in 1998.

Since that time the most significant subsequent development has been the setting up in Western Australia of a state-wide curriculum council created by the Minister. In November 1998 a curriculum framework, comprising a strong element of values education, was published, intended for use in all state schools in Western Australia and strongly recommended for use in all non-state schools (the council having representation from all sectors). This curriculum framework, while preserving the rationale of the original national curriculum framework in having eight key learning areas and extensively spelling out anticipated student outcomes, nevertheless diverges considerably from it, to the point of including many values statements in the framework and values outcomes in the assessment procedures. It also incorporates an explicit values framework that, in nearly 80 per cent of its entries, owes a direct or implicit debt to the concluding statement of the NPDP, the 'agreed minimum values framework'. This debt is openly acknowledged. Efforts are proceeding in the WA Education Department to develop case studies and work samples to help teachers implement these initiatives, and these developments again have been not a little influenced by similar work already done in the independent sector through the original project work of the NPDP.

The former chair of the NPDP, Reverend Dr Tom Wallace, continues to chair a 'values in education' cross-sectoral committee, which is providing training for school-based resource persons who can assist their school communities in working with the values issues raised in and by the WA curriculum framework. This committee is about to initiate some research work, which will document the progress being made in and by those schools that were involved in the original NPDP and have continued to grapple with the integration of values into the whole of school life. In addition, that committee is currently exploring the possibility of initiating a pilot project to work with upper primary students in developing a language that is more friendly to the expression of positive values.

Increasingly important issues and concerns

These then are some of the commonwealth and state activities in which issues of values and culture are currently under discussion and promotion in Australian education. But what of Australia in the 21st century? The following appear to be among the major issues on which schools and educating institutions will need to concentrate their educative endeavours. They may be illustrated as shown in the following sections (see also Aspin, 1999):

The economic issue

The question here is what knowledge and skills shall we mandate in our curriculum to prepare our students for facing the challenge of the knowledge economy and the learning society of the 21st century. We know that our students will be living in an increasingly global environment in which economic development and advance will be governed by exchanges of information, goods and services, knowledge, culture and ideas on an increasingly global basis. Yet Australia is a relatively small country in a relatively isolated geopolitical position, with a culture that is largely European in origin and yet with an economic environment that places it firmly and squarely in the Asia-Pacific region. How are we to prepare our children for the future of competing in the world's market-place by providing goods and services that people will want to buy from us and therefore enable us to lower our public sector borrowing requirement? And how shall we prepare our students for a life in which the nature of employment is changing, and in which they will have to achieve standards in those competencies and dispositions (flexibility, adaptability, team building, literacy, imagination and creativity), the exercise of which is going to be called for in an increasingly competitive and global economic environment? And how shall we prepare them for a future in which they can expect to have to change employment five or six times in their lifetimes and to have an increasing amount of non-salaried leisure time at their disposal? In short, what values are we to put upon changes in the culture of work and leisure in the Australian society of the 21st century?

The environmental issue

Australia is a signatory to many international conventions and protocols relating to environmental protection and the notion of environment-friendly sustainable economic development. Yet recent events suggest that some of our political leaders only feel themselves partially bound by the necessity of adhering to the full range of the content of those protocols. There is plenty of evidence that Australian citizens in general are deeply concerned about environmental protection – witness the power and success of our national campaigns of 'Clean Up Australia' day. Yet the fact remains that many aspects of our economic activities and enterprises militate against environmental concerns and values. How shall we educate our students to finesse the dilemmas caused by the need for utilizing our resources and developing our economy in the way that confers the greatest benefit on the Australian people at the same time as doing everything we can to protect the quality and riches of our natural and built environments? Schools will want to address the issue of helping their students to realize that we live upon a planet of finite resources and to consider how we can deal with the ways in which we should attempt not only to work out policies for sustainable development with respect for those resources but also to construct our future after they run out.

The social justice issue

The OECD and UNESCO, among many other educational institutions and agencies, are deeply anxious as to whether the issue of access to computers and information technology communication is going to widen the gap in the world and in our societies between the haves and the have-nots, between the class of those people who have access to educational opportunity and to employment, and the underclass of those who have not. We know already, for example, that students who are Anglo-Saxon, male and live in the south-eastern suburbs of Melbourne have a much greater chance of ensuring access to the opportunities open to them in higher education than the daughters of immigrants living in the western suburbs. This is a 'description' of an existing state of affairs but it is a statement that also carries normative overtones, implying that there is something unbalanced that ought to be redressed.

Although there have been great strides forward in the emancipation of particular social groups in Australian society – women, ethnic minority groups, rural dwellers, indigenous people – it is still clear that there is a long way to go before we can be regarded as having achieved emancipation and equality for all members of such groups.

The numbers of women in the highest positions in business and commerce, the law, education and the universities, politics, and even the arts and culture is still small and out of all proportion to the numbers of women participating in such activities and institutions at the lower levels. The same would be true of members of minority ethnic communities and people of non-English-speaking backgrounds and it is also true of members of Australia's indigenous community. The question here is: by what means can we ensure that all members of such groups have access to and are able to participate in the activities of such institutions and professions on an equal basis and in such a way that their number in the Australian community is reflected proportionately in their representation in the activities and processes of such bodies?

The issue of interpersonal relationships

In its publication *Learning: The treasure within* (UNESCO, 1996) UNESCO makes the knowledge of how to relate to other people one of its four main pillars of educational endeavour: learning to know; learning to do; learning to live together; learning to be. There is no doubt that the Australian community sets great store by such interpersonal values as tolerance, a fair go for all, equality of opportunity and respect for other people, with particular emphasis being placed by Australian males on the concept of mateship. Yet not withstanding these emphases, we may well be disturbed by some statistics that suggest that, among OECD countries, in the workplace for which we are preparing our young people, Australia stands high in the list for workplace disaffection and disagreement; one particular state in Australia stands very high in the list for domestic violence; another state stands high in the list for child abuse; and Australia overall for teenage suicide. These are disturbing statistics. They refer to existing patterns of behaviour, which we realize our educational institutions, among many other community institutions and agencies, ought to try and help to change. The question for educators in Australian schools is how to encourage our students to approach the important issue – a central one, as Haydon (1999) rightly remarks, in the enterprise of moral education – of developing positive relationships between themselves and other people in which the presence of such dysfunctional phenomena is attenuated or altogether dispersed.

The constitutional issue

The momentum for constitutional change may have slowed somewhat now that we have just gone through a government-sponsored referendum centring on the question of whether Australia should change its constitutional arrangements and become a republic. The issue was decided in the negative but many people feel that this outcome was more a function of the form in which the debate was framed and the style and manner in which the proposition was put. There is no doubt, however, that in the years ahead Australians will continue to ask questions about our preferred form of government, what kind of person we want to be head of our state and how that person is going to be selected. These will be questions to which answers will have to be given in the time of the adulthood of the people we are teaching now. And this is a very important consideration that will structure and define the content and mode of teaching in many of their lessons in social sciences, in history, in politics and democracy. This is the area in which our current programmes of education for citizenship and civics education will get an especial point of purchase and it will not be one confined solely to a historical approach. For central to this issue is the concern for students to acquire the knowledge from skills, dispositions, values and attitudes necessary for their engagement in the political process and to their learning how to exercise properly and fully their rights and responsibilities in the participative democracy that Australians are proud to declare their preferred form of government to be.

The issue of reconciliation

There can be no doubt that the concern for reconciliation between non-indigenous and indigenous Australians that has been rapidly developing over recent years will continue to exercise the thoughts of all Australians for many years to come. The legislative actions of the last commonwealth government and the decisions of the High Court of Australia (known as the Mabo and Wik judgments) have placed firmly on the table the issue of the necessity to move to a positive and mutually acceptable understanding and *modus vivendi* between the indigenous and non-indigenous peoples that constitute the body politic of the Commonwealth of Australia. The requirements of the Wik and Mabo decisions relating to ownership of lands; the realization that indigenous Australians were indeed the original inhabitants and custodians of the land (the legal rejection of the *terra nullius* view) giving the notion of some sort of return of and/or reparation for land originally in their guardianship an especial urgency; and the recollection of the harm done to the current generation of adult Aboriginal people by their having been forcibly taken away from their parents in the policy-dictated attempt to incorporate them into white Australian culture (the so-called 'stolen generation' problem) – all are matters of value and culture of critical concern.

Schools' attention to those matters will be affected by the awareness that, in public debates on this issue, there is considerable difference of opinion. There is a strong tension between those who believe that non-indigenous Australians should not adopt a 'black armband' view of Australia's past, that attempts should be made to extinguish some of the original indigenous inhabitants' land-rights, and that no responsibility should be taken nor apology offered for the conduct of our European ancestors towards Aboriginal and Torres Strait Islander people; and those who believe that Australia's record in these matters is one of which present-day non-indigenous Australians should be ashamed, one for which an apology should be extended and one in respect of which reparations should be offered as a necessary precondition for moving to an effectual system of relationships among all groups.

These matters and concerns will be a focus of attention in subjects such as economics and political science, legal and constitutional studies, social sciences such as sociology and anthropology, history and geography, personal and social development, and even the creative and performing arts. Indeed it would not be too much to say that in this one single issue, all the other main values issues are in one way or another comprised. Thus the issue of reconciliation is one that will provide a forum for the discussion of values issues and cultural concerns in Australian classrooms for many years to come.

These then are among the list of vital issues with which teachers increasingly have to concern themselves as they go about their work in our schools. And these are not matters of the future: they are matters with which we must be dealing now. The attention of students in educational institutions to such issues is being increasingly called, as educators and members of the community more widely realize their immediate or proximate relevance to students' future lives and all their main concerns.

Addressing the centrality of values in Australian schools

We have argued in this chapter that mention of values is found increasingly in many Australian policy documents, curriculum schemes and programmes of study. This is as it should be: for there is now a widespread realization that no schooling is value-free: that everything schools do – the nature of the School Councils they set up and the range of members they appoint to them, the curricula they adopt, the forms of their organization and administration, the leadership style of the principal and the senior teams in the school, the staff they appoint, the pedagogical approaches they take up, the relationships between teachers, students and outside stakeholders (NALSAS, 1998) – these are all shot through with value considerations of one sort or another.

This is particularly true in the case of the curriculum: in schools 'values' exist, are found, embodied and presented in subjects throughout the whole curriculum. As opposed to the views of some, who believe that subjects concerned solely with 'facts' may be separated from those the sole concern of which is with 'values', Australian educators are increasingly ready to accept that values are not a separate domain of discourse to be defined as an element in the curriculum, being a subject or interest on its own, with its own body of theory, cognitive content, typical activities, disciplinary procedures and criteria for success. Just as is the case for science, so too with the arts and the humanities: no subject is value-free: it is shot through with value elements that help structure and define it (cf OECD, 1994a, 1994b; Aspin and Chapman, 2000).

Many teachers are now concerned for the ways in which learning and activity in their subjects can provide their students with an understanding of the ways in which individuals, societies and cultures look at themselves, consider their origins and project their visions for the future. They appreciate, as do our education colleagues in New Zealand (see Ministry of Education New Zealand, 1999), that learning in their subjects will enable their students to affirm their cultural identities and understand their origins and histories; clarify and reflect on their attitudes, beliefs and values; understand and value the contribution they can make to society; value the contribution their education can make to their lives, their communities and the societies in which they live; reflect on the beliefs, values and attitudes of others; develop understanding about how people express their beliefs, ideas and feelings; and understand how other cultures and societies value their learning, knowledge and skills in a variety of contexts and for a variety of purposes.

All this is commendable, so far as it goes, but in our view such general statements of aspiration leave some important questions unanswered. To begin with, we might point to the use of such terms in the foregoing as 'affirm', 'understand', 'clarify', 'reflect on', 'value' and so on, and comment that, while it is obviously important that students be able to come to such understanding and reflection, reference to such terms, and the way they are written up give us no indication of what the students are *actually to do*: what are students to *do* when they have finished 'valuing' the contribution of their education to their lives and their community (come to that, how are they supposed to go about that process or activity?)? How is that valuing to be made manifest? To what kind of conclusion is their reflection on the beliefs, values and attitudes of others to come? Too often, all the value words are manifestations of an injunction to *re-*

flection rather than to *making judgements, forming conclusions* or *making plans for action* of any sort. We are not told how students will be encouraged to demonstrate their affirmations, understandings and reflections in any public forms of action, which will indicate not only that they have understood but also that they have drawn implications as to their future behaviour, beliefs and commitments.

Moreover, there is another question to be raised here. One of the values outcomes at which many educators now aim is that of helping students develop the ability to 'reflect on the beliefs, values and attitudes of others and how they may differ from their own (see also Foster, 2000)'. In a multicultural society it is certainly important that students can get clear about the differences between themselves and others in such matters and that reflection on such differences may make them better informed in developing their own values and being able to have some understanding of the causes and reasons behind different values adopted, held or exhibited by other people. But, we might ask, what *difference* is such reflection supposed to make? Are students *not* to be encouraged to make judgements in such matters? Is there to be no place for students to reflect on the possibility that the beliefs, values and attitudes of others might be discriminatory, divisive, inflammatory and so on?

The foregoing enables us to say something about what appears in the view of many in the education service in Australia as the main approach to be adopted in any form of values education – that of *values clarification* (cf Pascoe, 1996). Certainly we want to indicate our agreement with the general proposition that values – of whatever kind – are present throughout the curriculum and in all the work of educating people that schools do. This being so, schools need to be encouraged, not merely to identify the values that are already at work in education, and the ways in which institutions work to realize and present them. It is clearly important to pay overt attention to the place of values in the fabric of our schools' work of educating their students, and this will involve being ready to get down to the hard work of identifying and clarifying them. Now, the skill of learning how to clarify values, to analyse policies and issues, to see what value considerations and issues are at work in our handling of curriculum content and methods of learning and teaching, and to judge whether the behavioural reality matches the moral rhetoric, is certainly a vital and indispensable feature of our lives as educators having a moral responsibility (see Daveney, 1973) and it is important that all our colleagues in education – teachers and learners – should acquire it.

In our view, however (see also Aspin, 1999, 2000a), values clarification will only take us part of the way. It misses out on the crucial element of values education: for that enterprise to do its real work, it is not sufficient for people merely to clarify the things they value and approve of, to desire those things, to accept them, to prefer them, to incline towards them, perhaps even to seek to emulate them. People have also to commit themselves to the adoption and implementation of particular modes of conduct or kinds of choice (Wringe,

1999). Accepting that is part of learning how to become a member of a decent civil society (Krygier, 1997).

It is not sufficient merely to analyse, to identify or to clarify values. There has to be an outcome arising from such an enterprise that makes a difference to our lives and to the lives of others. It is not enough to tell people about the avoidance of risk-taking behaviours: we have also to try to alter their behaviour. That is the educational *qua* moral point of this whole approach. School leaders, subject teachers, educational policy makers in our community have the responsibility and task, not only to get their students to become a part of a particular community and to come to hold certain beliefs, to commit themselves to certain values: they have to secure that commitment in students' actions and conduct as well.

The point for us is that all work in values and discussions involving value words and expressions, such as 'ought', 'good' and 'wrong', has a force and a significance far beyond our own subjective reactions. Rather, values and value judgements function as bridges between us; they act as targets for emulation and as guides to judgement, choices and conduct. They are objective in that people agree (or disagree) about them interpersonally, even though different people place weight upon different ones. That objectivity is exhibited in the fact that matters of value are central to the lives of individuals, communities and their cultures, and in all their main concerns. And that is why they are central to the educating institutions of those cultures and communities.

Conclusion

This position enables teachers to call into question the views that are often expressed in school staffrooms or elsewhere – whenever discussion of values, value judgements or values education is taking place. Some people think it a very clever refutation of such teachers' views to voice what they take to be the irresistible rebuttal: 'Whose values?' By this question, such people are perhaps endeavouring to prove that values are individual, subjective, irreconcilably different, and in no way congruent, such that, on any matter of policy or practice, product or performance, absolute differences of opinion are to be expected. In our view, by contrast, values are objective because they are intersubjective, and our awareness of differences between us and our interlocutors on matters of value is the start, not the end, of all discussion and attempted resolution between us.

It is our institutions – and particularly our institutions of learning – in which such differences and disagreements can be articulated, developed and rationally resolved. The values embodied and at work in such institutions are agreed upon at the level of the culture of a community and they determine beliefs, actions and behaviours on a normative basis for a good deal longer than the mere utterance of the relativistic moment. In our society among the major institutions in which such matters can be broached and put into play are those of education – in those schools and colleges in which we seek the best ways in which we can institutionalize our educating practices and purposes. Values are instantiated in every word we select and speak, every piece of clothing we wear, the ways in which we present ourselves to one another, our reading of others' reactions to what we are saying, the cues we pick up and the actions we take as a result (and sometimes get wrong, too!) – they are embedded and embodied in everything we do, as part of the warp and weft of our and our community's whole form of life.

Teachers of all subjects in the curriculum have an especially momentous task to perform in exemplifying this concern. We misconceive the nature and consequence of their work *as educators* if we encourage them to believe that values are only subjective and we misrepresent the vital moral import of their work in educating their students about and in values if all they are to do is to teach them to clarify their own values without reference to the choices they make and the implications of those choices for themselves and their society. For in so doing they would be selling their students – and their community – short.

These are issues in the changing nature of culture and values in Australian education, which are yet to be seriously addressed.

References

Aspin, D N (1999) The nature of values and their place and promotion in schemes of values education, *Educational Philosophy and Theory*, **31** (2), pp 123–43

Aspin, D N (2000a) Values, attitudes and beliefs: their nature and place and promotion in schools, in vol II (*Institutional Issues: Pupils, schools and teacher education*), pp 130–43, *Education, Culture and Values*, Eight-volume symposium, ed M Leicester, C Modgil and S Modgil, Falmer, London

Aspin, D N (2000b) A clarification of some key terms in values discussion, in vol IV (*Moral Education and Pluralism*), pp 6–31, *Education, Culture and Values*, Eight-volume symposium, ed M Leicester, C Modgil and S Modgil, Falmer, London

Aspin, D N and Chapman, J D (2000) Values education and the humanisation of the curriculum, in vol VI (*Politics, Education and Citizenship*), pp 123–40, *Education, Culture and Values*, Eight-volume symposium, ed M Leicester, C Modgil and S Modgil, Falmer, London

Curriculum Corporation (1997) *Discovering Democracy*, DEETYA, AGPS, Canberra

Daveney, T F (1973) Education: a moral concept, in *New Essays in Philosophy of Education*, ed G Langford and D J O'Connor, Routledge & Kegan Paul, London

Foster, M (2000) Monitoring students' attitudes and values, Unpublished paper presented at the Thirteenth International Congress on School Effectiveness and Improvement, January, Hong Kong

Haydon, G (1999) Values, virtues and violence: education and the public understanding of morality, Special issue of *Journal of Philosophy of Education*, **33** (1), March

Hill, B V (1991) *Values Education in Australia*, Australian Council for Educational Research (ACER), Hawthorn, Vic

Kenny, A (1978) *The Aristotelian Ethics*, Oxford University Press, Oxford

Krygier, M (1997) *Between Fear and Hope: A hybrid thoughts on public values* (The Boyer Lectures), ABC Books, Sydney

Ling, L, Burman, E and Cooper, M (1998) The Australian study, in *Values in Education*, ed J Stephenson *et al*, pp 35–60, Routledge, London

Lovat, T and Schofield, N (1998) Values formation and citizenship education: a proposition and an empirical study, *Unicorn*, **24** (1), April, pp 46–54

Ministerial Council on Education, Employment, Training and Youth Affairs (MCEETYA) (1999) *The Adelaide Declaration on National Goals for Schooling in the Twenty-First Century*, MCEETYA, AGPS, Canberra

Ministry of Education New Zealand (1999) *New Zealand Draft Curriculum for Arts in Schools*, Learning Media, Wellington, NZ

NALSAS (1998) *Partnership for Change: The NALSAS strategy report of the National Asian Languages and Studies in Schools Taskforce*, MCEETYA, AGPS, Canberra

OECD (1994a) *The Curriculum Re-defined: Education for the twenty-first century*, OECD, Paris

OECD (1994b) *Quality in Teaching*, OECD, Paris

Pascoe, S (1996) Civics and citizenship education: the Australian context, *Unicorn*, Journal of the Australian College of Education, **22** (1), March, pp 18–29

Pascoe, S and Ferguson, S (1999) Discovering democracy: the story so far, *EQ Australia*, (3), Spring, pp 18–21

Popper, K R (1970) *Objective Knowledge*, Clarendon Press, Oxford

Quine, W V (1951) Two dogmas of empiricism, *Philosophical Review*, **60**, pp 20–45

Rorty, R (1979) *Philosophy and the Mirror of Nature*, Princeton University Press, Princeton, NJ

Ryle, G (1949) *The Concept of Mind*, Hutchinson, London

Stephenson, J *et al* (ed) (1998) *Values in Education*, Routledge, London and New York

Taylor, P W (1961) *Normative Discourse*, Prentice Hall, Englewood-Cliffs, NJ

UNESCO (1996) *Learning: The treasure within*, Report of the Commission chaired by Jacques Delors, UNESCO, Paris

Winch, C (1996) Practising valuable education and equality, quality and diversity, *Journal of Philosophy of Education*, Special issue: *Quality and Education*, **30** (1), March, pp 85 ff and 113 ff

Wringe, C (1998a) Reasons, rules and virtue in moral education, *Journal of Philosophy of Education*, **32** (2), July, pp 225–37

Wringe, C (1998b) Reasons, values and community in moral education, *British Journal of Educational Studies*, **46** (3), September, pp 278–88

Wringe, C (1999) Being good and living well: three attempts to resolve an ambiguity, *Journal of Philosophy of Education*, **33** (2), July, pp 287–93

8. Changing cultures and schools in Brazil

Candido Alberto Gomes and Clélia de Freitas Capanema

Introduction

A Contrasting Country was the title of a famous book on Brazil. In fact, recent industrialization, urbanization and secularization have caused so many changes that values, culture and education are in turmoil. The interface of cultural elements, and the complex interaction between them, is only one of the elements of a developing – or modernizing – society in Latin America. The emerging influential mass media, the social and regional differences aggravated by economic internationalization, the disjunctures between traditions and new technologies are some of the features of a society under transition. In such a context, education is in crisis, aiming to be socially significant, egalitarian and substantially improved from the qualitative point of view. Not being an exception, particularly in the southern hemisphere, Brazil is a challenge for comprehension and for action. This chapter is an attempt to understand the challenge, its historical roots, educational development and multiple dilemmas.

Social, cultural and political factors

Brazil, like other American colonies, entered Western history as a result of a double mission that European leading countries attributed to themselves: the mercantilist and the Christian expansion throughout the world. The Catholic Church and the Portuguese Crown were associates in that mission in that the religious power was charged with converting and educating the colonial populations, whereas the temporal power was responsible for management and defence. In the mid-16th century, Jesuits arrived in Brazil, at that time a colony made economically feasible by tropical agriculture (Furtado, 1976). These leading emissaries of the modernizing Catholic Reformation built a non-formal and a formal educational system. The former was tailored to the culture of the Native Americans, as the Jesuits sought to refine their new and dynamic mission: that of contextualizing Christian teaching within the cultural traditions of those groups whom they came to evangelize. The latter consisted of elementary and high schools and seminaries. The scattered primary schools were limited to literacy training and to teach 'good manners' to the sons of colonizers and Native Americans, more often in desegregated classes (Azevedo, 1950). High schools practised an elitist approach to influence the upper class so that the whole society could be conquered to adhere to the counter-reformist values. The most important goal of the curriculum was the transmission of humanistic culture, inspired by a modernizing and synthesization of the teaching of medieval scholars.

Religious values and moral education were the nerve, blood and flesh of education in Brazil. Jesuit priests wisely maintained this self-financed and independent system (they managed their farms very well) for two centuries until they became a threat to the Portuguese and Spanish crowns. In the middle of the 18th century, the Enlightenment arrived as a delayed intellectual stream to the Iberian Peninsula and its colonies. The authoritarian regime of the prime minister Marquis of Pombal not only conducted top-down innovations in all the fields of public life, but also expelled Jesuits from the kingdom. Although the movement was like an open window and a blast of fresh air for the metropolis, it was like a closing door to the colonies, since their confessional schools were not replaced by the state. There were no curricula, no qualified teachers, no school buildings and no effective sources of financing.

A gap of a century in education provision lasted until the Portuguese court, threatened by Napoleonic wars, moved to Brazil. The colony then became the metropolis. The state established several educational and cultural institutions, including colleges, and new intellectual winds started to blow.

When the independent country was founded some years later (1822), the most serious limit to education was its low priority. Brazil inherited an agrarian, outward-oriented economy, based on African slavery. Although the elites formally shared liberal ideas, education was not regarded as useful in a traditional society, in an oligarchic political system and in a scarcely productive economy. Different from Argentina, where liberalism inspired the diffusion of universal primary schools as a means to integrate immigrants and to construct nationalism, liberal values in Brazil led to decentralization and state withdrawal from education. As a result, private confessional and lay schools expanded to provide education for the elite and the emerging urban middle classes. Not only did the Jesuits return, but also other religious orders that founded schools, among them French congregations, which established the first schools for girls. Nevertheless, one of the changes was the arrival of Protestant churches. Inspired by American educational values, their schools introduced new patterns, especially co-education, which was something revolutionary in relation to the European traditions. Limited public education, as well as disconnected reforms, characterized the 19th century and the first three decades of the 20th century.

After the 1929 Great Depression, the Brazilian industrial revolution, based on import substitution, was the spur that led indirectly to the expansion of public lay schools, the organization of a real educational system oriented towards modern society. The coexistence of public and private education, as well as of lay and confessional schools, simultaneously reflected and diffused a new order of values, based on secularization, bureaucratization and modernization. Of course, the path from an agrarian to an industrial society was arduous. Old wine in new bottles and new wine in old bottles are metaphors that express the dynamics of change.

The construction of a modern society in Brazil, as in other Latin American countries (see, for example, Filmus, 1996), has plenty of contrasts. Despite the almost continuous increase in gross national product, social and regional differences were magnified or at least became more visible and unacceptable.

Economic crises have regressive effects on lower classes, particularly that of the late 1990s partially resulting from the opening of the economy to the internationalized competition, after several decades of import substitution industrialization. Unemployment, underemployment, urban deterioration, growth of slums and expansion of the parallel economy, particularly drug traffic, with its cohort of evil, are the dark side of modernization. As a consequence, secularization has tended to reduce the influence of traditional educational institutions such as the family, traditional churches in general (in spite of a revival), school, neighbourhood and community. In contrast, the mass media, specially television, and peer groups emerged as new powers in the country. Almost exclusively financed with resources from advertising, television is oriented toward the expansion of consumption, an increasing aspiration often unattainable by the majority of the population. One of its effects is the trend to the standardization of specific social dialects, habits and customs throughout the 5.3-million-square-mile country. Moreover, despite good projects and programmes, the exploitation of violence and sex is likely to acquire the same importance as in other countries (see, for example, Groebel, 1997). The final result of these factors' interaction is anomie for a large proportion of the population (Ribeiro, 1995) and a serious loss of values for the society as a whole.

Schooling, in opposition, is far from offering satisfactory responses or competitive methodologies and technologies. Brazil has neglected education, and particularly basic education, throughout its history. It is surprising that the country achieved so high an economic performance with such a low-skilled labour force (average of six years of schooling). In fact, access was the top priority of educational policies until recent years, whereas the substantive issues of quality, efficiency and equity were largely underestimated. Schooling reflects the unequal social stratification system with lower Socio-economic Status (SES) and non-white pupils; rural areas, the periphery of cities and the most deprived regions have access not only to fewer years of study but also to a lower quality of schooling. The exception, in comparison with other countries, is gender. Girls and women perform significantly better in educational indicators than boys and men (except in mathematics and science). Opportunity cost offers the best explanation for this difference: girls and women are often less in demand in the labour market; they also tend to enter the system at a later stage and thus gain extra time in school.

It is important to point out that the continuance of these educational asymmetries is largely an effect of still entrenched values in politics. Bureaucratization has not yet become strong enough to defeat patrimonialism, paternalism and populism. Therefore, public purposes and resources often give way to private interests. Tax revenues are used to improve the advantages of privileged groups, while education is a sort of currency (or gift) to be exchanged with votes (see Plank, 1996). Of course, educational quality and effectiveness, in such circumstances, are potential threats to the status quo, since they arouse consciousness. Nevertheless, it is possible to assess progress towards a better and more egalitarian educational system when it is compared with the situation one or two decades ago.

The precariousness and even alienation of schools created a gulf between curricula and life. Instead of education, with a complex, formative profile, schooling was often reduced to the transmission of content. At secondary level, the competition for college entrance examinations exacerbates this kind of instruction targeted towards knowledge and seldom to values, emotions and attitudes (see Gomes, 1999). Faced with a changing society with conflicting values, it is easier to omit sensitive matters.

Religious movements

The milestone for the beginning of the remarkable religious movements in Brazil was the Second Vatican Council, as far as the Catholic Church is concerned. For the Protestant churches different points of reference will be outlined later in this chapter.

Since Vatican II, a new form of lay participation has arisen in the vast and complicated world of politics, social reality and economy, culture, science and arts, international life and the mass media, in addition to other realities of life such as love, family, education of children and adolescents, work and suffering. The primary source of this important Catholic Church reform in Brazil was some hundreds of young newly ordained bishops, who had completed their studies in Europe and had been influenced by the ideas of German Dominicans, defenders of a less hierarchical and more missionary Church.

The first theoretical manifestation of these new trends, a theological reading of modern problems, was liberation theology, which can be considered to be the daughter of Vatican II, in the 1970s. It aimed at making the poor subjects of their own history. The consequent strategy was to put the Bible in the hands of the Catholic people who, until then, unlike the Protestants, were practically prohibited from reading it. The reading of the Bible represented a great revolution in Latin America as a whole.

As a concrete result, groups of laypersons were organized to study critically Brazilian history and reality in the light of the teachings of the Bible: the ecclesiastic base communities (CEBs). The theoretical framework of this movement was the social doctrine of the Catholic Church whose roots go back to Pope Leo XIII's *Rerum Novarum*, the encyclical that approached the social issue for the first time in the history of the Catholic Church. Cobo (1999) identifies those ecclesiastic base communities as the birthplace of the present Labour Party in Brazil (PT) specifically in Volta Redonda (National Metallurgy Company) and the industrial area of São Paulo, the ABC, which comprises the municipalities of Santo André, São Bernardo and São Caetano.

At the same time there existed a powerful organization called Catholic Action, created long before the military regime took charge in Brazil. Originally it was intended to assemble Catholic laypersons to help with the apostolic work of the clergymen. This organization gave birth to a radical branch called Popular Action that generated important labour and intellectual political leadership, forming an active leftist opposition to the political and institutional situation in Brazil in the1960s and 1970s. This politicization led to those leaders being persecuted and forced to lead a clandestine life and, in some cases, even exile. Many congressmen and Brazilians who are still active in political life are remnants of that movement.

The National Conference of the Brazilian Bishops (CNBB) was already an influential institution in the Catholic Church at that time. Noteworthy, for instance, was the prominent role played by the bishops during the hardest years of the military regime. Theirs were the only voices heard by the government in support of political prisoners, many of them members of the Church.

From the late 1970s, the Catholic Church's social doctrine has been to speak out about and have an impact on social, economic, political and cultural practice through the named fraternity campaigns, which were first conceived as a fund-raising mechanism. Having failed to reach that objective, it became a powerful instrument for the formation of Christian consciousness. From general Christian principles, these campaigns shifted attention to real situations of Brazilian life, resulting in clear cultural changes. Examples of this influence were the Pastoral of the Child and the Pastoral of the African Brazilian, which ensured new government policies dealing with the social, political, economic and cultural demands of these segments of society. Each year a different theme is addressed by the fraternity campaign, bringing up crucial issues such as social exclusion, violence, health, hunger, family life, solidarity, street children and unemployment. The theme for 2000 is peace, this time with an ecumenical character since it will be a movement endorsed by both the Catholic and other Christian churches. The 2001 campaign will focus on drugs, a universal concern, irrespective of religious beliefs.

The 1982 fraternity campaign dealt with the theme education, calling for the formulation of the progressive ideas generated in the councils held by CELAM (Latin American Episcopal Conference) in Medellín, Colombia, in

1968 and in Puebla, Mexico, in 1979. In Medellín it was stated that the Catholic Church should be committed to the transformation of Latin American people by education, in order to alert all to the structural injustice and oppression of which Latin America is victim. Puebla reinforced the educational and transforming role of the Church in the promotion of socio-cultural changes in the country through a liberating education, an educational concept very similar to that of Paulo Freire. The appearance of Paulo Freire's work on adult literacy with the poor in the north-east of Brazil, which came at the same time as those religious movements took place, should be seen as a coincidence. The ideological roots are the same. It is noteworthy that there is a close relation between each document elaborated by the Church and the historical, political and social moment when it has been produced.

Parallel to those movements, the Catholic Church has another channel of evangelization consisting of its network of schools, at all levels, from kindergarten to university. However, research carried out in Catholic high schools in the Federal District (Capital City) shows that Church norms, orientations and recommendations do not reach classrooms (Stein, 1998). Schools are too involved in conventional curriculum content to be accountable to parents, society and government. It does not mean that those educational institutions neglect the basic teachings of Christian beliefs and values. On the contrary, these elements are present in school life. As far as confessional universities are concerned, their stated mission is to act towards the full development of the human being and society as a whole, by means of generating and communicating knowledge, committed to Christian and ethical values, in the search of truth, as well as to the rigour of scientific research.

Religious movements focus on adapting religious doctrine to the multifarious effects of modernity in a societal ethos that embraces all from cradle to grave. One of these movements is freedom of choice having as a consequence ethical, cultural and religious pluralism. This phenomenon has led, since the 1970s, to a reduction in the percentage of people declaring themselves to be Catholics. The 1970 Census registered 91.77 per cent; in 1980 the figure was 88.95 per cent; and in 1991, it was 83 per cent. An opinion poll conducted by the newspaper *Folha de São Paulo*, in August–September 1994, showed that among 21,000 voters, 74 per cent were Catholics, 20.1 per cent were affiliated to other creeds and 4.9 per cent had no religious affiliation whatsoever (1 per cent missing data). Among those who professed to be other than Catholic, 3.4 per cent were historical or traditional Protestants; 9.9 per cent were Pentecostals; 3.5 per cent Kardecists; 1.3 per cent Afro-Brazilian cults; and 2 per cent affiliated to Islam, Judaism, Buddhism, Seicho-no-iê and Perfect Freedom (CNBB, 1999c).

From a sociological standpoint, it is fair to say that the retrogression in the traditional churches in the heart of a secularized society does not mean a diminution of the people's religiosity. There are a growing number of believers migrating to newer and smaller sects, which are spread throughout both urban and rural areas.

The law also guarantees religious pluralism in education. Schools are allowed to teach general religious and ethical principles but are legally forbidden from proselytism. This is the effect of a joint lobby of the traditional churches in the Congress, in 1997, under the principles that govern a democratic state separated from the Church. However, bureaucracy has put obstacles in the way of reinforcing this ecumenical ideal.

The statistics of religious affiliations in Brazil are problematic. The churches produce different figures to the IBGE, the Brazilian Geography and Statistics Institute. By and large those numbers are exaggerated. Kraft (1999) ascribes it to the priests' subtle ways of gaining political prestige, with the exception of the so-called historical churches such as the Methodist, Presbyterian and Lutheran whose statistics match the IBGE's. According to SEPAL, the Service of Evangelization for Latin America, the real figures show that there were 19,575,727 members of evangelic churches in Brazil in 1998 out of a total population of 161,383,000. The Assembly of God, with 14 million, and the Universal Church, with 4 million, are by far the largest evangelic denominations in Brazil. The latter has exhibited an amazing growth both in the numbers of affiliates and in economic and political power. In all cases, the churches have representatives in the House and the Senate, demonstrating their influence in politics.

In spite of that religious pluralism, the Catholic Church still maintains a strong influence on cultural change in Brazil. It is presently leading two movements. The first one is related to social exclusion, evident in the various walks of life in Brazil. The Church managed to assemble thousands of people in various parishes, calling for social justice, through a crusade called 'The cry of the excluded' (*Folha de São Paulo*, 1999b). The second is the publication of a document, subscribed to by at least a million Brazilians, demanding the eradication of corruption in politics. The outcome of this movement was a bill unanimously approved by the House of Representatives, in 34 days, and there is a high probability of it being in force in time for the next elections on 1 October 2000. As a result, the buying and bargaining of votes will be an electoral malpractice, and designated a crime. This latter movement had the approval and participation of the National Council of Christian Churches (CONIC) as well as the Order of Brazil's Lawyers (OAB), the most influential juridical organization in the country.

Economic trends

As in many other societies, the social prestige of academic education and selected areas of the curricula have affected the Brazilian educational system. Brazil's colonial roots have stressed the stigma of manual occupations so that education was (and still is) a means of ascending to the middle and upper classes through a white-collar job or a profession. Since educational opportunities to reach these aims were very scarce, secondary education, divided in two tracks, was a strategic filter. Whereas the academic track opened the doors to higher education, the vocational track locked its graduates from lower social classes into blue-collar occupations. The negative label traditionally attached to these occupations was so strong that, in the 19th century, vocational schools even required a formal proof of poverty, issued by the police, to enrol their applicants. It is not hard to understand why the demand for academic education has been so high and still remains so today.

However, during the industrial revolution, income growth, urbanization and other factors generated a contradiction. Although initially conceived for the elites, the academic schools were also attended by urban middle classes. The criticisms of academic school led to legislation and policies in the 1950s and 1960s gradually to soften the gap between academic and vocational education. Nevertheless, in 1971 the search for equity induced the country to reform education. Whereas Argentina chose the secondarization of vocational education, Brazil opted for the vocationalization of the secondary school (Gallart, 1988) but this led to strong opposition because of the prejudice against manual occupations. Middle-class values and cultural patterns were so strong in schools that an earlier attempt to offer pre-vocational education in the last grades of primary school (5th to 8th grades) had failed. According to research data, 1.5 per cent of the pupils enrolled in such schools actually intended to pursue a career of the same status as the pre-vocational component of the curricula (Castro et al, 1972). In addition, the demand for technicians and technical assistants by Brazilian companies was revealed to be much lower than expected. The role of these workers in production and services, contrary to the European and Japanese experience, in general was not clear. In fact, having had to meet the expectations of their clients, students and families, schools only minimally complied with the reform. Curricula, in fact, minimized vocational components, while they actually prepared students for college entrance examinations.

Not surprisingly, the system returned to dualism 11 years later. In the 1990s, the enrolment rate increased significantly (it almost doubled), opening the doors for major changes. Later, this chapter will focus on the new law on the policies and basis of education. The structure of the educational system is now similar to a tree, where the trunk is general education. At different stages, even in the last grades of the eight-year primary education, pupils may attend a vocational programme simultaneously while attending regular school. After compulsory education they may leave the school for some time and later return to it. The students also have the opportunity to follow a vocational programme and transfer part of the credits to their secondary schools. The final aim is to extend general education for all until the 11th grade as a means to strengthen the foundations for vocational education and on-the-job training.

In addition to these changes and a likely mitigation of prejudice against manual and technical occupations, recent trends for the diversification of the programmes and demands for vocational education at the secondary and tertiary levels have been detected. Interest for non-traditional occupations increased in the last decades of the 20th century so that the differentiation of alternatives might be broader if regulations were less strict, especially in higher education. Economic openings certainly played an important role in these processes. The requirements of new technologies, new management standards and competitiveness seem to have changed perceptions and expectations.

An interesting point relating to values and work is that increased competition also induces individualism. Vocational and higher education are predominantly a personal venture, instead of a contribution to a national project (Calmon, 1993). A national project may be neither clear nor attractive enough to most, since the social effects of economic development have been negative to a significant extent. Nevertheless, extension projects and programmes at the tertiary educational level have become valuable opportunities not only to integrate theories and practices but also to provide services to communities.

Students' participation in politics, as a consequence of the new individualistic society and the eclipse of community, was very active during the national development era (1950s and 60s) and at the beginning of the military regime (1960s). The latter changed the patterns of political socialization stimulating indifference to focused participation in public matters. However, rare but remarkable participation has occurred in relation to focal issues of the national life, such as the country's re-democratization (1980s) and the impeachment of a president of the Republic (1992), a rigorously constitutional and peaceful process. In general, students are very far away from the missionary activism of the 1960s.

Legal frameworks

The principles and values that form the basis of the rules and regulations of education are focused on the cultivation, protection and refinement of a reborn democracy in Brazil. The legal framework portrays an idealized nation whose political creed pledges to face up to the most challenging issues such as its place in a global economy by means of sustainable development, the amelioration of social inequalities and exclusion as well as the building of citizenship (see Capanema, 1996).

With these principles and values Brazil appears to have experienced a metamorphosis during the last two decades or so of the 20th century in the field of education, although at a slower than desirable pace. The euphoria following the proclamation in 1988 of a very optimistic constitution was replaced by a more realistic attitude by policy makers and educators. According to Bobbio's reasoning (1992: 25), the gravest problem faced by Brazil is to guarantee the protection of the human rights rather than to justify them. The right to fundamental education, included in the federal constitution as a subjective right, that is, inherent to the subject, is being exercised by means of a major increase in the enrolment rate. Progress in this respect is undeniable. The enrolment rate of children between 7 and 14 years of age increased from 76 per cent in 1981 to 86 per cent in 1991. Yet, in 1996, there were 4 million children between 7 and 14 years of age still out of school (IPEA/PNUD, 1996).

Failure to provide for equal educational opportunities is shown from other angles of analysis such as pre-school education, urban/rural differences and regional diversities. Schooling for children from 5 to 6 years of age was limited to 50 per cent of the cohort, according to 1990 data. The sharp cleavage between the rich and the poor in Brazil will not be narrowed unless these inequalities are replaced by signs of significant progress in the provision of good-quality basic education for all.

Even before solving the quantitative problem of enrolment, at least in secondary and higher education, Brazilian educational policy makers have to face the challenge of quality confronting the educational system at all levels. The gap between Brazil and the international context within which it is embedded is well known. Brazil is aware of the urgency of facing the demands of quality control and zero defects demanded by the modern world aiming at the preparation of a conscious citizen and an effectively productive person. Brazil must face the need of providing sufficient and good-quality public middle-level education, especially taking into account the needs of the poor, with more determination, since the well-to-do people resort successfully to private schools.

Innovations in the legal frameworks highlight the trends of educational reforms in this decade. As in many other countries, one pillar of these changes is undoubtedly school management and autonomy. They are prescribed by the 1988 constitution, the 1996 law on the policies and basis of education, the most recent important piece of educational legislation, the rules and regulations of the Ministry of Education and the National Council of Education, in the context of the Brazilian state's reform that followed the re-democratization process in the 1980s. The main character of the new democratic and autonomous school is the establishment of a governing body consisting of the headteacher and representatives of the teachers, parents, pupils or students and the administrative body. The law entrusts each school to develop its own educational plan, including the private schools network made up of either lay or religious institutions of every creed. Compared with the tight centralization of the past, the changes show a remarkable administrative and political improvement. Participation is the key word in these new times. There are already several surveys in different parts of the country showing the success of these democratic experiments, resulting in visible changes in the old attitudes of the community being alienated from the life of school. Of course, the meaning of success here is the improvement of the learning process, the sole rationale for changing the structure and the functioning of schools since this is the aim for which the main schools are accountable.

A significant innovation in Brazilian primary and secondary schools in the midst of decentralization is the introduction of national curriculum parameters, which provide directives on cross-curricular themes of study dealing with values inherent in ethics, the environment, cultural pluralism, health and sexual education, work and consumption. These themes are intended to shape behaviour alongside intellectual development since they combine cultural identity, pluralism and national diversities.

Conclusion

Changing cultures and values in Brazil reflect the ambiguities of the development process. Old and new patterns and values not only coexist, but also interact, bringing together the challenges of industrialization, late modernity and the traditional, agrarian societies. The difficulties resulting from these intricate processes involve the effects of economic development, the struggle for income distribution (and against entrenched privileges), the difficulties of consolidating a democratic regime and the crisis of secularization.

Following two decades of lower (or negative) economic growth, burdened by huge domestic and international debt, the country needs to be cautious, not exactly optimistic or pessimistic. A simplified view of our contradictions involves several questions. Will economic opportunities be adequately managed or will the process be discontinued, going back to the tradition of an introverted economy and extroverted finance? Will the elites at last renounce their old privileges, in favour of national integrity, or will social differences remain dangerously sharp? Will democracy remain or will this society accede to the temptation of authoritarianism to solve its economic and social problems, like other Latin American countries? Will anomie prevail, particularly in big cities, or will a relative consensus on values, secular and religious, be the axis of Brazilian society? Will the educational system pursue the goals of equity, quality and modernization or will it go backwards? Will schooling have a significant role in changes in values or will it remain directed towards conventional contents? These are some questions the future will answer. Brazil, despite many individual characteristics, is similar to at least some developing societies. Some of its lessons may be significant in the understanding of virtues and failures in the new international order.

References

Azevedo, F de (1950) *Brazilian Culture*, Macmillan, New York

Bobbio, N (1992) *Estado, governo e sociedade: para uma teoria geral da politica (State, government and society: towards a general theory of politics)*, Paz e Terra, Rio, Brasília

Brasil (1988) *Constituição da República Federativa do Brasil (Constitution of the Federative Republic of Brazil)*, Senado Federal, Centro Gráfico, Brasília

Calmon, J (ed) (1993) *A Crise na Universidade Brasileira: Comissão parlamentar mista de inquérito: final report (The Crisis of the Brazilian University: Congressional investigative ad hoc committee: final report)*, Centro Gráfico do Senado Federal, Brasília

Capanema, C (1996) Educação pós-moderna: os desafios para a formulação de uma política pública (Post-modern education: the challenges to the design of public policy), *Epistéme* (a publication of The Bandeirante University of São Paulo), 1 (2), Jul/Dec, pp 85–100

Castro, C *et al* (1972) *Ensino Técnico: Desempenho e custos (Technical Education: Performance and cost)*, IPEA, Rio de Janeiro

CNBB (1999a) Missão e ministérios dos cristãos leigos e leigas (Mission and ministry of lay Christians), Documentos da Conferência Nacional dos Bispos Brasil, 62, Paulina, São Paulo

CNBB (1999b) A fraternidade e os desempregados: sem trabalho... por quê? (Fraternity and unemployed people: why joblessness?), Texto-base da Campanha da Fraternidade 1999, Editora Salesiana Dom Bosco, São Paulo

CNBB (1999c) Diretrizes gerais da ação evangelizadora da Igreja no Brasil: 1999–2002 (General guidelines for the missionary action of the Church in Brazil), Documentos da Conferência Nacional dos Bispos do Brasil, 61, pp 99–100, Paulina, São Paulo

CNBB (1999) Rumo ao novo milênio: projeto de evangelização da Igreja o Brasil em preparação ao grande jubileu do ano 2000 (Towards the new millennium: the Church's missionary project in preparation for the great jubilee in 2000), Documentos da Conferência Nacional dos Bispos do Brasil

Cobo, J (1999) Movimentos Católicos no Brasil (Catholic movements in Brazil), August, CNBB, Brasília, Oral communication

Filmus, D (1996) *Estado, Sociedad y Educación en la Argentina de Fin de Siglo: Proceso y desafíos (State, Society and Education in Argentina at the End of the Century: Process and challenges)*, Troquel, Buenos Aires

Folha de São Paulo (1999a), 9 April, pp 1–6, Brasil

Folha de São Paulo (1999b), 4 September, pp 1–6, Brasil

Furtado, C (1976) *Economic Development in Latin America: Historical background and contemporary problems*, Cambridge University Press, Cambridge

Gallart, M A (1988) The secondarization of technical education in Argentina and the vocationalization of secondary education in Brazil, in *Vocationalizing Education: An international perspective*, ed J Lauglo and K Lillis, pp 203–18, Pergamon, Oxford

Gomes, C A (1999) New perspectives for secondary school: the case of Brazil, *International Review of Education*, 45 (1), pp 45–63

Groebel, J (ed) (1997) *New Media Developments: Trends in communication 1*, Boom Publishers, Amsterdam

IPEA/PNUD (1996) *Relatório Sobre o Desenvolvimento Humano no Brasil 1996 (Report on Human Development in Brazil– 1996)*, p 35, Published for the United Nations Plan for Development – PNUD, Brasília

Kraft, L (1999) Numeros evangelásticos (Evangelistic data), in *Vinde*, C Fernandes, p18 e 20, Setembro

Plank, D N (1996) *The Means of our Salvation: Public education in Brazil, 1930–1995*, Westview, Boulder, Colorado and Oxford

Ribeiro, D (1995) *O Povo Brasileiro (The Brazilian People)*, Companhia das Letras, São Paulo

Stein, G B (1998) A educação nos documentos da Igreja Católica Apostólica Romana e como suas orientações chegam às salas-de-aula, em Escolas Católicas no Distrito Federal (Education in the Roman Catholic Church: how its orientation reaches classrooms in the Catholic schools in the Federal District), Master in Education thesis, Catholic University of Brasília, Brasília

9. Changing cultures and schools in Canada

Geoffrey Milburn and Rebecca Priegert Coulter

Introduction

Canadians appear eager to debate value issues in schooling.[1] During the last
two decades, they have expressed divergent opinions on almost every aspect
of schooling: curricular aims, gender and racial issues, schools for minorities,
language services, religious observances, privatization, student violence,
teachers' duties and many others. Scarcely a day passes in which there is not a
relevant article about contemporary schools in one or more of Canada's major
newspapers. That popular interest is also reflected in the number of Royal
Commissions and major governmental studies of schools undertaken in the
last few decades. And these discussions are not confined to political or educational elites. Everyone seems to know what to do about schools and how to
change them for the better: students, parents, social activists, workers,
businesspersons, professionals and social theorists. Schooling, it seems, to a
much greater extent than heretofore, is everybody's business, and everyone
has opinions that he or she wishes to express.

To some extent, this interest in values in schooling is by no means new;
such debates have been a feature of Canadian political life since confedera-
tion. On the other hand, current debates have perhaps become more intense
because of changes not only in Canadian society but also in the technology of
communications. It is certain that previous understandings have come under
increasing scrutiny in the last 20 years. Some underlying principles of public
education, and the legislation that put them into effect, have been questioned
and challenged by groups within society whose opinions had rarely been considered.

In this chapter we identify the principal value issues and questions about
schooling in contemporary Canada, and examine some debates they have
prompted. Where important controversies exist, we outline briefly arguments
and counter-arguments surrounding them and, where appropriate, indicate
how those arguments may affect schooling in the future. We pay particular attention to those features that render the Canadian experience distinct. In
short, we assess how value discussions have focused on the moral purpose of
Canadian schooling. These tasks are far from simple. Schooling is a vast enterprise; the issues are complex and numerous. Evidence is scattered over many

jurisdictions, and locked in a web of policy statements, legislative action, administrative decisions and court cases. The contemporary climate in which discussions take place is frequently clouded by ideological posturing, partisan misinformation and political manoeuvring. Of necessity, we are selective in our discussions – and tentative in our conclusions.

After an outline of the historic context, we examine four very broad topics on which contemporary values debates have focused:

- equal treatment of students in schools;
- religious teachings in schools;
- business values in schools; and
- student behaviours in schools.

Historical legacy: the context for debates

Value discussions in schooling are constrained, at least in part, by several historic factors: previous agreements concerning constitutional rights and powers, cultural, religious and language patterns caused by successive waves of immigration, and shifts in economic development and social contexts. Although each new generation works with a different set of circumstances, it does not begin with a clean slate – a historic legacy persists through the generations and affects the character (and often determines the outcome) of decisions made in subsequent years. Canada is no exception. Several historic developments play a major role in discussions of schooling.

First, Canada is a vast country, and its population and resources are very unevenly distributed. It is home to two 'official' languages, French and English, derived from its Euro-colonial past. Federal services are provided in both languages. The province of Québec is officially French-speaking (while protecting minority English rights), New Brunswick is officially bilingual and the other provinces are English-speaking (with very varied provisions for French minorities). Canada is also home to a growing population of Aboriginal peoples who possess, or claim, historic and treaty rights to land, resources and self-government. In the last two decades, however, the traditional demographic structure of Canada has changed dramatically as immigrants have been welcomed from largely non-European sources, the greater part of whom have settled in the three major cities of Vancouver, Toronto and Montréal. Under the terms of the British North America Act 1867 (now called the Constitution Act 1867), Canada is a federal state in which governmental powers and responsibilities are divided – not always clearly – between a central government and (currently) 10 provincial governments. Education is a provincial responsibility, and special protection is given in the Act to certain denominational schools. Provision is made for amending the written constitution, but exercising that provision is not easy.

However, one constitutional amendment had both direct and indirect effects on schooling: the adoption of the Charter of Rights and Freedoms, after intense discussions between the federal government and the provinces, in 1982. Whereas an earlier Bill of Rights at the federal level had been relatively weak, and provision for rights within the provinces varied, the Charter encoded in forthright language a single set of principles that were now to apply to all Canadian citizens, no matter where they lived in the country (Department of the Secretary of State of Canada, 1987). Henceforth every citizen was to be 'equal before and under the law' and had 'the right to equal protection and equal benefit of the law without discrimination'. The Charter prohibited discrimination based on 'race, national or ethnic origin, colour, religion, sex, age or mental or physical disability'. It stipulated that the rights and freedoms in the Charter were to be 'guaranteed equally to male and female persons'. 'English and French' were confirmed as 'the official languages of Canada' and had 'equality of status' in federal government services. The Charter affirmed that all citizens, within certain historically determined conditions, had 'the right to have their children receive primary and secondary school instruction' in English or French, and ensured that in situations in which either language was spoken by a minority, those children also had the right to instruction in their own language, where numbers warranted. The Charter guaranteed freedom of conscience and religion, and freedom of thought, and affirmed existing rights and freedoms (and any that may be acquired) of Aboriginal peoples in Canada. A clause ensured that the Charter 'shall be interpreted in a manner consistent with the preservation and enhancement of the multicultural heritage of Canada'. Finally, the Charter provided for legal remedies if any rights and freedoms are 'infringed or denied'. It should be noted also that the federal and provincial legislatures were given limited power (under the terms of the 'notwithstanding' clause) to pass laws that contravene sections of the Charter concerning fundamental, legal and equality rights.

The prime target of the Charter was not the condition of the nation's schools. The right to education was not mentioned in its text (although it does appear in some provincial lists of rights). That omission leaves open the important question of what particular services are to be protected. But exercise of the rights embedded in the Charter had an immediate application to some of the problems previously identified in the school system. And instead of relying on provincial legislation (which may be uneven or non-existent) or on the discretion of local school authorities (which may be governed by other interests than the need for equal treatment), parents with grievances could now seek to obtain remedy in the courts (MacKay, 1995). And, in their turn, educational policy makers and local administrators found themselves subjected to legal tests engendered by a list of specific rights, and discovered that their use of discretionary powers was severely blunted by judicial review. It is worth noting, however, that the Charter was based on a liberal democratic tradition in which particular *rights* were identified and protected. How the Charter would be invoked and interpreted in questions involving *values*, especially those of cultural and religious groups, would only become apparent as particular cases, including those related to schools, came before the courts.

Such historic constraints – political, constitutional, legal, social and cultural – are more than a backdrop to current discussions on schooling; they influence all arguments and shape all resolutions. In this, Canada is no exception; discussions about values in schools are played out against a particular set of historic circumstances that, for better or worse, influence notions about both the purpose and provision of schooling. And many persons involved in these discussions profess various levels and forms of dissatisfaction.

Equal treatment of students in schools

Much of that dissatisfaction centres on the question of equality of treatment in schools. Forty years ago the school system seemed – at least in retrospect – to be much more certain of its values than it is today. The school population was viewed as relatively homogeneous, teachers were usually white, authority structures within schools were dominated by men, a rigid curriculum emphasized traditional academic subjects, and the religious ethic was largely (and officially) Judaeo-Christian in origin. In essence, the schools were monolithic and certain (and assertive) of their purpose. In those schools, certain groups – particularly white Anglo-Saxon males – benefited, and others suffered various kinds of impediments, both major and minor. Although this characterization is far too simplistic (there were many exceptions and atypical instances), it at least reveals the principal targets at which critics have aimed their arrows. Leadership in the social analysis of Canadian schooling was provided by many academics inspired by the pioneering work of John Porter in 1965. And students (and their parents) began to report that they faced unfair and discriminatory treatment: in other words, they claimed that schools were agents of inequality in society.

Arguments were made that students in schools faced inequalities on several bases, including language (Majhanovich, 1995), gender (Coulter, 1996; Gaskell, McLaren and Novogrodsky, 1989), race (Dei, 1996b), culture (Stairs, 1994), class (Curtis, Livingstone and Smaller, 1992), sexual orientation (Epstein, 1998) and disability (Lupart, 1998). These inequalities were experienced in various aspects of schooling. Some of the groups (eg disabled students) claimed that they were not given equal access to schooling, that provisions made on their behalf were sometimes grossly inferior to those available to others. Some (eg homosexuals, Aboriginal peoples or students from minority-language or cultural groups) maintained that the treatment they received in school was unfair, others (eg young women) pointed out that the curriculum did not meet their needs and expectations, while still others (eg working-class students) contended that they did not experience the same level of success as other students. Thus protests of unequal treatment in Canadian schools became focused on (but by no means confined to) several very significant features of schooling: access to schools and school services, treatment while in schools and the outcomes of schooling.

There were, and are, disputes about these claims. They revealed at times significant inherent contradictions (eg between conflicting rights claims based on gender or sexual orientation, and those based on traditional practices of cultural groups or belief systems of religious faiths). Some critics maintained that complaints of discrimination in schooling were not fully warranted by empirical data, and that claims of unfair treatment occasionally have been overwrought (Paquette, in press). Some contended that claims by certain minorities were infringing on the rights of majorities in the provision of schooling. Some claims had financial implications that could not easily be accommodated. Political parties on the left or in the centre tended to take very different positions from those on the right on such essential matters as definitions of inequality and purposes of schooling.

Nevertheless, the force of these complaints was generally recognized, and attempts were made to remedy at least some of the inequalities. Many provincial governments introduced or amended civil and human rights legislation and instituted commissions to ensure that complaints could be investigated and solutions provided. Efforts were made, for example, to include the female experience in the curriculum, and attention was paid to comparative test scores and achievements of male and female students.

But the result was uneven: some provinces took legislative action before others, and school boards exercised their powers of discretion in various ways. The different jurisdictions in the country assumed a patchwork pattern, and the remedies offered for existing inequalities did not always meet the expectations of protesters. Many ameliorative changes in curriculum content and school procedures were subject to discretionary implementation by local school authorities – and many of those authorities decided to postpone action for financial or other reasons. The passage of the Charter of Rights and Freedoms changed the rules: it did not end difficulties over the clash of values in schooling. Certain rights were now more clearly stated (and remedies more readily available), but disputes continued – including those over the claims of individuals and those of particular groups.

The issue of language (particularly the minority rights of English and French speakers in various sections of the country) is central to the entire Canadian experience – and to its schools. Québec in recent decades has taken legislative steps to protect the use of French by regulating the language of instruction in its schools, and when the Supreme Court, on a Charter challenge by an individual over the language of a commercial sign, ruled in the 1980s that sections of the provincial legislation ran counter to the Charter, the provincial government invoked the 'notwithstanding clause'. In this instance, the provincial government seemed to be contending that the collective rights of francophones in Québec took precedence. Indeed, in 1997 Québec moved to a system of schooling based on linguistic rather than denominational rights (Smith, Foster and Donahue, 1999).

The phrase in the Charter making minority-language rights subject to the condition 'where numbers warrant' has provoked – not surprisingly – many disputes. Provincial governments have reacted in various ways. Ontario in the 1980s, after a court decision, ruled that every French-speaking Ontarian has a right to education in his or her own language, an example followed in several other provinces. Whether that education should be offered in a separate school is another difficult question, especially in local areas of small minority-language populations. When Prince Edward Island, for example, refused recently to provide a local school for a group of francophone children (who were being bused about an hour each way to another French school), the Supreme Court, after a Charter-based appeal, ordered the province to open a local French school, whereupon English-speaking parents whose children faced similar bus journeys felt aggrieved, at least according to the provincial premier (Hamilton, 2000). At the same time, enrolment in French-immersion second-language programmes has grown significantly in schools across the country over the last two decades. Francophones outside Québec, however, remain very nervous about the survival of their language, a condition that is exacerbated by such perceived irritants as the Alberta provincial government delaying full implementation of a Supreme Court ruling giving francophones power to manage and control their own schools (Majhanovich, 1995: 90–94).

The question of the role of multiculturalism in the curriculum is also unresolved. Some provinces, especially those in western Canada, offer bilingual programmes to recognize the heritage languages of several different ethnocultural groups. In other settings, supplementary heritage language instruction is available either during or after the school day (Cummins and Danesi, 1990). In all provinces, some changes have been made to the curriculum to reduce the emphasis on the European heritage. But disputes persist about the nature of those changes. Some contend that the legitimate needs of various cultural groups within Canada (and in particular in the large cities) can only be met by ensuring that the curriculum reflects a multiple-culture perspective (MacKay and Richard, 1998). Some black Canadians, for example, recommend that black children receive an Afro-centric curriculum that includes acknowledgement of their own way of knowing and endorsement of their own cultural heritage (Dei, 1996a; James and Brathwaite, 1996). Such an Afro-centric curriculum would also demand its own pedagogies and methods of assessment. Others, however, warn that the adoption of a multicultural perspective could impair social cohesiveness and entrench a system of multiple solitudes (Bissoondath, 1994; Lund, 1998). Schools across the country seem to respond mostly to parental and local pressures – with some making greater provision than others.

Despite the Charter, some critics insist that Canadian schools continue to be racist. True, some progress is acknowledged: more members of visible minorities have joined the teaching profession. Legal steps have been taken to remove the accreditation of teachers found guilty of racial prejudice (Bercuson and Wertheimer, 1985). But many racial minorities continue to feel excluded. Some contend that students whose first language is not English or French suffer systemic difficulties in education (especially in the provision of second-language instruction). Others point out that some racial groups experience additional difficulty in standardized tests because the questions in those tests are biased against them on cultural grounds.

Aboriginal persons, in particular, given their dismal experience in residential boarding schools (Miller, 1996), demand that separate provision should be made for students from their cultures. A distinct Aboriginal consciousness, they assert, cannot be maintained if students are submitted to curricula – and to the pedagogical practices in relations between teachers and students – that are characteristic of non-Native schools. Over the last few decades, Native control over Native schools has gradually been asserted. But many contend that such control is still largely frustrated by governmental policies and bureaucracies (despite many declarations to the contrary), and First Nations 'continue to have some of the lowest rates of educational attainment, to have some of the highest drop-out rates, and to occupy the lowest positions of socio-economic status' (Brady, 1995: 364). On the other hand, attempts to require non-Native students to participate in Native studies programmes have not always been applauded (*National Post*, 1999).

Provision of equal education to students from working-class or minority-group families is another persistent difficulty (Curtis, Livingstone and Smaller, 1992). Given the statistical evidence that these students did not succeed in schools to the same extent as students from white middle-class families, some provincial governments have tried to ensure more equitable benefits from schooling. Measures have been taken by some governments to replace the 'streaming' of students (dividing them according to their assumed intellectual abilities) with 'de-streamed' classes in which students spend a greater number of years in undifferentiated classes with their peer group. Some provinces have gone further in their attempt to correct perceived imbalances between social groups, by focusing curriculum content upon 'outcomes' rather than 'objectives'. In other words, the emphasis in schooling would change from equality of opportunity for all students to equality of outcomes for all students, a frank acknowledgement that traditional ends for schooling had proved socially unacceptable. Such a notion was particularly attractive to a few social democratic political parties in Canada elected to government office in recent years. One such party, which (somewhat to its own surprise) took office in Ontario in the late 1980s, found such changes were neither easy to formulate nor to implement, and their ambitious plans foundered on such realities as administrative confusion, teacher resistance, financial restraints and, ultimately, voter rejection (by no means entirely related to educational matters) in a subsequent election. Some commentators complained that de-streaming and an outcomes-based curriculum were charged with social engineering, devoid of intellectual merit and destructive of traditional values in education (Gidney, 1999: 218–24).

Another particularly contentious issue has been the treatment of homosexuals in schools. Although statistics are difficult to locate, acts of overt harassment in Canadian schools may well have increased as issues related to homosexuality are openly discussed. Some school boards have attempted to adopt policies and take action to counter homophobia (Campey *et al*, 1994) – with limited success. The British Columbia Teachers' Federation ran a controversial campaign to highlight the existence of homophobia in schools and counter its effect (MacKinnon, 1997). On the question of acknowledging homosexual experience in the curriculum, there appears to be little agreement. Many people were uneasy about devoting more of the curriculum to the exploration of homosexuality, and some religious and right-wing groups were vehemently opposed. Gays and lesbians still complain that they are virtually invisible in the curriculum, although they are divided on the remedies: some are content to have specific content simply added to the curriculum, while others demand more significant changes. Some school boards (especially in the major cities) have failed to resolve such questions, even after spending more than a decade in examining them (Epstein, 1998).

Changes have also taken place in providing schooling for students with disabilities (Goguen and Poirier, 1995; Lupart, 1998). Such students, formerly viewed as a group requiring care and compassion, are now perceived by many as an oppressed minority. In this respect, treatment of disabled students has moved from a 'charity mode to the minority rights paradigm' (Smith and Foster, 1994b: 334), backed by Charter-based actions in the courts. But the question of equality of school services remains open to dispute. Not all provincial governments have provided school boards with the authority to order implementation of affirmative action programmes. Not all schools offer barrier-free access. Parents often do not have the right to choose a school for their disabled children, nor is the consent of parents always required in the assessment and placement of students. Provisions for placing students in schools are often subject to ill-defined criteria of practicability. Some jurisdictions have adopted the notion of 'mainstreaming' students without making available the financial and human resources to accommodate that policy successfully – as many teachers have experienced. In short, in most Canadian schools, the right of disabled students to obtain an education is universally acknowledged, but the moment those students enter a school, the services offered are generally subject to board discretion – and they vary significantly from province to province and board to board (Smith and Foster, 1994a, 1994b).

Not all changes in recent years have attracted universal support. Some critics contend that educational principles have been sacrificed on the altar of political expediency (Loney, 1998). They point in particular to some curricular changes that seem to encode socially relevant notions of knowledge. Others are opposed to curricular provisions that seem to separate students on the basis of cultural groupings. Emberley and Newell (1994), for example, claim that recent educational changes have reduced contemporary schooling to a 'shambles' (p 3) in which students are confined in 'ghettos' or 'theme parks of identities' (p 7). Much of contemporary schooling, they assert, is so 'irrelevant' and 'parochial' (p 4) that students are denied the essential purpose of education: to take them 'out of themselves on a journey of the soul, beyond the familiar world of our time and place' (p 137). As a result of such criticism, groups of parents across the country have banded together to demand a return to traditional disciplines within the curriculum. Their slogan, advocating 'quality' schools, has attracted some support, especially among right-wing provincial governments (Holmes, 1994, 1998; Meaghan and Casas, 1995).

Religious teachings in schools

When the founding provinces were confederated in 1867, the Constitution Act guaranteed the rights of denominational schools existing in the various provinces at that date. Thus special constitutional protection (and tax support) was given to Protestant schools in Québec and Roman Catholic schools in Ontario. Newfoundland, for example, which was admitted in 1949, brought with it a school system organized around five denominations. A variety of administrative provisions were made for denominational schools across the country. But until the 1960s, all school authorities required religious instruction in public schools, often involving such practices as repeating the Lord's Prayer and reading passages from the Bible.

Canadians not given constitutional protection concerning schooling, and atheists and agnostics, have either sent their children to public schools or established their own private schools for which they paid fees (in addition, of course, to their local educational taxes). While the country was largely Christian, the opposition to the original constitutional arrangement was relatively muted, but with the increased immigrant population from non-European sources, voices of protest became more vocal. Some parents found the Christian ethic of many school systems (reflected, for example, in curricular content and annual celebrations) to be unacceptable. Court challenges have been made to such observances as the public reading of the Lord's Prayer in schools (Peters, 1996: 244). The public system also found itself in difficulties over such matters as students wearing religious apparel (Todd, 1998) or requesting religious holidays (Dickinson and Dolmage, 1996: 373).

One direct result has been the removal of direct religious instruction from the curriculum in many Canadian public schools. Following court challenges in Ontario, for example, in 1988 and 1990, the provincial educational ministry decreed that teaching *about* religion would be acceptable but not the teaching *of* religion (and, in particular, no suggestion could be made about the primacy of any given beliefs). As a result, as one commentator has suggested (Peters, 1996: 245), 'it is fine for a school to provide information about religion – about any or all religions – but one must say absolutely nothing about the question whether one religion is better than another, about the goodness or the appropriateness or the value of any particular religion'. This effort to avoid sectarianism has been seen by some as a particular form of relativism – not to say 'blandness and sterility' (p 245).

Parents with particular religious faiths maintain that education is intimately and inextricably connected to religious values and norms. Religious education in the school environment, they assert, is essential for inculcating moral values, tolerance and trust. They perceive what they label the 'secular humanism' of the public schools as offering standards and norms hostile to their own belief systems.

But what strikes some groups within society as particularly unfair is the funding of one type of denominational school and not others (Peters, 1996). Recent constitutional amendments have permitted Québec (a province in which language is now a much more pressing issue than religion) to reorganize its schools on linguistic (English and French) rather than religious lines, and Newfoundland, after very divisive discussions within the province, to amalgamate all its publicly funded religious schools into one public system (DeMont, 2000). But Ontario, for example, continues to financially support two systems – Roman Catholic and public schools – on an equal basis.

Various groups have challenged that Ontario provision. Christian fundamentalists, Jews, Muslims, Hindus, Mennonites and Sikhs, among others, have labelled the original constitutional protection of the Roman Catholic system a historic anomaly that ignores important changes in society (El-Kassem, 2000). Appeals from these groups to the Ontario government were met with the argument that the province has a constitutional responsibility for the Roman Catholic system and no other. The Supreme Court of Canada, to whom Charter-based challenges to Ontario schooling have been made, simply confirmed the legality of the current arrangement, although it admitted that it was unfair (Green, 1998). The United Nations Human Rights Tribunal, acting on an appeal, has also directed Ontario to finance all religious schools, a ruling that the province thus far has declined to follow, despite a request from the federal government that it do so. However, the federal government also points out to its critics that it is powerless in this matter, education being a provincial responsibility.

What is clear in these debates is that the value systems inherent in individual faiths are not adequately accommodated, in some people's judgements, within the existing framework of human rights in Canada. In essence, the state has decided that its own view of rights shall take priority over the value systems of some citizens. As one Ontario judge recently stated: 'the public schools are open and accessible to all on an equal basis and founded upon the positive societal values that, in general, Canadians hold in regard as essential to the well-being of our society. These values transcend cultures and faiths' (cited in Wiltshire, 1996: 85). This type of statement gives force to the conclusion that the courts support common rights rather than group-identity rights in their approach to these issues, or, as Dickinson and Dolmage (1996) contend, a liberal-pluralist rather than a cultural-pluralist position. These are not sentiments that some religious and cultural groups find acceptable.

For example, this difficulty found expression in a recent debate over teacher education (Chwialkowska, 1999). The Council of the British Columbia College of Teachers, in a decision that ran counter to the college's own review of the programme in 1996, refused to accredit the teacher education programme at Trinity Western University because the university ban on 'sexual sins' included, among others, premarital sex and homosexual behaviour. The college claimed that graduates of such a programme may discriminate against homosexuals. Values, the college seems to be saying, are articulated by parliament, and sexual orientation is a protected right. The university (supported by religious leaders in many faiths) has suggested that such a stance may well disenfranchise any college or university that affirms religious beliefs. The issue, the university maintains, is one of religious freedom (Gatehouse, 2000). To this point the issue is unresolved: two British Columbia courts have struck down the College's decision, but it has made a Charter-based appeal to the Supreme Court of Canada, which has not yet heard the case.

Many deplore what they perceive as the religion of secularism in Canadian public schools. One critic (Hunter, 2000) has wryly observed that schools seem to be suggesting that mathematical tables can be relied on, but not moral laws, thus reinforcing the view that children have a body and not a soul. 'I am not persuaded', he adds, 'that the silence of the schools on matters spiritual contributes to education, broadly understood, or to social betterment.' Given the terms of the Charter, and decisions of the courts, any solutions to major problems in this aspect of schooling seem to lie, *faute de mieux*, in the hands of the country's federal and provincial politicians.

Business values in schools

Canadian educators have watched, often with concern, current shifts in international economic development towards freer trade and harmonization. Given the country's participation in both the North American free trade community and the World Trade Organisation, it is not surprising that economic determinants have affected social policy. In recent years at both the federal and provincial levels, right-wing governments have adopted programmes designed to enhance the corporate state. To that end, spending on social services has been dramatically reduced (a policy encouraged also by burgeoning debts and deficits at all levels of government), and attention paid to a narrow and ideologically focused delivery of government services of all kinds – including education. This change in policy on government services has been justified by an ideology favouring individual choice and responsibility, furtherance of private enterprise and loosening of government regulations in favour of market-driven forces. In that notion of corporatism, state-governance is depicted as the problem, and individualism and private enterprise as the saviour (Wideen and Courtland, 1996).

Schools have not escaped either the rhetoric or the effects. Several commentators (and senior government officials) have depicted schools as monopolistic in their authority, overstaffed by (often incompetent) teachers and administrators, hostile to academic knowledge, protective of trendy pedagogies, unsympathetic to the expressed wishes of parents and unsuccessful in meeting the educational goals and contemporary needs of students – in short (and pointedly), schools have been labelled 'inefficient' (rather than, say, 'dynamic' or 'free') (Delhi, 1998). The results of Canadian students in recent international tests of reading, mathematics and science have been a particular source of obloquy. These arguments have succeeded in positioning contemporary schools as being not only 'the problem' in attempting to make society more efficient and productive, but also in need of significant (perhaps even root-and-branch) change. However, such change in Canada is difficult: schools are resistant, and ultimate authority is vested in 10 provincial governments.

But many governments in various provinces (especially Newfoundland, New Brunswick, Ontario and Alberta) have tried to meet this corporate agenda (Calvert, 1993). Standardized tests have been introduced at several grade levels to check students' progress and compare schools' records. Responsibility for managing schools has been shifted from local boards to individual schools. New Brunswick has abolished school boards and Ontario has reduced their number and powers. Parents have been encouraged (and empowered) to participate in school governance, teacher recruitment and curriculum decisions. In Alberta, parents have been given the right to apply for a charter to the provincial government to establish their own (publicly funded) schools that will express the particular philosophies of their creators – and several groups have done so (Dobbin, 1997; Wagner, 1999).

Many commentators have noted ways in which public school programmes and curriculum have been adjusted to meet the expressed needs and goals, not of the students, but of the corporate economy. Students have begun to spend more of their time in school partnership programmes with local businesses. Attempts have been made to infuse every subject in the curriculum with goals derived from career education. The task of guidance counsellors has become virtually indistinguishable from government employment bureaucrats. In particular, schools have been accused of surrendering their educational integrity to the worst types of corporate invasion (Barlow and Robertson, 1994; Moll, 1997; Overton, 1997; Robertson, 1998; Shaker, 1998). School services (even at the humblest level of fast-food machines) have been auctioned to the highest bidder. Gifts from international companies (especially of computer equipment and services) have been Trojan horses (Robertson, 1995). In some jurisdictions students are required to watch commercial messages prepared by corporations that provided the television sets in the classroom. On (perhaps rare) occasions, the means of student evaluation have been dictated by the work ethics of local businesses (Palmer, 1995). In short, students in school have been tied, whether they like it or not, to the demands of the marketplace. At the same time, curricular allotment to the traditional disciplines has been reduced. Study of the fine arts and music in many jurisdictions has been reduced to a shell, and the humanities (but not the sciences) have been severely diminished (Natale, 1998: 32–33).

The question of the effect of corporate ideology on essential educational goals has engendered intense public debate (Kuehn, 1999). Are students in public schools, as Barlow and Robertson (1994: 79) contend, being indoctrinated into holding 'a free-market world view on issues of the environment, corporate rights and the role of government'? Are schools being transformed 'into training centres producing a workforce suited to the needs of transnational corporations'? Or, as supporters of recent changes maintain (Bloom, 1996: 120), do businesspeople simply seek to improve education by 'linkages... based on consensual ties with educators and students in their educational institutions, not coercive efforts to infiltrate and dominate the halls of learning'?

Student behaviour in schools

Two aspects of student behaviour have attracted some attention in recent years in Canadian schools: what students read and how they behave in schools. These concerns have raised questions about the state governance of student reading habits and conduct on the one hand, and student freedoms, rights and personal choices on the other.

Some school boards, for example, have taken action to restrict the type of reading material provided for students. In 1995 a group of parents in Milton, Ontario organized a petition to remove Joyce Carol Oates's *Foxfire* from a school reading list because it contained four-letter words and plot events considered amoral and contrary to what were labelled community standards (Pastoor, 1997). After lengthy debate, the local school board approved the book for small-group discussion or for independent study. In 1997, country-wide attention was drawn to the Surrey school board in British Columbia when it banned, as a result of pressure from religious groups, three children's books depicting children with gay and lesbian parents. This decision was appealed to the Supreme Court of British Columbia, where the board's decision was quashed (Shariff, Case and Manley-Casimir, in press). Court action in this case confirmed the need for school officials to check carefully their administrative decisions against the requirements of the Charter.

Access to the Internet also presented some boards (and teachers) with a different set of control problems, especially in light of the violent, racist and pornographic material available from that source. The use of so-called 'filters' has not been particularly successful, although it has raised several important questions about their appropriateness for public as opposed to private locations (Johnson, 1998). The use of so-called 'blockers' to bar access to selected sites raises the issues of who controls the blocking system and what principles are used for selecting sites to be blocked. Blocking by identifying words deemed inappropriate has not produced desired results, and suggesting that local police forces exercise this particular duty has not been widely supported. Others with more libertarian views suggest that the Internet should be accessible to all students who should then be encouraged to make their own educated choices. On the other hand, a school principal in British Columbia chose to suspend eight elementary-school students for creating an 'offensive and dangerous' Web site, and police in Ontario took similar action (Fournier, 2000).

Exercising control over students in schools is a matter of grave concern to administrators and teachers – especially in light of what the public perceives as a dramatic rise in gun-related and violent incidents in high schools in North America (MacDonald, 1997; Roher, 1997). Public attention has been drawn to such incidents as the hanging of a 10-year-old boy in 1998 in an Ontario school washroom. Some have noted a significant decrease in the average age for violent offenders in the past 40 years, and an increase in such offences as schoolyard bullying and other acts of aggression. Some experts ascribe such changes in part to increasing incidents of mental problems, while others note the effects of growing rates of marriage breakdown, availability of drugs and economic inequalities (Sims, 2000).

The reaction of administrators and teachers to questions of how they should govern student behaviour has been varied. Several programmes intended to teach conflict resolution have been introduced into school curricula (Bickmore, 1999). Encouragement has been given to students to share in class differing perspectives on social problems, and classroom pedagogies have included a greater reliance on stories, simulations and debates on violence-related incidents. Curriculum materials have been provided on peace education and value-related international material.

Some school authorities have gone further. Surveillance cameras are an increasingly common sight in Canadian secondary schools, especially in the major cities, as part of 'safe-schools' programmes. Some steps have been taken towards adopting school uniforms as a means of exercising social control (Sher, 2000). Others have adopted various restrictions under the rubric of a 'zero tolerance' policy – usually involving automatic suspensions for unwanted or aggressive behaviour. Punishable offences include possession of offensive weapons and fighting. Others have gone further. A school in Manitoba has prohibited mass hugging, another outlawed kissing in the hallways, a third banned touch football and games of tag (all involving 'touching') and another suspended four students who were alleged to have committed 'playful pushes' in the snow. In this last case, the school involved is reported to have suspended more than 100 of its 585 students during the current year (Prittie, 2000).

These actions have not gone unnoticed by critics. Some see current policies as an attempt to regulate the very nature of childhood on an unprecedented scale. One school board official observed that the close scrutiny of student behaviour that has followed several acts of violence has led to the 'legislating of childhood', and suggested that outlawing kissing would put half the current student body on the wrong side of the law (Prittie, 2000). One reporter suggests that schools are 'gripped by a puritanical certainty that deviance and evil lurk everywhere in the young human soul, and must be nipped in the bud' (Wente, 2000). When a successful student was suspended from school for throwing snow, the same critic observed that the student 'learned a big lesson, about respect for authority, the rule of law, and the wisdom of adults. I suspect it's not the one the school set out to teach her' (Wente, 2000). After a careful study of the evidence, another critic (Dolmage, 1996) has concluded that the notion that school violence in recent years is increasing is a myth, and that perpetuating that myth is a major disservice. Furthermore, he contended (p 204) that zero-tolerance policies violate basic principles of justice:

> By assuming that it is not necessary to hear the students' side of the story and that no latitude need be given for extenuating circumstance, we deny the basic principles that underlie our justice system. It is inappropriate to teach, by example, that fundamental freedoms, such as the right to procedural and substantive due process, can be ignored if one believes the end (safe schools) justifies the means (zero-tolerance).

If Dolmage's forebodings are given further justification, then state regulation of student behaviour in Canadian schools may supply ample fodder for the courts.

Conclusion

The historical context in which discussions of values in Canadian schools take place is of first importance. Given the country's colonial history of two founding peoples, its communities of First Nations and its legal system, a particular school configuration was set in place. Recent changes – social, economic and legal – within the country have led to pressures for change.

Those pressures are apparent in important debates over a great many questions related to values in schools: what does it mean to give equal treatment to students in schools, and how can policies on equal treatment be effected? What is the role of religion in schools? To what extent should schools accommodate the wishes of the corporate sector? And to what extent should the state regulate student behaviour in schools?

Answers to such questions are not easily obtained. Public attitudes and opinions are not always well informed, well intentioned and principled. Statements of human rights often run counter to deeply rooted value systems. Although citizens with grievances often resort to the courts, the judicial system is not always perceived as able to satisfy those grievances. Whether the federal and provincial legislatures will be able to offer additional solutions is not always apparent.

Note

1. Readily accessible sources include recent issues of three journals, *Our Schools/Our Selves*, *Education & Law Journal* and *Canadian Journal of Education*, and two national newspapers, the *Globe and Mail* and *National Post*. For introductory discussions, see also Dickinson and MacKay (1989), Erwin and MacLennan (1994), Ghosh and Ray (1995) and Roberts and Clifton (1995).

References

Barlow, M and Robertson, H-j (1994) *Class Warfare: The assault on Canada's schools*, Key Porter, Toronto

Bercuson, D and Wertheimer, D (1985) *A Trust Betrayed: The Keegstra affair*, Doubleday, Toronto

Bickmore, K (1999) Teaching conflict resolution across the curriculum, *Orbit*, **29** (4), pp 30–34

Bissoondath, N (1994) *Selling Illusions: The cult of multiculturalism in Canada*, Penguin, Toronto

Bloom, M R (1996) Corporate involvement in curriculum: Partnership not coercion, in *The Struggle for Curriculum: Education, the state and the corporate sector*, ed M Wideen and M C Courtland, pp 119–24, Institute for Studies in Teacher Education, Simon Fraser University, Burnaby, British Columbia

Brady, P (1995) Two policy approaches to native education: Can reform be legislated?, *Canadian Journal of Education*, **20** (3), pp 349–66

Calvert, J with Kuehn, L (1993) *Pandora's Box: Corporate power, free trade and Canadian education*, Our Schools/Our Selves Education Foundation, Toronto

Campey, J et al (1994) Opening the classroom closet: dealing with sexual orientation at the Toronto Board of Education, in *Sex in Schools: Canadian education & sexual orientation*, ed S Prentice, pp 82–100, Our Schools/Our Selves Education Foundation, Toronto

Chwialkowska, L (1999) Court fight billed as battle for religious freedom, *National Post*, 16 December, p A3

Coulter, R P (1996) Gender equity and schooling: linking research and policy, *Canadian Journal of Education*, 21 (4), pp 433–52

Cummins, J and Danesi, M (1990) *Heritage Languages: The development and denial of Canada's linguistic resources*, Our Schools/Our Selves Education Foundation, Toronto

Curtis, B, Livingstone, D W and Smaller, H (1992) *Stacking the Deck: The streaming of working-class kids in Ontario schools*, Our Schools/Our Selves Education Foundation, Toronto

Dei, G J S (1996a) The role of Afrocentricity in the inclusive curriculum in Canadian schools, *Canadian Journal of Education*, 21 (2), pp 170–86

Dei, G J S (1996b) *Anti-Racism Education: Theory and practice*, Fernwood, Halifax, Nova Scotia

Delhi, K (1998) What lies beyond Ontario's Bill 160: the politics and practice of education markets, *Our Schools/Our Selves*, 9 (4), pp 59–78

DeMont, J (2000) The bitter reality of reform: massive changes to school system are still dividing Newfoundland, *Maclean's*, 113 (2), 10 January, pp 54–55

Department of the Secretary of State of Canada (1987) *The Charter of Rights and Freedoms: A guide for Canadians*, Minister of Supply and Services, Ottawa

Dickinson, G M and Dolmage, W R (1996) Education, religion, and the courts in Ontario, *Canadian Journal of Education*, 21 (4), pp 363–83

Dickinson, G M and MacKay, A W (ed) (1989) *Rights, Freedoms and the Educational System in Canada: Cases and materials*, Emond Montgomery, Toronto

Dobbin, M (1997) Charting a course to social division: the charter school threat to public education in Canada, *Our Schools/Our Selves*, 8 (3), pp 48–82

Dolmage, W R (1996) One less brick in the wall: the myths of youth violence and unsafe schools, *Education & Law Journal*, 7, pp 185–207

El-Kassem, M (2000) Religious schools deserve fairness, *The London Free Press*, 5 February, p F6

Emberley, P C and Newell, W R (1994) *Bankrupt Education: The decline of liberal education in Canada*, University of Toronto Press, Toronto

Epstein, R (1998) Parent night will never be the same: lesbian families challenge the public school system, *Our Schools/Our Selves*, 9 (1), pp 92–117

Erwin, L and MacLennan, D (ed) (1994) *Sociology of Education in Canada: Critical perspectives on theory, research & practice*, Copp Clark Longman, Toronto

Fournier, S (2000) Grade school pupils suspended for 'offensive' Web page, *National Post*, 9 March, p A4

Gaskell, J, McLaren, A and Novogrodsky, M (1989) *Claiming and Education: Feminism and Canadian schools*, Our Schools/Our Selves Education Foundation, Toronto

Gatehouse, J (2000) B.C. university takes legal battle to court of public opinion, *National Post*, 5 January, p A7

Ghosh, R and Ray, D (ed) (1995) *Social Change and Education in Canada*, 3rd edn, Harcourt Brace Canada, Toronto

Gidney, R D (1999) *From Hope to Harris: The reshaping of Ontario's schools*, University of Toronto Press, Toronto

Goguen, L and Poirier, D (1995) Are the educational rights of exceptional students protected in Canada?, in *Social Change and Education in Canada*, 3rd edn, ed R Ghosh and D Ray, pp 310–22, Harcourt Brace Canada, Toronto

Green, M A (1998) No constitutional right to public funding for Ontario private schools, but is the public system better protected?, *Education & Law Journal*, **8**, pp 227–38

Hamilton, G (2000) Court ruling on francophone school could raise tensions, Binns warns, *National Post*, 15 January, p A6

Holmes, M (1994) *Canada's Educational Crisis: Problems, causes & solutions*, Ontario Organisation for Quality Education, Waterloo

Holmes, M (1998) *The Reformation of Canada's Schools: Breaking the barriers to parental choice*, McGill-Queen's University Press, Montréal and Kingston

Hunter, I (2000) What if school prayers mattered?, *National Post*, 2 March, p A19

James, C F and Brathwaite, K (1996) The education of African Canadians: issues, contexts, and expectations, in *Educating African Canadians*, ed K S Brathwaite and C F James, pp 13–31, James Lorimer, Toronto

Johnson, D (1998) Internet filters: Censorship by any other name?, *Emergency Librarian*, **25** (5), pp 11–13

Kuehn, L (1999) Globalization and the control of teachers' work: the role of the OECD indicators, *Our Schools/Our Selves*, **9** (6), pp 117–29

Loney, M (1998) *The Pursuit of Division: Race, gender, and preferential hiring in Canada*, McGill-Queen's University Press, Montréal and Kingston

Lund, D E (1998) Social justice and public education: a response to George J. Sefa Dei, *Canadian Journal of Education*, **23** (2), pp 191–99

Lupart, J L (1998) Setting right the delusion of inclusion: implications for Canadian schools, *Canadian Journal of Education*, **23** (3), pp 251–64

MacDonald, I M (1997) Violence in schools: multiple realities, *Alberta Journal of Educational Research*, **43** (2–3), pp 142–56

MacKay, A W (1995) The rights paradigm in the age of the Charter, in *Social Change and Education in Canada*, 3rd edn, ed R Ghosh and D Ray, pp 224–39, Harcourt Brace Canada, Toronto

MacKay, A W and Richard, M C (1998) Multiculturalism: who needs it?, *Education & Law Journal*, **8**, pp 265–93

MacKinnon, K (1997) The BCTF anti-homophobia campaign and the right-wing backlash, *Our Schools/Our Selves*, **8** (6), pp 82–93

Majhanovich, S (1995) Official and heritage languages in Canada: how politics translate into practices, in *Social Change and Education in Canada*, 3rd edn, ed R Ghosh and D Ray, pp 84–101, Harcourt Brace Canada, Toronto

Meaghan, D and Casas, F (1995) Quality education and other myths: a new face for an old conservative agenda, *Our Schools/Our Selves*, **7** (1), pp 37–53

Miller, J R (1996) *Shingwauk's Vision: A history of Native residential schools*, University of Toronto Press, Toronto

Moll, M (ed) (1997) *Tech High: Globalization and the future of Canadian education*, Fernwood, Halifax, Nova Scotia

Natale, C (1998) Social Darwinism comes to education: the career education scam, *Our Schools/Our Selves*, **9** (1), pp 26–42

National Post (1999) Feathers and clam shells, 13 November, p B9

Overton, J (1997) The business quest for 'total re-education' in Newfoundland, *Our Schools/Our Selves*, **8** (6), pp 94–116

Palmer, B (1995) Capitalism comes to Napanee High, *Our Schools/Our Selves*, **6** (3), pp 14–41

Paquette, J (in press) Cross-purposes and crossed wires in education policy-making on equity: the Ontario experience, 1990–1995, *Journal of Curriculum Studies*

Pastoor, B (1997) Joyce Carol Oates' *Foxfire*: a book-banning battle reconsidered, *Our Schools/Our Selves*, **8** (6), pp 132–45

Peters, F (1996) The changing face of denominational education in Canada, *Education & Law Journal*, **7**, pp 229–56

Porter, J (1965) *The Vertical Mosaic: An analysis of social class and power in Canada*, University of Toronto Press, Toronto

Prittie, J (2000) Schools are ruining childhood, critics charge, *National Post*, 28 February, pp A1–A2

Roberts, L W and Clifton, R A (1995) *Crosscurrents: Contemporary Canadian educational issues*, Nelson Canada, Scarborough, Ontario

Robertson, H-j (1995) Hyenas at the oasis: corporate marketing to captive students, *Our Schools/Our Selves*, **7** (2), pp 16–39

Robertson, H-j (1998) *No More Teachers, No More Books: The commercialisation of Canada's schools*, McClelland & Stewart, Toronto

Roher, E M (1997) *An Educator's Guide to Violence in Schools*, Aurora Professional Press, Aurora, Ontario

Shaker, E (1998) Marketing to captive students: corporate curriculum in Ontario, *Our Schools/Our Selves*, **9** (1), pp 17–25

Shariff, S, Case, R and Manley-Casimir, M (in press) Balancing competing rights in education: Surrey School Board's book ban, *Education & Law Journal*

Sher, J (2000) Catholic schools opt for uniforms, *The London Free Press*, 15 January, pp A1, A12

Sims, J (2000) Aggression among children shows steady rise, *The London Free Press*, 4 March, p A4

Smith, W J and Foster, W F (1994a) Educational opportunity for students with disabilities in Canada: a platform of rights to build on, *Education & Law Journal*, 5, pp 193–223

Smith, W J and Foster, W F (1994b) Educational opportunity for students with disabilities in Canada: beyond the schoolhouse door, *Education & Law Journal*, 5, pp 305–34

Smith, W J, Foster, W F and Donahue, H M (1999) *How Does the Québec Education System Work?: A primer for school governing boards*, Office of Research on Educational Policy, McGill University, Montréal

Stairs, A (ed) (1994) *Culture and Education: Aboriginal settings, concerns, and insights*, Special issue of *Canadian Journal of Education*, 19 (2)

Todd, S (1998) Veiling the 'other', unveiling our 'selves': reading media images of the hijab psychoanalytically to move beyond tolerance, *Canadian Journal of Education*, 23 (4), pp 438–51

Wagner, M (1999) Charter schools in Alberta: Change or continuity in Progressive Conservative education policy?, *Alberta Journal of Educational Research*, 45 (1), pp 52–66

Wente, M (2000) Zero tolerance and zero sense: the Fall River Rebellion and other dastardly school-yard crimes, *The Globe and Mail*, 4 March, p A28

Wideen, M and Courtland, M C (ed) (1996) *The Struggle for Curriculum: Education, the state, and the corporate sector*, Institute for Studies in Teacher Education, Simon Fraser University, Burnaby, British Columbia

Wiltshire, R (1996) The right to denominational schools within Ontario public school boards, *Education & Law Journal*, 7, pp 81–87

10. Changing cultures and schools in Denmark

Thyge Winther-Jensen

Introduction

This chapter is based on the assumption that education in Denmark has been challenged particularly on two fronts. On one hand, what we normally understand by Danish national culture has come into closer contact with other cultures through an increasing immigration from other, mainly Islamic, cultural spheres. According to the statistics office in the EU, Eurostat, Denmark has 4.2 per cent foreigners, concentrated in and around the major cities. The cultural differences stemming from this have not only led to education being involved as a means to assimilate and integrate refugees and immigrants into the Danish society, but it has also intensified the awareness towards what might be particular and valuable in Danish culture.

The Danish economy, on the other hand, is to a greater extent than earlier being integrated into a worldwide economy where labour is competing on the global market. The private market, which has functioned within the national state since the late 18th century, can no longer be contained within that framework today. Companies find themselves compelled to be looking for a European or a world market to be able to sell their increasingly more specialized products, if the production is to continue to be profitable and competitive. This so-called economic globalization makes demands on education different from those caused by internal cultural differences, namely a demand to improve future generations' capacity for living and working in a world that reaches beyond the national state.

The predominant task for education in Denmark today is to meet these challenges – of increasing internal cultural differences and equally increasing external economic and cultural influences.

Internal cultural differences

In 1952 the prominent US social theorist, Talcott Parsons, characterized the concept of culture by suggesting 'first, that culture is *transmitted*, it constitutes a heritage or a social tradition; secondly, that it is *learned*, it is not a manifestation, in particular content, of man's genetic constitution; and third, that it is

178

shared. Culture, that is, is on the one hand the product of, on the other hand a determinant of systems of human, social interaction' (Parsons, 1952: 15). This way of viewing the concept of culture is an analytical definition originating from the social sciences. It presupposes an observation of the cultures from the outside and does not give priority to one particular culture, but it enables us to analyse without prejudice any culture from three different angles: 1) What is the social tradition that is to be transferred? 2) What explicitly are its demands for learning? 3) What values does it have in common? It also makes it possible to compare cultures.

This definition should be compared with another, which to a greater extent originates from the experience of a culture as seen from within. An example of this definition is the following one drawn from an older edition of the *Shorter Oxford English Dictionary*, where culture is defined as 'the training and refinement of mind, taste and manners;... the intellectual side of civilization'. According to this, culture is more an educational concept. It presupposes training in and learning the norms, values and mentality of a *particular* culture. Though it does not give priority to one culture at the expense of another, it does assume, however, that cultural education takes place within the frames of a particular culture, ie the one you belong to. Furthermore, emphasis is laid on the intellectual aspect, not on the norms and customs that are connected to that culture.

The two attitudes to culture as a concept described here are illustrative of one of the dilemmas that have influenced the debate in Denmark. On one hand have been the endeavours to comprehend the new cultures that increasingly make themselves felt in our everyday life. On the other hand there is a growing interest in establishing what Danish culture actually is, and what qualities it has for integrating foreigners into a Danish-speaking civil society with rights and duties.

In the educational field this two-pronged endeavour, the analytical and the pedagogical, was expressed in the objectives clause of the Folkeskole Act of 1993. It says, for example, that 'the Folkeskole shall familiarize the pupils with Danish culture and contribute to their understanding of other cultures' (Section 3: 3). In the explanatory memorandum this is qualified in this way: 'The school must familiarize the pupils with Danish culture, including Christianity and create sympathy for other cultures, ie the culture of other European counties as well as the cultures from which immigrants are coming.' The difference between the choice of words: 'to familiarize with' and 'to create sympathy for' nicely illustrates the two concepts of culture described.

This was not only the first time the term 'culture' had appeared in the objectives clause of a Danish school act, but it was also the first time in which the words 'Danish culture' appeared. This proves, if nothing else, that 'Danish culture' is now on the agenda of politicians and government. Until recently 'Danish culture' was taken for granted by everybody. It was an all-pervading phenomenon seldom talked about and if it were, the tone was relaxed and ironic. It was tacitly agreed that 'Danish culture' was a culture of consensus, an acceptance of the fact that conflicts were solved through dialogue, since this was the country with a *folk*eskole and a *folk* high school.

More than anything the task of these institutions was to bridge the gap between internal cultural awareness and social clashes to create a feeling of social and national unity. It might also be the reason why Danes have a predilection for equality and democracy. In the field of education this is reflected in anti-elitist policies, eg the postponement of the streaming of children for as long as possible, few examinations at the early stages and the extensive influence of parents.

In the late 20th century this self-esteem came under pressure owing to the conflict between 'old' and 'new' Danes, and this found expression in the electorate and on the political scene. The integration of the old and the new has not run as smoothly as expected, to which a number of recent unfortunate episodes bear witness. It began with violent fighting between police and demonstrators in Nørrebro on 18 May 1993 after a referendum had accepted the Maastricht Treaty (with certain provisos); later followed by clashes between police and second-generation immigrants in Vollsmose in Odense; and in August and September 1999 there was the scarf debate about whether owners of supermarkets and shops can forbid Muslim women to wear scarves at work, and whether a mayor can ban halal meat in public childcare institutions. The government's wish to distribute refugees and immigrants among the 275 municipalities to facilitate integration and to avoid concentrations and ghettos has not been very successful either. The smaller municipalities have felt strained and have been confronted with the argument that refugees and immigrants must also be allowed to settle down where they want.

At the same time, schools with many non-Danish-speaking pupils have seen Danish-speaking children leaving the folkeskole to seek admittance to some kind of private school (in 1998, approximately 13–14 per cent).[1] And also, it has been difficult for applicants with foreign-sounding names to enter the private labour market.

The government has reacted by supporting a strengthening of aspects of Danish culture on the paradoxical assumption that such a strengthening will create a greater sympathy for the foreigners. The Danes are not so open, liberal and tolerant as they ought to be and this must be due to our neglect to cultivate our particular Danish qualities. In keeping with this line of thought the minister of culture announced recently:

> We must develop our Danish identity in such a way that it does not become a
> defence against the outside world, but rather enables us to meet the rest of
> the world with open minds and hearts because we feel assured that we
> Danes will not only be able to cope, but might even benefit from and also en-
> rich the surrounding world. In order to make this happen we must keep in
> better touch with our roots and we must develop joint dreams for the future.
> I can contribute to the strengthening of our roots by a goal-oriented culture

policy, which opens a wider and better access to our cultural inheritance, ie museums and libraries. I can help to strengthen our Danish language, and I can contribute to the protection of our Danish qualities: tolerance, kindness, a relaxed attitude – and, may I add – broad-mindedness [my emphasis]. It is precisely on that foundation our dreams must grow. But the demand is that we do not drivel about when we describe ourselves. They do come from somewhere, our cultural inheritance, our art, history and language, and we must develop a closer relationship to them. Otherwise they will become empty phrases. *Jyllandsposten* (1999)

The cultural policy here referred to implied the minister's intentions of tabling a motion in the Folketing in the autumn of 1999 to continue to link state subsidies to demands for more Danish television, theatre and music productions:

I will go through our entire legislation relating to music, theatre and the media with reference to a boosting of all that is Danish. Regarding TV I want more Danish news productions and TV drama... The TV stations have a particular responsibility towards Danish culture – this is in the objects clauses even today. But it must be improved... it has become even more important to stick to Danish culture, Danish values and Danish attitudes.

This line of thought is the fairly simple one that if there is a clash of interests between 'old' and 'new' Danes, and if the integration appears not to have been successful, it must be due to the fact that the Dane has forgotten or neglected the values that are a part of the Danish cultural heritage. If the Danes will only keep that in mind then the open, tolerant and broad-minded disposition, which we all know to be theirs, will reappear and smooth out all the differences.

However enticing this way of thinking may sound it does call for the following comments. When we talk about Danish culture in the sense of Danish language, history and literature, there is something quite concrete to relate to, but as soon as we equate 'Danish culture' with ideas like broad-mindedness, tolerance and democracy, it is justifiable to ask whether these ideas are specifically Danish. Are they not rather of common European origin, mainly from the Age of Enlightenment? And what would the advocates of specific Danish values say if the Germans began to talk about specific German values, the French about specific French values, the English about specific English values? Would that not wrinkle a few brows? Moreover, would the eloquence not appear to be an attempt to preach and moralize ourselves out of a conflict leaving the heart of the matter unsolved? Where do we draw the line between what we can and cannot accept according to our Danish/European norms? Where do we draw the line regarding the suppression of women, arranged marriages and corporal punishment, for example?

This approach does not exclude the need to stress the importance of Danish language, literature and history. However, the biggest threat to Danish language and literature has sprung from the circles of changing governments and decision makers from the 1960s and which the minister herself comes from. 'In that space of time an extensive and not altogether fruitless effort has been made to deprive future generations of an insight into their historical and cultural backgrounds', as a feature writer put it recently:

> Danish culture was considered to be the culture of the bourgeoisie and, consequently, had to be eliminated. The subject history was minimized in primary and secondary schools; the subject Danish also, both the language and the literature aspects. At the same time great pains were taken to ensure that no young people received a coherent insight into Danish history and culture, which fact has left them without an identity and therefore vulnerable. It was recently confirmed that pupils in primary school had an appalling lack of knowledge about Christianity. (Hvorslev, 1999)

If this statement is to be believed maybe the task should be limited to the recovery of the Danish language and culture through a concrete implementation of the current curricula without resorting to concepts like openness, broad-mindedness and tolerance.

Danish society is a welfare society, which is based on economic equality as well as a fair distribution of the goods we produce in common. It is the society where 'few have too much and fewer too little'.[2] But from being a tool that creates economic equality the concept of welfare has developed further into becoming a moral ideology. It is not enough that we pay our taxes; we must also feel it to be morally wrong if we do not, even though this is the most heavily tax-burdened country in the world. It is not enough to work; we must also feel it morally wrong if we do not, even though an unprecedented number of the population are living on income support. It is not enough that children accept they should learn what they are being asked to learn at school; they should also feel it to be morally wrong if they do not feel 'responsible for their own learning'. It is no coincidence that the present prime minister talked at the beginning of the 1990s about a decade of morality. The foundation of this morality of consensus and equality in the field of education was laid down in the so-called *Blue Report* of 1960 (an advisory national curriculum), which made it the prime task for schools 'to further the opportunities for children to grow up being harmonious, happy and good' (Undervisningsministeriet 1960). This pietist morality, which so easily turns into paternalism, care and hands raised in admonition, is probably what representatives from other cultures find most difficult to understand. But it also raises problems for the Dane, because when foreign cultures will not allow themselves to be assimilated into this almost religious philosophy it is the Danish self-esteem that cracks (are we not as good as we thought we were?). The reaction is either disillusion or apathy or an even stronger, almost hysterical, demand for 'old Danish values'.

To conclude this part of the discussion let us return to the two definitions of the concept of culture already mentioned. Cultural changes have in the Danish context caused unpleasantness on the analytical as well as the pedagogic

front. It is apparently not easy to understand foreign cultures nor what is particularly Danish. The two attitudes to culture have not yet manifested themselves in a concrete and assimilative practice. The solution could be a
concentration on academic standards, less anxiety from the state and more
confidence in the different cultures being able, on their own, to move forward
towards a common new culture. Culture is, like other ideas, not static in its
contents.

Globalization and internationalization

The second challenge comes from the number of trends that it has become
customary to gather under the designation 'globalization'. Globalization can
be both economic and cultural. A common factor, however, seems to be a tendency to break down the framework laid down by the nation state; it also
points to a new social order, so to speak, or a new kind of community where
previous definitions of state, market and civil society are no longer valid.

Economic globalization

The reason for economic globalization is a competitive global economy, which
has brought along a hitherto unseen integration of product development,
production and financing across existing borders. This development was first
started by multinational companies, but increasing specialization has also
forced medium-sized companies to look beyond their national markets in order to make their production profitable. An important precondition for the
economic globalization is, consequently, development in transport and information technology.

The move from national economies to a world economy has not happened
overnight. It would be possible to point to different phases in that development
from the middle of the 19th century. The last phase, based on high technology,
multinational companies, free movement of capital and improved communication, followed in the wake of the 1974 oil crisis. Globalization has made our
world smaller; the discussion is now more and more frequently about a common economic global market, which even the non-globalized markets outside
the United States, Europe and the Far East will have to depend on.

Although economic globalization has its positive sides, it is, however, not
altogether without problems. For instance, it widens the gap between the
higher educated and the short-term trained because knowledge and an education will increasingly be the criteria for how the individual and the society
will be able to manage in the global marketplace. According to Robert Reich
who in 1991 published his book *The Work of Nations* (with an obvious allusion
to Adam Smith's *The Wealth of Nations*), globalization will, in the long term,
lead to radical changes in the structures of society and classes. According to

him three social classes will appear: routine workers, service workers and what he calls symbolic analysts.

The first category, the short-term-trained routine workers, competes with its opposite categories in other countries and is, consequently, very sensitive to wage fluctuations. To a lesser degree this is the case for the second group, which includes servants, shop and hotel staffs, police, security guards, etc. For this category the face-to-face relationship is of vital importance. But it can be difficult to predict which jobs in this group will be immune to international competition. Teaching, for example, which has traditionally depended on the direct contact between teacher and student, may be forced into some kind of distance teaching, if, that is, the technological development can make this kind of teaching pedagogically and economically competitive compared to traditional teaching. The third category, the symbolic analysts, includes engineers, media and advertising experts, research people, journalists, politicians, economists, lobbyists and lawyers. These are directly involved in the global economy.

In many respects, Robert Reich paints a disturbing picture of social fragmentation in the United States. The rich fifth, the symbolic analysts, 'are selling their expertise on the global market' and increase their living standards 'even as that of other Americans declines' (p 250). The rich United States is, according to Reich, moving away from the rest of society, as are the less privileged groups, each in their different ways. What is going to hold society together? Or as he puts the question: 'The question is whether the habits of citizenship are sufficiently strong to withstand the centrifugal forces of the new global economy' (p 304).

If only a fraction of this scenario is true, it is to be feared that the modern societies may break up into a privileged minority and a majority with far less opportunities. Some have called it the 20/80 society.

Cultural globalization

Parallel with economic globalization, a cultural globalization has taken place. News and information spread through modern mass media with lightning speed. Electronic aids like Internet and e-mail bring us instantaneously into contact with family, friends and colleagues on the other side of the world. Foreign cultures no longer seem far away and exotic. The pop culture is international; film and TV inform us about customs and norms in other countries and cultures. Modern cities are intercultural metropolitan centres, where the original character fades away more and more. It is fair to claim that the world has developed into a global village and has become more uniform.

The tendency of this uniformity must, however, be compared with the fact that globalization also opens up greater diversity and more differences than those hitherto known. As we witness traditional communities and affiliations being put under pressure by the oncoming global culture we also see that nationalities held down by the national states come into the open again. Nothing will prevent the two tendencies – the tendency towards a greater uniformity and a greater diversity – thriving side by side.

But reasonable doubt may be raised as to what this diversity actually means. Do we witness the appearance of new rationally founded communities as a sensible supplement to an internationalized and, for many people, alienated world? Will we also be experiencing new tribal cultures, which will turn their backs on the surrounding world and which internally will gather around purely emotional and irrational values?

On the individual level the same ambiguity is valid. Is a new kind of human type being developed, one who at the same time belongs in a global as well as a local, family-related community? Or are we rather going to see the egoistic wo/man without a homeland, a cultural relativist, who lives in a world of her/his own construction, with no roots in a national or local community?

At the present time nobody will probably be able to give the final answer to such questions. But nobody will probably doubt either that education will be playing a vital part if the further development must be directed along rational lines.

Consequences for education

In the educational field the dilemma, on one hand, is to educate a minority, adequately skilled to compete on the global market and thereby create jobs, and, on the other hand, to create a feeling of a cultural solidarity. The latter demands general, the former specialized knowledge.

General knowledge distinguishes itself partly by being something everybody must have, partly by being broad, ie including a greater number of subjects. From the almost unlimited amount of knowledge and information available today it is also an obvious pedagogical task, within the different subject areas to distil and abstract that which will offer the greatest degree of insight. Such ideas of general knowledge are by no means new. The Czech educator Comenius (1592–1670) must have been thinking along these lines when he wrote his famous encyclopaedic educational ideal: to teach everybody everything. He did not imply, of course, that everybody should learn everything, which would be impossible, but as he says in *The Great Didactic*, 'anyone who enters the world, not only as an observer, but also as a future actor, must be taught about foundations, causes and purposes behind the most important facts and events, so that they will not in this dwelling meet anything to such a degree unknown that they cannot with modesty evaluate it and without unpleasant delusion apply it; *this* must be taken care of, and *this* must really be achieved'(my translation) (Comenius, 1960: X, 1). General qualifications and knowledge have an important function in creating a common background for discussions and dialogue between all groups in society.

The specialized competencies are for the few with special interests and qualifications. They are normally sited on a narrow knowledge base, which studies a single subject in depth. In a modern society with a clear division of labour this must, of course, be reflected in the educational system, especially in higher education, but the demand for specialization is already making itself felt on the level after primary school. It is still an open question how early specialization should be introduced. In other words it is still debatable whether school systems with earlier or a later specialization will turn out to be most suitable for the challenges of globalization.

The Danish school tradition has always been characterized by its relatively late specialization. An objective of a high degree of competence has never been compatible with an elitist objective. High educational competence has been equated with a solid foundation of general knowledge. The encyclopaedic ideal of education is therefore much closer to Danish education than early specialization. The introduction of optional subjects has greatly individualized the curriculum, but a real break from the encyclopaedic principle has not occurred. A faith in comprehensiveness has been a fundamental principle in Danish curricula.

When, in the early 1990s, Danish schoolchildren were ranked relatively poorly in international tests in basic subjects like reading and arithmetic this created a national state of shock. In the biggest international reading test ever in 1991 Danish children from year 3 and year 8 classes participated. The test was conducted in 32 countries including the Nordic countries. The problems were characteristic for the age groups with an emphasis on concrete texts and the understanding of what was being read. The results were extremely discouraging from a Danish point of view. The Danish year 3 classes read more slowly and less precisely than the pupils in all the industrialized countries taking the test. In the year 8 class the Danish pupils did relatively better but still clearly worse than pupils from Sweden and Finland.

A major problem with the slow reading development among Danish children is the unreasonably long time it takes before the children can make any use of their reading. If the school took account of this development profile the problem might be overcome, but the school expects that year 3 children begin to read not only Danish literature but also history and other subjects. Moreover, they are expected, as a matter of course, to be able to read the instructions in mathematics books. And then in year 4 they are exposed to English texts. The best Danish children read just as well as children in other countries, but the main problem is that a quarter or maybe a third have not become reasonably independent readers by the middle of year 3. New words make them uncertain, they read slowly and find it difficult to learn as well as read (Elbro, 1996). In a new comparative test (Sommer, Lau and Meiding, 1996) of 1,200 pupils from 60 Danish, Swedish and Finnish classes 1–3 from 1995 it was unfortunately again confirmed that Danish pupils performed poorly. Recently it was reported that 420,000 Danish adults between 18 and 67 (out of a total population of 5.2 million) have such reading difficulties that they have problems in managing at work.

In 1996 the so-called Timms survey was published. Here Danish standards – like the reading tests from 1991 – were compared with standards in approximately 30 other related countries, and again the result was clearly unsatisfactory, though not as disastrous as in the reading test.

The results of these surveys developed near-national shock (sometimes called the Togo-shock, as the tests proved that Danish schoolchildren in an international context were on the same level as those in the African state of Togo; cf the Sputnik and Toyota shocks that hit the United States in the 1960s and 1980s) and this may be owing to two things. First, it hit the centre of what the Dane considers good education: a broad and solid foundation of general knowledge found in all the citizens. The criticism was not aimed at some elite; it was the ordinary Dane's education that had failed the test. Secondly, the surveys proved that globalization has had its effects. How would we be able to compete with nations on the same footing if our level of knowledge was lower? And if we believed that a means to counter globalization was a generally high level of knowledge in all members of our society and not only a highly specialized elite, how would we possibly be able to survive when our educational system apparently produced neither?

It is hardly too much to claim that the surveys have clarified the entire pedagogical agenda. The primary school, the teacher training colleges, Denmark's Lærerhøjskole as well as naive politicians have been accused of having neglected the school system through a one-sided cultivation of a local variety of the child-centred pedagogics that culminated with the Folkeskole Act of 1993, adopted in the Folketing just prior to the publication of the surveys.

The accusations and the criticisms have found expression in the press and in a number of influential books. In 1996 Henning Fonsmark published a book with the characteristic title *Kampen mod Kundskaber* (*The Struggle against Knowledge*), which described the gradual dilution of curricula from 1960 (the year of the *Blue Report*, which introduced child-centred education). At the same time educational rhetoric has been on the increase. This is how the book ends:

> What this essay has been focusing on – and been polemic against – is the motives which were presented or hidden and the arguments put forward by those people who persistently fought for an academically uncommitted comprehensive school with a clear aim of keeping all children together, if possible till the age of 18, to leave it to the school to indoctrinate the children with any kind of 'politically correct' norms, to focus on the performance of the group, rather than of the individual, to make it difficult to evaluate the level of attainment at all levels. On the other hand, in the name of equality and evenness, to discriminate the value of basic skills and fairly consequently to downgrade the respect for general knowledge. (Fonsmark, 1996)

In May 1997 Maj Cecilie and Niels Chr Nielsen (father and daughter) published the book with the (semi)ironic title *Verdens Bedste Uddannelsessystem* (*The Best Educational System in the World*), which exactly included 'the international development as a challenge'. The book also contains a chapter about 'The vision of the best educational system in the world'. It states, among other things and fitting well with the Danish tradition, that 'high competence must be measured in breadth' and that 'the high level lies in broad competence'.

Finally in 1998 Jørgen Lund published *Sidste Udkald* (*Last Call*). Here he dissociated himself from the demand for early selection (streaming): 'We must not be put into little boxes too early; this can happen soon enough. An élite without a developed social gift is not good enough for a society with our ideals. Early streaming is not bad for the weak only. Also for the strong' (p 16). He emphasizes again that increased competition must be matched by broad general knowledge: 'The competition is real. But nothing is so dangerous as to aim a society's strategic educational planning at the present conditions on the market; it will lead to poor preparation, and to a stagnation that will narrow the opportunities. General knowledge, basic know-how and practical skills are needed at all levels. But also people who can communicate' (p 22). But the importance of cultural continuity is also underlined. It does not come on its own; school must take a responsibility – even though the relevance to the pupils appears not to be evident, because (p 64):

> to many people school is the only opportunity for acquiring a feeling for different historical periods, and the same goes for an overview of the artistic forms of expression. Is it too much to demand that the pupils within a period of 9–10 years get an opportunity to meet literature, music, and art from different ages, put into a context which is adapted to their development and interest? Is it unreasonable that Christianity has a central position in the presentation of the religions of the world, which ought to be a matter of course? Does it matter that not all modes of expression from different periods are equally obvious for all pupils? Does it matter that everything is not just to be experienced, but that something must be fingertip knowledge? Is it not reasonable to expect that e.g. Shakespeare, Holberg, Mozart, Thorvaldsen, Kierkegaard, Carl Nielsen, Martin Andersen Nexø, Ingmar Bergman, and Per Kirkeby can be placed in the correct century, even though the reach of their production is not realized by all?

The Danish answer to Robert Reich's question of how to avoid society splitting into two will undoubtedly be to stiffen the demands for general skills, particularly reading, and by recovering respect for general and basic knowledge founded upon a general curriculum principle. This will still be based on breadth. But an actual canon in cultural subjects like literature and history has not been agreed on yet. The streaming of children as was the case before 1960 will probably not be considered – yet. But the present law does allow for dividing classes into groups using certain criteria. It will be the force of future global competition that will decide to what extent these will be applied. A first step has been a tightening of teachers' training, which was introduced in 1997, bringing professionalism to the fore.

Conclusion

The answer to many of the questions that this chapter has raised will depend on how the future will interpret the concept of solidarity. Culture is based on solidarity as it appeared from Talcott Parsons's definition. It is from the cultural community that we select what we want transferred to the next generation, what we want to be learnt and what we have in common. There is no doubt about the fact that old communities are breaking up, but what do the new communities consist of? It is from this uncertainty that the problems that we are facing in the educational field today originate.

Notes

1. An investigation from *Kommunedata* shows that 26 per cent of the parents in the folkeskole thought of moving their children to a private school.
2. Often-quoted line from a song by N F S Grundtvig (1783–1872), Danish priest and founder of the folk high school.

References

Comenius, J A (1960) in *Grosse Didaktik* (*The Great Didactic*), ed A Flitner, pp X, 1, Verlag Helmut Kupper Vormals Georg Bondi, Düsseldorf and München

Elbro, C (1996) in *Læs Her* (*Read Here*), Ministry of Education, Copenhagen

Fonsmark, H (1996) *Kampen mod Kundskaber* (*The Struggle against Knowledge*), Gyldendal, Copenhagen

Hvorslev, B (1999) Lecktor, cand. mag, *Jyllandsposten*, 27 September

Jyllandsposten (1999) 28 August

Lund, J (1998) *Sidste Udkald: Om dannelse og uddannelse* (*Last Call: On education general and specific*), Gyldendal, Copenhagen

Nielsen, Maj Cecilie and Nielsen, Niels Chr (1997) *Verdens bedste uddannelsessystem*, Fremand, København

Parsons, T (1952) *The Social System*, p 15, Tavistock Publications, London

Reich, R (1991) *The Work of Nations: A Blueprint for the future*, Vintage, New York

Sommer, M, Lau, J and Meiding, J (1996) *Nordlæs: En nordisk undersøgelse af læsefærdigheder 1.–3. klasse* (*A Nordic test of reading skills from class 1–3*), Ministry of Education, Copenhagen

Undervisningsministeriet (Ministry of Education) (1960) *Vejlende Læseplan for Folkeskolen* (*National Guidelines for the Folkeskole*) (the *Blue Report*)

11. Changing cultures and schools in England and Wales

Brian Davies and John Evans

Introduction

Education systems are built to contain and resist change yet, everywhere, they are expected by policy makers to initiate it. This apparent paradox is part of their condition. Our schools must motivate, acculturate, instruct, select, adjust children to their local context, provide opportunity for them to wind up, intellectually and morally, elsewhere and ensure economic growth while resisting moral decay engendered by lack of religious faith, family breakdown and economic dislocation. All of these things are to be achieved without significant disturbance to existing distributions of economic and social power and resources. Other social agents produce; schools are among those that reproduce. They have some autonomy but it is fragile and comes easily under pressure.

Modern state systems are, above all, relatively recent inventions and highly institutionalized, 'made up of rules providing sweeping standardisation across social and physical space' and 'true by definition' (Meyer, 1987: 158). Bernstein (1996: 112) enjoins us to look for 'the sponsors and shapers of pedagogic discourse' located in the fields of production and symbolic control, whose complex division of labour 'were the products of new technologies of the twentieth century relayed by the education system' (p113). They can be shown empirically to be engaged in competition and struggle for the truth of definitions, for control of the 'pedagogic device', the rules that govern what forms of knowledge and consciousness shall be distributed to different social groups and the criteria that govern how that official knowledge may be offered and received. In this pedagogic discourse, instructional intentions and practices always presuppose and are constrained by their regulative context. Students come from families, communities and classes within societies that precondition and have expectations as to what is usual and possible. Two important considerations follow. Change that occurs in social practice and belief may flow into schools and alter what is possible and expected, while change that schools attempt, including borrowing what appear to be successful ideas and practices from elsewhere, are likely to founder for want of recognition and the means of realization by either teacher or taught. In Meyer's terms, 'in a system in which institutional rules are a driving force, *appearances matter*, and maintaining them may be a central means to effectiveness' (p 170, emphasis in the original). Students show up because of the institutional control education exerts over their futures; school conservatism and curriculum inertia arise from active reliance on this institutional authority. Variability and the inter-personal tend to be concealed by low classroom visibility, the front of stan-dardized content and individual grading. As successive analyses of our whole-class-method-dominated pedagogy have shown, children know that they have been taught even when they have learnt little or nothing (Dahloff, 1971; Evans, 1985; Westbury, 1978).

While quiet indifference to, enjoyment, or rejection of their life in class-rooms and schools may be key points of difference in the fates of students passing through them, the public debate about why we send them there ap-pears to have lost some of its historic meaning. As nation states have always sought to control their populations through schooling, so the modern notions of education as release from the accident of birth and local content into wider forms of understanding, as preparation for the social mobility required by in-creasingly knowledge-based production forms and as a route to common identity have been of great importance. They have always competed with views of school as carrying out parents' will, creating each generation in their image. Private schooling predates state provision and continues to reach com-plex accommodations with it, predominantly through religious and ethni-cally based agencies. As Coleman (1987: 180) put it:

> struggles for control of the school... show that schools are not merely for children, regarded as individuals whose interests and goals can be assumed. Schools are for families, for communities, for cultural groups, for societies, for religious groups, for local governments, and for central governments... school policy is not solely aimed toward goals for children as individuals, however insistent the rhetoric surrounding policy.

Coleman draws a distinction between functional and value communities, the former built around either 'traditional' or merely work and residence groups, the latter simply involving those sharing values about education and child rearing. He contrasts both with the 'unintentional' communities that most US schools serve, and outlines the likely consequence of having more or less value consistency and intergenerational closure between and within families and community and school. Coleman refers to areas where little or no British educational research either has ventured or now ventures. If it did, it would involve worlds where once schools might have expected and received orderly acceptance of the dominant values that they embodied, even from those who felt them wrong or oppressive or those whom they 'selected' on attainment or class criteria. Many more likely sites now exist where material and value dif-ference and dissensus within their messy zones or catchment areas, the non-functional 'communities' that schools serve, are reflected in their troubled disciplinary regimes, where neither value consensus nor publicly acknowledged pluralism exists. These thrive alongside the schools of value communities long established by religious bodies and by the state, with screened or selective or linguistically distinct intakes, reinvigorated by recent policies of 'choice'.

We would do well when considering 'changing cultures' and values in schools in England and Wales, or anywhere else, to remember, as Bidwell (1987: 206) enjoins us, that our dominant 'resource analysts have not paid much attention to the social structure of the school, even though this structure organises not only the way schooling resources are distributed but also the way they are combined to affect what students learn'. In particular, he reminds us that the Durkheimian task of moral education is a real one involving not simply the content of what is taught but the shape and character of the message systems that contain it. Its *summum bonum*, in his view, is engendering capacity for reflective moral judgement, commitment and conduct, which he sees to be complexly related to the existence of 'community' within the school and its degree of closure among staff and students. How this community is contrived is a matter for school policy in relation to staff and staff groupings, whose messages to students may differ significantly depending upon, particularly in secondary school, the 'openness' of the school student body, the continuity of school and home, community and media values and school differentiation processes. Bidwell's colleagues (eg Dreeben and Barr, 1987; Gamoran, 1987) have shown us convincingly that children going to the same building may only in a limited sense be attending the same school. Their experience of different tracks or routes, of differentiated reputational or identity universes within them, may quite overwhelm any experience of similarity planned by school. Indeed, when schools refer to themselves as communities, we may suspect, more than usually, an excess of appearance over reality, a moment of humbug.

The same is broadly true of talk of educational change. The president of the British Educational Research Association put it very succinctly. 'No doubt all generations feel that their lifetime is a period of unprecedented change' but consideration of our granny's experience should give us pause for thought in the matter (Mortimore, 2000: 7). Change there is, both with and without progress, some of it relevant to and penetrating education. While recognizing and dealing with it is a task among many for schools, policy makers invoke its necessity, in defence of national priorities, as part of their apparatus of control. We shall see how particular conditions of change in globally inspired economic conditions has underlain the huge, recent increase in centrally imposed innovation on British schools, prefaced by the establishment of a regime of truth that positioned them as largely responsible for national decline and failure.

The urge to reach for the intellectual holster should also grip us when politicians, preachers and educationalists talk of values as causes, as they frequently do. While moral judgements exist, *sui generis*, values and behaviour or action have an entirely empirical relationship. We need no complex theory of ideology to tell us, as Blake and Davis (1964) did, that holding motives, intentions and values and not acting in terms of them is as likely as any of the other three possible relations between them. Moreover, our understanding of how interests, power, knowledge and ideology work ought to leave us with the irremediable suspicion either that values may be epiphenomena of material conditions or that evincing them may not create more than desired appearance.

All of these considerations make clear that values, meanings and practices, that is to say, culture, in any social context, let alone those of schools, cannot be understood apart from considerations of power, control and institutional or structural relationship. The 'values education' that goes on in our schools consists of a whole array of messages transmitted by their practices concerning who gets in, how they are organized when they do so, what they are taught and how, under what resource conditions and how they are assessed. Each one will embody value and provide source for identity. Their purposes are explicitly cognitive, moral, social and political.

By way of final introductory note, it must be understood that the United Kingdom is not an educational entity. The systems of England, Wales, Scotland and Northern Ireland all show considerable difference, though those between England and Wales are relatively limited, except for the existence of Welsh-medium provision and a number of other, minor differences in the rest of the curriculum and some real resistances to aspects of market-oriented change supported, not least, in Wales by a collegial rather than punishment-centred inspectorate (Fitz, 2000). All our references to schools are confined to those of England and Wales. While our focus has to be delimited in this way, we are also aware of not offering a separate section on 'global' influences, for central to our argument is that worldwide economic forces are precisely those that have, locally adapted, altered and shaped our system, particularly since the 1960s. Somewhat at our imperceptive peril, we borrow practices, particularly from those systems that we believe are 'outperforming' ours.

Economic trends

In the second half of the 20th century, Britain completed its shift in economic base from primary and manufacturing production to a service economy. Farming, though still in the main under heavy European Community (EC) subsidy, now employs fewer people than the education system and will shrink further. Mining and heavy industry are vestigial, and manufacturing is predominantly assembly-based and highly penetrated by foreign capital, particularly in vehicles and electrical goods. The service sector, in areas like travel, hotel and catering, leisure and entertainment, and banking and finance, is the dominant employment area. The old public services have been privatized, wherever politically possible, including telephones, electricity, gas, water and public transport. High technology, information and communications-based activity, whose development successive government policies has privileged, is small and it is not simply to caricature to say that Britain exports rather that develops technical and commercial ideas.

The post-Second World War consensus upon the centrality of full employment to public policy lasted barely a generation. US post-Vietnam devaluation and the oil shock produced Britain's first serious post-war recession in 1974–75, neatly dividing the period into one where jobs were almost impossible to avoid and one where they were almost impossible to find, especially for the unqualified school-leaver. A period began under Callaghan's Labour government and continued under the successive Thatcher and Major administrations, barely assuaged by Blair, of blaming schools and teachers for British uncompetitiveness and unemployment identified as stemming from lack of training and skills. Thatcher's earliest moves in 1979 were to free the pound, end industry-wide labour training schemes and abolish teachers' industrial bargaining and representation rights. The first led directly to the recession of 1990–92 and defection from the European Exchange Rate Mechanism with Britain, chronic international overspender, left with high interest rates and low investment, incapable of improving a weak domestic market, and high taxation required to finance the cost of high unemployment and its concomitants. The pursuit of low inflation acted as a final disincentive to job creation, though it was instrumental, along with labour deregulation, in providing the low-cost, easy planning environment that was attractive to foreign capital. Britain became, particularly on its highest-unemployment productive periphery, a major site of attraction for US, Pacific Rim and European capital. Only at the end of the 20th century had manufacturing capacity regained the levels of 30 years ago. Only now has a much-massaged unemployment rate approached 4 per cent at the national level and 'full' (though not necessarily 'full-time') employment re-entered the political vocabulary. We maintain low inflation as the central policy objective at the cost of high interest and exchange rates. Having refused at Maastricht to accept the European Social Chapter, we now waver about rejoining the Exchange Mechanism.

For education, we must note three categories of effects. Firstly, throughout this period of relative economic bust rather than boom, the extent and character of the labour market has been under stress and change. Government-financed training, regarded, particularly by its consumers, as being of dubious quality except as a stopgap, has replaced work for the unqualified school-leaver, with significant backwash effect upon schooling. Government policy has increasingly been oriented toward the role of schools in enhancing competitiveness and flexibility in the labour market, imposing 'business values' on their activities where possible. Secondly, although public sector expenditure has risen almost continuously, both in absolute terms and as a share albeit of a GNP more than 10 per cent below the OECD average for most of the period, health and social service expenditure has been under constant relative pressure, education's share, having peaked at 7.6 per cent in 1976, barely sustaining 5 per cent since. Thirdly, the repositioning of teachers as a workforce through a concerted campaign of blaming their 'producer interest' for barring the way to educational improvement led to crisis in their relations with government and their substantial withdrawal of industrial goodwill in response to the 'discourse of derision' (Ball, 1990) that they faced. This has left its marks upon the micropolitics of schools, as well as their extra-curricular activities, particularly games, long officially regarded as central to the shaping of community and individual character and further sacrificed to the demands of the national curriculum core. It has also been central in realigning their relationship with the state. For further elucidation of the centrality of economic conditions and policy to British life, Hutton's (1995) account is particularly apposite, and for analysis of their economic consequences Avis et al (1996) develops most themes.

Social, cultural and political factors

Behind any school system, the rhythms of economic life are always intertwined with demography's blind grope. Compulsory school education must cope with those who come forward, providing them with places and teachers. The bass note of many of the changes and policy initiatives in our schools and teacher training is to be found in the bulges and dips in the age cohorts passing through schools. At the same time, schools respond to the shape and pressure of the changing class structure. Changes in the occupation structure that underpins it and in state fiscal policy that adjusts real income and wealth levels have been marked over the last half-century. The traditional class pyramid has become onion-shaped. Unskilled work has declined, and service classes have also grown and become more differentiated. The character of work in what is referred to as a post-Fordist system (Williams, 1994) has shifted. Labour is required to be more 'flexible' and 'adaptive', its character 'intensified'. Class identities have, arguably, shifted in the direction of a more consumption-oriented lifestyle rather than a production, work-related basis engendered by post-war affluence and Welfare State provision, where income and social differentials appeared, in some respects, to be declining (Cahill, 1994). While never without their critics, some aspects of these views now, certainly, seem to be erroneous. Britain is now a less equal society in terms of income distribution (often measured in terms of shares of national wealth of top and bottom percentiles) than 30 years ago. At the same time, incomes have risen so that the reality is of relative wealth and poverty commingling, both by region and social category. Child poverty and the size of a persistently growing pensioner group dependent on state income support are central focuses of government policy.

By contrast, the apparently runaway phenomenon of autonomous youth culture in the third quarter of the century has been doused by youth unemployment. The single-parent family and the teenage mother, drugs being perceived as an affliction of all social classes, have taken the place of folk devil, in large part. The former is largely the product of rising divorce rates, in turn the output of complex social and legislative change. Marriage is more avoidable and conditional, and teenage motherhood, arguably linked not only to unemployment but to exigencies of social benefit and housing policies, as well as changing family structures and the weakness of sex and social education in our families and schools, is the highest in Europe. The 'usualness' of growing up continuously in a two-parent family has become no more than a two-in-three chance, varying significantly by class and ethnic group. The definition of the importance of school and training to employment prospects has, with little exception, strengthened, even where their links appear to be most tenuous, as in areas of highest unemployment and poorest skill formations and job structures. Post-compulsory school participation rates are also among the lowest in Europe at less than 60 per cent. As with income distribution, we have the reality of plenty and shortage coexisting in respect of qualifications and employment nationally. The UK Skills Survey for 1997 estimated that while 42 per cent of those in employment were 'adequately educated', more were 'over educated' (32 per cent) than were 'under educated' (20 per cent). The positive link between 'more' education and earnings remained in all categories. At the same time, most small and medium businesses complained of skill shortage, suggesting either that the skills available were of the wrong type or level or in the wrong place or that they failed to find or attract such that existed.

Britain has also become a multi-ethnic society, more in urban England than elsewhere. The majority of inward migrants in the period of relatively open entry until the series of immigration and race relations acts from 1962 to 1971 were from Commonwealth countries in the Caribbean and Indian subcontinent and located in unskilled and semi-skilled jobs where shortages were most acute. While the obvious common feature of their experience has been the prejudice that they have encountered during successive policies of assimilation and multiculturalism, they constitute an extraordinarily diverse set of communities of whom Phillips (1999) suggested, on the evidence of Modood *et al* (1997), there has been a:

> decoupling of material disadvantage from cultural (in this case racial) inequality at least for some minority groups. On a range of economic indicators relating to income, qualifications, housing and employment, it no longer makes much sense to describe African Asians (those whose families were expelled from Kenya and Uganda in the late 1960s or early 1970s) or the Chinese as economically disadvantaged groups; and while Pakistanis and Bangladeshis are seriously and consistently disadvantaged, those of Caribbean and Indian origin are edging closer to parity with the white population.

So, though it would be mainly, it was and is far from exclusively, true that the experience of these groups of British schooling has been of working-class, relative failure. Gender differences in responses to school have also been a salient feature among these groups. Overall, their under-representation in higher education and courses of professional preparation remains evident.

The final crucial social category that must be recognized is gender. The position of women in Britain's mainstream cultures has shifted, somewhat unevenly, across a number of fronts. Formal gender equality in wage rates, conditions and benefits have often been nominally achieved, though part-time and discontinuous employment contribute to female lifetime earnings under the glass ceiling still languishing around 25 per cent below those of men. Despite evidence of sexism in school, classroom and curricular practices, female progress within education has been substantial, the long-established cognitive superiority of girls by early adolescence now translated into continuing better performance than boys at school-leaving examinations at 16 (the General Certificate of Secondary Education – GCSE) and higher education entrance at 18 (Advanced or A level). Female participation in higher education and their final examination performance there has now moved marginally ahead of parity with males. Among our current preoccupations is the 'underperformance of boys' and its possible linkage to economic and occupational changes that may have altered traditional masculine identities. While this almost certainly rests on statistical mythology (Gorard, Salisbury and Rees, 1999), it is interesting how rapidly there was an official 'awakening' to this issue in comparison with the length of time that it took for female 'underperformance' to lead to corrective action. At the same time, there are still huge differences in subject participation that begin in school and become crystallized in post-16 and higher education and continue to underpin male hegemony over most key economic activity.

There is a good deal in the argument that the terms of debate about equality of opportunity have shifted from class to categories such as gender, sexual orientation, disability and ethnicity, the prospects for economic equality having been seriously lowered by loss of confidence in radical or socialist economic reform in the last quarter of the 20th century and the organized force of women's, black, gay and other minority movements, initiated particularly in the United States, succeeding, in their turn, in redefining access to the political agenda. In our schools, provision for students with special educational needs (SEN) of various sorts has, since the Education Act 1970, moved decisively in the direction of inclusion, as far as possible, in mainstream experience. While the division between mental and manual labour may remain the villain of the piece in sustaining lifetime political and social hierarchies, access to education and training is seen as a vital ingredient in its assuaging. While such access has made only halting progress, in Phillips's (1999) terms it is recognition of equal human worth, avoiding the misrecognition, cultural domination and disadvantage experienced by Western minorities as diverse as the

Muslim and the homosexual and accepting its economic concomitants, that matters to political and other equalities.

A shift in the division of labour to place those who control the means of enunciation alongside those who merely own the means of production, the rise of the 'symbolic worker' and the new middle classes who live on little more than words alone in a global rather that a national economy, has had a profound and interactive effect on governance and politics, culture and schools. These changes, which were well under way in what we might call the dream-world of British politics in the third quarter of the century, became the nightmare of calling in the International Monetary Fund and the serious deterioration in industrial relations that followed.

Beginning in 1979, Thatcher contrived 'the "counter-revolution" to Keynesianism, known as Monetarism' (Keegan, 1992: 51). The boundaries of the state were to be rolled back; government was to facilitate rather than conduct business. Denationalization, outsourcing and competitive tendering would, as far as possible, characterize the more than one-third of economic and transfer payment activity in the public sector. Public expenditure on welfare would, thereby, be reduced, and trade unions required to relent in the face of managers' 'right to manage' in pursuit of the employment and financial disciplines of the private sector. Considerable state apparatus was to be dismantled, including much of the power and operations of the local government that Thatcher's 'one best way' policies found awkward, even immoral, their daring departures from class politics giving particular offence (Davies, 1994). In a state already the most centralized in the Western world, apparently without sense of shame or contradiction and in the name of 'choice and diversity', the local state was steadily replaced by a galaxy of quangos, revolving only about the source of political heat and light at the centre. Esland (1996: 40) depicted these 'New Right' political strategies 'in relation to education and training policy' as reliant 'on both a narrow, protectionist view of nationhood and a Taylorist form of managerialism designed to maintain a tight regulatory control over the culture, content and practice of education', where 'internal divisions within the Conservative Party have ensured that the determined defence of Britain's cultural sovereignty has prevented any serious engagement' with 'a more international concept of citizenship' that might be expected to flow from the prioritization of globalization. The spate of school, as well as further and higher education, legislation that flowed from this mixture of restorationist and new trainer (Williams, 1961) oriented convictions has been unparalleled in British experience.

Religious movements

At the same time as formal participation in Judaeo-Christian worship has reached historic lows in modern Britain, we have also developed relatively substantial Muslim, Hindu, Sikh and other communities associated with our growing ethnic minorities. While the state and monarchy remain Anglican, church membership and attendance has been in steady retreat and nothing remotely like the US religious right has manifested itself in British life or politics. A nationally conducted poll has suggested that among 13–15-year-olds belonging to Christian faith communities, two-fifths claimed to believe in God, one-third were agnostic and the remainder atheist (Francis and Kay, 1995). To judge by the character of our premature millennium celebrations, religious ritual has little significance in national life, having been substantially replaced by media-contrived and managed celebrity. In our schools, while the privileged position of Christianity has been preserved, its impact has also waned. Parochial schooling, almost exclusively Anglican and Roman Catholic and amounting to nearly 7 and 5 per cent of provision respectively, continues to have the protection of the forms of autonomy initially settled in the 1944 Education Act, including control of pupil intake.

Religious education lies outside the national curriculum described below. The daily religious worship required of schools has long become, in many establishments, neither daily nor worshipful. An attempt to strengthen and revive this aspect of school collective life was embodied in the Education Act 1993, which reconfirmed the 'mainly Christian character' of school assembly, required secondary schools to provide sex education as part of 'basic' education, as well as RE, while not tampering with parental rights to withdraw their children from any of these. In most non-religious foundation schools, RE lessons are few in number and agreed local syllabuses tend to include teaching about many faiths. Their lack of popularity among the majority of children is shared by the schemes of personal, social and health education (often referred to as PSE or PSHE) found in virtually all state schools, though also outside the national curriculum. The instatement of 'family values' as central to the policies of all major political parties, initially identified with the Thatcherite belief that there was 'no such thing as society', has intertwined with resurrection of attitudes in public policy that see the poor and unsuccessful as, if not simply undeserving, untapped sources of self-righting self-help. The 'normality' of families consisting of cohabiting, heterosexual married parents is enshrined in successive curricular requirements, most famously represented in Section 28 of the 1988 Local Government Act, which prohibited the promotion of ideas of the normality of homosexual forms of relationship. The fury of the current debate about New Labour's attempt to repeal it provides the most characteristic noise about 'values' in our schools at the turn of this century, bus owners and archbishops experiencing a meeting of homophobic minds that leaves most teachers wondering about what images of classroom practice furnish them. Even the typically immoderate English chief inspector of schools is reduced to stating the obvious with regard to the centrality and difficulty of schools' moral educative role.

The fact that Islam now has as many, if not more, practising adherents – there are notorious problems of computing the number of followers of religions and denominations – than Anglicanism in Britain's has not yet led to any great inroads either in school provision or the curriculum that might match its growth. The first state-supported Islamic school has been established but otherwise there has been clear resistance to public funding and legitimating of not only Islamic but black evangelical Christian and other thriving voluntary forms of schooling. Here, as elsewhere in educational policy, the British are steadfast; those who have shall hold.

Legal frameworks

Selection and measurement, both between and within schools, have characterized British provision throughout the period since the 1944 Education Act. It had provided for primary, secondary and further and higher 'stages' to which pupils should gain access according to 'age, aptitude and ability'. Administrative exigency modified the stock of schools in existence, for what was to become an escalating age group, in terms of selective grammar and residual modern schools for which the streamed primaries prepared. Technical education during compulsory schooling remained vestigial, technical schools or streams only marginally penetrating the system in the period up to the 1960s and initiatives like TVEI after 1983 and NVQs later in the 1980s becoming rapidly absorbed into mainstream curriculum and funding.

In retrospect, the trend toward reorganizing secondary schools on 'comprehensive' lines, driven by local initiative and indicative planning and avoidable central funding constraints, led to enormous LEA variation and subterfuge and has proven a quite short-lived and imperfect interlude in our selective history. 'Common' secondary schooling, particularly in our urban areas, has never led to schools with ability intakes any more equal than the neighbourhood primary schools that feed them. At the same time, in the period predominantly from the 1960s to the 1980s, primary schools were places where (in Bernstein's 1973 terms) the pedagogic code had shifted, in some degree, from visible to invisible: from strong subject boundaries and tightly framed, teacher-centred methods, with overt public testing and considerable pupil–teacher hierarchy, towards content juxtaposition, if not mixing, more individualized and pupil-centred styles of working, feedback rather than assessment and more relaxed adult–child relationships. Notwithstanding work, especially that of Galton, Simon and Croll (1980), that showed that '[primary] teachers value the 3Rs as much as they ever did' (Delamont, 1987: 11) and that secondaries remained untainted by its presence, 'progressivism' was already under attack. Moreover, unduly egalitarian and simultaneously self-regarding teacher producer interests, held to imbue schools with anti-industry and enterprise values and practices, were rediscovered to fuel the attack from 1976 onwards (Ahier, 1988). While, not unexpectedly, this led to a number of industrial education and economic awareness projects that schools took in and denatured as easily as they dealt with TVEI, their most important upshot became the simultaneous policies of nationalizing the curriculum while denationalizing the schools, whose centrepiece was the 1988 Act. Its claim to enhance 'diversity and choice' barely concealed the party and class basis of Thatcher's populism (Jessop, 1990), an appeal to an insular nationalism that eased an inward slide of foreign capital and international control of British assets.

All schools were required to 'locally manage' their own essentially pupil-number-driven budgets and to offer 'open enrolment' based on 1979 intakes. Their widened governance privileged parental and local enterprise interests. Schools were to wax and wane as parents preferred and those who wished to leave LEA supervision altogether might opt for grant maintained (GM) or city technology college (CTC) status. Though not initially allowed to change the character of their intake, schools were, by degrees, allowed to increase their selectivity. These policies ran alongside the assisted places scheme (now phased out, along with GM schools), introduced in the 1980 Education Act, which, essentially, subsidized the entry of lower-middle-class children to independent schools.

The Act had also given parents new rights in choosing schools and such a policy of 'choice' required market information about 'standards' in the system, which in turn required a national curriculum to which they might sensibly relate. Out of this, a since regularly modified 10-subject (11 in Wales, including Welsh) curriculum finally emerged in the 1988 Act, made up of three core (English, maths and science, and Welsh in Welsh-medium contexts) and seven foundation (modern language, including Welsh as a modern language in non-Welsh-medium schools in Wales, humanities, design and technology, music, art and PE) subjects, to be regularly tested by teacher and 'standard' or national assessment across three 'key stages' at 7, 11 and 14 and a fourth by GCSE at 16. The national curriculum was presented in terms of broad programmes of study and national attainment targets. There was no accompanying apparatus of textbooks or teachers' guides or specification of timetable or teaching methods. Apart from introducing science and technology to many primary classrooms where there had been little or none, it did little more than confirm established content and practice for, in its devising, despite unsubtle attempts at intervention by Thatcher in English, maths, history and physical education (see, for example, Evans and Penney, 1995), it fell into the hands of subject panels dominated by professional educationalists. Teachers railed at losing autonomy, while, with little exception, being not uncomfortable with the national curriculum content. The same could not be said concerning national testing, which has produced an onerous regime of recording assessment at eight levels through the stages and which has provided the core of a burden of discontent such that in 2000 an ICM opinion poll conducted for the *Guardian* (Carvel, 2000) showed that more than a third of teachers under 35 expected to quit within 10 years and nearly a half within 15, particularly in primary school and this in a context where, given their bulge in numbers over the age of 40, 40 per cent of them will be expected to retire 'normally' over the next 10–25 years anyway.

The 'heavy workload' that inclined three-quarters of the primary teachers sampled towards thoughts of early quitting has been accentuated by the even more recent policy of nationalizing their pedagogy. A pervasive managerialism has settled on the schools through target setting, benchmarking, publication of league tables of results, insistence on the centrality of the leadership of heads and senior mangers, regular external national inspection and, in prospect, performance-related pay. It has been substantially sanctified by the 'findings' of a school effectiveness literature that has neither conceptualized, let alone measured, pedagogic process and whose pliant, latter-day discovery has been of the improving properties of whole-class teaching, putative key to the secret of high-performing elementary classrooms in some Pacific Rim systems. This has become the promised means of effecting what the national curriculum and testing system, introduced in the name of 'improving standards', failed to.

Alexander (1997: 193) in a fascinating discussion, not least with respect to how his talents as an academic were used and misused by politicians, contended that it was not until 1991, after the initial round of national curriculum innovation, that government gave first sign that it recognized 'that content and pedagogy are indissolubly linked'. By 1995, the English school inspectorate, OFSTED, had provided in its *Guidance on Inspection of Nursery and Primary Schools* an official quasi-orthodoxy on primary pedagogy, organization and resourcing with built-in means of enforcement. It linked positive factors in standards of achievement to subject knowledge, direct teaching, a mixture of teaching strategies and grouping by ability, and negative ones to non-instructional, facilitative teaching, poor time management, increase in the use of undifferentiated worksheets and dull, unchallenging work tasks. The conditions for the creation of the 'literacy hour' for English, with similar arrangements for maths, were now present to complete the over-recording, planning and monitoring of a narrowed and assessment-led curriculum.

Meyer's world of that which is 'true by definition' was never more complete than in our present one where neither British major political party any longer questions fundamental structures of education or the distributional effect of its practices. Our much-competed-for 'middle England' electorate is held to dislike tampering with their educational privileges as much as their taxes, so both are avoided. Every classroom in the school becomes capable of untold but targetable improvement, out of existing resources. Secondary schools are told that unless they can achieve 25 per cent 'good GCSE' pass rates they will be closed, without the slightest reference to policies that have allowed schools to come into existence that cannot normally achieve them. Having systematically dismantled local (LEA) democracy, school autonomy and such professional associational resistance as has ever existed in Britain, the state may now, as a perfectly normal occurrence, indulge in such pronouncements and mainline the fad of the day, month or year as statutory requirement. The wilfulness of its misunderstanding of and necessity for and character of change in a system built to absorb and resist it in the greater interest of social and cultural reproduction could be regarded as a key system value and immoral. Public policy actually celebrates processes of 'naming and shaming' teachers, schools and LEAs who fail to meet performance standards, while being unwilling to question the structures and institutional practices that generate them. It may hardly be surprising that teachers experience stress in their expected work of 'raising and praising' their charges under such conditions though we do not say this with any sense of belief that there was some previous golden state of the system.

What must be asked, indeed, is how the changing character of school as it impinges on teachers is experienced by pupils and their parents. To glance back at a collection such as Lester Smith's (1954) where headteachers depicted their secondary school as 'Christian communities' is to inspect a mythic world of order, service and vibrant, extended extra-curricular experience that was far from normal then and is unusual now. The ability, social, ethnic and gender diversity of many schools make them unlikely close communities, more likely places where differences sharply coexist and become invidiously ranked. School peer cultures, always differentiated, are complex identity worlds formed not only by the home, community and the media, teachers and subjects, ambition and occupational prospect, but perhaps, more than ever, attainment. Schools are more instrumental places, their images of appropriate conduct, character and manner more open, their forms less ritualized. The purposes of their often-vestigial pastoral systems are procedural rather than didactic. The manner and practice of teachers and subject departments, particularly in secondary schools, are likely not only to be different, as they have long been, but openly critical or antagonistic of one another or of school policies. In these senses, schools have become more like society: less deferential, more honest, slightly less given to cant, potentially open to the celebration and enjoyment of their differences.

On the evidence of the *Guardian* poll, the great majority of parents rightly believe that standards have been maintained or improved in them over the past 10 years and are fairly or very happy with their own children's schooling. But schools are not like families except in the rhetorical, regulative discourse of headteachers nor are they democratic nor particularly given to unconditional positive regard. The values that curriculum carries tend to be more explicit, less socially biased and often form the objects of study. The curriculum is also generally more open to outside experience, though highly deficient for the great majority of pupils in consideration of the social sciences, including economics and politics. Social studies being expunged and economic awareness having died, the final loss of English empire through devolution to Scotland and Wales has brought forth the prospect of civics in the compulsory curriculum by 2000. Quangos and spin doctoring may well yet become the commonly shared and understood heritage of key stage 3/4 students alongside their well-honed and closely tested phonic reading and mental arithmetic skills. It would be nice to think that this would enable them to penetrate the character of their experience, as Bidwell hopes, more reflectively. Perhaps even more urgently, we need to consider the case of our new primary teachers, who know nothing but change, as part of a group that has had its autonomy, including the habit of questioning official orders, so eroded that we put them in jeopardy of the ultimate professional downfall, that of not knowing how to answer back. Few things could be more dangerous to our school cultures and values.

References

Ahier, J (1988) *Industry, Children and the Nation*, Falmer, London

Alexander, R (1997) *Policy and Practice in Primary Education*, Routledge, London

Avis, J et al (1996) *Knowledge and Nationhood*, Cassell, London

Ball, S J (1990) *Policies and Policy Making in Education: Explorations in policy sociology*, Routledge, London

Bernstein, B (1973) *Class and Pedagogies: Visible and invisible*, OECD, Paris

Bernstein, B (1996) *Pedagogy, Symbolic Control and Identity*, Taylor and Francis, London

Bidwell, C E (1987) Moral education and school social organisation, in *The Social Organisation of Schooling*, ed M T Hallinan, pp 205–19, Plenum Press, New York

Blake, J and Davis, K (1964) Norms, values and sanctions, in *Handbook of Sociology*, ed R E L Faris, Rand McNally, Chicago

Cahill, M (1994) *The New Social Policy*, Blackwell, Oxford

Carvel, J (2000) Teacher crisis – half plan to quit in 10 years, *Guardian*, 29 Feb, p 1, *Education*, pp 1–2

Coleman, J S (1987) The relations between school and social structure, in *The Social Organisation of Schooling*, ed M T Hallinan, pp 177–204, Plenum Press, New York

Dahloff, U (1971) *Ability Grouping, Content Validity and Curriculum Process Analysis*, Teachers' College Press, New York

Davies, B (1994) On the neglect of pedagogy in educational studies and its consequence, *British Journal of In-Service Education*, **20** (10), pp 17–34

Delamont, S (1987) The primary teacher 1945–1990: myths and realities, in *The Primary School Teacher*, ed S Delamont, pp 3–17, Falmer Press, London

Dreeben, R and Barr, R (1987) An organisational analysis of curriculum and education, in *The Social Organisation of Schooling*, ed M T Hallinan, pp 13–39, Plenum Press, New York

Esland, G (1996) Education, training and nation-state capitalism: Britain's failing strategy, in *Knowledge and Nationhood*, ed J Avis *et al*, pp 40–70, Cassell, London

Evans, J (1985) *Teaching in Transition: The challenges of mixed ability groupings*, Open University Press, Milton Keynes

Evans, J and Penney, D (1995) The politics of pedagogy, *Journal of Educational Policy*, **10** (1), pp 27–44

Fitz, J (2000) Local identities and national frameworks: the case of Wales, in *Ethnicity, Race, Nationality and Education: A global perspective*, ed K Shimahara and I Holowinsky, Lawrence Hillsdale, NJ, Erlbaum

Francis, L J and Kay, W K (1995) *Teenage Religion and Values*, Gracewing, Leominster

Galton, M, Simon, B and Croll, P (1980) *Inside the Primary Classroom*, Routledge & Kegan Paul, London

Gamoran, A (1987) Organisation, induction and the effects of ability grouping: comment on Slavin's and 'best evidence synthesis', *Review of Educational Research*, **57** (3), pp 341–45

Gorard, S, Salisbury, J and Rees, G (1999) Reappraising the apparent underachievement of boys at school, *Gender and Education*, **11** (4), pp 441–54

Hutton, W (1995) *The State We're In*, Jonathan Cape, London

Jessop, B (1990) *State Theory: Putting capitalist states in their place*, Polity Press, Cambridge

Keegan, W (1992) *The Spectre of Capitalism*, Radius, London

Lester Smith, W O (ed) (1954) *The School as a Christian Community*, SCM Press, London

Meyer, J W (1987) Implications of an institutional view of education for the study of educational effects, in *The Social Organisation of Schooling*, ed M T Hallinan, pp 157–75, Plenum Press, New York

Modood, T *et al* (1997) *Ethnic Minorities in Britain: Diversity and disadvantage*, Policy Studies Institute, London

Mortimore, P (2000) Does educational research matter?, *British Educational Research Journal*, **26** (1), pp 5–24

Office for Standards in Education (OFSTED) (1995) *Guidance on the Inspection of Nursery and Primary Schools*, HMSO, London

Phillips, A (1999) *Which Equalities Matter?*, Polity Press, Cambridge

Westbury, I (1978) Research into classroom processes: a review of ten years' work, *Journal of Curriculum Studies*, **10**, pp 283–308

Williams, F (1994) Social relations, welfare and the post-Fordism debate, in *Toward a Post-Fordist Welfare State?*, ed R Burrows and B Loader, pp 49–73, Routledge, London

Williams, R (1961) *The Long Revolution*, Penguin, Harmondsworth

12. Changing cultures and schools in France

Olivier Cousin

In France schooling is based on two principles: the desire for a democratization of education and the will to integrate individuals into modernity. Throughout the 20th century, schooling has historically been concerned with making education more democratic by endeavouring to base selection uniquely on criteria of merit and by attempting to turn individuals into full citizens. Today, these two principles are still considered as fundamental aims. But their meaning has changed and the school has to resolve problems of another nature. The democratization of the system no longer refers to the access of all pupils to secondary education (an aim that has practically been fulfilled). Rather it entails the administration and management of an extremely diverse population – from the point of view both of its educational level and of its relationship to schooling and knowledge. Integration no longer raises only the question of citizenship. It also raises questions regarding the recognition of the individual and his or her subjectivity. It is no longer simply a question of transmitting the universal values that help to mould individuals. On the contrary, the question today is how to preserve the uniqueness of all individuals in order to protect them from a system that, in many respects, appears to brutalize them.

Today, changes in French schools result not so much from structural reforms, as from transformations in society's relationship to the school system and in expectations regarding education. Presently school has become part of everyday life and debates over education are in fact discussions about society itself. Discussions about violence or immigration in schools (in the case, for example, of the Muslim girls wearing headscarves) convey both the decline of the school as an institution and the need for it to face social problems. In this chapter, I shall first present the organization of the school system and then I shall go on to discuss three major topics that reflect the challenges facing the school system: democratization and the question of mass education; competition at school in the present situation of widespread unemployment, and the socialization of young people in the context of the decline of the institutions.

Recent developments in the French school system

In France, the history of schooling can be regarded as a quest to achieve uniformity. As in many other countries, the school system was initially divided into several distinct educational units. The vast majority of pupils left school at the end of the primary cycle. Only the most 'deserving' continued on to secondary school, depending on which social class they belonged to. There was, however, an enormous difference in probable school careers. Middle-class children attended the primary classes in the *lycées*. This ensured that they would get into secondary school. Working-class children were educated in the primary schools. Access to secondary schooling depended on passing an examination. Middle-class children went on to university, whereas working-class children left school during early adolescence. Thus, educational success, measured here in terms of length of schooling, was not so much due to pupils' capacities as to the circumstances of their birth.

The successive reforms implemented throughout the 20th century were aimed at unifying the system to enable all pupils to extend their studies further than primary schooling, regardless of their place of birth or social origins. The issue at stake was mainly the *collège*, that is to say the intermediate level between primary school and *lycée*. The question was to know which form it should take. Should it be an extension of primary school and be concerned mainly with pupils' needs, regardless of the gap between scientific knowledge and popular culture? This orientation was at the forefront of a new form of humanism, based more on technical knowledge and less on elitism. The idea was that it would adapt to the pupils, and also modernize the school by legitimating technical culture. Or, should the *collège*, on the contrary, resemble the *lycée* and give preference to classical culture and to the form of excellence that is based on the humanities? The question was not settled directly. To begin with, several different models of *collège* coexisted. Some, like the CES (*collège d'enseignement secondaire*), offered classical streams, as well as the so-called modern streams, which did not include Latin and Greek. The others, the CEG (*collège d'enseignement général*), did not have classical streams. Later there was to be only one type of *college*, the CES, comprising different streams. It was not until the 1970s that the various streams disappeared and that the *collèges* offered the same type of education to all pupils. With the creation of the *collège unique* the school system was said to be unified. The French school system is therefore a three-tiered structure composed of the primary school, the *collège* and finally the *lycée*, with the latter including three types of education – classical, technical and vocational.[1]

In form and structure, the *collège* is closer to the *lycée* than to the primary school, because it is primarily the gateway to the latter. On the one hand its teaching lays the basis for a broad general culture by means of a common core syllabus. The knowledge acquired in primary school is reviewed and explored in greater depth. On the other hand, it plays a decisive role in the orientation of pupils, which presently takes place at the end of *troisième*. Sometimes these two functions are incompatible because orientation (tracking) has now become one of the priorities of the *collège* since almost all pupils go on to further study. As in the past, streaming has appeared once again, but by way of optional courses (rare or prestigious languages such as German, which are chosen in order to have the best chances of succeeding). In theory, however, the classes remain undifferentiated. Moreover, orientation implies a degree of competition between schools, because some *collèges* are more efficient than others and, as a result, give the pupils a better chance of reaching general secondary schooling than others.

The creation of the *collège unique* was partly a response to the problem of introducing more democracy into schooling, since it made it possible for all pupils to continue their education after primary school in a common structure offering the same type of education for all. However, the reform of the school system has not solved all the problems. Paradoxically, it provoked what is today referred to as the 'crisis' of the school system. Now that all the pupils are accepted in the *collège* and the *lycée*, in particular those who previously would have been sent to specific programmes (such as apprenticeship) or who would have dropped out altogether, schools are faced with new challenges. These are of at least two types. The first is selection, and the second concerns mass education. Selection is a new challenge because now it is an integral part of the school system. As long as the school was organized as a separate educational entity, selection took place prior to entry into the school system. Now that a whole age group attends *collège*, selection takes place within the system itself. The school, previously perceived as a fair institution in contrast to a society regarded as unfair, is now criticized for being a source of injustice. The more opaque the rules and the arguments for selection, the greater the distance between the school and society. The highly selective nature of the school system is one of the causes for the malaise amongst teachers who feel that their mission is no longer to transmit knowledge but rather to select pupils.

The second challenge is that of mass education; this is not simply due to the considerable rise in numbers, but also to the arrival of pupils with very different social and educational backgrounds from the mainstream. Nowadays the school has to manage a heterogeneous and previously ignored population. This heterogeneity appears through social and educational differences, diversity in degrees of aspirations, and variations in attitudes and expectations concerning schooling. It means that the school, and more precisely the teachers, are faced with difficulties that they do not know how to resolve. On the one hand the school must deal with an unfamiliar population, and on the other it continues to apply an educational model that is ill suited to this new public. The advent of mass education stresses the need to introduce difference as a means of taking into account the specificities of each pupil without having this lead to an unequal treatment of pupils. It is therefore a question of diversifying without excluding, which was not the case with streaming. The advent of mass education meant that the creation of the *collège unique* had to be revised, for until then the principle was that to ensure equality of opportunity all that was needed was to ensure equality in the educational offer. In order to respond to the problems posed by heterogeneity, the school system had to embark on a huge reform based on the autonomy of each school and on a policy that encouraged every school to have its own plan. Since the schools welcomed specific populations, they were given the opportunity to implement specific actions in response to the problems that they themselves had identified (Cousin, 1998). This policy was part of the larger trend towards decentralization, which began in 1982. This represents a genuine change in French society, ie the recognition that to achieve a common goal the initiatives of local actors must be encouraged. One of the pillars of this policy was the designation of educational priority areas (ZEP – *zones d'éducation prioritaire*), setting the way for positive discrimination of socially deprived schools.

Democracy and the school system

Sociological studies of the 1960s and 1970s cast doubt on the idea of the link between a democratic school system and meritocracy (Baudelot and Establet, 1971; Bourdieu and Passeron, 1964, 1970; INED, 1970). These analyses were carried out before the creation of the *collège unique*. What has happened since then? An overview reveals the extent to which the school has changed. After primary schooling, all children enter the *collège* and most of them continue further. Almost 70 per cent of an age group obtains the *baccalauréat*, and 60 per cent of young people over the age of 20 are in further education. As a result of the opening up of the system, the democratization of education has become a reality. The fact that streaming no longer takes place in the *collège* has enabled a large majority (89 per cent) of working-class children who entered the *sixième* in 1989 to complete the whole cycle. Democratization is primarily demonstrated by the narrowing gap between working-class children and middle-class children. In 1980, 96 per cent of the middle-class children who entered *sixième* finished *collège*, as compared with 58 per cent of working-class children. In 1989 there was only a 10-point difference (99 per cent and 89 per cent respectively). Access to the *lycée* has also become widespread and, among the pupils who began *sixième* in 1989, 22 per cent of the working-class children enter the general or technological final year without having repeated a year, as compared with 60 per cent of middle-class children.

Democratization is only relative and numerous forms of inequality are still to be found. The educational careers of working-class children are not the same as those of middle-class children. The former repeat classes more frequently and are much more often found in the technological and vocational *lycées*. Moreover, if they do get into the general education *lycée*, they are always under-represented in the most prestigious options. This shows that pu-

pils have different strategies depending on their social origins. It indicates too
that the workings of the educational system are also a function of the type of
population being dealt with. Thus the options demanded by and offered to
equally successful pupils will depend on their social origin. For example,
working-class children who obtain average results will tend to underestimate
their capacities and their chances of succeeding, and will therefore be less
likely to request entry into a higher class or into a selective stream. This tendency of pupils and their families to underachieve will be communicated by
the actors in the school system who will also minimize such pupils' capacities,
therefore preventing them from entering the best courses. For middle-class
children, however, the situation is reversed. These pupils make more ambitious demands and the teachers encourage them to do so, anticipating the
likelihood of their chances of succeeding.

The same remarks apply to the educational achievement of girls. Generally
speaking, they do better than boys; this is true at all levels of the school system.
They also gain access to the general education more frequently. However,
girls do not have the same opportunities as boys. They are subject to discrimination that is revealed in orientation. The scientific and technological courses
remain fairly inaccessible, and in order to gain entry into them they have to get
better average results than the boys. They tend to practise self-selection in
their choices of orientation. Girls are less likely than boys with the same qualifications to request admission for which selection is made. By so doing, they
conform to the gender stereotype according to which girls are considered less
ambitious than boys. The school does nothing to reverse this situation. The educational institutions perpetuate the dominant social models, reinforcing the
social role of girls by over-selecting them and maintaining them in 'women's'
sections.[2]

The question of the democratization of the school system has therefore become more complex. Inequality persists but has been displaced. The main issue is no longer access to the *lycée*, or to the *baccalauréat* or to the university,
since they have become part of mass education. Now the issue is one of the
type of course followed, the type of school or university attended, the type of
baccalauréat obtained. Inequality is now to be found in the choice of options
and courses. The unification of the school system has resulted in the introduction of forms of differentiation within the school itself. Previously, the difference was between those who continued their studies and those who did not.
Today the difference is between those who have access to the selective
streams and the others.

These new forms of inequality change the relationship between society and
the school. The school is now the object of special attention by families who
hope that the school will not only teach something, but also deliver a diploma
that will give access to the job market. In a system that aims to get 80 per cent of
an age group up to baccalaureate level, the issue is no longer access to the *lycée*,
but rather the choice of a 'good' *lycée* and of a 'good' course, ensuring the best

possible chances of success. Complex strategies are developed and the pupils and their families behave like consumers managing their best interest. Schooling has not actually become a market, since attendance at a given school is subject to strict rules and schools are grouped in catchment areas. Nevertheless there are pressures and real competition between schools (Ballion, 1982; Ball and van Zanten, 1998). Well-to-do families want their children to attend the schools with the best reputation in order to increase their chances of success as well as to avoid bad company. Sometimes schools themselves create fast-track courses to attract the best pupils. Thus one of the effects of the democratization of schooling, in a context of mass unemployment, is to introduce new forms of behaviour. While in theory all schools are the same, in practice there are considerable differences. In the long run, this may lead to an increase in social and ethnic segregation and to further inequality between the deprived social categories and the middle classes in access to schooling. Working-class schools situated in educational priority areas (ZEP) or the peripheral suburbs are the main victims of this reality. There is a real risk of developing a dual system with schools for the middle classes and schools for the peripheral suburbs (Payet, 1995).

School, employment and the economy

Since the beginning of the 1990s, French society has faced mass unemployment affecting approximately 13 per cent of the active population. Young people are over-represented among the unemployed (25 per cent). The rate is even higher if one counts all those in precarious economic situations, for instance those who can find only part-time or temporary employment, or those who are no longer considered as officially unemployed but who depend entirely on social welfare payments. However, the length of time spent in education is rising steadily as is the number of people with qualifications. There is a strong and positive link between levels of qualification and economic integration. The higher the level of qualification, the less risk there is of being unemployed and the shorter the period of unemployment. Those who leave the school system with no qualifications have little chance of finding a job. They make up the majority of the long-term unemployed. This highlights the contradictory relationship between the school and the employment market.

The obsessions with success at school, and with the search for the best courses and the best schools, are not so much indications of a concern for modernization of the economy as they are for the desire to curb unemployment. While the target of bringing 80 per cent of an age group up to baccalaureate level may have been chosen with a view towards improving productivity in firms and in order to face the challenge of international competition with countries such as Japan, it was mainly understood as the best protection against unemployment. Both pupils and parents expect the school to be efficient. Their relationship to knowledge is strictly instrumental (Charlot, Bautier and Rochex, 1992; Dubet, 1991). It is not so much the content of the subject that matters as its utility for the pupil's future educational career. The same is true for the choice of languages. German, for example, is considered more efficient than other languages. This choice ensures that the pupil will be in a good class and represents a better guarantee for entry into the selective streams. The choice of scientific streams in the *lycée* is made on the same basis. Pupils do not wish to continue in this path but they know that a scientific baccalaureate leads to the best options. Pupils' choice during orientation, their relationship to studies and the modes of selection, do not reflect economic and vocational perspective as much as the concern with unemployment. This leads a great many pupils to have absolutely no illusions about school. While the actors in the school system try to keep the myths of free knowledge in being, and learning as pleasure alive, the pupils stress efficiency. They appear as cynical consumers who are uniquely interested in the utility of their studies.

Does this concern with success and the utility of studies pay off? Unemployment among young people does seem to suggest that this is the correct perspective, since qualifications are a protection against exclusion from the employment market. One form of inequality does, however, persist, since girls are more likely to be unemployed than boys with the same educational qualifications, except after the baccalaureate. On the other hand, if the relationship between school and social mobility is examined, the answer is more complicated. In France, as elsewhere, there is no direct link between the level of qualification and the social standing of individuals. Compared to their parents, schoolchildren today stay in school longer, go further in their studies and, generally, have a better level of education (Baudelot and Establet, 1989). However, an overall rise in the educational level and a net increase in the number of qualified people does not necessarily mean greater social mobility. The two structures are independent of each other and are only indirectly linked (Boudon, 1973). The employment market has not undergone the same evolution as the school. It has not opened up to the newly qualified. Therefore they cannot directly convert their qualifications into jobs (Baudelot and Establet, 2000). Between 1960 and 1980, for example, the percentage of managers in the active population rose from 5 to 8 per cent, whereas the proportion of young people leaving school with the baccalaureate rose from 10 to 30 per cent. The structure of employment has therefore not followed the rise in education. Thus in 1993, 160,000 young people left the educational system with a level of qualification at least equivalent to a first university degree, whereas, in the same year, the number of employees in management under the age of 28 did not exceed 77,000 (Duru-Bellat and van Zanten, 1999).

As a result of the overall increase in qualification, we have witnessed a relative devaluation of educational awards. While to invest in an extra year is always financially advantageous, this bonus has decreased constantly since the 1970s. The difference in salary is closing between those who leave the educational system with the baccalaureate and those who obtain a qualification after two years of further study. This drop in status reinforces disillusionment with the educational system, leaving young people feeling trapped. They know that qualifications are a protection against unemployment but they do not always give access to the most desired jobs. Above all, the rise in qualification levels induces tension and competition between the different streams. The university institutes for technology (IUT – *instituts universitaires de technologie*) are an example of this. They are highly rated because they deliver qualifications as technicians after two years of study and because the failure rates are relatively low as compared with the universities. They were originally set up to deal with the students who had a technical baccalaureate. Now, in reality, numerous courses, and in particular the most sought after, are attended by students with a general education baccalaureate. This phenomenon, which concerns many streams, reinforces the dominant position of the general education baccalaureate, in particular the scientific options, at the expense of the other types of baccalaureate, which have absorbed the main brunt of qualifications for all.

The fragile and complex link between qualification, unemployment and social status intensifies the instrumental relationship to studies. The vast majority of pupils – those who are only average students and who do not have the symbolic resources of Bourdieu's 'heirs' at their disposal – experience school as something of an obstacle race in which they are more likely to lose (repeat classes, negative forms of orientation) than to win. In such a context, efficiency is more important than interest in studies, even for 'good' pupils. Above all, the system appears to be opaque and the pupils are never sure of the validity of their choices or of being able to control their destinies. Pupils in technical education are undoubtedly the worst off. Their sections are socially devalued. What will become of them in educational terms is uncertain.

Socialization by default

The task of the school is not restricted to the distribution of places. It also aims at socializing individuals. Its duty is to transmit norms and values that will ensure social cohesion and the formation of autonomous individuals. School became compulsory at the end of the 19th century, not so much for reasons of education but to ensure national unification, which was still fragile at the time. School was considered to be an institution concerned with socialization of the individual. This was achieved through self-imposed discipline and conformity with rules. Such a necessary constraint enabled the individual to become autonomous (Durkheim, 1958, 1990). This vision of the school was strongly challenged by the critical sociology of the 1970s, which departed from such an 'enchanted' vision and denounced the social domination that it exerted. According to this critique the school does not make way for the construction of autonomous beings but only gives the impression of so doing (Baudelot and

Establet, 1971; Bourdieu and Passeron, 1964, 1970). Later, the effect of mass education on the system was to make way for another image of the school. It no longer appeared as a system, but rather as fragmented comprising several forms of activity. From one perspective the school is a place for learning that, as we have seen, ranks individuals hierarchically. It is therefore a place of intense competition where failure is experienced as a permanent threat. From a second perspective school is a social organization, with its rules and its codes, in which pupils develop a juvenile form of sociability and enjoy considerable autonomy. Finally, from a third perspective the school is the place in which individuals are moulded. In their relationship to knowledge and the school culture, pupils become individuals and construct their personalities as individual beings (Dubet, 1991; Dubet and Martuccelli, 1996).

These three spheres of activity are not necessarily compatible. This is particularly true of the *collège* or the *lycée*. Pupils must be at one and the same time good pupils, with competent strategies, good friends, integrated into their peer groups, and autonomous beings. Any one sphere of activity may conflict with the other two. For example, peer pressure, or the push toward conformity, conflicts with the need to be competitive at school, which stresses difference. Moreover, conforming to the group weighs heavily on the construction of the individual personality, which demands authenticity. Conflict between various spheres of activity is not specific to schools, but what is specific is that the educational institution itself no longer has a guiding principle. It hesitates, for example, between striving for efficiency in its preoccupation with selection of elites and economic integration, and a desire to give preference to the relationship with young people and the development of their personalities (Derouet, 1992).

These conflicts between various spheres of activity have changed the role of the school in the process of socialization. The school no longer has the means to impose itself on individuals; it is no longer the model for social roles. On the contrary, socialization has become an activity by default. It is the pupils who try to articulate the various dimensions of the experience of schooling. They attempt to construct themselves as autonomous individuals by giving a meaning to their actions. Socialization then becomes a sort of individual process, which varies with the social and educational position of each person and the type of school. In reality, instead of the world of the school imposing itself on the pupils, it tends to adapt to them. For middle-class children who attend schools that maintain a good reputation, the experience of school tends to be highly integrated. By and large the pupils have an instrumental relationship with their studies. Utility rules over interest, and some behave like consumers investing in their future. Usually, these schools do not have any particular problems and have a low degree of control over their pupils. A juvenile form of sociability develops without provoking a clash between adolescent culture and the culture of the school. The autonomy and freedom that is permitted rather than given to the pupils may in this case be perceived as a compensation for pressures suffered at school. The pupils play the game because they hope that today's investment will pay off tomorrow. They defer gratification and accept sacrifices. The situation of pupils who experience problems is more awkward. They do not always fit in to this type of school, and their educational status marginalizes them in the eyes of young people. In order to save face, some of them resort to stereotyped forms of behaviour thus reinforcing their marginality.

In the *collèges* and *lycées* situated in deprived catchment areas, the experience is more fragmented and often dominated by tension between the world of school and that of the young. The attitude towards studying is conditioned by the constant threat of failure at school. Selection appears to be brutal, sometimes unfair and almost always negative. In this context, the weakest pupils feel that they are defined uniquely in terms of failure. This stigma gives them a sense of being both bad pupils and bad individuals. In order to construct a more positive image of themselves, some of them choose to take refuge in a juvenile culture and identify only with their peer group. They construct an identity for themselves that clashes with what the school expects. They adopt ostentatious forms of behaviour, challenging the authority of the school, through the use of provocative and sometimes outrageous language. The world of school stands for civic-mindedness to which they oppose the use of force. They adopt the appearance of rebels (Lepoutre, 1997). Thus, for a great many pupils who experience school failure, far from helping them to become autonomous individuals, the school seems to be a blind and brutal machine that destroys them.

Educational institutions have lost their leading role and this contributes to the school's heightened vulnerability. On the one hand, it no longer has the monopoly of knowledge and the distribution of culture. The school now has to compete with other worlds, particularly since one of the characteristics of its adolescent population is the high degree of autonomy of their lives. This is another feature of their socialization by default. Points of references in the world of adolescents are often totally foreign to the world of the school. Nowadays, the school is characterized by the development of two parallel cultures that tend to overlap and ignore each other. The school has little control over adolescents beyond the relationship of teacher and pupil. In this respect, it is liberal in the same way as society is towards adolescent culture and the habits of individuals. For adolescents, school is as much a world in which the cohesion of the peer group and juvenile sociability is at work as it is a place for learning. These two instances almost never meet. In most cases they are juxtaposed. There is therefore no continuity; on the contrary, there are sometimes conflicts. Generally speaking, the coexistence of the world of school and the world of juvenile culture is not a problem. But it can generate conflicts in some schools when the experience of school is dominated by failure.

On the other hand, those who represent school feel invaded and threatened by the local environment, particularly in working-class areas and in the suburbs. They are no longer successful in marking the boundary between the school and the surrounding area and in keeping practices that they do not tolerate outside the school. In some schools violence has become a major issue, dominating the whole question of education. The school spontaneously rejects responsibility for the causes of violence and attributes this phenomenon to the outside world of the social and urban crisis, or accuses the parents of being incompetent. But violence also emerges when the pupils are too frequently faced with educational failure. They experience their situation as an indication of the lack of respect for them. They attack the school because they are rejected (Debarbieux, 1996). School is no longer a sphere for the construction of the self, but rather becomes an institution that excludes and stigmatizes the weakest. This situation is made all the more unbearable since any form of failure is synonymous with future unemployment.

Finally, as its power declines, the school allows for practices that are contrary to its principles, as indicated by problems relating to ethnic discrimination. While in its general approach and its ways of selecting pupils the school does not discriminate against pupils of immigrant origin (Vallet and Caille, 1996), at the local level some schools practise an emerging form of segregation. These start with the ways in which classes are formed. Their composition is not a question of chance and the end result is that pupils are grouped together by ethnic origin on the basis of the optional subjects available (Payet, 1995). Segregation is rarely intended. It is sometimes the consequence of a project that aims at the contrary. This is the case of *collèges* in the working-class suburbs, which attempt to attract good pupils but which then isolate them from the others. In some schools in the working-class suburbs, the question of immigration has become a problem in itself and policies aimed at the integration of immigrant children are set up. This is illustrated by the increasing use of 'mediators', themselves often of immigrant origin, and who, as a result, are better placed to support the young people and to help them to become pupils. In doing so, the schools often classify these pupils into categories in which they do not necessarily recognize themselves since they are defined uniquely by their ethnic origin. There is a risk of the racialization of social relations (Bouveau, Cousin and Favre-Perroton, 1999).

Conclusion

The image of the French school system is often one of paradox and contrasts. It has been through a sea of change. Although it has demonstrated that it is capable of adaptation, it is very frequently presented as a very unwieldy administration, impossible to reform. On the whole, the school system has succeeded in absorbing mass education and, objectively, the school is more democratic. However, it is on the subjective side that difficulties emerge. Failure, which was very widespread, is now more marginal, but it has also become more unbearable. The consequences are no longer the same. Now, young people are marginalized by educational failure and the school is made to feel guilty about it because it is held responsible for the situation. Moreover, by extending schooling at secondary level to all the children from the same age group, the school not only welcomes pupils, but it also receives adolescents. The focus on success in schooling and the division of labour within schools are not conducive to assuming this responsibility. The school seems to be a divided world in which the organization of education and the social and cultural world of adolescence never meet. The breadth of the gap between the two worlds varies. It becomes a problem when it creates a feeling of self-destruction in the pupil, that is to say when he or she cannot merge the two worlds. This is one of the challenges facing the school if it wishes to mould individuals.

Notes

1. For a general approach to the history of the French school system, see Prost (1993) and Lelièvre (1990).
2. For an overall view and an evaluation of pupils' school careers, see Duru-Bellat and van Zanten (1999).

Translator's note

Collège: The term *collège* refers to the type of state secondary school French children attend between the ages of 11 and 15 (ie after *école primaire* and before *lycée*). *Collège* covers the school years referred to as *sixième, cinquième, quatrième* and *troisième*. At the end of *troisième*, pupils take the examination known as the *brevet des colleges*.

Collège d'enseignement général et professionnel: general and vocational college.

Lycée: the state secondary schools where pupils study for their *baccauleuréat* after leaving the *collège*. The *lycée* covers the school years known as *seconde* (15–16-year-olds), *première* (16–17-year-olds) and *terminale* (up to leaving age at 18). The term *lycée professionel* refers to a *lycée* that provides vocational training as well as the more traditional core subjects (*Dictionnaires Le Robert*, 1998, 5th edn, Le Robert & Collins).

References

Ball, S and Van Zanten, A (1998) Logiques du marché et éthiques contextualisées dans les systèmes français et britannique, *Education et Sociétés*, (1), pp 47–71

Ballion, R (1982) *Les Consommateurs d'Ecole*, Stock, Paris

Baudelot, C and Establet, R (1971) *L'Ecole Capitaliste en France*, Maspéro, Paris

Baudelot, C and Establet, R (1989) *Le Niveau Monte*, Ed du Seuil, Paris

Baudelot, C and Establet, R (2000) *Avoir 30 Ans en 1968 et 1998*, Ed du Seuil, Paris

Boudon, R (1973) *L'Inégalité des Chances: La mobilité sociale dans les sociétés industrielles*, A Colin, Paris

Bourdieu, P and Passeron, J-Cl (1964) *Les Héritiers*, Ed de Minuit, Paris

Bourdieu, P and Passeron, J-Cl (1970) *La Reproduction*, Ed de Minuit, Paris

Bouveau, P, Cousin, O and Favre-Perroton, J (1999) *L'Ecole Face aux Parents: Analyse d'une pratique de médiation*, ESF, Paris

Charlot, B, Bautier, E and Rochex, J-Y (1992) *Ecole et Savoirs dans les Banlieues... et Ailleurs*, A Colin, Paris

Cousin, O (1998) *L'Efficacité des Collèges: Sociologie de l'effet établissement*, PUF, Paris

Debarbieux, E (1996) *La Violence en Milieu Scolaire: 1. Etat des lieux*, ESF, Paris

Derouet, J-L (1992) *Ecole et Justice*, Métailié, Paris

Dubet, F (1991) *Les Lycéens*, Ed du Seuil, Paris

Dubet, F and Martuccelli, D (1996) *A l'Ecole*, Ed du Seuil, Paris

Durkheim, E (1958) *Education et Sociologie*, (first edn 1922), PUF, Paris

Durkheim, E (1990) *L'Evolution Pédagogique en France*, (first edn 1938), PUF, Paris

Duru-Bellat, M and Van Zanten, A (1999) *Sociologie de l'Ecole*, 2nd edn, Armand Colin, Paris

INED (1970) *Population et Enseignement*, PUF, Paris

Lelièvre C (1990) *Histoire des Institutions Scolaires (1789/1989)*, Nathan, Paris

Lepoutre, D (1997) *Cœur de Banlieue: Codes, rites et langages*, Odile Jacob, Paris

Payet, J-P (1995) *Collèges de Banlieue*, Méridiens-Klincksiek, Paris

Prost, A (1993) *Education, Société et Politiques: Une histoire de l'enseignement en France, de 1945 à nos jours*, Seuil, Paris

Vallet, L A and Caille, J-P (1996) Les élèves étrangers ou issus de l'immigration dans l'école et le collège français, *Les Dossiers de l'Education et Formation*, (67)

13. Changing cultures and schools in Germany

Manfred Kwiran

Introduction

According to Samuel P Huntington in *The Clash of Civilisations* (1996), history is always the history of cultures. The development of mankind cannot be thought of in any other way. At all times cultures were a possible means of identification (p 49), which were and are always inseparably connected with the history of a nation. Even though the two parts of Germany, East and West, had been forced to develop separately from one another culturally and educationally, and under two entirely different political ideologies, they did share a common history and a common ruin. During the last 50 years of the 20th century each developed its culture and school system apart from the other and this became quite apparent after 1989 and can still be seen and felt at the beginning of the 21st century.

Glaser (1997) has tried to identify changes in the 'German culture' over the period 1950 to 2000. It is a detailed account and evaluation of the history of the two separate states, with an emphasis on post-1989. He shows how difficult it is for the two Germanys to try to understand one another after this long period of separate development. Not everything that had happened culturally and educationally could be rejected by either side. Only the acknowledgement of the 'two' historical developments, and the attempt to understand and respect one another, can help to develop a unifying culture and educational system serving one united nation as part of Europe.

The problems of new technologies and unemployment, and social welfare system questions, are being discussed by all institutions and people of the changing new Germany (Glaser, 1997). Out of their different opportunities to develop culture, one democratically, the other dominated by Soviet ideology, the estimate given in an overview of culture in 1981 speaks of a situation of freedom and democracy, but does present a view of German culture as such: 'Cultural life in the Federal Republic of Germany, marked by a great diversity of forms of expression and inherent natural contradictions, has its roots in centuries of history and German traditions. Developments in the cultural sphere in this country are also a part of European culture, even where political frontiers make divisions apparent' (Fetzer, 1981: 5).

The diversity of culture in Germany today arises from the re-establishment of democratic ideals and the new constitution of 1949, which guaranteed the freedom of art, of scholarship, of research and of teaching. As far as the state is involved at all in the development of culture, the individual states have responsibility for culture. That which has been taken to be freedom since 1949 in West Germany also holds for the Eastern part after reunification:

> Apart from looking after cultural policy directed abroad, the federal authorities have few powers, limited to drawing up general guidelines, which never encroach on the rights of the Länder. The resultant polycentrism within cultural life in the Federal Republic of Germany is a continuation of German traditions going back for centuries. From the Middle Ages onwards, a many-sided cultural existence developed in provincial capitals large and small, in principalities temporal and ecclesiastical, without being focused on a single metropolis. That only changed with establishment of the Reich in 1871, but the member states of the German Reich were, however, still left a large degree of independence in the cultural sphere. (Schmidt, 1981: 5)

The Nazi regime and the East German government forced their own ideological dimension on the development of German culture, and cultural regeneration in West Germany was part and parcel of rapid development in the political, social, economic and scientific areas in the early 1950s:

> The literature of the Fifties, the years of political, economic, and social reconstruction, of rearmament, of joining NATO, and of the Economic Miracle, is characterized by on the one hand a continuation of facing up to the implications of the legacy of fascism (including its literature), and on the other by the attempt to make a literary impact on the present day... The literature of the 1960s, the years of the declining Economic Miracle and the Grand Coalition, of the Vietnam war and the Extra-parliamentary Opposition, was marked in all its forms by far-reaching politization, making literature functional. Literature was meant to serve the political struggle... Politization was followed by a de-politization, which was nevertheless in no way unpolitical. Instead the literature of this period of blocked reforms (70s) became a medium concerned with individual (political) experience even if not with complex political problems any longer. (Fetzer, 1981: 15)

In 1972 there were already 7,200 self-employed authors and in 1977 some 50,000 books were published. Artistic activities flourished as never before and showed an impressive diversity throughout these years. In the early 1980s the Federal Republic alone had over 1,500 museums and 85 city and state theatres with a varied programme not only for adults but also for the young: 'Theatre for children and young people has become of great importance in recent years. The fairy-tale tradition has been slowly shaken off, and adventurous subject matter from our own age is being discovered and performed alongside emancipatory and educational activities' (Schmidt, 1981: 79).

In the Federal Republic of Germany in the early 1980s there were more than 100 orchestras, some working in theatres or opera houses, others being attached to radio or television stations, which have also flourished and are the most important mass media today. 'The great expenditure on "saturation" cultivation of concerts and opera – to which must be added an equally extensive infrastructure of centres for musical training – has led to the flourishing of German musical life and frequent exchanges across the national frontiers' (Wittich, 1981: 79). In addition to the amateur music scene, in the early 1960s the German Music Council was already paying much attention to the development of a network of music schools.

German architecture, which today is comparable on an international level, had tremendous problems after the end of the Second World War after the destruction of most historic buildings. Important cathedrals, churches and representative buildings, opera houses and museums have been reconstructed and restored. Some buildings were reconstructed on the outside and on the inside rebuilt using new materials and for functional needs only. Many of the historic centres of the cities were reconstructed but this took place primarily in the Federal Republic and was neglected in East Germany. At present the reconstruction and restoration of important historical monuments is making great progress in the East, being highly subsidized by the Western states. German culture is at best diverse also because of cultural federalism with many different cultural centres:

> There are no cultural backwaters in Germany. No one must travel hundreds of miles to see good theatre or hear good music. Even in some small towns, one can find valuable libraries or interesting art collections. This goes back to the days when Germany was made up of many principalities whose rulers sought to make their residences centres of culture, and when civic-minded citizens patronized the arts and sciences in their towns. (Kappler, 1996: 483)

When we speak of 'culture' in Germany, we realize that the concept has several meanings. We may describe the characteristics of the people living in Germany, but it is also related to different stages of Germany's history. We may look at the customs, ideas, behaviour and values that influenced and formed its life. It would be asking for too much to go into the smallest details, since it would then be necessary to differentiate still further between the different German states each having its own culture and school system, although there are many similarities between them. In spite of the awareness that each German state, each region, has its own peculiarities, it was only in the last decade of the 20th century that we have been able to speak of a multicultural society, although it cannot be compared with pluralistic societies like the United States or Canada. Nevertheless, one can see different ethnic, religious, economic and geographical subgroups, at least in the larger cities like Munich, Hamburg, Frankfurt and Berlin. The subgroups accept the principles of the dominant culture and the laws, the main language, the economic system and the educational institutions that are shared by all, without eliminating their particular customs and traditions and other aspects of their 'previous' cultural tradition. So when we speak of culture in Germany, we refer to 'the blending of all the composite, generally held, valued ideals of a group sharing a common identity' (Wise, 1990: 174).

Social, cultural and political factors

In an introduction to German culture in 1964 Professor Helmut Arntz described in brief what still holds today:

> Cultural life in present-day Germany is rooted in a rich and abundant past. Bach, Mozart, Beethoven, Brahms and Wagner in music and Goethe, Schiller, Kleist, Heine, Büchner and Hauptmann in literature have their secure place among many other composers, poets, painters and sculptors of the classical, romantic and modern ages. Germans today eagerly study, discuss and share the music, poetry, painting and sculpture of all countries. While much of the 'old Germany' may still be found, there is in addition in the deeper strata of cultural life much that is new and urgent – many a significant reaching out towards a fresh horizon side by side with intellectual need. In the present tensions between East and West, relationships of Germans to neighbouring European cultures – in particular the French – pose a new problem, just as do the attraction and repulsion of Russia and the eastern countries, and the mighty challenge of the American civilization. (Arntz, 1964: 105)

Arntz's evaluation and description point to basic ingredients of the German culture from a perspective of the Federal Republic and the time when West Germany was doing well economically. The ideology and censorship in East Germany and other Soviet satellite states are not mentioned, but the tension between different influences of cultures of other nations is obvious. Arntz also pointed out that in looking at Germany from a cultural viewpoint we would have to note that it is 'trilingual', including terminology not only of Christianity, but also of Marxism and liberal humanism:

> In the Federal Republic, Marxist intellectual thought – apart from interesting contributions to popular education made by the labour movement – has hardly come to the fore since the war. Almost everything that can be said about cultural life may be divided between the various contributions to the humanitarian tradition which is part of the heritage of classical times, the German middle classes, and of Christianity, whose influence has grown extraordinarily since 1945. (Arntz, 1964: 105)

This was surely the result of the situation at the end of the Second World War, when most other institutions apart from the churches had ceased to exist. But we would fail in our estimate, were we to claim that German culture and schools were able to start anew without picking up their traditions of the past before the Nazi regime. Even the most horrible experiences and cultural cut-backs during the Hitler period made the people the more aware of their rich cultural and school tradition. They had been forced to become sensitive to the reform-pedagogical perspectives of the 1920s, of the freedom of art, of the theatre, of life, and even the religious educators like Helmut Kittel 'swore' never to allow an ideology to take hold of education again. So it is true:

> No one would assert today that the end of the war in 1945 marked a completely 'fresh start' for German literature. There was no new beginning without reference to the past, either for the authors of 'inner emigration' (Gottfried Benn, Werner Bergengruen, Hans Carossa, Friedrich Georg Jünger, Ernst Wiechert) or for those returning from exile whether in person or through their works (Bertolt Brecht, Hermann Broch, Alfred Döblin, Heinrich Mann, Thomas Mann, Stefan Zweig). Even for the younger authors of the 'deforestation' (Wolfgang Weyrauch) fascist language and literature were the polemical negative to their poetics of a consciously impoverished language concentrating on the realistic detail... Modern German post-war writing was shaped and determined by the 'literature of the ruins'... poetry was the poetic forms of a literature that sought to come to terms with both the reality of ruins and rubble, and the downfall of ideals and hopes. (Wise, 1981: 12)

Similar, but also different, was the situation after the reunification of the two German states. Many authors and poets, many artists could only be creative by reflecting upon the previous decades under the socialist-communist government. Their reflections and writing brought to the fore not only critical aspects of their former situation, but also a sensitivity for the new without losing the critical perspective that had been won.

Like all cultures, the German culture has been transmitted through social institutions, the schools, the churches and religious groups and the political structures or systems. In the past, the family was one of the most important factors in cultural transmission. 'The basic institution in all cultures is the family. In the nuclear family the traditional pattern is that the children live and are reared under the influence of the father or mother. This type is more prevalent in Western industrial cultures' (Wise, 1990: 174).

The grandparents and relatives who were very important for cultural transmission in an agricultural society now in Germany play almost no role at all, not even in regions where farming remains. The values and expectations with which children grow up are often those imbibed in a one-child family, one-parent (either mother or father) family or with changing parents in a family, where partners change (stepfather, stepmother etc), sometimes more than once for the growing children.

We have already seen the important part that has been played in the culture of Germany by different political movements throughout its history. Political structures and processes changed in such a radical way that the development of culture was strongly restricted, moving from kingship to democracy, being stifled by a dictatorship and then opened to a free democracy after the Second World War. A new opportunity was then opened for the Germans with the reunification of East and West Germany: democracy. In a short period of time many aspects of life of the Federal Republic were shared with the East Germans and a new infrastructure and industry started to pave the way toward the goal of social and economic equality. During the decades of separate ideologies, the culture and people had aligned themselves accordingly. Under Hitler's dictatorship, freedom of speech, the arts, literature, theatre etc was impossible. In a similar way the socialist-communist government allowed only its own philosophy to guide every aspect of daily life.

Religious movements

In a recent statement by the Evangelical Church of Germany on the question of 'Protestantism and culture' (Gestaltung und Kritik, 1999) it was claimed that the church cannot withdraw from culture without forfeiting its very Christian self-understanding. Faith and culture are inseparable and part of the task of the church, which involves the encouragement of life and a critical awareness of suffering. The church must accept a responsible position and participate critically in cultural development. Inculturation is therefore an essential aspect of Christianity, which again and again needs to be filled and defined anew (p 9). In Germany the churches have always been active, sometimes intensely, in changing culture and schools, in the development of society and at other times to a lesser degree (eg during National Socialism or in East Germany).

In the preamble to the Basic Law (constitution of 1949) 'responsibility before God' is explicitly mentioned with state authority and human action being directly related. Article 4 of the Basic Law not only guarantees the free practice of religion, but also challenges the churches to be actively a part of the society: 'Freedom of faith and conscience as well as freedom of creed, religious or ideological, are inviolable. The undisturbed practice of religion shall be guaranteed' (Kappler, 1996: 431). More than 55 million people in Germany are members of a Christian church (28.2 million Protestants, 27 million Roman Catholics). The churches are independent public-law corporations and their social and charitable commitment is an integral part of public life.

Religious institutions as vehicles for transmission of culture show how they themselves are also active in developing and influencing culture through their forms of worship and educational methods as they attempt to transmit their religious faith. This happens by having children and members participate in the activities of their faith community, by their formal nurture and teaching (eg Sunday school etc) and by formal religious education in public schools.

Whereas religion and freedom of worship have had a long tradition in Germany, under National Socialism Hitler and his demagogues steadily forced the churches and their influence toward the periphery of life and used parts of the teachings of the churches to back their policies. In all subjects in school, and also in religious education, the arts, theatrical production, architecture and the film industry, the National Socialists used censorship and control. The National Socialists spoke of cultural politics 'against the un-German spirit' and in 1933 books were openly burnt in Berlin (Pfändtner *et al*, 1996).

After the Second World War and denazification, freedom of speech and the complex cultural and educational system were guaranteed by the Western allies, whereas in East Germany the Soviet regime replaced the National Socialist ideology by their own. East Germany had to serve Communist ideology in every aspect of culture and school life. The aim of the East German education system was to create 'a fully rounded socialist personality' (MacNeill, 1999: 215). Attempts were steadily made also to undermine church institutions by party agents, to influence church decisions and to hinder members of the churches from studying at the university.

For centuries the churches have been very influential in transmitting culture and also in influencing its development. The Evangelical-Protestant Church of Germany, including the Lutheran and Reformed churches, and the Roman Catholic Church are dominant in Germany. Only in recent years have free churches and other small Christian churches (Orthodox Russian, Greek churches, Methodist, Baptist etc) grown in such a way that they have their own particular traditions and customs, contributing in part to the dominant cultural process.

The return of German Jews, and the migration of Russian Jews and those from some of the other East European countries, have led to the Jewish people again having an important voice. Religious sectarian groups, New Age groups, occult groups and youth-culture groups contribute to the growth of plurality in German culture and society.

Religion and values education in German public schools, and to a lesser extent in private schools, has played an important part in developing culture. Religious and values education is guaranteed by the federal constitution and by the education laws of each state. Article 7, section 3, of the German constitution of 1949 declares that religious education must be a regular compulsory subject in the public school at all age levels and is mandatory for all pupils. School children at age 14 can decide for themselves to opt out of the confessionally oriented religion classes and the parents of younger pupils decide for their children but the children must attend values education classes, where the values of the constitution are the guide for the curriculum. The responsibility for the content of confessional religious education rests with the churches, here primarily the Evangelical and Roman Catholic, although confessional Greek and Russian Orthodox religious education is also available. Children of other religious groups, such as sects, can either participate in confessional religious education or in values education. Their own religious development is usually provided by their fellowship groups. A very important movement was started in the late 20th century by different Moslem groups for Islamic religious education in public schools, to be equal to the confessionally oriented religious education of other churches and religions.

After 1945 a new chance was given to German society as well as the schools system. The Western allies encouraged political–societal development toward a federation of states, whereas the Soviet model opted for a one-party-rule and totalitarian state model. These developments resulted in the Federal Republic of Germany and the German Democratic Republic with their different societal orders being reflected in their school and educational systems. In the western part of Germany liberation from the National Socialistic rule and the 're-education' and democratization of society allowed the development of a school system on the basis of a democratic–pluralistic perspective. Walter Stahl in 1961, some 12 years after the Basic Law was introduced in Germany, reached a conclusion that: 'The Germans, old and young, have learned that democracy works. The prestige of Parliament has, in contrast to the Weimar Republic, increased steadily since its establishment' (p 6).

The responsibility for culture and the school system was now again in the hands of the individual states. Several institutions or commissions organized the cooperation of the states, for example the 'permanent conference' of the ministers of culture of the different states. Every two years a report is made on the politics of culture of the states. Here once more the plans and the developments of the individual states are described, comparisons are made and a new impetus given for reforms.

The ministers of culture cooperate closely with the cultural section of the Ministry of Foreign Affairs over cultural agreements with other lands and states. These experts provide recommendations, evaluations and declarations to accompany the development of the education systems: 'A large number of important research centres, among which the Max Planck Society is particularly outstanding, were placed by the "Königstein Agreement" in the joint care of the Länder. The Federal Government has set up a "Department for the Cultural Affairs of the Government of the Federal Republic" in the Ministry of the Interior' (Arntz, 1964: 97).

Quite early in this new Republic the Federal Ministry of Scientific Research was founded (1962). But already in 1953 the Federation [Bund] and the states had appointed a 20-member committee for educational affairs [Deutscher Ausschuss für Erziehungs- und Bildungswesen]. Here the basic design for freedom in education, the arts and sciences was developed with few essential changes, as government changes occurred over the last 50 years. Hitler had in a criminal fashion used culture as an instrument of propaganda against his people. After the war the belief gained momentum that culture and schools should be open equally for everyone (Jonas, 1999: 72–73).

In 1945 the churches were the only remaining institutions and saw to it that religious education was again to have an important place in the public school curriculum. Being critical of the National Socialist influence in religious education, they now called the religious education 'evangelical nurture' (1945–58). Some church leaders and theologians and teachers wanted this school subject to be watchful so that never again could an ideology enter the schools. At the end of the 1950s religious educators emphasized textual work and critical biblical studies and religious education received a hermeneutical emphasis. At the end of the 1960s, it became very obvious that too much attention had been paid to textual work and very little to the interests and abilities of the pupils. Reformers pleaded, in the other school subjects as well, for renewed attention to be given to pupils and their interests. This resulted in a phase of problem-oriented religious education. Since then many other emphases have been added, eg pupil orientation, symbolic religious education, therapeutic religious education, ethics, values education (also within religious education). Today a healthy pluralism allows all these and other perspectives, even a multi-religious or inter-religious aspect and confessional cooperation between the Evangelical and Catholic religious education.

Again and again reforms have been encouraged to modernize school subjects and the school system in line with developments elsewhere as well as technological progress and economic growth, giving education a priority on which the future of state and society will depend (Rupp, 1999: 591ff).

Compulsory education is from 6 to 18 years old with the elementary school to age 14 and thereafter three years of vocational training. In 1969 a new type of school, *Gesamtschule* (5–10, similar to a US high school), was introduced parallel to the *Grundschule* (basic school 1–4), *Orientationschule* (5–6), *Hauptschule* (main school 7–9/10) and *Realschule* (7–10 with possible transfer to *Gymnasium* (7–12/13)*, leading to the entrance to university studies after the successful passing of the 'maturity' examination (*Abitur*). Although the German school system does opt for equal opportunities for all children, children of the workers are under-represented in schools leading to university studies. This tendency also degrades the *Hauptschule*, originally a school for the major part of the population, to become a so-called 'rest school'. Those pupils not going to the *Gymnasium* move into the vocational schools until the age of 18.

Private schools exist by permission of the state and are responsible to it for quality education. The private schools also have to abide by the general educational laws and curriculum, training of teachers, continued education and in-service training regulations of the state. *(Figures indicate school years/grades)

Since the 1950s there has never been a year when the reform of aspects of the German schools has not been discussed. This shows that an awareness of changes within society, changes of technology and changes on a European and international level do lead to a critical review of the educational system. School development, teacher training and teaching itself again and again have faced the challenge of democratic and humanistic education.

One of the best-known German educators in the recent past has been Wolfgang Klafki. In his essay on a democratic and human school, he presents 10 theses underscoring different aspects that are to guide the process of a democratic school (Klafki, 1988: 15ff). In his first thesis he claims that a democratic and human school that wants to be responsible to the coming generation is an institution that allows teachers and pupils a consciousness of the tensions and discrepancies between the constitutional text and its reality. He then adds in other theses that such a school needs to pay adequate attention to the demands, the different interests, the different abilities and the conflicts within society and to help the pupils on the basis of their abilities to achieve their own position in the economic, social, political, cultural and religious sectors. A continuous and open dialogue is necessary in the schools to prepare pupils for democracy and to practise democracy within the schools. Pupils are guided to look for alternatives to that which is. Such a school would encourage and challenge the fantasy, to see the discrepancy between the self-understanding of a society and the reality, to opt for more justice, more equality, more humanity, more solidarity among people, more peace, more common decision making and for greater quality of life. Such a school would help pupils as well as teachers to identify new perspectives for the future, striving more than before to reach such goals, the perspective of peace and ecology and a perspective that includes the needs of all people throughout the world. In such a school experiences must have their place free of anxiety and fear, including models of solidarity to help in the learning process and non-competitive cooperation, where one helps another. Such a school needs to keep contact with the environment outside without losing its critical distance to it. Such a school would pay more attention to the different interests, the different learning dimensions and abilities of the pupils. Such a school would have a rich repertoire of instructional and non-instructional learning situations. Practice, observation and experience, experiments and trials, reflection also upon questions of meaning and thinking about basic questions and the societal existence of the people would have a place. Exemplary learning should involve questions of the life experience of the pupils, but also questions that are of national and international dimension. In recent times, all these different aspects of a humane and democratic school have entered the reform of schools as institutions and are part of every syllabus – content and method – and of every subject area, be it history, language or religion (Wilhelm, 1970: 33ff, 124ff).

Karl Ernst Nipkow, educator and religious educator, recently pointed out that the church is always involved in education. He does not just talk about church and culture, church and education, but 'church as an educational institution'. A democratic school needs to remember the painful past of a country's history and culture, but also be open for religions and confessions and the earnest dialogue between them. All this is an opportunity for our schools, for our pupils and for our culture, and provides help to face the challenges to come (Nipkow, 1999: 116ff).

Legal frameworks

One important step for German culture and schools was the law of 1794, which declared that the schools and universities were state institutions and that the state was responsible for their supervision, even though in practice representatives of the churches took care of this task. This law stated: 'Schools were to be supported by public funds and attendance was compulsory. Children were to attend from the age of five until they had reached a state of learning which the supervisor (regularly the pastor) considered proper for their particular status in society' (Helmreich, 1959: 34). This still holds true to-day.

State compulsory education applied to all people, regardless of which religion. This was especially made clear by the law, the Prussian Allgemeine Landrecht of 1794. Here it was stated that no one should be denied an education (entrance into a school) even if he did not hold the religion of the dominant group, and that no one should be forced to attend religious instruction if he belonged to another group. 'It was not until the law of June 23, 1847, that Jewish schools were recognized in Prussia and entitled to some public support. This was, however, done under the proviso – which was clearly in contradiction to the Allgemeine Landrecht – that attendance at these schools should be limited to Jewish children' (Helmreich, 1959: 45).

Since the Prussian school system was based on the Christian tradition, it was difficult to arrange for Jewish religious instruction. The law of 1847 demanded that the synagogue was to make sure that every Jewish child would have Jewish religious instruction during compulsory school attendance.

Conclusion

We need to differentiate between European and global developments. The European ideas, values and ideals have had both political and economic foundations, whereas global trends have emphasized the international economic possibilities. Cooperation with other countries in cultural and educational exchange and dialogue is normal in Germany. International cultural exchanges are organized mostly by legally independent groups. The Federal Foreign Office is interested to help finance the initiatives as part of Germany's cultural relations.

A multicultural world cannot be avoided, since a global empire is impossible. The safety of the world demands the acceptance of a multicultural world. I think Huntington is correct when he states that, in a clash of cultures, Europe and America need to work together or divided they will be overcome (Huntington, 1996: 551). This also means that the large world cultures with their great heritage in the field of religion, art and literature, philosophy, science and technology, morality and empathy, also need to speak and act in unison.

This will be the essential battle between civilization and barbarism, between culture and non-culture. The influence of Western cultures upon all others of the world cannot be overlooked. It is, however, questionable if Western cultures can keep their dominant role in the future. Perhaps this dominance would even stifle future developments. In this case it would not even be desirable to have such dominance prevail.

The challenges of a global nature demand new answers and the walls between cultures, states and societies begin to weaken. Modern communication systems bring about a new type of global transparency. Pictures, insights, understandings of other cultures, other traditions and cultures flow into one's own cultural context, relativizing, strengthening and enriching one's own culture. The modernizing processes led by Western models of civilization show the pluralism in one's own culture and allow the experience of pluralism of cultures on a global level. A global culture would not be desirable, or possible. It is more likely that the developing nations in the globalization process, via economic, technology or educational competition, will also have their legitimate part in showing their cultural influence. Together, the cultures of all countries can shape the future of our globe, hopefully for the benefit of all.

The question of culture is the key and the dialogue about culture is inseparably tied to the dialogue of the religions. On a global perspective for a just, peaceful coexistence of the churches, cultures and religions, and more, for a united effort for the well-being of all, all participants have their legitimate part to play and need to work together. The former chancellor Helmut Schmidt wrote in an article about the rights and responsibilities of individuals and of nations. He emphasized that, since the end of the Soviet bloc and the reopening of China, the number of people involved in the open world economy has almost doubled. In the new millennium, nations and their economies will be more dependent upon one another than ever before, but this globalization will also lead to previously unknown competition. The temptation to influence competition by power politics for one's own benefit will gain momentum. If politicians, nations and the leaders of religions fail to learn to respect one another's religious, cultural and civilization heritage, if people will not learn to hold the two categorical imperatives of freedom and responsibility in balance, then peace will be in danger and the global political net and the social–economic well-being of nations may be in trouble. Therefore, we need an inter-religious and international conception, 50 years after the Universal Declaration of Human Rights, to speak of human responsibilities. In Germany, rights are more emphasized than responsibilities.

The need to avoid a clash of cultures and civilizations has encouraged politicians of the five continents to devise a draft of a universal declaration of human responsibilities (Schmidt, 1997: 17–18). The first article of this general declaration states that all human beings, no matter what their gender, ethnic heritage, social status, political persuasion, language, age, nation or religion, have the duty to deal with all humans in a human way. In the preamble it was also stated that global problems demand global solutions. This can only be reached when all cultures and societies respect one another's ideas, values and norms (p 18). International cultural exchange, collaboration and true cultural dialogue among nations and people are today more important than ever before. An ethic of responsibility and a radical self-responsibility are needed to face future challenges. This means that a responsible consciousness and a corresponding feeling need to develop more and more to change culture and education in a pluralistic world (Nipkow, 1998: 175). Science cannot take away our fear of the future challenges, of the unknown, but it can help us to trust our spiritual and technical strength, which are necessary for the solving of coming problems. Our educational and cultural endeavours can help us and especially the young generation to have the courage and knowledge necessary to confront future tasks as we keep on building a human civilization for the welfare of all people (Markl, 1999: 203ff). 'Learning in times of globalization' for UNESCO includes four aspects: 1) learning how to acquire knowledge; 2) learning to act and use it; 3) learning to live with one another, and having respect for people of other cultures; 4) learning for life, for the total development of each individual. Global learning will have to provide a sensitivity and ability for the welfare of all people throughout the world, always opting for sustainable development (Gugel and Jäger, 1999).

References

Arntz, H (1964) *Germany in Brief*, 3rd edn, Press and Information Office of the Federal Government of Germany, Bonn

Fetzer, G (ed) (1981) *Cultural Life in the Federal Republic of Germany*, Heinz Moos Verlag, Inter Nationes, München, Bonn

Gestaltung und Kritik (1999) Zum Verhältnis von Protestantismus und Kultur im neuen Jahrhundert, Evangelischer Pressedienst, Frankfurt a M

Glaser, H (1997) *Deutsche Kultur 1945–2000*, Hanser Verlag, München, Wien

Gugel, G and Jäger, U (1999) *Welt... Sichten: Die Vielfalt des Globalen Lernens*, Verein für Friedenspädagogik, Tübingen e V

Helmreich, E C (1959) *Religious Education in German Schools*, Harvard University Press, Cambridge, Mass

Huntington, S P (1996) Kampf der Kulturen (The clash of civilisations), in *Die Neugestaltung der Weltpolitik im 21. Jahrhundert*, Europa Verlag, München, Wien

Huntington, S P and Kampf, K (1996) *Die Neugestaltung der Weltpolitik im 21. Jahrhundert*, Europa Verlag, München, Wien

Jonas, P (1999) Elitäre Kultur für die ganze Öffentlichkeit, in *Eliten und Demokratie*, ed M G Dönhoffe, H Markl and R von Weizsäcker, Siedler Verlag, Berlin

Kappler, A (1996) *Facts of Germany*, Societas Verlag, Frankfurt

Klafki, W (1988) Thesen über eine demokratische und humane Schule, in *Ist die Schule noch zu retten? Plädoyer für eine neue Bildungsreform*, ed A Dannhäuser *et al*, Beltz Verlag, Weinheim, Basel

Kwiran, M (1987) *Religionsunterricht in USA – ein Vergleich*, Peter Lang, Frankfurt a M

MacNeill, D (1999) State education and religion: comparing three European approaches – England, France and Germany, in *Informationes Theologiae Europae*, ed U Nembach, Peter Lang, Frankfurt a M

Markl, H (1999) Die Herausforderung durch das Unbekannte, in *Eliten und Demokratie*, ed M G Dönhoff, H Markl and R von Weizsäcker, Siedler Verlag, Berlin

Nipkow, K E (1998) *Bildung in einer Pluralen Welt*, Chr Kaiser/Gütersloher Verlagshaus, Gütersloh

Nipkow, K E (1999) Schule in der Demokratie und der Beitrag der Kirche, *Zeitschrift für Pädagogik und Theologie*, (2), 116 ff

Pfändtner, B *et al* (1996) *Deutschland zwischen Diktatur und Demokratie: Weltpolitik im 20. Jahrhundert*, C C Buchners Verlag, Bamberg

Rupp, H F (1999) Schule/Schulwesen, in *Theologische Realenzyklopädie*, Bd 30, S, Walter de Gruyter, Berlin

Schmidt, D N (1981) Theatre, in *Cultural Life in the Federal Republic of Germany*, ed G Fetzer, Heinz Moos Verlag, Inter Nationes, München, Bonn

Schmidt, H (1997) Zeit, von den Pflichten zu sprechen, *Die Zeit*, (41), 3 October

Stahl, W (1961) The present status of democracy in West Germany, *Education for Democracy in West Germany*, Frederick A Praeger, New York

Wilhelm, T (ed) (1970) *Demokratie in der Schule*, Vandenhoeck & Ruprecht, Göttingen (see also, for the development within religious education in the German context of political changes and challenges, the basic texts presented by K E Nipkow and F Schweitzer (ed) (1994) *Religionspädagogik*, vols 2/1 and 2/2, Chr. Kaiser/Gütersloher Verlagshaus, Gütersloh)

Wise, F F (1981) in *Cultural Life in the Federal Republic of Germany*, ed G Fetzer, p 174, Heinz Moos Verlag, Inter Nationes, München, Bonn

Wise, F F (1990) Culture, in *Encyclopedia of Religious Education*, ed I V Cully and K B Cully, Harper & Row, San Francisco

Wittich, G (1981) Music, in *Cultural Life in the Federal Republic of Germany*, ed G Fetzer, Heinz Moos Verlag, Inter Nationes, München, Bonn

14. Changing cultures and schools in Japan

Yoshiko Nomura

Introduction

The relation between education and the development of values has been closely sustained in Japan since ancient times. In fact, education has always reflected these values, which in turn were virtually synonymous with education. In the first of the so-called 'Seventeen Articles', Japan's first constitution, which was promulgated in 604 ce by Prince Shotuku, it was proclaimed that 'Harmony shall be revered'. The importance of unity and harmony based on Buddhist thought was thus presented as national policy. Accordingly, formal education was initiated in the hall of Horyuji, a temple dedicated to education, erected in 607.

The imperial court at Yamato sent three missions to Sui China in the 7th century and a dozen or more to Tang China during the two centuries that followed, to study the classics and absorb Chinese culture. Confucianism and Buddhism introduced in this way from the continent had a profound effect on Japanese ethics and morality, which are the cornerstones of education. The fundamental nature of Japanese culture continued along these lines with little change as history swept around it, and was reflected in the education prescript promulgated on the basis of the Meiji Constitution more than 10 centuries later.

I wish to emphasize that prior to the introduction of foreign thought, there was an indigenous spirituality, an animism that could be identified as a national characteristic nurtured by the climate of the country, which provided the basis for accepting and absorbing it.

This ancient animism continues to flow as an undercurrent of the culture even today in the way of thinking and enduring spirituality of the Japanese people, conscious as they still are of being an intrinsic and symbiotic part of the natural world. The spirit of animism is the consistent and unchanging essence that enables us Japanese to accept, not reject, foreign and heterogeneous cultures and dissolve them, as it were, into our own cultural bloodstream, creating our own multi-layered culture that makes up our national constitution. It is this spirit that underpins and pervades the foundations of Japan's history, culture and education.

Characteristics of Japanese education

There are two principal characteristics of Japanese education having this spirituality as a basis. The first characteristic is that the object of education has always been holistic, with moral education at its centre. The prime objective of all areas of education, not just formal education but in domestic service, learning of manners, apprenticeship in trades and the arts (as well as the martial arts) and so on, was in training a person to become a good human being. The other characteristic was the diffusion and equalization of education.

The earliest anthology of poems, the *Manyo-shu*, is a collection of poems selected from a wide range of poets, from members of the imperial family to military men and ordinary people, during the period that spans the 4th to the 8th centuries. Their eloquent sensitivities and poetical imagination as well as the outstanding works of women as literary figures that added to the court culture in the 10th and 11th centuries speak of the equality of education and cultural excellence achieved regardless of sex, social rank, family or region.

The literary masterpieces of women of the Heian period (794–1185) may be quite unique compared with their counterparts of the same historical period anywhere. The emergence of outstanding women writers such as Murasaki Shikibu, who wrote *The Tale of Genji* (*Genji Monogatari*), identified as the oldest full novel in the world and one of the finest, and Sei Shonagon, the author of *Pillow Talk* (*Makura no Soshi*), described as a work combining both sophistication and charm, characterize the maternal nature of Japanese society.

Fruits of the continuous importance given to education are to be seen in the high levels of culture reflected in the literature of the Kamakuru and Muromachi periods that followed, such as *waka* (31-syllable poems), *renka* (45-syllable poems) and *haihai* (*haiku*), as likewise in *Noh* and *Kyogen* and the arts of the tea ceremony and flower arrangement.

The 260 years of the Edo period (1603–1867) were marked by what would have been an unusually long period of peace anywhere. During this time the shogunate government's Confucian school, called Shohei Ko, and 300 other clan schools established by the feudal lords, came into being. In addition, there were over 50,000 private and temple schools devoted to the education of the people. Sailors could not become master seamen unless they qualified in reading and arithmetic. In the large cities of Edo (Tokyo) and Osaka, people read newspapers printed on baked tiles to keep up with current events. Education was spread from the ruling class to the common people. Education was thus widespread in Japan long before the establishment of a modern school system, unthinkable perhaps in societies where the level of education often reflected class.

Changing times and educational reform: three major changes in Japan

It is possible to detect a great cause-and-effect relationship between education and the cultural and other historical circumstances of a given period. A period demands an education appropriate to the nature and requirements of that period, and education in turn helps to form the period. In its contribution to this ongoing relationship, education has played a pivotal role in human history.

At a time of revolutionary change, education necessarily undergoes a momentous corresponding transformation: and the reverse is also true. Whenever an educational system is reformed it is a long time before society is affected and before all its ramifications are felt. All of us are made painfully aware that humankind faces unprecedented changes in the 21st century, as evidenced by the violent social convulsions and tumultuous world events that we learn of daily.

The Meiji Restoration – from temple education to school education

With the Meiji Restoration, the military regime of the Tokugawa shoguns was brought to an abrupt end, ushering in a constitutional monarchy. As the nation took steps towards modernization, education underwent a major change, namely it shifted from temple school education to school education.

On 2 August 1872, the Meiji government promulgated an act introducing Japan's first modern school system, abolishing what might be called the voluntary education system that had been run by the clans, private educators and temples. And in accordance with Western school systems, free education was provided at the primary level for all citizens. As a result, Japan's level of illiteracy became the lowest in the world.

This required the state to participate directly in education, and as a consequence school-centred education was introduced throughout the country. As described, while the fundamental philosophy of education since ancient times had been based on a national policy, the actual education of the common people was left to their discretion and in practice took on varied forms not unlike lifelong education as we understand it today. However, the transition to modern school education created a strong relationship between education and the state.

In November of the same year at the same time as the inauguration of the new school system, military conscription was initiated, suggesting that Japan had embarked on its modernization not only with the pen but with the sword as well. In the drive to become a rich country with a strong army and, in imposing on its citizens three national duties of compulsory education, conscription and taxation, we may glimpse the impatience of the country to awaken from its long isolation and to catch up with the world.

Modernization took place amidst domestic turmoil and a climate of external threat. The military rule that had lasted for about 700 years since the opening of the Kamakura shogunate in the 12th century had given way to the restoration of the imperial reign. Within its borders Japan was experiencing a historic upheaval with all the adjustments that attended the resumption of constitutional monarchy following the dissolution of the feudal system under the shogunate, while a raging storm of colonization was engulfing the peoples of Asia and Africa, threatening their survival.

Japan, however, not only escaped the humiliation of colonization but also was able to maintain the dignity of an independent state through a combination of determined leadership and rapid progress to achieve security and prosperity. In this feat I see manifested the accumulated result of our cultural conditioning and educational traditions.

Defeat in the Second World War – loss of the fundamental spirit of education

A serious collapse of Japan's traditional spirituality was brought about by the defeat in the Second World War. The defeat and subsequent occupation by the forces of a foreign country were an unprecedented experience for Japan in its nearly 2,000 years of history as a nation.

It was the victorious occupying power that imposed on the country the far-reaching educational reform that followed the ending of the war. The school system was divided into six years for primary and three each for junior and senior high schools. The most radical aspect of the reform was 'the drawing ink over lines in textbooks', which amounted to censorship and repudiation of elements now disapproved of. What had been taught up to that time as right was now considered wrong; what was once good was evil. It was nothing less than the eradication of education as we had known it and the consequent uprooting of our identity as individuals and as a nation.

The principles of Japan's traditional education were drawn from the spiritual lessons of Buddhism, Confucianism and Shintoism, and consisted of a holistic approach to instruction focused on nurturing a spirituality based on morality and ethics. This objective, which was the province of the church in the West, was the essence of all public education and every form of private study. For this reason, its eradication from the curriculum dealt a blow that in a Western context might be analogous to liquidating the church. The seeds sown at this time have had a lasting effect on education to this day. This, to me, is the greatest tragedy of the defeat in the war.

After regaining independence with the conclusion of the San Francisco Peace Treaty, Japan promulgated a Peace Constitution that contains in Article 9 a renunciation of war for all time. In accordance with the new constitution, a Fundamentals of Education Act was enacted dedicated to fostering the personal development and dignity of the individual so that s/he may contribute to peace and the welfare of the society, the country and the world.

The revival, however, of the lost traditional spirituality continues to be a challenge. I am frequently asked why I clamour for a drastic reform of Japanese education when it is commanding favourable attention worldwide. My reply is that education does not produce an immediate effect. What achievement there is today is the accumulation of the past, not the result of current education. What worries me is the result, much of which remains to be seen, of the rootless system of education adopted after the war. The loss of the fundamental spirit of education cherished from ancient times can be likened to sailing rudderless in the open seas. It is an education without a fixed course. It is the future that I worry about, when the results of the present system of education make themselves felt.

Having lost the authenticity preserved by virtue of the profound relations education had with history and culture, Japan in the post-war period was a nation without spiritual values. It was washed away without the life-jacket of spirituality in the current of which Western rational thinking and scientific education had become the mainstream.

With diligence and sincerity the farming community rescued the nation from the brink of starvation. Under an economic policy predicated on production and material values they succeeded in achieving a dramatic economic success. However, without confidence and direction in life, the older people were bewildered by their contemporary life and uncertain about the future in the face of the rapid changes in their lives brought about by the scientific revolution of the 20th century.

It was in this social climate that children were raised by adults who had no sense of self or redeeming spirituality but only economic values to depend on. They grew up with values that encouraged self-centred egoism and ambition for material possessions, money, status and honours and, mirroring their parents and teachers in their values and attitudes to life, a total lack of discipline, rules, modesty and morality.

This is what I mean when I say children are the reflection of adult society.

The scientific revolution of the 20th century – from school education to lifelong education

The third period of change occurred as a result of the scientific revolution of the latter part of the 20th century. This time its scope was global and it forced an unprecedented change in values and attitudes. In 1988, the Ministry of Education published a white paper titled *The Present Status and Future of Educational Reform*. It first pointed out the need to correct the predominant emphasis placed on academic records. It also stated categorically the need to shift away from school-centred education, emphasizing that school should be treated as one of the elements in a lifelong education. It marked, from the policy standpoint, a departure from school education to a system of lifelong learning.

This was a step in the right direction, but the reality is far from what was envisaged. The concept of lifelong learning intended to correct the overemphasis on both academic records and school-centred education is merely treated as running parallel with school education without much change in the latter's conventional preference for academic qualifications.

It is asking too much of a closed and narrowly defined school education system to address all issues of human existence in a period fraught with changes. After all, the school system has been with us a mere 100 or 300 years, depending on whether one includes clan and temple schools during the feudal period. In contrast, lifelong integrated education stands for the principles that have been created with the large mission of addressing the inevitable and disrupting consequences of the scientific revolution.

Towards a value-creating education

My original motives in starting volunteer educational activities on the principle of lifelong integrated education were sparked by what I saw as the tragedy of youth growing up in Japanese society during the rapid economic growth of the early 1960s. As I grappled with each individual case, I began to see that the root of the problems of youth went far deeper than I had at first supposed. These young people were the victims of an adult society, which in turn was a victim of the rapid social changes brought about by the scientific revolution we were living in with far greater implications than those of the Industrial Revolution of the 18th century. And I could see we were witnessing the onset of social changes of historic proportions.

The tragedy of Japanese youth was being at the crest of a wave of complex factors being experienced for the first time by humankind. The unhappiness of the young in Japan is not theirs alone. It is now a common phenomenon alike in advanced and developing societies. By making commodities of them, treating them as if they were part of a machine and evaluating them by their monetary achievements, they have been robbed of human sensitivities. Their loss of ethical and moral values has resulted in their dehumanization and loss of humanity.

This worldwide pathological phenomenon poses educational challenges shared by all who live in the 21st century. There is, I believe, a strong rationale for making the 1960s a turning-point in education around the world.

Education is primarily a process of nurturing and drawing out the human qualities with which every person is born. At the same time, it has the historical role of contributing to the creation of new cultures and civilizations and setting the direction of a period in time. In this context the present narrow framework of existing school education cannot possibly deal with the milliards of issues faced by human society today.

The turbulent times we live in that are the cause of individual unhappiness and the collapse of social standards around the world necessitate a totally new vision that will transform existing concepts of education. The Coperni-can-scale revolution required of today's education must inject an entirely different dimension into its system, content and methodology. It is for this reason that I believe the concept of lifelong integrated education has emerged to provide the comprehensive and integrating principles now so urgently needed in the field of global educational reform.

Lifelong integrated education, born out of the demand of our times, has not been understood in its full significance. The focus in developing countries is on informal education emphasizing the need to improve literacy. In the industrial countries the focus is on recurrent education and vocational retraining. In Japan it has taken the form of cultural refinement courses offered at various cultural centres. In other words, in many countries, lifelong integrated education is simply acknowledged at the same level as the opportunities for adult education that follow school education. However, education in a globalizing society should not only fulfil individual needs; it must respond to social needs. It must have a cosmic mission to meet the needs of our times and that of humankind as a whole.

Changing culture and unchanging values

Most important in considering education in these turbulent times is to recognize that there exist unchanging universal values. At a time when all at last must learn to respect the differences and peculiarities that distinguish the various nations and cultures and their histories and seek ways to coexist, what we need most at the heart of education is to acknowledge and accept the universal and unchanging values.

As seen earlier, the loss and breakdown of humanity is a worldwide phenomenon, a tragedy common to all. Terrorism, violence, social injustice, pollution of every type, depletion of natural resources, and nuclear proliferation that threatens the very survival of our kind and the rest of life on earth are but some of the dangers shared by all.

The irreducible, universally indispensable values are the sacredness of individual lives and of the totality of the cosmos, of which our small planet and we who live on it are a part. It is their dignity and survival that must be placed at the heart of education as unchanging values to be respected beyond all differences between us.

Direction for global development of education

It is now the scientific and material civilizations that are leading the world. These civilizations have clearly reached their limits. Internally, humanity is threatened and externally the ecological and cosmic systems are being destroyed. I believe that the world is in search of a new philosophy. In the 17th century René Descartes developed his theory of the dualism of mind and body in his attempt to find a clue in the eternal search to understand the human being and the spirit that inhabits him. This was the basis on which modern science was developed. The sciences have shed light on the natural order and natural law and enabled mankind to rule nature and to enjoy unprecedented abundance, convenience and efficiency.

The grave mistake of modern science that sprang from this theory of dualism was to seize upon the natural world as a mere object and to fail to take into account the equally indisputable fact that humans are also part of the object perceived, the natural world. Herein lies the ignorance and foolishness of modern human beings, who are virtually passing a sentence of death upon themselves.

In initiating a new education I sought to draw principles from the structure and order of the natural world and the monistic concept of the unity of mind, body and environment, based on the oriental view of nature that has been my own belief and term of reference for all things. In order to restore education to its original purpose for those whom it was meant to benefit, human beings designed a framework for its reform by placing the human being at its heart and examined the relationship between the person and the natural world. Rather than studying human beings through their own eyes I made observations from the perspective of the natural and cosmic worlds that give and sustain life. And by identifying the place of the human being as an intrinsic part of the natural order within the earthly and cosmic structures, and by emphasizing the unique value of each person as the first principle of education, I have developed the Nomura Theory of Lifelong Integrated Education. It was in order to put this theory into practice that I founded the private volunteer educational organization that operates under that name. The circle now covers the whole of Japan and has expanded its network beyond its shores to 80 countries, transcending all ethnic, religious and ideological differences. We now have overseas branches in Germany, India, Egypt and Palestine.

I am convinced that the new education based on the unity and integration of mind, body and environment that transcends dualism and enables humanity to coexist with all things in the cosmic and natural worlds will make a huge contribution to the creation of a new civilization.

If the Renaissance meant the rebirth of humanity that had been buried under the yoke of the church, the contemporary renaissance, the rebirth of human beings, will be their liberation from the grave of material and machine civilization, and from their own insatiable greed, ignorance and arrogance. It will be a rebirth from the pit of their own foolishness at allowing themselves to be enslaved by material goods and machines and losing themselves so utterly that unwittingly they may end by pushing the button that will send us all unto oblivion.

I pray for the rebirth of humankind and its rescue from its arrogant surrender to the illusion that it is acting on behalf of all creation to rule nature and other people. I pray too for a renaissance that will enable them to master science and to coexist with all non-human living things, with nature and transcendent existence; and for a rebirth of mercy and wisdom.

The development of global education should have the following objectives:

- the renaissance of humankind;
- the establishment of an order for coexistence;
- the creation of a new civilization.

My prayers are for the revitalization of the universal values found in Japanese history and culture within and beyond the nation that nurtured them for the future of our entire global family.

15. Changing cultures and schools in the People's Republic of China: tradition, the market and educational change

Kai-ming Cheng

Introduction

China is often identified as a society of collectivism and this contributed to the extreme collectivism during the Cultural Revolution (1966–76). China is also known for its traditional values of education. Scholarship has always been something treasured by society and has contributed to the rapid expansion of education in the two decades of reform after the Cultural Revolution. However, it is exactly that reform that has given rise both to a growth in individualism and to education having an economic dimension. Both developments have gradually eroded the traditional culture of education.

Culture of collectivism

Writers in various disciplines (eg Hofstede, 1980, 1991; Kim *et al*, 1994; Hsu, 1985) tend to use China and Japan as typical cases of collective societies. Typically, in such a society, individuals are seen to be born into a social configuration in which they occupy respective distinct positions. Such a social configuration is also hierarchical in nature. Fei Hsiao-tung, a student of Malinovsky, who is still seen as *the* pioneering anthropologist in China, observed in 1947[1] that Chinese society is a *hierarchy configuration*, as compared with the *group configuration* of the West. In the former, individuals are highly conscious of their own position in the society, are very conscious of the social expectations and behave according to such expectations. In the latter, individuals are born independent, and form social associations contingent on interests and needs. This contributes to the observations that, compared with people in other cultures, the Chinese submit more readily to rituals and disciplines (Redding, 1990), which reflect social norms that bind individuals. They care more about grace or 'face' (Ho, 1976) and hence are more vulnerable to social pressure. Chinese exist only as part of the social fabric, and hence they seek to solve problems through social relations (*guanxi*) (King, 1991) rather than legitimate procedures. As such, they are therefore more concerned with relationship building and reciprocity (Yan, 1996) as a way of enhancing participation in the social network.

Hsu concludes that the notion of *self* that is understood in the West is non-existent in Chinese societies. The Chinese *self* is not independent, but is a *small self* that submits to the benefits of a *large self* (Hsu, 1985). Such a *self* is a relative concept, such that individuals, families, the nation and the entire world are consecutively a smaller self within the next larger self. There is a general framework of conceptualizing personal developments along the paths of *cultivating the self, harmonizing the family, managing the nation* and *harmonizing the world* as the legitimate vision of a person's development.

During Mao's era, the collective paradigm was reinforced in a Marxist framework, where citizens were expected to see themselves as brothers and sisters of the proletariat, with individuals expected to submit themselves to the state for the development of the nation. Hofstede (1991: 40) identifies the irony that 'Mao Tse-tung tried to wipe out Confucianism but in the meantime his own rule contained Confucian elements', a conclusion that concurs with that of many analysts in China.

However, Hofstede hastens to add that collectivism does not mean a negation of the individual's well-being or interest; it is implicitly assumed that maintaining the group's well-being is the best guarantee for the individual (Hofstede, 1980: 216, quoting Ho, 1978: 2). This is very much the basic argument for the planned system in Chinese socialism. As is highlighted in a basic 'self-cultivation' reader in the high times of the Great Leap Forward during the late 1950s:

> Our state fully protects the common interests of the nation and the society. Such common interests are the foundations for fulfilling the interests of the people as well as the individuals... Collectivism is the only correct principle for handling the relations between individuals and the collective. The collectivistic principle requires to place collective interests in the primary position; individual interests are secondary. When there is a conflict between individual and collective interests, the former should submit to the latter. (Hubei Department of Education, 1958: 111–13)

Culture for education

In such a hierarchical configuration, education plays an essential role. Education is the means, and the only means, to achieve mobility in the hierarchy. To become a scholar is the only way to change one's social status. If one wanted to identify any consensual national hero in ancient China, it would be a scholar. Over the dynasties, the folklore, as presented in novels, operas and storytelling, is largely about how poor scholars worked through difficult circumstances until they became champions in the civil examination at the imperial court. Typically, the scholar went through '10 years by the cold window' – '10 years' as a matter of long-term perseverance, and 'cold window' (ie without heating) to highlight the unfavourable environments.

Formal civil examination started in the Shui dynasty in around AD 606, but similar arrangements had emerged a few hundred years before that. The system could be analytically described as follows (see Liu, 1996; Huang, 1992; Miyazaki, 1963):

- The civil examination system was designed for recruitment into officialdom.
- In ancient China, joining officialdom was the only path of upward social mobility.
- The reward to success in the examination was tremendous. Annual champions were often appointed to high positions in government ministries, or were sent back to head local governments. Luckier ones married into the royal family.
- It was a simple system. All that mattered in the system was the examination. There were normally three tiers of examinations. Local examinations sifted and selected candidates for higher-level examinations. The lucky few sat the central examination at the imperial court.
- There was a simple curriculum: the *Four Books* and the *Five Classics*. The examination was simply on the interpretation of the classical writings in the context of government.
- It was a low-cost system. The classical writings were commonly available at trivial prices. It involved no practical work. It was all about reading, thinking and writing. It was affordable by any family.
- It was a highly individualized endeavour. Although at different times there were 'schools' to prepare the potential scholars collectively for the examination, schools were never a necessity.
- The examination itself was simple. It involved mainly the writing of an essay. The essay was an interpretation of the classics in the context of public administration or national development strategies. The candidates were judged according to the ideas expressed in the essay. Finalists were sometimes interviewed by the emperor.
- It was also an open system. Nobody was debarred from taking the examination. It therefore enjoyed high legitimacy as a fair system for social mobility. Indeed, as is mentioned earlier, the success stories from poor families are the favourites of folklore.
- It was, none the less, a tight system. It was rigorous and strict. There were tight security systems for the examination. In some cases, candidates worked in closed cabins (see descriptions in Miyazaki, 1963). Plagiarism and cheating in civil examinations were seen as serious crimes. Examinations were exceptionally 'clean' in a society that often suffered from serious corruption. That further enhanced the legitimacy of examinations.

Solomon (1971) has a very vivid description of how, in a traditional Chinese society, a child's life is governed by the honour of the family, and how the child's success in examinations is symbolic of the family glories.

All this helps explain the high values the Chinese place on education. However, a second look may also reveal that the notion of *education* in such a context carries with it a particular meaning that may not be shared by other societies, particularly those in the West. The following is an attempt to summarize such an observation:

- 'Education' in ancient China was assigned a special meaning that was explicitly related to social mobility. Social mobility was almost the only aim of 'education'. As is noted by Schirokauer (1976: 7): 'In traditional China, government service was by far the most honourable and, in every sense, the most worthwhile occupation; and... the system of civil service examination stood alone as the preferred route to success'.
- 'Education' in traditional China was not related to 'knowledge learning' as is common in the West (Gardner, 1984). The meaning of education was inherited from the times of Confucius when 'education' meant socialization into rituals and ceremonies. Education was not about knowledge and skills. There was at times the teaching of knowledge-based subjects such as arithmetic and medicine, but these were seen as peripheral.
- It is not surprising that motivations for learning, even now in Chinese society (and in Japanese society), are basically extrinsic in nature, as has been identified by contemporary psychologists (see Lynn, 1988; Biggs, 1996). Enthusiasm for learning was not driven by intrinsic interests in discovery and understanding of reality. It was driven by extrinsic incentives such as praise or a reprimand from the parents, the aspiration for a higher social status and/or university entrance, the wish to leave the rural villages and the like.
- Examination success was not a matter of right and wrong. Rather, it was how the interpretation of the classics met with the approval and appreciation of the examiner, sometimes the emperor. There was therefore a subtle expectation of conforming to authority. The examination trained respect for authority rather than objectivity. It trained political sensitivity rather than analytic capacity.
- It was open to all, and was indeed seen as fair to all, although in the final analysis, success belonged to the few. There were only a few prizes for the massive number of competitors. There were indeed opportunities for social mobility, but the gate to such opportunities was understood to be narrow. Hence, although effort paid off, it was on a competitive basis. There was no guaranteed success for hard work.

Education in contemporary China

Schools in China were an imported idea and this Chinese heritage was carried forward to the contemporary school system. However, the school system in China is relatively young. Although there were scattered 'schools' in most of the ancient dynasties, a national system of schools was established only at the turn of the 20th century. The system was modelled on German schools in the beginning, but was also influenced by the Japanese system that came about as part of the Meiji Restoration. In the 1920s, the Chinese school system was also influenced by US thought through Dewey and his disciples.

During the last years of the Qing Dynasty (ie the first decade of the 20th century), reform movements prevailed. The basic thinking in those days could be best summarized by the motto, 'the Chinese framework as the main body, a Western framework for utility'. It could be interpreted as a pragmatic use of the Western model to serve Chinese purposes, or to use the Western skeleton to support the Chinese flesh.

The school system was established in such a context. Before such schools were established, education was limited to private tuition. Typically, a private tutor was employed by a large family and was responsible for the education of all the children. Reciting and understanding the classics was still the basic activity in the small classes, although arithmetic was sometimes added because of the increasing importance of commerce. The new schools adopted a Western curriculum and they began to teach subjects such as geometry, algebra, trigonometry, physics, chemistry and geography, all those knowledge-based subjects that were never part of education in ancient China. In terms of structure, they were not very different from schools in the West. However, there was the conspicuous addition of social elements in the curriculum and school life. Even in their early days, schools in China had an unambiguous emphasis on *moral education*, sometimes even with a subject known as moral education, ethics or life education. But moral education was inculcated more through school life, using discipline as a fundamental element, sometimes accompanied by military training, student unions, weekly themes on moral virtues and so forth.

The establishment of schools had given more people the opportunity to study in groups. The first schools in China also inherited the traditional ideas of social mobility and attempted to extend it to the grass roots. Schools were never conceived as places for the elite.

Such a paradigm of schooling lasted for much of the 20th century. School education was relatively developed in the first half of the century, and with the establishment of the Communist regime school education spread into the rural areas. As in other socialist nations after World War II, China developed a fairly sophisticated system of education, and without the rapid growth of the population China could have achieved universal primary education in the 1960s.

Development in education was disrupted in the 1960s when China underwent a period of de-schooling during the Cultural Revolution (1966–76). In most of these years, universities were closed down, or functioned as training grounds for Mao's ideology. Secondary and primary schools were reopened after the initial years of turmoil but suffered from an ideological reinterpretation of the curriculum and teaching, and normal learning was resumed only at the end of the Cultural Revolution.

The disasters during the Cultural Revolution, however, served as a catalyst for the rapid reconstruction of the education system immediately after its end. Universities reappeared in 1977, and universities in China have replaced the imperial examination as the target goal for studies. There was also a rapid development of basic education and there has been a nationwide campaign for universalizing nine-year basic education, although this has been more successful at the primary than the secondary level. A number of traditional beliefs about education still remain, however, and some of them are supported by the system. The following is a summary of the situation in the 1990s.

Education, especially the university, is seen as the gateway to social success and social mobility. In the socialist system, citizens in China are divided into *urban* and *rural* household registrations. This was established in the 1950s and was seen as an effective way of containing unwanted drift of the rural population to cities. This has become ineffective since the 1980s, because food is marketed and any control of food (which was the main means of control) has become ineffective. Even in the 1990s, people with a rural registration remained in a rural status (and hence not officially employable and allowed to enjoy urban benefits) unless they had graduated from university or senior secondary technical schools (known as specialized schools). The only other alternative to gain mobility is retirement from the military, which is not always favoured. Education, therefore, is still the most legitimate way of changing one's status from rural to urban, and the change carries with it lifelong benefits such as welfare and children's education.

Even among the urban population, education plays an overt screening function. Graduates of universities and senior secondary technical schools are given the status of 'cadre'. Those with lesser educational qualifications remain as 'workers'. These are the only two categories of citizens in the Chinese system who enjoy a different economic and political status. Hence the mobility function of formal schooling is not only a matter of belief and general practice. It is also legitimized by the employment structure. The reform in recent decades has blurred the actual difference between the two categories, but the majority of people who are employed in state enterprises are still classified as urban.

Parents are enthusiastic about the education of their children. China is known for its high enrolment ratio in basic education. Primary enrolment is around 98 per cent (Ministry of Education, 1999). The remaining 2 per cent represents the small pockets of remote or mountainous areas (where access is a problem) and the minority communities (where the traditional values do not apply). All studies seem to agree that parents have taken for granted the importance of education, that is, although parents all see education as a way to climb the social ladder, their enthusiasm for children's education is not always a matter of economic calculation. Attending schools is simply part of the culture (see Cheng, 1996b).

Parents' enthusiasm is also reflected in the supply side of education. The rapid expansion in primary education in the decade after the Cultural Revolution was largely due to the mobilization of local resources. Reform in rural areas, which heralded economic reform in the following two decades, had given rural farmers the opportunity to contribute to the education of their children. Among others, starting in the 1980s, while the school system was still all publicly supported and administered, farmers in rural villages began to provide resources for local schools. Such precedents, seen as illegal in the old system, were later taken as models of mobilizing community resources. With a policy of decentralization, local collections and donations have become the major means of financing the construction of school buildings. In many villages, the best buildings are the school buildings, mostly built with donations from a large number of villagers who individually could afford only a small amount. Meanwhile, parents demonstrated a high degree of tolerance during the reform when education was no longer free and schooling involved high private costs.

The curriculum remains uniform and academic. It is uniform in the sense that there is only one path of student development and all students are expected to achieve the same. It is academic in that relevance to local lives, such as practical farming skills, is either absent from the curriculum or unpopular among the parents. 'Schools are not for farming skills,' parents would say. 'School should certainly not train students to lead rural lives,' they would say if they spoke their mind. 'Scholarship', which was treasured in ancient times, is translated into examinable subjects in the higher education entrance examination.

The reform

In 1985 (*Reform*, 1985), the state promulgated an overall policy of reform (Cheng, 1986). The reform capitalized on the new aspirations for education as well as new opportunities of mobilizing the society in constructing the formal education system. The main theme of the reform was the decentralization of schools in terms of both finance and administration.

In the years since then, China has seen a rapid development of nine-year compulsory education. By the end of the 20th century, universal primary education had become a reality in most parts of China, and junior secondary education had extended to almost all urban areas and the majority of rural areas. Meanwhile, there has been an expansion of vocational education at the senior secondary (Grades 10–12) level, such that in most cities the majority of youth at that age attend schools of one type or another. There has also been expansion in higher education, although expansion at this level is more politically sensitive. None the less, there has been a significant expansion in higher education over time. The enrolment ratio at the post-secondary stage has increased from around 1 per cent during the early 1980s to around 6 per cent by the end of the 1990s. More spectacular expansion has occurred in the non- formal sector. Adult higher education has grown to a learner population that is comparable to the formal sector. There are also all kinds of non-institution-based continuing education schemes, the most significant being the self-study examination, which attracted around 10 million candidates in 1999. Among others, there are all kinds of non-governmental or private educational institutions mushrooming in the 1990s. The latest figure was around 60,000 such institutions at all levels.

Such expansion is but one of the more apparent aspects of the reform. The scale of the expansion is by no means surprising, given the context of a much more fundamental overhaul in the economy. In order to understand the cultural aspect of the change, it would be useful to examine the essence of the reform in education. The expansion of basic education was made possible by the mobilization of private resources as an alternative to government funding. Take a village primary school as an example. Such a school used to be totally funded and administered by the county.[2] The county was no more than the administrative representative of the provincial government, which in turn represented the central national government. The reform has fundamentally changed the structure of governance. Local governments at all levels retain most of the revenues, and are then responsible for local expenditures. After the reform, the typical funding situation in a village primary school is (Cheng, 1994):

- that the state (meaning the local government) pays teachers on the government payroll, using the local general revenue;
- that local tax (often in the form of education surcharge) covers community teachers;
- capital construction is supported by community donations, often with some government matching; and
- non-recurrent expenditures such as maintenance and repair, are paid for by income generated by the school (through economic activities such as small-scale manufacturing, agriculture or renting).

In essence, the school has become a community school. Although teacher education and teacher appointments are still administered by the higher-level government, the day-to-day running of the school is in the hands of the villagers. For the first time in China's history, the community has a stake not only in the education of their children, but also in the schools that educate them.

This has brought about a fundamental change in the conception of the state. For thousands of years, the state was the supreme collective above all collectives. Everybody, and every school, was no more than part of the huge state machinery. In that conception, education was given by the state. In the reformed situation, schools are virtually owned by the community, although nominally that is not the situation. Like many other aspects in China, the substance changes faster than the names.

Parents pay for education indirectly through taxes, but the marketized economy has also given rise to other unprecedented private costs. Textbooks, for example, which were supplied by the state, are now purchased by parents but through commercial publishers, and the prices escalate every year. During the compulsory years (Grades 1–9), schools are not supposed to charge fees. However, most schools charge what are known as miscellaneous fees that are by no means trivial. Such fees have become a significant source of income for the schools. It is not unusual for a lower-income family to spend about a quarter to a third of the household income for children's schooling, even though there is usually only one child in the family (because of birth control).

After primary education, private costs for education increase. Senior secondary education is non-compulsory and is not free. Schools charge higher fees and it is also common for schools to charge 'entrance fees' (often known as sponsorship) for admissions. Such fees are often non-refundable, and the price varies with the popularity of the school: an entrance fee could be as high as 20 or 30 times the household income if the school is popular. Even in cities where neighbourhood attendance is introduced as a reflection of new thoughts about fairness, it is not unusual for parents to pay a fee so that their children can attend good schools.

In quite a number of cities, public examinations for transition between levels of schooling have been abolished. Neighbourhood attendance is practised. However, often, students are admitted across neighbourhoods on payment of a fee. This becomes another source of income for the schools, and is also an addition to the parents' private costs. In other places, when students are still distributed among schools according to public examination scores, students are admitted below the cut-off for a fee. All these fees would be seen as scandalous in other systems, but are generally accepted by the public in an immature market economy. They all none the less increase the economic implications of education for families.

Fee charging is now extended to higher education. Since 1997, all universities have started to charge fees. The only exception is teacher training programmes. The fees vary from programme to programme, and are often dependent on the potential income of the graduates rather than the costs of the programmes. English language learning, for example, charges much higher than physics.

Fee charging is but one dimension of 'reforms' in higher education. More dramatic is the change of funding (Cheng, 1997). All higher education institutions used to be state institutions, although the governing body could be the Ministry of Education (known as the State Education Commission in 1985–98), other ministries at the central government, or provincial authorities. They are still this in name with only a few institutions being recognized as private institutions. However, most higher education institutions receive only a small percentage of their funding from the state (at various levels) and institutions are expected to generate their own incomes. Such incomes are generated through industries operated by the institutions, joint ventures with enterprises, commissioned training or consultancies, sale of research products and, more recently, all kinds of public or venture investments.

Even before the funding situation changed, institutions had undergone serious reforms in terms of management and personnel policies. As with other units in the socialist system, higher education institutions were allocated resources and personnel by the state and the institutions were again no more than part of the state machinery. In particular, all funding was earmarked for special expenditure, and institutions were only expected to implement the spending. They were not supposed to be worried about income/expenditure relations; they were not given room to manipulate the resources in order to enhance efficiency. Indeed, efficiency was not a concern in a state-owned system.

In the early 1980s, following the reforms in the economic sector, higher education institutions were given 'block grants' and institutions had to plan their own expenditure. With that came the gradual reduction of the relative weight of state funding and the emergence of self-generated income. All these prompted the institutions to change their ideology and become real managers of resources.

Central to such reform was the change in personnel policies. In the socialist system, individuals were assigned to the institutions on their graduation, as part of the state plan and as a consequence of strict human resource planning. This had reinforced and indeed developed the collective culture among people. In higher education institutions in particular, the academics seldom changed jobs. They were actually 'owned' by the institutions from the day they were assigned to the job. Not only were they supposed to be loyal to the institutions, but the respective institution was supposed to take care of all aspects of the individuals' lives. A typical university in China, for example, was a mini-society that ran all the functions of a society – staff quarters, restaurants, barber shops, baths, kindergartens, homes for the aged, clinics, post offices, food markets and so on – 'with the exception of funeral homes', as presidents of Chinese universities would humorously claim.

Academics in higher education institutions were therefore 'domesticated'. They would work in the institution for life; they had no threats of unemployment; there was no performance appraisal as such. Performance was driven by state goals and visions. When they retired, they stayed in the same quarters on campus, and were given 75 to 100 per cent of their original salaries. Even their children were normally taken care of by the institution: sent to the attached schools for education, and assigned jobs in the same institution or related work units.

It is conceivable that under such a system, collective culture was not only a matter of belief but an institution with a comprehensive social structure. The individual academics were part of the institution. Their lives were part of the institution, and hence the goals and fate of the institution were also the individuals' goals and fate. But since the institution was only part of the nation, the nation's goals and fate were also the goals and fate of the individuals. This was perhaps collectivism at the extreme.

An experiment of an 'accountability system' in Jiaotong University, Shanghai, in 1979 started the collapse of the system, though slowly. Accountability systems were introduced into most institutions in one form or another. Such accountability systems, which allowed the allocation of tasks to individuals by way of a contract, have given rise to appraisal systems and incentive systems, which have given rise to a culture of 'hire and fire' closer to what would occur in a market economy.

The cultural implications

The reforms and their consequences have serious implications for values in education. The following are some obvious implications. First, the effect of fee charging on people's values of education is far-reaching. For thousands of years, education in China did not carry a price tag. The legitimacy of the ancient civil examination was exactly that it was free and fair to all social classes and families of all income levels. Fee charging is a challenge to that legitimacy.

When Chinese parents send their children to schools, they take it for granted that education is good. It is not to be doubted. As was evident in some of the studies among rural parents, the desire for education was beyond understanding (Cheng, 1996a); because it was such an established concept it was never challenged within the culture (LeVine, 1984). In other words, the emphasis on education was never subject to rational analysis, because there was supposed to be no financial cost. The fee charging, higher education fee charging in particular, has forced the parents to apply economic analysis to their children's schooling, that is, in addition to working hard, parents have to worry about whether or not they can afford university studies, even if their children obtain high scores in the examinations.

In the few years that have passed since the introduction of fee charging in 1997, there has not yet been any significant deterrent effect on university entrance. However, some signs of change are observable. First, the popularity of teacher training programmes and teacher training institutions has increased dramatically. This is largely because these programmes and institutions do not charge fees. Second, there are reports that many students take private loans from relatives and friends in order to attend university.[3] Third, in rural areas in general and in poorer provinces, there have been reports that it has become increasingly difficult to retain students who intend to drop out, since parents are no longer sure of the returns from schooling.

The desire for education is a very strong tradition in China. The introduction of university tuition is only recent. The inertia of the tradition may still sustain the aspiration for some time. In the longer run, however, if the fees become intimidating for rural families, it is not certain whether the traditional aspiration for education would still remain. On all counts, the introduction of university tuition and school fees has placed parents in the role of private investors. This is very different from the high times of socialism when study was an honourable national mission, or in ancient times when investment was only in terms of effort.

The second implication for values in education is that the long-standing legitimacy that education is *fair*, as was symbolized by the civil examination, is lost. The desire for incomes has eroded the integrity of schools and institutions. Admissions to schools preferred by parents, in particular, require a financial dispensation for the parents. In many places, some form of 'fairness' is built into such a 'transaction', for example that the entrance fees could be proportional to the students' scores short of the required cut-off. None the less, only those who can afford the fee can aspire to the better schools.

In higher education before 1997, institutions admitted students beyond the quota only when they could pay the fee. This was somewhat rectified in 1997 when all students had to pay fees and hence there is a common cut-off for students within or outside the state plan, that is, admissions are now more a matter of merit. However, given the very limited supply of higher education places, and given the vast number of potential candidates, a large number of candidates are still deprived of places in higher education purely because of financial difficulties.

The third implication is that, with the changed funding situation, the role of the state *vis-à-vis* institutions has changed. In Chinese society, which respects authority, the state still maintains direct influence over the policy and management of institutions. However, since the state provides only a small percentage of the funding, the actual control of the state over the institution has diminished. Reciprocally, institutions increasingly do not see themselves as owned by the state. While the state dictates the quota for student admissions in virtually all institutions, institutions can be highly flexible in admitting fee-paying students beyond the quota. Theoretically, the state still has control over the curriculum in higher education. However, most institutions offer programmes on commission, or through non-formal modes of learning on contract with employers, and such income-generating programmes normally do not go through state scrutiny. In reality, the institutions have substantial autonomy. However, such autonomy is also an indication that education is no longer such a sacred mission of the state. The institutions have their own axe to grind.

In other words, not only do the learners have to calculate economically, but the suppliers of education now have to be economically conscious, even if they are supposed to be public institutions. This is perhaps inevitable given the strong marketization trends in other sectors of the society, but is none the less another betrayal of the long tradition that education is for the common good of society.

The change of role of the state to individuals is even more significant. Individuals used to be part of the state workforce. They were virtually owned by the state, through the work units (eg higher education institutions), and there was no economic transaction between the individuals and the state. In crude terms, individuals were 'fed' by the state. They were not even 'employees'.

Starting in the early 1980s, private enterprises and self-employment began to emerge and became legal and there was then the first generation of 'employees' in the capitalist sense of the term. They are paid to perform their duties as specified in their contract. Their employment can be terminated if circumstances so require. Nevertheless, higher education institutions are already the slowest among all sectors of the society. All state enterprises are undergoing serious re-engineering, and job security is becoming a bygone issue. The state has now become very remote from the individual.

The fourth implication is that the reforms in education, and indeed in society, have increased the sense of the market in education, and hence have developed among students the sense of *choice*. In the high times of Chinese socialism, the 1950s and 1960s, strict workforce planning required graduates to abide by state plans in their job assignments. This was the case in higher education as well as in schools during transition between levels. A junior secondary graduate (that is at Grade 9) was assigned to do further study in general or vocational schools, and in a specific type of vocational school, according to the state workforce plan. The state machinery was so strong that students in those days were indeed indoctrinated to take pride in following the call of the state. The graduation song during the 1950s started with: 'To the rural, to afar, to where the motherland needs you most.' Under those circumstances, very able students were assigned to jobs in difficult industries or remote areas with a mission to reconstruct the nation. Over the first 30 years of the People's Republic, a culture was developed among students that they should not have their own choice for the future. It was not that individuals' desires were suppressed, but that they were educated to align their personal needs with the needs of the nation. They were not exposed to alternatives and hence were unable to conceive of personal choices about their future.

The situation has dramatically changed since the reform. The breakthrough emerged in the very late 1970s, when for the first time the state allowed farmers to retain most of their products and self-employment was allowed in urban cities. These were soon followed by other opportunities for employment outside the state, either by joint ventures or in enterprises beyond the state plan. Farmers were then also given the opportunity to work in cities on temporary contracts (for example, as construction teams) for wages. At the time of the breakthrough, few realized the most dramatic expansion of the market in the years to follow. The state sector in the economy has shrunk tremendously. Although disparity (over the nation as well as among individuals) is growing as significantly as the size of the market, the state sector decreases further because of strong policy interventions and thus the market has become the most active factor in shaping changes in the economy.

Changes in the economy have led to changes in society and, indeed, in people's ideology. In a study conducted in the mid-1990s (Cheng, 1996b), it was found that students in Shanghai who were finishing compulsory education (Grade 9) chose to go for high-risk options, that is, they went for studies with no job guarantee in return for high returns and high flexibility. The idea that their careers would be arranged by the state had almost totally disappeared. Among their criteria for choice, national needs were almost never mentioned. Moreover, students revealed that they made their decisions independently, at times even rejecting what their parents or teachers preferred.

The change in ideology is apparently a reaction to the extreme collectivism highlighted by the Cultural Revolution, but it is also a deviation from the traditional culture where individuals submit to the will of the family, the community or whatever is the collective. The implications of such a change of ideology are far-reaching. When individuals are expected to make decisions independently of the state, they become experienced decision makers and it is individual decision making that forms the very basis of the democracy that prevails in the international community.

Conclusion

China is an old civilization that has developed a strong cultural tradition. Among others, and sometimes taken as central to the culture, is the value of education. Such a value has been developed over the dynasties for many years, much more than a millennium, and is crystallized in the system of civil examinations. The value of education has remained despite the change of political regimes and even under the radical Cultural Revolution. It is the market that has caused fundamental changes to the values of education, and to the culture of collectivism. At the change of the millennium, it is no longer easy to predict how China will change further, given that it will evolve in a changed culture. However, education indeed could be used as a very good window or thermometer to understand the dramatic cultural changes in China.

Notes

1. See Fei (1947). Fei's works are mostly translated into English and other languages. However, this book, which is a collection of 13 lectures, remains available only in Chinese.
2. The administrative hierarchy comprises national government – provinces – prefectures – counties – townships – villages. Villages are non-governmental communities.
3. There is a public student loan scheme. However, it is yet to be commonly accepted. It is handled by the Industrial and Commercial Bank, which has little incentive in promoting the loans.

References

Biggs, J B (1996) Western misperceptions of the Confucian-heritage learning culture, in *The Chinese Learner: Cultural, psychological and contextual influences*, ed D A Watkins and J B Biggs, pp 45–68, Comparative Education Centre/Australian Council for Educational Research, Hong Kong/Melbourne

Cheng, K M (1986) China's recent education reform: the beginning of an overhaul, *Comparative Education*, **22** (3), pp 255–69

Cheng, K M (1994) Issues in decentralising education: what the reform in China tells, *Alternative Policies for the Finance, Control, and Delivery of Basic Education*, Special issue of *International Journal of Educational Research*, **21** (8), pp 799–808

Cheng, K M (1996a) Changes in student choice: consequences of economic reform in Shanghai, Paper presented at the 9th World Congress of Comparative Education, 1–6 July, University of Sydney, Australia

Cheng, K M (1996b) *Quality of Basic Education in China: A case study of the province of Zhejiang*, International Institute for Educational Planning, Paris

Cheng, K M (1997) Markets in a socialist system: reform of higher education in China, in *Educational Dilemmas: Debate and diversity*, vol 2, *Higher Education*, ed K Watson, S Modgil and C Modgil, pp 238–49, Cassell, London

Fei, H (1947) *Xiangtu Zhongguo (Earth-bound China)*, (reprint 1985), Joint Publishers, Hong Kong (in Chinese)

Gardner, H (1984) The development of competence in culturally defined domains: a preliminary framework, in *Culture Theory: Essays on mind, self, and emotion*, ed R A Shweder and R A LeVine, pp 257–75, Cambridge University Press, Cambridge

Ho, D Y F (1976) On the concept of face, *American Journal of Sociology*, (81), pp 867–84

Ho, D Y F (1978) Psychological implications of collectivism: with special reference to the Chinese case and Maoist dialectics, Presented at the 4th Congress of Cross-Cultural Psychology, Munich, July

Hofstede, G (1980) *Culture's Consequences: International differences in work-related values*, Sage, Beverly Hills

Hofstede, G (1991) *Cultures and Organizations: Software of the mind*, McGraw-Hill, London

Hsu, F L K (1985) The self in cross-culture perspective, in *Culture and Self: Asian and Western perspectives*, ed A J Marsella, G Devos and F L K Hsu, pp 24–55, Tavistock Publications, New York

Huang, XX (1992) *Zhongguo Kaoshi Fazhan Shilue (A Brief History of the Development of Examinations in China)*, Fujian People's Press, Fuzhou

Hubei Department of Education (1958) *Qingshaonian Xiuyang (Self-cultivation for Youths)*, vol 1, Hubei People's Press, Wuhan

Kim, U *et al* (ed) (1994) *Individualism and Collectivism: Theory, methods, and applications*, Sage, Thousand Oaks

King, E (1991) Kuan-hsi and network building: a sociological interpretation, *Daedalus*, **120** (2), pp 63–84

LeVine, R A (1984) Properties of culture: an ethnographic view, in *Culture Theory: Essays on mind, self, and emotion*, ed R A Shweder and R A LeVine, pp 67–87, Cambridge University Press, Cambridge

Liu, H F (1996) *Ke-ju: Kaoshi de jioayu shijiao (Civil Examinations: An educational perspective)* Hubei Educational Press, Wuhan (in Chinese)

Lynn, R (1988) *Educational Achievement in Japan: Lessons for the West*, Macmillan, London

Ministry of Education (1999) *Educational Statistics Yearbook of China*, Educational Science Press, Beijing

Miyazaki, I (1963) *China's Examination Hell: The civil examinations of imperial China*, tr C Schirokauer (1976), Yale University Press, New Haven, Conn

Redding, G (1990) *The Spirit of Chinese Capitalism*, Walter de Gruyter, New York

Reform of China's Educational Structure: Decisions of the CPC Central Committee (May 1985) (1985) Foreign Language Press, Beijing

Schirokauer, C (1976) Introduction, in *China's Examination Hell: The civil service examinations of imperial China*, by I Miyazaki (1963), tr C Schirokauer, pp 7–10, Yale University Press, New Haven, Conn

Solomon, R H (1971) *Mao's Revolution and the Chinese Political Culture*, University of California Press, Berkeley

Yan, Y (1996) *The Flow of Gifts: Reciprocity and social networks in a Chinese village*, Stanford University Press, Stanford

16. Changing cultures and schools in Poland

Janusz Tomiak

Introduction

Interest in Poland, her place in European history, both the more remote as well as the more recent, her role in the process of the disintegration and the ultimate collapse of Communism, has evidently grown in the course of the last few years. So has the interest in the Polish people's culture, their artistic and scientific achievements, their past political predicament as well as their present difficulties and dilemmas (see, for example, Neal Ascherson's 1981 *The Polish August*, Zbigniew Brzezinski's 1989 *The Grand Failure*, Norman Davies's 1982 *God's Playground* and his 1984 *Heart of Europe* as well as his 1996 *A History of Europe*). All these issues are very closely linked to the visions the Poles themselves have of their own future as an integral part of the European Union but, at the same time, as a people determined at all cost to preserve their distinctive cultural and spiritual identity in the world exhibiting powerful globalizing tendencies (Tomiak, 1997: 426–36).

At the very heart of this are the values that the present generation, deeply divided and often utterly confused by the mounting social, political and economic pressures, tries to clarify, redefine or reaffirm. Tradition, a genuine and near-universal and ever-present respect for the values that enabled the Polish nation to retain its cultural identity in the long period of the partition of the country among its powerful neighbours in the 19th century and the more recent foreign domination, has always been and still is today a factor of great consequence (Jedlinski, 1999: VII–XXVII). But modernity, with its materialistic and consumeristic tendencies, has recently also become an influence of a major significance for many ambitious and aspiring members of the younger generation, increasingly interested above all in personal advancement and immediate gratification. Postmodernist ideas, gradually making headway among the younger intellectuals, have now equally begun to play a role by relaxing the grip of firmly held beliefs and convictions upon the thinking habits of the leading individuals. The cynics have in the meanwhile managed to undermine many of the prevailing values by pointing out that frequent acceptance and rejection of different sets of values by people of consequence simply prove beyond any doubt that only too many of them are really careerists and opportunists at heart, espousing – as the circumstances require – values that ostensibly guarantee to make them popular and influential in society.

This kind of situation demands, however, a more penetrating analysis to reveal the complexity of the changing balance between the transmission and transformation of values and, in particular, of the role played in it by education. A careful scrutiny of the features of the recent social, political and economic developments in Poland is likely to reveal their profound influence over the system of values dominating the minds and the attitudes of the young generation, in whose hands will rest the future of the country in the 21st century. This should lead to a clearer understanding as to why education has become in many ways a battleground between the past-oriented traditionalists and the future-oriented modernizers and why the recent debates concerning a reform of the system of education in Poland have revealed quite significant differences of opinion concerning the character and substance of education and upbringing of the younger generation and the cultivation of values upon which they ought to be based in the immediate future (Mieszalski, 1995: 207–13; Szymanski, 1995: 214–22; Turnowiecki, 1995: 200–06).

At the roots of the traditional values

If one takes into account a longer perspective of time, it becomes clear that the values that dominated the inner life of the previous generations were rooted in the peculiar character of the history of the country. Poland, a powerful and important country in the 16th and 17th centuries, disappeared altogether from the map of Europe as an independent state towards the end of the 18th century for well over 100 years. The partitioning of the country among her neighbours was without doubt a calamity of the greatest consequence for the Polish nation. Forced to live under three very different kinds of political regimes, interested primarily in their might and grandeur, the Poles had to devise a defence mechanism that would enable them to survive foreign rule and to regain political independence. That mechanism could only take the form of a system of values that would permit them to retain their national identity despite all the attempts at Germanization or Russification. Every effort was made to defend the Polish language by memorizing and passing on poems and stories of bitter resistance in the face of persistent attempts by the occupiers to eliminate once and for all Poland as an independent country. In addition, the memory of past victories, heroic deeds and memorable events in the history of Poland were portrayed as a bulwark of Christianity and Western values by Polish writers and thinkers.

As two of the great powers that took most of the Polish lands tended to be considered by the Poles as the promoters of Protestantism and the Orthodox religion, a permanent and lasting alliance was formed between Catholicism and Polishness, which nothing could seemingly dissolve. In the context, a value system was bound to centre around the family, the Catholic religion and the cultivation of national tradition and national pride in the sanctity of the home and not in the schools, controlled by what the people considered to be alien and unacceptable influences.

One could see parallel developments during the four decades of Communist domination in the second half of the 20th century. Once again, it was the home, the Catholic religion and the national traditions that represented the trinity of sources of the values that were seen by an overwhelming majority as the only available means for retaining the nation's spiritual and cultural distinctiveness. As long as Communist domination in its overt or crypto-dirigistic form exercised its influence over the country, this phenomenon was bound to continue, even if the number of those who decided to pretend to conform and even to support the official policies pursued in order to gain personal advantage tended to increase with time. For the majority of the people, loyalty to the national tradition and all that it stood for, that is, deep attachment to the past, never allowing the atheistic or even the agnostic or secularizing ideas to undermine the faith of their fathers and maintaining the closest possible ties among the members of each family, became the imperatives of the highest order.

Remarkably, the course of history confirmed the hopes of the people. The Polish Pope, in the days of euphoria following the collapse of the Communist power in the country, came to be seen as the national hero of independent Poland and the final fulfilment of all Polish hopes.

The crisis of values

The collapse of Communism created an entirely new situation in all Central and Eastern European countries. In Poland, the regaining of full political independence was initially greeted with enormous joy and enthusiasm. It rekindled the hopes not only for the re-establishment of political liberties and of an open society but, rather naively, also for the creation of a flourishing economy with full employment and lasting prosperity for all. The shock of the transition from the planned to the free-market economy, from the strictly controlled patterns of production and distribution of goods and services to a highly competitive labour market without any guarantee of jobs for a lifetime, from a highly centralized to a decentralized state administration and from the monopoly of political power to a bewildering multiplicity of political parties of all shades of opinion and varying priorities, caused widespread confusion and vacillation.

The validity and relevance of the traditional values to the new situation came, increasingly, to be questioned and challenged. But the action taken to discard them brought about a reaction in the form of a determined attempt to defend the old values against the new constellations of modernizing and globalizing tendencies. The sources of the traditional values, that is the parents, the Catholic Church, the nationalistically oriented political leaders, all turned their attention towards the proclaimed need to reaffirm and re-emphasize such values.

But this time, the critical voices of those who were interested in the propagation of new values corresponding more closely to the newly emerging political and economic reality could be heard with much greater clarity. They were the voices of the older adolescents, aspiring to a greater personal freedom of opinion and action, and the voices of the secular humanists protesting against the growing influence of the Catholic Church and religious dogmatism. They were the voices of some of the new enterprising businesspeople and entrepreneurs, objecting to protectionist policies and against what they considered to be the unnecessary measures to maintain at high cost many uneconomic and inefficient units of production. They were also protesting against excessive concern for those sections of the population, such as the farmers, the miners and the workers in heavy industry, who had been adversely affected by the declining demand for their products. The ambitious modernizers, critically disposed against the traditional values, came to espouse new values that were very different in character. These included respect for material advancement, for the ability to succeed even against the fiercest forms of competition, for unrestricted freedom of action as well as the courage openly to profess and manifest one's power and importance and to enjoy without any restraints the advantages that they bestow upon those who succeed. Such a conflict of the traditional and the modernizing values has inevitably involved all social, political and economic institutions and affected all individuals and all families.

One is, naturally, aware of the fact that the central values associated with either orientation are to a considerable degree well integrated within each category. This fact makes them interdependent and supportive of each other within the confines of either system of values. Thus, within the traditional values system, the family circle tends to strengthen the religious commitment of its members, while the Church always emphasizes the importance of the family. Similarly, for historical reasons patriotic feelings tend, in the Polish case, to reinforce the nation's religious feelings. This is clearly explained by the fact that it was the Catholic Church and the Catholic priests who, in the past, not only defended the Polish language and national tradition but frequently also helped to organize effective measures of collective self-defence, be it in the times of the partition or under the Communist rule.

Similarly, the values of liberalism and open society go well together with the reassertion of the spirit of individualism. They legitimize the tendencies towards personal enrichment, promote the cult of efficiency in general and are all increasingly seen as indispensable conditions for a smooth and speedy entry of Poland into the European Union. This is so, even if such a tendency is often portrayed by its opponents as a most regrettable effort to 'change poets into cold businessmen and transport Alice from her Wonderland into "Bankland"' (Kotusiewiczowa, 1995: 191).

The two very different value systems have, inevitably, clashed with each other in many arenas of social, political and cultural life of the country. One of these has been the parliamentary debates concerning the legislative measures to be taken. Quite naturally, reforming the educational system was bound to reveal fundamental differences of opinion between the defenders of the traditional values and the determined promoters of the new ones. It could hardly be otherwise, considering the importance of education for all citizens, parents and their offspring alike, as well as for the nation as a whole.

Values and the reform of the system of education

The recent reform of the Polish educational system, its first major reform in post-Communist Poland, began in September 1999. It was envisaged as a far-reaching attempt to change in a very fundamental way the principles of control and administration as well as the structure of the system, to revise and modernize the contents and methods of education and to formulate clearly new educational aims and objectives. The reform had been carefully prepared by a number of experts familiar with the way in which the national system of education operated and by numerous specialists who were able to cover all the subjects of the curriculum. The real promoter of the reform was Professor Miroslaw Handke, since October 1997 the Minister of National Education, a prominent member of the ruling AWS–UJ coalition (the Solidarity Electoral Action and the Freedom Union). Representatives of the teaching profession, school directors, parents and older pupils had taken part in the debates preceding the introduction of the reform. Comments on the proposed changes had been received from numerous professional associations, non-government organizations, the episcopate of the Roman Catholic Church and the representatives of other churches that were represented in the Polish Ecumenical Council. The proposed changes were also discussed with OECD educational experts in meetings in Warsaw and Paris. The principal ideas upon which the reform was to be based were thus made quite explicit and the values to be emphasized were explained and justified on a rational basis.

A document published by the Ministry of National Education in 1998 and entitled *The Reform of the System of Education:– A proposal* contained Section Four, dealing with the fundamental principles upon which the education and upbringing of the young were to be based. This was preceded by the identification of what were seen as the most significant weaknesses and shortcomings of the Polish educational system so far:

- undue attention being paid to didactic considerations instead of a proper concentration upon the educational process;
- the existence of a great variety of educational slogans and contradictory pedagogical principles;

- chaos in the sphere of values, making ethical understanding difficult for young people;
- lack of cooperation between the home and the school;
- low prestige of the teacher.

This led to the identification of the educational priorities in the reform to be undertaken:

- helping the young to formulate ethical principles and to decide upon a hierarchy of values;
- placing special stress upon personalization in family life, in peer groups and in the community at large;
- cultivating work ethics.

(Ministerstwo Edukacji Narodewej, 1998: 36-37)

In the section dealing with the axiological foundations of education, special emphasis was placed upon the necessity to answer several fundamental questions. These included the following: What sort of guidance could be offered to the young? What sort of life should they be prepared for? What features of human personality should be cultivated and receive the greatest emphasis? These were said to be difficult questions, but it was considered that the school could not possibly evade them. At the very heart of the matter was the desire to enable the young persons to make rational choices in respect of the values they themselves selected, having first acquainted themselves with the alternatives available (Ministerstwo Edukacji Narodewej, 1998: 38).

Of key importance here was the statement given prominence in the proposed legislation concerning the proposed reform of education. This runs as follows:

Education and upbringing, while respecting the Christian system of values, adopts as a basis the universal system of values. Education and upbringing aim at developing a young person's sense of responsibility, love of the mother country as well as respect for the Polish cultural heritage, while at the same time preparing all individuals for the opening up towards the values of other cultures of Europe and the world. (Ministerstwo Edukacji Narodewej, 1998: 105).

Moral values, civic virtues and personal integrity

The role of the school was said to include – in addition to assisting all pupils in mastering the knowledge and skills indispensable for each individual in his or her life – helping the pupil in the search for spiritual values in life; preparing the pupil for active participation in the process of shaping the world, finding one's own place in it and developing a national and cultural identity; and, in addition, assisting the pupils in adopting patriotic attitudes while also developing the awareness of each person being at the same time a member of a local community, an ethnic group, a nation as well as the international community.

It was further specified in the document that, in the teaching of Polish language and culture, history and civics, mathematics, nature study, arts and crafts, a foreign language, physical education, religion and ethics to all pupils aged 10 to 13, special consideration should be given to patriotism and citizenship, preparation for family life, health education and information technology. The Fatherland and the family are, therefore, identified as the key values. The existence of religion as a school subject is an indication that religion as such must be added to the first two (Rapacz, 1995: 93–100).

In giving further consideration to the contents of education for that age group, a number of values are specifically listed as requiring a special stress in the teaching of history and civics. They are: truth, goodness, justice, beauty, family, society, work, Poland. A more detailed scrutiny of the tasks of education at school shared in common by teachers of all subjects in respect of patriotic education, education for citizenship and preparation for family life confirms the key importance of these values for both the younger and the older adolescents, attending a *gimnazjum* for the age group 13–16 and a *lycée* for the age group 16–19 (Ministerstwo Edukacji Narodewej, 1998: 123–67).

The current reform underlines the need to weaken the strong traditional lines of division between the different school subjects and to introduce blocks of subjects in order to integrate the contents of learning. It also recommends that promoting certain kinds of tasks, skills and competencies should be shared by teachers of all subjects. An important area here is – among others – preparation for family life. This, again, confirms particular concern with this value. Of special interest are the following important tasks of the teachers at the *gimnazjum* level:

- promoting the vision of an integrated human person and offering assistance in the choice and realization of values that help the development of personality;
- promoting the process of self-education of the pupils;
- supporting moral development and the process of forming a hierarchy of values by each pupil;
- creating an atmosphere of respect for brotherhood, friendship and love;
- promoting an integrated vision of human sexuality by portrayal of unity between sexual acts, love and responsibility;
- cooperating with parents in order to develop a positive relationship between them and their children;
- assisting young people to find answers to the fundamental questions of human existence.

(Ministerstwo Edukacji Narodewej, 1998: 147)

It should be added that the sense of sharing in the common European cultural heritage is, as a value of great importance, considered indispensable for all pupils. This is clearly seen from the inclusion in the contents of learning in the *gimnazjum* of the sources of European culture embracing the Bible and Greek mythology, the writings of Homer, Sophocles and Horace as well as the literary texts representative of the best works in literature, including those by Dante, Shakespeare, Cervantes, Molière, Goethe, Pushkin, Dickens, Conrad, Twain, Hemingway and Camus (Ministerstwo Edukacji Narodewej, 1998: 129).

In the *lycée*, the oldest pupils are expected to scrutinize alternative value systems, the principles of moral behaviour as well as the main philosophical movements: Marxism, existentialism, phenomenology, psychoanalysis, behaviourism, modern tomism, analytical philosophy, hermeneutics, the philosophy of dialogue, and postmodernism (Ministerstwo Edukacji Narodewej, 1998: 169).

At the very foundation of this educational strategy lies, one can argue, proper respect for personal integrity, the moral autonomy of all human beings and the recognition of their capacity for making rational choices in life. That is of paramount significance and direct relevance to overcoming major cleavages in a society in which a crisis of values and the initial stage of confusion leads on to the second stage. This may prove to be the establishment of a democratic pluralist society based on every person's right to attempt to lead a good life through a completely open and free choice of values and the corresponding philosophy of life.

Conclusion

In recently published articles several Polish educationalists and sociologists have paid considerable attention to the findings of social research about changes in the values of Polish young people. These suggested that with the growing loss of confidence in socialist values, repeatedly proclaimed, but in reality largely ignored by many members of the older generation, 'the young people have become politically and socially apathetic' (Lewowicki, 1994: 279). The main reasons for this have been identified as the growing political instability, frequent changes in the government, conflicts in parliament, economic difficulties and endless difficulties in clarifying the model of the state. As a result: 'The young generation... threatened by social crisis, economic crisis and values crisis was overwhelmed by feelings of doubt and lost hope' (Lewowicki, 1994: 277).

Opinions have also been expressed that the end of the millennium brought with it growing anxiety and deepening worries about the future, the weakening of traditional norms and values as well as chaos and the disintegration of personality. 'Under the growing pressure of modernizing tendencies even the best intentioned actions lead in the world of increasing complexity towards the destruction of what for man is most important of all: his dignity, his freedom and his individuality' (Wojnar, 1995: 55). These pessimistic observations are not entirely without foundation, but the current reform provides concrete evidence that determined attempts are being made to create a climate for positive educational measures and injecting a new dose of much-needed optimism into the social framework.

It has also been an obvious exaggeration to argue that the Poles always tend to adhere to one form of authoritarianism or another and the disappearance of Communist fundamentalism sponsored by the Soviet Union can only be followed by religious fundamentalism sponsored in the country by the Catholic Church. The suspicion that 'by the time the objective processes that characterise democratic and market systems will develop in Poland, the Catholic Church may well dictate control over the Polish school system' (Kruszewski and Kruszewski, 1994: 104) has proved to be ill founded. Rather to the contrary, the spirit and the substance of the current reform suggests that, as in several other societies, 'the intelligent Christian of our secular age... can overtly accept that we have autonomous moral understanding and that, at least as judged on moral terms, Christian teaching is rationally defensible... [and] overt acceptance of secular rational morality means that the contemporary Christian need no longer begin to imagine that there should be something about his moral principles that rational non-Christians must reject. The rational humanist and the rational secular Christian can expect to be in full agreement' (Hirst, 1974: 53).

A thoroughgoing and far-reaching reform of the national system of education is never easy. Its ultimate success is conditioned by political, social and economic developments in the country. But the prospects for the future of Polish education and the place of Poland as a credible partner within the enlarged European Union in the near future have been substantially enhanced by the changes proposed.

References

Ascherson, N (1981) *The Polish August*, Penguin, Harmondsworth

Brzezinski, Z (1989) *The Grand Failure: The birth and death of Communism in the 20th century*, Scribner's, New York

Brzezinski, Z (1993) *Out of Control:– Global turmoil on the eve of the 21st century*, Scribner's, New York

Davies, N (1981) *God's Playground: A history of Poland*, vol I, Columbia University Press, New York

Davies, N (1982) *God's Playground: A history of Poland*, vol II, OUP, Oxford

Davies, N (1984) *Heart of Europe*, OUP, Oxford

Davies, N (1996) *A History of Europe*, OUP, Oxford

Hirst, P H (1974) *Moral Education in a Secular Society*, London University Press, London

Jedlinski, J (1999) *A Suburb of Europe:– Nineteenth century Polish approaches to Western civilisation*, Central European University Press, Budapest

Kotusiewiczowa, A (1995) Education for democracy in search of new values in teacher education, in *Education in Europe: An intercultural task*, ed C Wulf–, pp 189–92, Waxmann, New York, Munster

Kruszewski, K and Kruszewski, K B (1994) Playing Monopoly Polish style, in *Education and the Values Crisis in Central and Eastern Europe*, ed V D Rust *et al*, pp 89–105, Peter Lang, Frankfurt am Main

Lewowicki, T (1994) Changes in Polish youth values: between doubt and hope, in *Education and the Values Crisis in Central and Eastern Europe*, ed V D Rust *et al*, pp 267–79, Peter Lang, Frankfurt am Main

Mieszalski, S (1995) Trzy pytania o polska szkole w okresie przemian (Three questions concerning the Polish school in the period of transformation), in *Szkola i Pedagogika w Dobie Przelomu (School and Pedagogy in the Period of Upheaval)*, ed T Lewowicki *et al*, pp 207–13, Zak, Warsaw

Ministerstwo Edukacji Narodewej (Ministry of National Education) (1998) *Reforma Systemu Edukacji:– Projeckt (The Reform of the System of Education:– A proposal)*, WSP, Warsaw

Rapacz, A (1995) Wychowanie religijne w Polsce dzisiaj: kontynuacja czy zmiana? (Religious education in Poland today: continuation or change?), in *Szkola i Pedagogika w Dobie Przelomu (School and Pedagogy in the Period of Upheaval)*, ed T Lewowicki *et al*, pp 93–100, Zak, Warsaw

Szymanski, M (1995) Polskie spolecaenstwo i szkola w dobie przelomu (Polish society and school in the period of upheaval), in *Szkola i Pedagogika w Dobie Przelomu (School and Pedagogy in the Period of Upheaval)*, ed T Lewowicki *et al*, pp 214–27, Zak, Warsaw

Tomiak, J (1997) Looking back, looking forward: education in central Eastern Europe on the eve of the XXIst century, in *Vergleichende Erziehungswissenschaft: Herausforderung – Vermittlung – Prazis: Festschrift fur Wolfgang Mitter zum 70. Geburtstag*, pp 426–36, Band 1, Deutsches Institut fur Internationale Padagogische Forschung, Frankfurt am Main

Turnowiecki, W (1995) Edukacja a proces transformacji w Polsce u progu lat dziewiecdziesiatych (Education and the process of transformation in Poland in the early 1990s), in *Szkola i Pedagogika w Dobie Przelomu (School and Pedagogy in the Period of Upheaval)*, ed T Lewowicki *et al*, pp 200–06, Zak, Warsaw

Wojnar, I (1995) Kulturowy wymiar edukacji jako szansa i alternatywa (The cultural dimension of education as an opportunity and an alternative), in *Szkola i Pedagogika w Dobie Przelomu (School and Pedagogy in the Period of Upheaval)*, ed T Lewowicki *et al*, pp 55–62, Zak, Warsaw

17. Changing cultures and schools in South Africa

Pam Christie

Introduction

The last decade of the 20th century stands as a dramatic watershed in South African history, signalling the demise of apartheid and the establishment for the first time of a democracy based on human rights and equal citizenship. A new constitution proclaimed equal rights and outlawed discrimination in education as in other spheres of public life, and a swathe of new legislation cut through the edifice of apartheid, replacing it with the ideals of a modern, national democratic state.

In education, the apartheid state had built an elaborate structure of inequality, which was evident in all aspects of school life. It could be argued that inequalities of race, class, gender and locality were in fact constitutive of the structures and cultures of schooling. Despite an impressive suite of new policies and frameworks for education, reversing the injustices of apartheid proved to be a complex task. In 1999, education minister Kader Asmal, while praising the policy achievements of the first five years of government, described the education conditions of the majority of South Africans as 'a national emergency'. In his assessment, large parts of the system were 'seriously dysfunctional' and there was rampant inequality, low teacher morale, failures of governance and management, and poor quality of learning.

This chapter will argue that legal frameworks and idealist policies for change, such as those developed by the post-apartheid government, are important but not sufficient to change schools and their cultures. What the South African experience in this period has shown is just how complex it is to manage change and to shift resources to remedy deep structural inequalities. Changing schools is not simply a matter of developing the right policies and planning more accurately for their implementation. Policies are mediated by social, economic and political influences, including powerful global trends. They are also mediated by the capacity and will of education bureaucracies and schools, as well as by institutional cultures and contexts. Far from being rational and predictable, as legal frameworks may suggest, changing cultures and schools is a complex, contradictory and often contestational process.

Social, cultural and political factors

The first post-apartheid government in South Africa began as a 'government of national unity', which brought together the African National Congress (ANC) and its alliance partners with apartheid's architects, the National Party, and other smaller political groups. This government placed a premium on negotiated settlements, shared agreements and political compromises, which inevitably curbed some of the more radical visions of social transformation that had emerged in the latter years of the liberation struggle (see Christie, 1999; de Clercq, 1997). Moreover, the new bureaucracy was something of a hybrid: new appointees, some of them political activists who lacked experience, worked side by side with bureaucrats of the previous order who were able to block changes they did not support.

The new government's vision for transformation in education was a complex reform agenda, with policies that would shift the values and practices of apartheid education into a democratic, rights-based approach to social and economic development. An early task was to restructure the racially based apartheid education departments, and to set out governance relationships between the national Department of Education and the nine provincial departments. Under the new constitution, the national Department of Education was given responsibility for developing norms and standards as well as framework policies for the system as a whole, and the nine provincial departments were given responsibility for policy implementation and the delivery of schooling.

The educational inequalities inherited by the new government were massive. The 1996 Schools Register of Needs (which was the first inventory of all schools in the country) showed the stark deprivation of the majority of black schools, particularly those in rural areas. Nearly all of these schools needed serious development and repairs. Most were inadequately resourced for learning, without libraries or learning materials. In the three most rural provinces, half had no water, even fewer had toilets and most did not have electricity and telephones (Bot, 1997). These schools stood in strong contrast to the much smaller number of historically advantaged white schools, almost all of which had good physical plant (including electricity and telephones), to say nothing of libraries, learning materials and often computer laboratories and media centres. The task of redressing inequalities of this magnitude is a daunting one. It requires political will, resources, redistributive policies and implementation capacity, and it cannot be speedily achieved. Certainly, the experience of the first term of office of the new ANC-led government showed how difficult it would be to make significant inroads into these deep inequalities.

The national Department of Education approached its task by developing a set of framework policies that covered most aspects of schooling. Symbolically, these policies were designed to break the assumptions of apartheid and provide an alternative vision for education. For example:

- A new outcomes-based *curriculum* framework (Curriculum 2005) and new assessment policies were developed from 1995, interlacing with a new national qualifications framework and South African Qualifications Authority.
- New frameworks, norms and standards for school *governance* were set out in the South African Schools Act (1996) and subsequent acts and regulations.
- Norms and standards for *school funding* were drawn up to redress past imbalances (1998).
- Frameworks for *teacher employment* were set out in the Education Labour Relations Act (1998) and accompanying agreements.

These new national framework policies drew directly on international experience and 'best practice'. Symbolically, they provided a paradigm-switching alternative to apartheid education, but in practice they proved difficult to implement. There were two major difficulties: firstly, the policies were drawn up as ideal-type frameworks, with little or no consideration given to actual conditions in schools; and secondly, they required greater capacity to implement than existed generally within the education bureaucracy and schools.

For example, the initial framework policies in the areas of curriculum and school governance contained few, if any, guidelines for implementation, and no provisions for targeting equity and redress. Importantly, they were not drawn up with budgetary considerations, with the consequence that provinces did not have adequate resources for proper implementation. Consequently, the new curriculum was introduced without adequate materials or teacher preparation, and without consideration of the widely different classroom conditions of apartheid schools. It is hardly surprising that research has shown that the generally well-qualified teachers in the well-resourced historically white schools were more confident in using the new curriculum than the often less-well-qualified teachers in poorly resourced schools and classrooms (Jansen, 1999). Similarly, the new governance ruling that all schools should have governing bodies with majority parent representation was implemented regardless of the fact that many schools had illiterate and untrained parents. Thus, problems were experienced because policies were developed and implemented without adequate strategies to take into account the very different circumstances of schools.

In short, an unfortunate and unanticipated consequence of these new policies was that they operated to the benefit of schools that had the capacity and resources to take advantage of the opportunities they offered, while adding extra burdens to under-resourced communities and schools. Ironically, rather than enhancing equity, these policies heightened differences of historical privilege between schools.

In 1998, the National Policy Review Conference on Education affirmed the importance of the new legislative framework in setting the basis for a unified, non-racial, non-sexist and democratic education system. At the same time, it identified implementation difficulties as a major weakness of the new policies. (Other problems included insufficient funds, a lack of fiscal capacity, poor Initial Teacher Training (ITT) and generally weak management capacity.)

Once the national Department of Education began to develop more targeted policies, it soon emerged that few provinces had the management capacity to implement them. For example, in 1999, a new approach to school funding was developed, which aimed to link levels of funding to a poverty index of schools. To implement this, provincial administrators needed accurate data and information systems on schools and their communities, technical capacity to work with this data, and strong administrative competence to work between head office, districts and schools. In the majority of provinces – and particularly in those with the highest concentration of historically black schools – this bureaucratic capacity was simply not in place. Provincial departments themselves required management development and capacity building in order to work with technical policies at school level. Again, this highlights the difficulties of working with and changing the profoundly unequal legacy of apartheid.

As mentioned earlier, the government approached educational change through a complex reform agenda, developing a suite of policies designed to shift the values and practices of apartheid education into a democratic, rights-based schooling system. Whereas national-level policies are useful in setting frameworks and leveraging resources to support change, international experience has shown that they are not particularly effective in bringing school-level changes in culture and pedagogy (see Heneveld, 1994; Elmore, 1993; Fullan, 1991). Ideologically and culturally, apartheid schools enshrined and normalized racial and ethnic identities, as well as urban–rural and gender differences. Curricula were produced bureaucratically, content and textbooks were strictly defined, there was a pervasive ideology of Christian nationalism and rote learning was common. New education policies envisaged a thoroughgoing transformation of teaching and learning: a curriculum framework that enabled school-level curriculum development, continuous assessment and learner-centred pedagogy. However, progress in achieving changes of this depth has been slow. A number of indicators illustrate this. In relation to the new curriculum, the initial timetable for the implementation proved too ambitious and had to be slowed down. Partly due to budgetary constraints, there were insufficient learning resources and very little teacher support. In relation to teaching and learning in classrooms, senior certificate and school-leaving results continued to show massive racial disparities. In relation to school integration, although classrooms in previously whites-only schools showed greater racial mix, the majority did not reflect the racial demographics of the country. In this context, Minister Asmal's assessment of the education conditions of the majority of South Africans was accurate: rampant inequality remained, and the quality of learning was often poor.

Perhaps the most powerful example of the difficulties of changing school-level practices is to be seen in the so-called 'breakdown of the culture of learning and teaching' in a number of black schools, particularly in poor and disrupted township communities. These schools had ceased to function under apartheid, and problems persisted under the new government. A number of problems characterized school dysfunction: irregular attendance by students and teachers; poor results; disputed authority relations between principals, teachers, students and parents; low morale and general demotivation; conflict and violence in and around schools; vandalism, criminality, gangsterism, rape and substance abuse (see Christie, 1998). While it was clear that the breakdown of schools originated in the poverty and deprivation of apartheid education and the resistance struggle against it, what was less clear was how to intervene to change these schools. One of the strategies developed by the national Department of Education was a campaign for learning, teaching and service, including a television and newspaper series depicting life in these schools. While this raised awareness of problems, it did not generate intervention strategies. Certainly, what the South African experience of school culture has shown is that once schools have reached this level of institutional and cultural breakdown in teaching and learning, it is extraordinarily difficult to remedy them (Christie, 1998). There is no doubt that Minister Asmal's statements about 'serious dysfunction' and a 'national emergency' were appropriate for these schools.

Any overview of the social, cultural and political factors at play in post-apartheid education needs to include consideration of the vexed issue of teacher retrenchment and redeployment. Two main factors influenced policies on teacher provisioning. Firstly, the apartheid system had produced an unequal distribution of teachers in relation to learners, with widely different class sizes, and this needed to be addressed for reasons of equity and redistribution within the system. Secondly, financial considerations drove the agenda: teachers' salaries absorbed more than 90 per cent of the education budget, leaving little over for other needs such as the introduction of new learning materials.

Unfortunately, however, the process of changing teacher provisioning was badly mismanaged by the government, and stands out as a major failure in education change during this period. The government began the 'right-sizing' process by setting out norms for class sizes in primary and secondary schools, and offering voluntary severance packages to teachers. However, it had no accurate headcount of teachers and their distribution through the complex system of apartheid departments, and no management plan to control the numbers and areas of expertise of teachers leaving the system. Far more teachers than anticipated took the opportunity to leave, costing the government more than R1 billion instead of the anticipated R6 million. Among those who left were well-qualified teachers in areas of need such as mathematics and science. Retrenchment policies brought the government into conflict with teacher unions across the political spectrum, and profoundly unsettled many teachers and schools. Though labour relations agreements were reached regarding teachers' hours and conditions of work, teacher morale was undermined and relationships between teacher organizations and the government were strained. In addition, these changes to the conditions of teachers' work cut across attempts to introduce changes in curriculum and school management, illustrating the new government's lack of experience in managing system change. Problems in the management of teacher redeployment not only brought political and financial losses to the government, but they also undermined the education transformation process. In the view of Jonathan Jansen, little was achieved in terms of redistribution (1999: 34): 'It can now safely be concluded that the teacher redeployment plan not only exacerbated the fiscal crisis of the state but sustained the resource inequalities between white, privileged and black, disadvantaged schools.'

So far, this chapter has sketched the social, cultural and political context in which the post-apartheid education agenda took shape. It has illustrated the difficulties of shifting resources to remedy deep structural inequalities, and the limitations of policy frameworks in achieving changes to cultures and practices of schooling. The chapter now turns to an examination of economic factors influencing changes in South African schooling.

Economic trends

The overall economic context for educational change in South Africa is characterized by profound structural inequality. The new government inherited an economy with high unemployment, skewed income distribution, a high level of poverty, negative economic growth and a negative balance of trade. Scenarios of this sort are not easy to turn around, and policies to do so were a major challenge for the government. Arguably, the options for macroeconomic policy were powerfully constrained by the global context of the 1990s; had political change come a decade earlier in South Africa, other options might have been possible.

To address the profound structural inequalities of apartheid, the first post-apartheid government attempted to introduce a comprehensive transformation strategy in the reconstruction and development programme (RDP), which favoured growth through redistribution. However, this redistributive agenda was not sustained. Firstly, the neo-liberal global context was not supportive of a transformation agenda based on these principles. Secondly, the agenda was too complex and unwieldy to be implemented as envisaged, and little headway was made in shifting resources or changing the operation of government to enable cross-sectoral programmes. By 1996, the RDP was replaced by the growth, employment and redistribution (GEAR) strategy, a blatantly neo-liberal macroeconomic framework of deregulation, privatization and fiscal restraint. This framework – amounting to self-imposed structural adjustment – put pressure on social spending, including spending on education.

Although the budget allocation to education remained high (approximately 20 per cent), there were cuts in real terms. All of the provinces struggled to keep education spending within budget limits. As mentioned earlier, with more than 90 per cent of the budget being absorbed by personnel costs, there was little over for recurrent expenditure such as purchasing textbooks and stationery (in 1999, R100 was allocated per learner per year), and providing in-service teacher education to support the new curriculum. In GEAR terms, the government's view during this period was that the problems were not straightforwardly financial; rather, they were the result of poor managerial capacity and mismanagement of resources. In these terms, solutions did not lie in increasing an already high budget allocation, but in improving internal efficiencies and in developing management competence at departmental and school level. Whatever the logic of these arguments, resource constraints and inefficiencies impeded the implementation of a systemic education reform agenda. With education planning strongly influenced by fiscal planning, the broader redistributive agenda was given second place.

While inherited backlogs have persisted, it is also important to point out that gains were made during this period: school enrolments increased, with near universal primary school enrolments; there were improved teacher qualifications and improved learner–teacher ratios; and there was greater equity in expenditure per learner (Bot, 1999). However, conditions in the poorest and most marginalized communities and their schools have not significantly shifted.

The 1998 census provided a depressing picture of unemployment and income distribution in South Africa, with more than a third of people unemployed and higher rates in the rural provinces. Within this, racial inequalities were stark, with 54 per cent of the African population considered to be poor, compared with 0.5 per cent of whites. Unemployment of youth between 20 and 29 was estimated to be 60 per cent (Motala, 1998). In the face of huge disparities between poverty and wealth, it has proved very difficult to redistribute economic and social opportunities. This has led theorists like Motala to argue that a comprehensive approach is necessary if education reform is to be effective.

What this section of the chapter has illustrated is that the new government's agenda for equity and redistribution was profoundly shaped by the global and local economic context, and the macroeconomic policies adopted to direct the development of the economy. It has been argued that an agenda driven by fiscal restraint has overshadowed moves towards systemic education reform.

Legal framework

An early move of the ANC and its alliance partners was to develop a new constitution and bill of rights (1996), which was intended to establish a society based on democratic values, social justice and fundamental human rights. In stark contrast to the fragmented racial and ethnic identities of apartheid, the new constitution provided a framework of common citizenship and common values. It enshrined the liberal rights of equality, human dignity and freedom, and it outlawed discrimination on the basis of race, gender, sex, ethnic origin, sexual orientation, age, disability, culture, language and so on. In education, it set out the right to basic education for all, and outlawed apartheid exclusions by setting out the right of equal access to educational institutions, protection from unfair discrimination on the basis of disability, and rights to language, culture and religion.

There is no doubt that the values of the new constitution, if fully implemented, would bring fundamental changes in education. This can be easily illustrated in the area of education governance and management. As the report of the Task Team on Education Management Development pointed out, the new approach based on these principles and values would transform the process by which authority is mediated in the system, from the level of the national ministry to the individual school (Department of Education, 1996: 13). Democracy and participation would replace hierarchical, rule-driven control of apartheid; accountability and transparency would replace non-consultative and secretive management approaches; and gender equality, flatter organizational structures and teamwork would be part of a more developmental and systemic approach towards capacity building (1996: 20). Schools would be given fuller powers for self-management, for controlling budgets, for employing staff and for developing curricula, within the framework of nationally developed policies.

As with other areas of policy discussed in this chapter, the principles and values of the new constitution and legal framework for education are laudable and offer a vision for thoroughgoing transformation of education. However, implementation of changes flowing from this legal framework needs time to work through the system, and is mediated by social, political and economic forces. In many cases, the *will* to change exists in government departments and schools, but the *capacity* is lacking.

Religious movements

The new constitution declared South Africa to be a secular state, and enshrined religious freedom for all. It stated that public schools could not discriminate on grounds of religion, including in their admissions practices. The implications for schools were potentially enormous. Under apartheid, religious instruction in Christianity was compulsory at school, and an ideology of Christian Nationalism underpinned the curriculum. This applied not only in obvious areas such as history, social studies and religious education; it also reached through to a creationist approach in biology, one of the most commonly studied subjects at senior certificate level. Reforming the ideological and religious dimensions of the curriculum was a priority for the new government, but because of slow progress of curriculum change generally, it is safe to predict that it will not be achieved by the early 2000s. Many schools continue to offer religious education through a Christian framework, but participation by staff and students is not compulsory. In a court case in 1998, a Muslim girl student established the right to wear a headscarf in a previously whites-only school. This incident may be read as an indication of the interrelationship between race and religion in identity issues, and illustrates the need for constant vigilance if equality is to be achieved in a society so deeply embedded in a legacy of discrimination.

Global trends in educational development

Most of the framework policy documents of the national Department of Education reflect state-of-the-art thinking on Western schooling, drawing explicitly from what was judged to be the best of international policy directions. This raises issues about the nature of education policy borrowing in the current context.

In his analysis of the patterns of late-modern education, Cowen (1996) points out that a gradual sense of crisis has stimulated education reform movements in countries such as Australia, Canada, New Zealand, the UK and the United States. These reform movements have a number of features in common. Firstly, the state has sought to diversify the sources of those who provide and pay for education. Education has been articulated more closely with the needs of the economy, and the state has assumed the role of controlling qualification structures and licensing arrangements in a marketplace of providers and consumers. Secondly, the contents and structure of education have been recast. Within an ideology of choice and diversity, curricula are defined by skill specification, pedagogic transmission is organized into modules of small pieces of knowledge, and frequency of assessment increases. Thirdly, 'the international' is broadened from being a source of policy borrowing. In Cowen's words, 'the international economy becomes a crucial definer of the purposes, efficiency and effectiveness of the education system, its content and its structures and even some of its pedagogic modes' (1996: 161).

It is worth noting that the post-apartheid government turned explicitly to the education systems of the countries mentioned by Cowen in searching for policy models for itself as a modern, national democratic state. Not surprisingly, therefore, the patterns identified by Cowen are to be seen in South African policies. In terms of governance and finance, the South African Schools Act (1996) and subsequent amendments endorsed the move to school-based management, in direct contrast to the centralist policies of apartheid. Attempting to draw as widely as possible on potential sources of funding for schools, the principle of 'user pays' was introduced alongside a commitment to free education. Unfortunately, however, this market orientation to schooling widened the gulf between rich and poor communities and their schools, in spite of the government's equity agenda. In terms of the content and structure of education, the patterns outlined by Cowen are to be seen in the new national qualifications framework, with outcomes-based curricula, modularization and assessment geared towards mobility and portability of learning. Concerns with the international economy and the need for education to support international competitiveness have echoed through new policies.

That said, it is important to recognize that global influences on South African education policies were the result of active borrowing, and policy borrowers were concerned to adapt global policies to fit local circumstances and interests. It is important to recognize local agency in policy borrowing, rather than to assume an automatic transfer or a global imposition (see Christie, 1997).

Conclusion

This chapter has sketched the educational agenda of the post-apartheid state, outlining the suite of policies and legal frameworks it put in place to achieve systemic change in education and to reverse the injustices and structural inequalities of apartheid. The chapter has shown how these policy frameworks have been mediated by social, economic and political influences, as well as powerful global trends. A clear lesson from the South African experience in this period is how difficult it is to develop and implement policies to change schools and their cultures, particularly in conditions of deep structural inequalities. Formulation of policy documents proved reasonably straightforward, but shifting resources within the system proved extremely difficult, particularly in conditions of resource constraints and limited managerial capacity. The chapter has argued that changing cultures and schools goes well beyond the rational process of producing legal and policy frameworks; it is a complex, contradictory and often unpredictable process.

References

Bot, M (1997) School Register of Needs: a provincial comparison of school facilities, 1996, *Edusource Data News*, (17), August, Education Foundation, Johannesburg

Bot, M (1999) *Macro Indicator 1997: Update of baseline study*, Centre for Education Policy Development, Johannesburg

Christie, P (1997) Global trends in local contexts: a South African perspective on competence debates, *Discourse: Studies in the cultural politics of education*, 18 (1), pp 55–69

Christie, P (1998) Schools as (dis)organisations: the 'breakdown of the culture of learning and teaching' in South African schools, *Cambridge Journal of Education*, 28 (3), pp 283–300

Christie, P (1999) Inclusive education in South Africa: achieving equality and majority rights, in *World Yearbook of Education 1999: Inclusive education*, ed H Daniels and P Garner, Kogan Page, London

Cowen, R (1996) Last past the post: comparative education, modernity and perhaps post-modernity, *Comparative Education*, 32 (2), pp 151–70

de Clercq, F (1997) Policy intervention and power shifts: an evaluation of South Africa's education restructuring policies, *Journal of Education Policy*, 12 (3), pp 127–46

Department of Education (1996) *Changing Management to Manage Change*, Report of the Task Team on Education Management Development, Government Printer, Pretoria

Elmore, R (1993) What knowledge base?, *Review of Education Research*, 63 (3), pp 314–18

Fullan, M (1991) *The New Meaning of Educational Change*, Teachers College Press, New York

Heneveld, W (1994) *Planning and Monitoring the Quality of Primary Education in Sub-Saharan Africa*, Technical Note 14, Technical Department Africa Region, World Bank, Washington

Jansen, J (1999) *Education After Apartheid: Intersections of politics and policy in the South African transition, 1990–2000*, Centre for Development and Enterprise, University of Durban-Westville, South Africa

Motala, S (1998) Reviewing Education Policy and Practice: Constraints and Responses' in *Quarterly Review of Education and Training in South Africa*, 5 (5) Johannesburg; Education Policy Unit, University of the Witwatersrand

18. Changing cultures and schools in South Korea

Meesuk Ahn and Paddy Walsh

Introduction

In the late 19th century, the Yi Dynasty (1392–1910), long associated with a strongly centralized and administratively efficient Confucian state, opened its doors to the outside world. From the massive influx of Western ideas that followed, national institutes and private schools began to emerge, founded by Christian missionaries and patriotic leaders. Koreans were exposed to new world-views and awakened to the need for an educational system that would be fitting and proper for the changing society and 'the modern world'. However, the independent development of this system was rudely interrupted when Japan annexed Korea in 1910. It is difficult to be enthusiastic about the Japanese influence on Korean education in the following 35 years. It was oppressive in the extreme, even if it also involved some expansion and modernization. Jayasuria explains their policy:

> One [aim] was to expand the government system of primary schools on a large scale, and the system of secondary schools on a very small scale... as a foil to foreign missionary enterprise and local Korean enterprise in education. The second line of attack was to destroy the non-governmental school system, namely the missionary schools and the Korean private schools... the Japanese knew very well that the private schools were breeding places of nationalism, and stood for the independence of the nation. Their curricula gave a predominant place to Korean cultural heritage, and this, too, was anathema to the Japanese who wanted to destroy the distinctive cultural identity of the Koreans. (Jayasuria, 1984: 37–38)

Independent once more from 1945, central government control of education was nevertheless retained in the interests of nation building in the new Republic of Korea. Thus the Educational Law of 1949 specified the school curriculum for each level of formal education, and between then and now Koreans have had a succession of six national curricula, all designed principally by bureaucrats and more or less given over to uniformity as an ideal. Hong comments on centralized decision making as a norm in Korean education generally:

> Historically, multi-layered combinations of Confucianism, patriarchy, colonialism, authoritarianism, and military dictatorship institutionalised the 'centralisation' norm in Korea's everyday life including politics and education. Under the highly centralised education system, educational reform plans, educational goals, curriculum developments, curriculum materials, teacher education, learning objectives, time allotment of school subjects and entrance tests were all predetermined at the national level and handed directly down to schools, teachers, and students. (Hong, 1996: 1)

Of course, this last half-century has been an eventful one for Korea: the Korean War followed by a sometimes uneasy peace, a military coup and 30 years of dictatorship giving way in the early 1990s to democracy, economic growth on a scale to earn 'tiger' status, which was then rebuffed by a sudden and serious recession from which Korea is now only slowly recovering. In education, free and open access to primary education was introduced from 1945, to junior secondary from 1968 and to upper secondary from 1973. These large national events and processes impacted upon the centre's policy making regarding such matters as curriculum, pedagogy and teacher education – as also upon the responses to policy of other sectors of society. We shall also see in this chapter that international trends and fashions in education – even apparently antithetical ones like progressivism and decentralization – have had their hours of influence, though usually in heavily 'filtered' forms.

It is illuminating to consider ongoing cultural change in Korean education as the product of certain interacting forces or value-sets. The first of these is traditional values, long shaped by Buddhism and Confucianism in particular (and therefore, having a provenance in Chinese civilization):

> The gradual introduction of Confucianism and the later introduction of Buddhism in the 4th century brought two powerful and lasting influences on Korean culture. Buddhism and Confucianism have exerted a profound impact on social, political and educational institutions throughout ancient and contemporary Korean history. Confucius set up an ideal ethical-moral system intended to govern all the relationships within the family and the state in harmonious unity. Scholarship and aesthetic cultivation were regarded as the prerequisites for those in governing and other official positions. (Adams and Gottlieb, 1993: 4)

Buddhism, officially recognized as the state religion of Koguryo in AD 372, involved an appeal to reason and some significant acknowledgement of the ideal of objectivity in setting spiritual standards. The Confucian tradition also, it is commonly argued, provided Koreans with a rational way of thinking and a strong moral sense, but we should note two of its more particular characteristics. Its recommendation of education – one can become a whole person through education (Park, 1991) – combines with its perception of schooling as a critical factor in upward social mobility and helps to explain the modern Korean's zeal for education. Whatever their socio-economic background, parents give first priority to their children's education, often sacrificing their own standard of living to it. Secondly, Confucianism includes the teaching that the people should follow the established leadership without question, and should not be concerned about acquiring the knowledge necessary for the exercise of leadership (Jayasuriya, 1984). As well as rationalizing an aristocracy in society, it envisages teachers as simultaneously leaders and powerful loyalists who transmit both obedience and knowledge to the masses. One consequence has been the public respect in which teachers have been held in Korean society. Never well paid in comparison with other professions, teaching has yet been an attractive career choice throughout the centuries (KEDI, 1992). Thus a 19th-century foreigner saw the Korean teacher as follows: 'He is treated politely by everyone, but he is looked upon very much as a pensioner. He receives no salary, but the boys bring him frequent presents, and he ekes out a living in some way. But there is a more dignified side to the question. Teaching seems to be looked upon as a thing that cannot be estimated by its money value' (Homer, 1969: 337).

Two other kinds of value jostle – sometimes combining, sometimes competing – with these traditional attitudes and values. One is the economic interests and associated assumptions, and the other the political considerations (latterly, democratic ones) already alluded to. Certainly, such a triangle of forces is not unique to modern Korean education. Even when we attach particular broad definitions to the 'corners' – a Buddhist/Confucian tradition, the dramatic rhythms of a paradigm 'Pacific Rim tiger economy' and a politics of cautious democracy recently emerged from authoritarian rule – we evoke parallels with other countries at each point. This triangle in motion, we contend, is a useful prism for viewing Korean education in its individuality as well as its shared features, and we shall keep it close to hand in what follows.

It is from another triangle, however, that we take the main divisions of this analysis. From the point of view of young learners, the curriculum, teachers and parents are the three things they have to contend with day to day. They are the tangible (if sometimes mysterious) front-line agencies of their education. By considering them in turn, our analysis can achieve a reasonable coverage and organization. We shall start with curriculum, focusing more on issues of control and form than content, and taking the time to give some historical context to present priorities.

The curriculum

Six national curricula

The outbreak of the Korean War in 1950 forced a postponement in the project of a national curriculum for creating national identity. South Korean teachers continued to rely on temporary syllabuses they wrote for themselves, or those bequeathed by the US military administration, to promote democratic education. This autonomy was restricted in practice, however, by the intense competitions for entry to lower and upper secondary schools and the requirements of the national standard admission tests introduced at this time to regulate those competitions.

In 1955, when the war was over, South Korean educationists constructed the first revised national curriculum. In its stated general guidelines and goals, it was influenced by John Dewey's progressive ideal of a curriculum based on the lives and interests of children. However, that spirit was certainly not carried over faithfully into the form and content of the curriculum actually prescribed which, like all the subsequent national curricula, based itself on traditional subject divisions and defined in great detail what should be taught, and how and when it should be taught:

> The focus of the first National Curriculum in the classroom was not on the needs and interests of children but on the subject contents of the curriculum or textbook. The discrepancy between the goals or aims and the contents or methodology of the curriculum increased the need for the identification and critical examination of the theoretical framework used in the first curriculum development. (Jo, Hwang and Ahn, 1994: 49)

But the sense of a gap between rhetoric and reality – as also of double-mindedness regarding Western educational fashions – would persist through later revisions.

The second revision came in 1963, a year of political turmoil in South Korea in which the April students' revolution led to the collapse of the First Republic and a military coup in May in turn overthrew the Second Republic. The resulting military dictatorship feared Communist influence and the newly revised curriculum stressed anti-communism and the traditional moral ethos of the community. It was promulgated as a 'life-oriented' curriculum, and officially defined in correspondingly broad terms as 'the total "experiences" that the students undergo under the guidance of the school' (MOE, 1963: 1). Though 'localism' was trumpeted as its management principle, the central system continued not to leave room for local definition of any real substance. On the other hand, schools and teachers of this period were still being prevented from actually implementing the centrally prescribed curriculum fully and faithfully by the requirements of the secondary admission tests. Lee refers to the primary scene:

> The excessive competition resulted in the implementation of abnormal or distorted curricula. When the competition was at its peak, the time allocation of curricula was quite abnormally unbalanced: the national language, science, mathematics, and social studies were considered to be included in the curriculum. Music, art and practical activities were neglected... The entrance examinations for the lower secondary schools thus adversely affected the proper objectives of compulsory education and made primary education insubstantial. (Lee, 1974: 9)

This is, of course, another example of the well-researched 'high stakes' curriculum distortion that occurs when teachers are 'distracted from their real purpose in order to teach to the test and produce good results' (Lawton, 1996: 8). Korean teachers, however, were being doubly burdened: not only their own educational consciences but the legally enshrined national curriculum reminded them of what test preparation was forcing them to omit in practice. These burdens were lifted from primary teachers when the lower secondary school test was abolished in 1968, and eased for secondary teachers when the upper secondary test was abolished in 1976. Since then there has been no formal national assessment system in compulsory education other than a centrally run college entrance examination, so that the primary curriculum, in particular, has been remote from the influence of national assessment. It is interesting to note, given the deliberate use of national testing to control curriculum in some countries, that in Korea at that time central control was enhanced by the abolition of national testing.

The national curriculum was revised again in 1973. Alongside the continued pursuit of anti-Communism, national identity and national spirit – for which the government now offered the slogan 'the curriculum with nationality' – the need for rapid economic development was emphasized. The curriculum expression of this composite philosophy was an emphasis on science and technology on the one hand, and on ethics and national history on the other. An additional feature was a move towards Jerome Bruner's 'discipline-oriented' curriculum (Bruner, 1960). The 'structures' and 'basic concepts' of each subject were emphasized, and 'discovery' and 'enquiry' were officially promoted as excellent teaching methods (Jo, Hwang and Ahn, 1994).

In 1981, the national curriculum was revised for the fourth time, as ordered by the government of the new Fifth Republic, which came to power in 1980. This revision was the first to be entrusted to a professional curriculum institute, the Korean Educational Development Institute (KEDI), and so it has been sloganized as a 'research and development [R & D] curriculum'. KEDI is both bureaucratic and pro-government, however, and in practice its involvement implied no great change in curriculum control. The government's intention, we may presume, was rather to provide professional legitimacy for continued highly centralized curriculum decision making than to alter it.

A significant feature of this fourth revision was the introduction by KEDI of an integrated subject curriculum in the earlier years in primary schools. However, though this was under the general aegis of a more 'humanistic-oriented' curriculum that would educate the whole person, scholars generally see the fourth revision as theoretically eclectic, a mixture of subject, experience, life and discipline orientations (Jo, Hwang and Ahn, 1994).

The fifth revision in 1987–88 – a 'golden time' for the nation: political stability, a roaring economy and the 24th Olympic Games – emphasized 'creativity to cope with social changes' and 'diversity of content and methodology' with respect to the individual differences, abilities and needs of pupils. However, these goals were not so much matters for individual teachers to interpret according to their own professional judgement as features newly (and somewhat uncomfortably) imported into the framework of the national curriculum, in which more teaching strategies than before were indicated to teachers.

The sixth – and present – national curriculum was introduced in 1992 when a civilian and more democratic government had inaugurated the Seventh Republic and displaced the military dictatorship, and it seemed to offer a firmer commitment to change. The socio-political context included ongoing democratization, the staging of the country's first local elections and the introduction of a partial local autonomy system. The new curriculum emphasizes moral character, human individuality and democratic citizenship, and the purposes particularly highlighted are 'democratization' and 'decentralization'. In previous revisions, reform had been restricted to content and methodology but now it is extended to the mode of control.

The new spirit was intimated from the beginning by entrusting the drafting of the curriculum to an 'independent' curriculum research committee in which teachers made up 74 per cent of the membership. However, these teachers were government-appointed, and mostly teacher-administrators no longer involved in teaching rather than classroom teachers. Furthermore, the major decision makers who evaluated drafts and defined final versions were of exactly the same type as before: the majority were from the Ministry of Education and KEDI (Ahn, 1996). All the same, this larger involvement of teachers can still be seen as a positive step towards engaging teachers in Korean curriculum development.

Let us now consider the structure of this present curriculum further, noting its more innovative aspirations, and then suggest an estimate of how well it is living up in practice to its promises of liberalization.

The sixth national curriculum and decentralization

The prescribed curriculum for each level of school is packed into a single volume, which comprises a common set of 'general guidelines' and a level-specific set of 'guiding principles' (MOE, 1992a; 1992b).

The general guidelines consist of the following four parts:

1. *The status of the curriculum.* This is a newly introduced section prescribing basic guidelines for the new curriculum roles of the local authorities and schools.
2. *The general framework.* This section identifies the well-educated person as healthy, independent, creative (a new emphasis in the interests of a more democratic society) and moral, and one who can also cope with information technology, international ideas and 'high-tech' industrialization. The individual pupil's in-built potentiality and creativity are stressed. There is a new encouragement to vary both contents and methods in accordance

with pupils' individuality, ability and careers as well as some measure of tolerance towards the preferred approaches of individual schools and teachers.

3. *The organization of the curriculum* refers to the subjects, extra-curricular activities and optional courses (a new feature) to be offered by schools. A nice touch is the integration in the first two grades of the bulk of the curriculum under the three headings of: 'disciplined life' – the precursor to 'moral education', and now allocated two hours a week rather than one at this level; 'intelligent life', which integrates social science and science; and 'pleasant life', which includes physical education, music and fine art. This improves upon some previous attempts at integration in the early years curriculum. For all ages, it is emphasized, social and moral education is a matter for every subject and for extra-curricular activities. The content of practical arts has been changed to heighten its applicability in real life and its starting time moved back from Grade 4 to Grade 3.

4. *Time allocations.* Here are prescribed the teaching hours for each subject across all grades. For illustrative purposes, the allocations for the primary level are reproduced in Table 18.1.

Table 18.1   Subject areas and time allotment by grade in primary school

Subject Areas		Time Allotment* by Grade					
Grade 1–2	Grade 3–6	1	2	3	4	5	6
Disciplined Life	Moral Education	60	68	34	34	34	34
Korean Language		210	238	238	204	204	204
Mathematics		120	136	136	137	170	170
Intelligent Life	Social Studies	120	136	102	102	102	102
	Science			102	136	136	136
Pleasant Life	Physical Education	180	238	102	102	102	102
	Music			68	68	68	68
	Fine Art			68	68	68	68

Practical Arts	-	-	34	34	34	34
Extra-curricular Activities	30	34	34	68	68	68
Optional Courses**	-	-	34	34	34	34

* The minimum numbers of total 'instructional hours' (= x 40 mins), by subject and grade, during 34 school weeks a year (30 for Grade 1). ** Optional courses depend completely on the individual school's choice. Source: MOE (1992a).

The guiding principles provide a five-part outline for each subject, whether at the primary or the secondary levels, as follows:

1. The *rationale* describes why and how a subject should be taught, and presents general guidelines for teachers in determining the direction of their teaching.
2. The *objectives* are the specified targets that pupils should achieve. They are indicated rather by contents to be mastered than by level of performance.
3. The *contents* section is generally seen as the most important part of the whole curriculum document. It states the level and the scope of the knowledge required for each subject at every level, presenting what is to be taught, and how, in great detail. Subjects are divided into general units, sub-units and individual topics, providing a step-by-step analysis of the prescribed contents. These structures, furthermore, are replicated in the official textbooks (see the illustrative comparison in Table 18.2), which – still – are either developed or approved by the Ministry as an integral part of their curriculum work and constitute, as it were, their final advice on how to implement the national curriculum in daily classroom teaching. (Textbook policy is overdue for attention, in our view. Teachers generally feel obliged, and are often in any case more than willing, to follow the official textbooks closely, indeed to identify them with the curriculum itself. Granted this textbook culture, should it not have been clear that decentralization called not just for pointers towards supplementary aids and exercises but for a rethinking of the design of textbooks themselves? No such rethinking seems to have occurred.)
4. The *instruction* section offers general guidelines to teachers. It shows how to develop a lesson plan, how to prepare and use teaching aids, while – in this revision – it moderates the assumption of textbook-driven and whole-class instruction by encouraging experiments, small-group discussions, enquiry strategies and field trips. (An unsurprising effect of these novelties has been to draw attention to class size – still above 40 pupils per class in primary schools. A recent study, conducted by one of the present authors, found Seoul primary teachers enthusiastic in principle but frustrated in practice. And, virtually unanimously, they believed the sixth national curriculum has been inadequately resourced (Ahn, 2000).)

5. The *assessment* section recommends a variety of methods, and a diagnostic and formative rather than a summative approach – especially in primary schools, in which the standard numerical grading from 1 to 5 ('*Su*' to '*Ga*') is abolished, as are pencil-and-paper tests in the first two grades, and school-wide tests are reduced from four times to twice a year. Teachers' annual reports are based on general and broad descriptions of each pupil's performance in relation to the prescribed contents, generally taking the form: 'x needs to do better at such and such' (Han, 1995). Control is exercised through prescription and a textbook adoption policy and, as intimated earlier, not through assessment. In terms of the 'three message systems' of 'content, pedagogy and evaluation' (Bernstein, 1975), the Korean curriculum continues to be 'content and pedagogy' driven.

Table 18.2   Curriculum and textbook compared

Social Science for Grade 3 (one semester)	
The Sixth National Curriculum	**Official Textbook**
Specification of contents	**Table of contents**
* Local community	1. Local community
** landscape and maps	(1) Figuring out our local area
*** land and fields	(2) Drawing our local area
roads and houses	
relics	
drawing our local area	
** utilization and preservation	2. The life of local people
*** land	(1) Utilization of land and water
water	(2) Improving life of the local area
** facilities	
*** public facilities	
their utilization	
* Resources of the local community	3. Resources for local life
** necessities for life	(1) Necessities for life
*** resources	(2) Production
job	
** production	
*** production from nature	
production in factories	4. Markets in the local area
** markets and stores	(1) Markets and stores
*** goods	(2) People and work
people and work	

* general units ** sub-units *** individual topics

Introducing this curriculum in 1992, the government declared: 'we intend to turn away from stigmatized monotony, exclusiveness, and rigidity of curriculum content and, at the same time, enlarge the discretion of local educational authorities and schools in curriculum decision-making' (MOE, 1992a: 99) – a bold statement of a policy that, in the Korean context, was itself bold – at least at the level of principle. There would be (some) democratic, professional and site-based curriculum decision making; (some) new powers and responsibilities to the local authorities, for example to provide schools in their areas with research-based guidelines for meeting their special needs and circumstances; (some) devolved authority to schools in planning and monitoring their overall curricula; (just a little) timetable room for school-selected optional subjects; and (a little) reduction in most teachers' contact hours to facilitate school-based curriculum development. The system remained a centralized one, certainly, but its movement was towards decentralization.

In practice, however, the momentum generated so far may have been less than was hoped for. The study already mentioned found both confusion and disagreements among Seoul primary teachers regarding the policy – what it was, whether it had made a real difference, whether it had been a good idea and what was the most desirable role for Korean schools and teachers in curriculum development (Ahn, 2000). This may be illustrated by the observations, each fairly representative, of three teacher interviewees from schools in that study:

1. What is new? There has been change in some contents as usual. Besides that, I do not see any difference from the fifth National Curriculum or the other earlier ones. Decentralization or giving power to teachers? I do not see any changes at all.
2. Korea is a small country with one nationality and we do not have a national melting-pot as in America. It means that we do not need their diversity, which can cause confusion. Most of all we need national standards in every sense of the word.
3. The sixth national curriculum is a useful framework. It's actually what we need, although it is still too specific and does not give enough flexibility to individual teachers.

Such differences may remind us of the efforts, persistence and clarity needed to change school and teacher culture. A lot will depend on how decentralization is sustained and taken forward in the next revision – whether, for example, textbook design is overhauled and textbook options are opened up this time round. It is still too soon, then, for a definitive evaluation of the central plank of the sixth national curriculum.

Teachers

Our focus here will be the professional identity of Korean teachers at the start of a new millennium. How is it maintained in terms of tradition, professional education and regulation? How do teachers themselves see their current status, and more especially their role – including their relationships to pupils, curriculum, one another (laterally and hierarchically) and government? What differences of view exist among them on these matters, and what changes may be afoot? In our necessarily selective and brief comments on these questions we shall draw further on Ahn's recent findings regarding Seoul primary teachers.

Education

Formal teacher training began in 1895, was consolidated and carefully controlled during the Japanese occupation and has continued as a function of central government since liberation. In terms of level, its evolution has followed a fairly standard international pattern. Primary teachers were trained to upper secondary level in special 'normal schools' up to 1961, when these were upgraded to national teachers' colleges offering a two-year post-secondary programme. In 1981 the programme was further upgraded to four-year degree level and some universities joined the national colleges in providing primary training – to add to the secondary training they had been providing since 1962.

National colleges are financed by central government, which also strictly controls all their institutional arrangements: personnel selection, funding, curriculum, admission policies, graduation requirements, calendars, events, enrolment patterns and degree offerings are all under its purview. Among the required qualities of teachers, humane character, warmth of heart and an altruistic attitude are seen as most important dimensions, in addition to the expertise and skill of teaching (KEDI, 1992; MOE, 1997). The university curriculum, also directed by government, includes broad foundational courses in educational theory and history, a major enrichment course in a teaching subject or subjects, and a school internship of at least eight weeks: four weeks of observation and four weeks of actual teaching. The minimalism of this practicum has been a recognized weakness for some time (KEDI, 1992).

Teachers are licensed at four levels: grade II on graduation, grade I after three years of experience plus 240 hours of in-service training, deputy headteacher and headteacher. Eligibility for the two latter requires at least 15 years of teaching experience. Teachers are transferred to other schools within their school district every three or four years.

In-service education has been a legal requirement since 1953. The site-based and practical approach that much of it has been taking since the 1970s (KEDI, 1987) remains under the auspices of approved teacher training institutes, three at the national level and many more that are immediately local in jurisdiction (but still Ministry-sponsored). In-service training programmes are classified into four types: *qualification* training relating to promotion to higher grades; *enrichment* training for keeping abreast of the rapidly advancing frontiers of knowledge (educational administrators and school managers are the main participants here); *adjustment* training for those who resume teaching after a long leave of absence; and *general* training to broaden overall knowledge of educational theories and practices and to prepare for introducing new national curricula. As to the last category, the head and at least one other teacher for each school attend the programme and then pass on what they have learnt to their colleagues – in theory. In practice, teachers perceive this process as tokenistic and only occasionally helpful; most acknowledge no in-service preparation for the current national curriculum (KICE, 1998).

Hierarchy

Teachers' salaries, in common with Korean salaries generally, rise automatically with age and experience, reflecting a deeply rooted association of age with wisdom and already making for an orientation toward authority, order and discipline. Beyond that, many teachers believe that advancement depends less on their teaching competence and more on the scrupulous management of administrative tasks and, thereby, of their credit with the hierarchy (Ahn, 1996).

As informal organizations outside this system, there are also five advisory bodies that have professional functions: the planning committee, the grade-level council, the whole staff meeting, the school operation advisory committee and the personnel advisory committee. These bodies function not as decision-making but only for consultation.

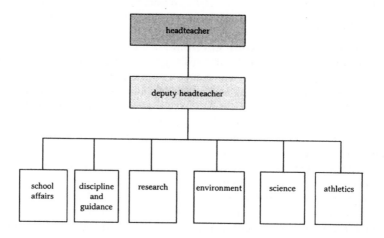

Figure 18.1 The organization of a school in Korea

The organizational pattern of all schools is as in Figure 18.1 (with small variations for size). The headteacher is assisted by a deputy headteacher and six
master teachers with the responsibilities indicated. This hierarchy is regulated
in law and ordinance and it is interpreted much more in terms of administrative efficiency than of curriculum leadership. Headteachers have the exclusive right to decide on school affairs. Of particular significance, they appoint
the 'master teachers', a coveted role among teachers and a step on the way to
further promotion. Teacher appraisal, which provides data relevant to promotion, is carried out in practice by the headteacher, according to criteria long
thought rather vague (KEDI, 1988). Since 1996, a substantial merit bonus is an-
nually available for up to 10 per cent of teachers. Here, too, headteachers generally nominate the deserving teachers.

The inspector is a person of rather less importance to the teacher. The independent division of 'supervision' ('janghak' in Korean) has had a regulatory
rather than a research or an advisory function: it monitors policy and project
implementation through to class instruction, identifies examples of success
and assesses the reorientation of values (APEID, 1984b). Once or twice a year
each school is inspected, in whole or in part, but the focus is bureaucratic com-
pliance rather than educational effectiveness. The school is judged by its conformity to official orders, including the national curriculum and the official
textbooks. There is no detailed rating form and no feedback, other than warn-
ings and instructions regarding non-conformism. The service has been
heavily criticized for excessive control, unjustified interventions and orders,
and being a liability to schools (Kim *et al*, 1994; KEDI, 1986, 1988). It is perhaps
unsurprising that teachers regard it as more authoritarian than supportive
(KEDI, 1992; Ahn, 2000).

Organized teachers

The struggles and debates over teacher unions are a deeply revealing strand
in the unfinished story of the Korean teacher. Authoritarian governments
were reluctant to allow trade unions to their civil servants. But, also, a teaching
force wedded to a Confucian interpretation of its own public role and dignity
did not press too univocally for them – nor welcome them wholeheartedly
when at last they came.

The Korean Federation of Teachers' Associations (KFTA), founded in 1947,
represents all kinds and levels of teachers from nursery schools to universities,
and currently claims 72 per cent of the nation's teachers as members. It is a federation not of trade unions, however, but of professional associations. The first
attempt at a trade union proper for teachers in the 1960s was quickly crushed
and its members imprisoned. A more sustained campaign started in the late
1980s with the 'Korean Teachers' Union' (KTU: 'Chunkyojo'), which promoted
'naturalistic, democratic and humane education' and a broadening of the understanding of teacher professionalism to embrace negotiating conditions of

service and influencing educational policy. Its demonstrations for a change in the law that would allow the right of civil servants to form a union led, in 1989, to the dismissal of 1,500 teachers and the imprisonment of over 100 teachers on charges of illegal assembly.

Relief came with the more liberal 1990s. In 1991 a special law gave rights of negotiation and consultation on material matters to the KFTA, while taking care to exclude school administration and curriculum implementation from the deal. In 1993 the new civilian government reinstated most – but not all – of the dismissed teachers. In 1998, after the election of the veteran democracy campaigner Kim Dae-Jung as president, the government, yielding to international representations and the ongoing campaign of KTU teachers, conceded the principle of unions. Though – in consideration of teachers remaining civil servants – industrial action is still not permitted and though some matters are off limits for negotiation, this legal recognition may prove of historic significance for Korean education and for Korean democratic society more generally.

On the other hand, the ambivalence of teachers themselves regarding unionization has to be noted. It is estimated that prior to recognition, 2 per cent of all Korean teachers participated in the KTU and that its membership has since increased to about 4 per cent (15,000). The day after the law was passed, the leader of the KTU spoke in a press interview of it being time for teachers to become 'owners of education', but he knew that the KFTA had campaigned openly against the change. They had maintained it would be socially destabilizing and professionally divisive. So far from being a concession, it might well be part of a hidden government agenda to undermine the traditional job security of teachers (this was the year of the recession). Most important of all, teachers are neither labourers nor an 'interest group': teaching is something both professional and sacred (*Chosun Daily Newspaper*, 1998). Older and senior teachers, in particular, feared that unionism would erode the traditionally honoured status of teachers.

Status, vocation and a changing role

As in many other countries, teaching in Korea has been an important avenue of upward social mobility. Free tuition, room and board, and a guaranteed teaching post on graduation have long meant a competitive entry to the teachers' colleges, and bright, motivated students from lower-class and poor country areas have particularly been attracted (APEID, 1984a). As recently as 1992, 40 per cent of teachers had come from a poor farmer background (KEDI, 1992). The equalization from 1981 of primary training programmes and qualifications with secondary has enhanced both self-image and stability among primary teachers, who before that had frequently directed their in-service energies to moving 'upwards' into secondary teaching (Smith, 1992).

Probably the single most important determinant of status, however, is that teachers are civil servants, a sector well regarded by Koreans generally. In financial terms, this has meant job security, freedom from income tax, and numerous health and retirement benefits. All this has had to compensate for relatively low salaries, however, and in the 1960s and 1970s, as rapid economic expansion led to the development of many new professions and as economic values came to dominate society, teachers started to feel underpaid in comparison to professions with equivalent levels of education and training. A tendency grew for male teachers in particular to 'escape' from teaching into something more lucrative. Continuing to recruit and retain able and dedicated people and a perception in some quarters of personnel deterioration became controversial issues in Korean society. Ironically, the economic downturn of the late 1990s and the emerging problem of unemployment highlighted the advantages of traditional civil service job security.

More than its material conditions, 'civil servant' signifies a set of relationships with government and society. Korean teachers are servants of nationally accepted values. Article 53 of the law for civil servants lays upon them the duties of obligation, sincerity, dignity and obedience – in their private as well as their public lives. The resultant relationship with government is complex – 'subordination' indeed, but also the 'power' of agency: Korean teachers play the role of government agents (KEDI, 1992) and take some pride in it. The ambivalence we noted earlier regarding the progress of unionization should be seen in this light.

Ambivalence has other manifestations. Ahn found that slightly more than a third of her sample of primary teachers felt teachers should not be civil servants (against barely half who were sure they should be). This proportion was surprisingly high – as was the (probably related) scale of teacher dissatisfaction with government: two-thirds refusing the proposition that 'government supports teachers well', and twice as many supporting as opposing the proposition that 'government gets in the way of good teaching'. On a wider front, virtually all felt that 'society does not respect teachers enough' and that 'teachers deserve to be paid more', and rather more felt their status as teachers to be in decline than did not (Ahn, 2000: 178ff).

If this is gloom, however, it was lit up by one remarkable shaft of light. No less than 97 per cent of the sample would still choose teaching if they were starting out again (Ahn, 2000). One is alerted to the likelihood that something more is going on in teachers' minds than thoughts of material reward and social respect,– important though those things are to them:– that, as it might be put, 'vocation' operates in a different dimension from 'status'. This fits with other research which shows Korean teachers retaining a 'sacred' view of the teaching profession, valorizing their affection for pupils and sacrifices made for their calling (KEDI, 1992).

We are also the more encouraged to put a positive interpretation on those teacher discontents, to see them as perhaps the growing pains of a new independence, assertiveness and confidence in the profession. One possibility here is that the contradictions between the decentralizing rhetoric, intention and indeed some practical aspects of the sixth national curriculum on the one hand, and the many systemic constraints on its implementation on the other, may have had the effect of forcing the issue of teacher autonomy. Let us refer one last time to Ahn's study. She found the large majority of teachers in her study, including the majority of occasional critics of government, were content to define their professional role and autonomy in restricted 'own-classroom' terms. But she also found evidence of a small but significant minority who had been led to conceive of professional autonomy in a broader and deeper way (though by no means anarchically) and felt correspondingly more frustrated. It is likely that the continuation of this trend will be intimately connected with future curriculum policy (and both developments with key decisions about resources).

Parents

Underwood has commented shrewdly on a key limitation in the Korean enthusiasm for education (1991: 63–64):

> The Korean people's eagerness for education is in many ways an eagerness for status rather than content, for certification rather than for education, for membership in an elite department of an elite university rather than following a particular field of study… Starting at the kindergarten level, parents try to enter their children in 'prestigious' schools in order that they may eventually have a better chance to enter a prestigious university.

Most parents take this 'external' view of education and are relatively unconcerned about what and how schools should teach. Their zeal focuses, instead, on getting their children to do well (high test scores) at the business – on the way to 'doing well out of it' in later life – and in that they are prepared to invest very heavily indeed.

The intensity and prevalence of private tutoring is one consequence. Through the 1990s, supplementary education activities accounted for significant proportions of national GNP (eg 2.7 per cent in 1994). Overwhelming majorities of affluent children and, even more tellingly, large majorities of poorer children were involved in private tutoring after school. And extra 'breadth' was not the main product of this industry. Tuition may have ranged across English, maths, computing, fine art, music instruments and so forth, but the concentration was on the more academic areas. Particularly at the primary level, parents wanted private tutoring in cramming schools that focused mainly on test-driven and rote-memorization learning designed to improve their children's performance in main school.

Another consequence, one that particularly clouds the parent–teacher relationship in Korea, is the giving by parents and the receiving by teachers of gifts in cash or in kind. The nature and surrounding culture of this practice is all too well captured in its familiar Korean name, '*Chonji*', meaning 'exceeding gratitude'. Hong points out its power to corrupt and damage (1996: 107):

> In some cases, parents meet teachers periodically to hand over their 'bribe' money as a token of great gratitude. Parents give money or expensive gifts, expecting teachers' special attention and care toward their own children at the expense of classmates. If a teacher gives special attention to certain pupils, the teacher's limited attention and caring power are monopolized by those affluent pupils. Usually pupils know well whose mom did it and why that pupil is especially minded by their teacher. Pupils feel their teacher's biased attention and feel deeply hurt. The practice has spoiled some teachers and destroyed the sound relationship between teacher and parents and among pupils.

Though clearly incompatible with appropriate relationships between teachers and parents, and though prohibited by law, *Chonji* is still common and still regarded as natural. Counter-campaigns like the joint parent–teacher 'No *Chonji* Movement' have been unable to end it. Indeed, the sixth national curriculum replacement of paper-and-pencil tests with performance-related assessment at primary level may well have strengthened the practice, by making teachers' judgements a more critical factor. Most parents believe that *Chonji* will affect those judgements (KEDI, 1993).

The *Chosun Daily Newspaper* for 12 May 1999 reported that the primary headteachers' association in Seoul had decided that all Seoul primary schools should close for Teachers' Day. Officially, teachers were said to have earned a holiday. Privately it was acknowledged that the headteachers wanted to subvert *Chonji*, for which Teachers' Day had become a good opportunity. However one views this decision, it constitutes a depressing progress report on the campaign for a healthy parent–teacher relationship.

We would like to suggest that the key to progress lies in more positive measures, starting with the ongoing redefinition of the roles of parents in schools and a consequent intensification of parent–teacher contacts. This has been brought home particularly to one of the present authors by her experience of being for some years a parent at a London primary school.

Paradoxically, for all their interest and zeal where education is concerned, Korean parents have participated very little in the life and the practices of their children's schools. Parent–teacher associations were introduced in 1945 mainly with fund-raising in mind, and in practice have continued to operate primarily as financial support agencies. Since 1995, some parents have been participating in new school management committees – set up at all schools under the local educational governance system that came into operation in 1991 – alongside teachers, headteachers, community leaders, alumni representatives and educational specialists. These committees have indeed a wide range of functions, relating to discipline, curriculum and staffing as well as to finance. However, parents are not yet very active in them. They are quite likely to feel uncomfortable expressing their opinion in front of their children's teacher and they may worry that their criticisms or suggestions will affect their children negatively. So they are inclined to restrict their role here too to funding matters.

In any case, the management committee, like the PTA, can accommodate only a fraction of a school's parents. English schools address this point by the multiplicity and variety of their communications with parents generally and, most particularly, by holding regular quasi-public parents' evenings at which all parents are expected to show in order to discuss their children's school life and academic progress with their teachers. That Korean parents lack this kind of official opportunity may be one reason why the majority feel obliged to visit teachers unofficially – to show their face as well as to give *Chonji*.

Over time, multiplied contacts with schools and teachers should lead parents to an appreciative and critical interest in what and how the schools are teaching their children – to the benefit of the schools as well as the parents. And such a more developed concept of education should, in its turn, lead to some reworking of parents' own indirect and direct contributions to the education of their children.

References

Adams, D and Gottlieb, E (1993) *Education and Social Change in Korea*, Garland Publishing Inc, London

Ahn, M S (1996) An analysis of decision-making process in the curriculum development: a case study on the technical and vocational curriculum development in Korea, Unpublished PhD dissertation, Ewha Woman's University, Seoul

Ahn, M S (2000) The relationship between teachers and government in curriculum development in Korea and England, Unpublished PhD dissertation, Institute of Education, University of London, London

APEID (1984a) *Toward Universalization of Primary Education in Asia and the Pacific: Country studies – Republic of Korea*, UNESCO, Bangkok

APEID (1984b) *Diagnostic Studies on Educational Management: Country studies – Republic of Korea*, UNESCO, Bangkok

Bernstein, B (1975) *Class, Code and Control*, vol 3, *Towards Theory of Educational Transmission*, Routledge & Kegan Paul, London

Bruner, J S (1960) *The Process of Education*, Harvard University Press, Cambridge

Chosun Daily Newspaper (1998) Our claims, 17 November

Chosun Daily Newspaper (1999) What a shame for Teachers' Day, 12 May

Han, J (1995) The quest for national standards in science education in Korea, *Studies in Science Education*, (26), pp 59–71

Homer, B H (1969) *The Passing of Korea*, (reprinted), Yonsei University Press, Seoul

Hong, H (1996) Possibilities and limitations of teacher participation in curriculum development under a loosely centralized national curriculum: the case of the Korean primary school curriculum, Unpublished PhD dissertation, University of Wisconsin, Madison

Jayasuria, J E (1984) *Education in Korea: A Third World success story*, Korea National Commission of UNESCO, Seoul

Jo, Y, Hwang, G and Ahn, M S (1994) *A Study on the Curriculum Organization and Implementation at the Municipal and Provincial Education Authority and School Levels:– In relation with the sixth national curriculum*, KEDI, Seoul

KEDI (1986) *A Study of the Autonomy of Educational Administration*, KEDI, Seoul

KEDI (1987) *The Development Strategies in Education toward the Future Industrial Society*, KEDI, Seoul

KEDI (1988) *Educational Development in Korea 1988–1990*, The Korean National Commission for UNESCO, Seoul

KEDI (1992) *Comprehensive Understanding of Korean Education and its Future (III): Teachers and teaching profession climate*, KEDI, Seoul

KEDI (1993) *A National Survey on the Educational Enthusiasm of Korean People*, KEDI, Seoul

KICE (1998) *A Study on the Development of Teacher Training Programme for Implementation of National Curriculum and Evaluation Policy*, KICE, Seoul

Kim, J et al (1994) *New Theory of Teaching*, Educational Science Ltd, Seoul

Lawton, D (1996) *Beyond the National Curriculum*, Hodder & Stoughton, London

Lee, Y (1974) *Educational Innovation in the Republic of Korea: Experiments and innovation in education*, No 12, The UNESCO Press, Geneva

MOE (1963) *The Second National Curriculum*, MOE, Seoul

MOE (1992a) *The Sixth National Curriculum*, MOE, Seoul

MOE (1992b) *The Sixth National Curriculum: Primary curriculum guiding principles*, MOE, Seoul

MOE (1997) *Education in Korea*, Samwha Printing Co, Seoul

Park, S (1991) Confucianism molds core of the system: its legacies cast deep influence, *Koreana*, 5 (2), pp 13–22

Smith, D C (1992) *Elementary Teacher Education in Korea*, Phi Delta Kappa Educational Foundation, Bloomington, Indiana

Underwood, H G (1991) Merits and demerits of Korean education, *Koreana*, 5 (2), pp 63–69

19. Changing cultures and schools in the United States of America

Susan Douglas Franzosa

Introduction

Benjamin Barber has written that, 'As any careful reader of American history cannot help but notice, America has always been a tale of peoples trying to be a People, a tale of diversity and plurality in search of unity' (Barber, 1992: 41). Historically, the task of forming 'a People', of transmitting the knowledge, dispositions, values and skills associated with democratic participation, fell to the nation's public schools. From the first, this task had inherent tensions. How would a common citizenship be defined and what would constitute a curriculum for its realization?

Early advocates of public education defined the parameters and articulated the principles of ensuing national debates on these questions. From the nation's beginnings, the democratization of educational opportunity was linked to political and social aspirations. The provision of publicly supported schools that could educate succeeding generations for responsible citizenship was deemed essential to national stability, prosperity and cohesion. Although educational priorities have shifted in response to the nation's political, economic and social circumstances, these ideals have continued to contour US perspectives on the role and responsibilities of schools.

However, the decentralized nature of control in US public education has worked against the formation of national educational agendas that would define a common citizenship for all students. Under the United States constitution, the provision of education and its regulation are the responsibilities of the individual states and not the federal government. As the history of educational reform movements demonstrates, abiding conflicts between commonality and diversity, private and public interest, and excellence and equity have been difficult to mediate within this context. With growth and expansion – state systems currently represent 15,000 school districts and enrol over 44 million students in 60,000 elementary and 23,000 secondary schools that differ significantly in size, ethnic, racial and class composition, financial support and per-pupil expenditures (Cookson, 1994: 493) – the need to mediate these conflicts has become even more acute.

Historic rationales for citizenship and public education

Although the effort to secure national unity was a foundational influence in the emergence of public schooling in the United States, an education that served merely to further the interests of an elite or maintain the government's power through indoctrination was clearly contrary to the ideals of the US constitution and bill of rights. Consistent with the principle of government by and for the people, initial models for public education in the United States defined schooling not only as a means to political and social continuity but also as a way of cultivating individual improvement that would ensure one's rights and liberty. That is, public schooling was conceptualized as being able to meet the educational needs of both the society and the individual.

To that end, following national independence in 1776, Thomas Jefferson introduced a proposal for publicly supported state schools in Virginia that were intended to foster 'a more general diffusion of knowledge' to 'illuminate the minds of the people at large' (Jefferson, 1779: 84). In Jefferson's proposal, state schools would offer three years of instruction in literacy and numeracy, the rules of social association, and the rights and duties of citizenship to all white children 'without regard to wealth, birth or other accidental conditions or circumstances' (Jefferson, 1779: 91). Public education beyond the first three years, however, was intended only for those who would become full citizens and members of the electorate. Only talented, white, male children who had proven their abilities during the first three years of schooling would be eligible to continue their education at state-supported secondary schools and colleges. In the first stage of Jefferson's plan, then, the system would address the need for basic literacy and socialization for 'the people at large', while in its subsequent stages it would offer education in the liberal arts and statecraft to students 'naturally endowed with genius and virtue' who were expected to distinguish themselves as political leaders or in the professions.

While Jefferson's plan was essentially aristocratic in its delineation of hierarchical stages within the system, it nevertheless established a basis for an institutional structure that would determine success through proven ability rather than inherited privilege. Although his proposals were never fully realized in 18th-century Virginia, this early meritocratic model remained important because it continued to frame US understanding of public schools as 'nurseries of citizenship' that function to transmit common civic values and provide an equal chance to acquire the knowledge and skills necessary to participate successfully in public life.

The practical realization of the Jeffersonian model for public education within the nation as a whole was made difficult by the decentralized nature of legislative control over education in the United States. Under the constitution, regulatory and fiscal responsibility for education had been delegated to the individual states and not the federal government. There was no formal centralized government mechanism for instituting one uniform system of education

throughout the country. Thus progress toward free universal public schooling had to be accomplished state by state. Despite the difficulties, most states'
founding documents and charters did contain statements acknowledging
their commitment to educate the citizens within their jurisdictions and by
1800 a majority of the states had enacted legislation establishing tax support
for some form of public schooling (Butts, 1978: 50).

There was considerable variation in the extent and organization of educational provisions between states and even between townships within individual states at the beginning of the 19th century. This situation began to change
by mid-century during a period of increased immigration and the beginnings
of a transition from an agriculturally-based to an industrial-based economy.
Public demands for schools increased significantly within this context, and a
common school movement emerged, which was influential in advancing the
country toward an expansion of educational opportunity.

The common schoolers concentrated their efforts on what had comprised
the first stage of public education in Jefferson's plan. They maintained that
students of both sexes and all classes should receive eight years of schooling
and stressed the need to teach civic obligations and responsibilities to 'a general public'. Horace Mann, the leading proponent of the movement, argued
that a free universal education should not only teach literacy and the values
that would 'enable each citizen to participate in the power of governing others' but should also function to uplift character and inculcate a work ethic
(Mann, 1957: 56). The common school's curriculum would include lessons in
reading, writing, numeracy, health, geography, and United States government and history. Texts that portrayed the exemplary values of thrift, hon-
esty, self-discipline, hard work and social responsibility would be integrated
throughout the curriculum and modelled by teachers in their classrooms.
While the education of an informed electorate remained a central goal, the arguments of the common schoolers repeatedly highlighted a need for training
in character and the dispositions required of work as components of preparation for citizenship. Foreshadowing contemporary discourse on public education, Mann maintained that a system of common schools would 'expand the
institutions and fortunes of the state, increase popular intelligence, and ele-
vate general morality' (Mann, 1957: 109).

The common school movement was successful in winning support for publicly financed education in part because it addressed widespread concerns
about the social and political consequences of industrialization and an increasingly divisive cultural pluralism. Older rural communities had changed
as workers moved from farm to factory and there were fears that 'the educational functions traditionally carried on by family, neighbourhood, or shop
were no longer being performed; somehow they must get done; like it or not,
the school must take them on' (Cremin, 1962: 117). In addition, the number of
foreign-born had increased from 12 per cent of the population in 1830 to 25 per
cent in 1880. By 1918 it would reach 35 per cent and, in the major cities of the

north-east, immigrants' children would comprise up to 85 per cent of public school students (Tyack, 1974: 230–32). Reflecting a popular sentiment of the time, one commentator wrote, 'Unless we educate our immigrants, they will be our ruin' (Butts, 1978: 236).

By the end of the 19th century, most states had increased their educational expenditures in order to provide more years of schooling to an increasing number of students and 31 of the 45 states had passed compulsory attendance laws. Public schools were now becoming less differentiated in structure and organization. However, at both national and local levels, profound differences emerged concerning the role of public education and the appropriate content of schooling for a common citizenship.

Contested definitions of democratic citizenship

At the beginning of the 20th century, reflecting the distinctions between the Jeffersonian emphasis on political citizenship and the common schoolers' emphasis on character and vocational dispositions, increasingly diverse constituencies called alternatively for informed political participation, socialization and cultural assimilation, or workforce preparation as educational priorities. 'Businessmen and labour unions were insisting that school assume the classical functions of apprenticeship. Settlement workers and municipal reformers were vigorously urging instruction in hygiene, domestic science, manual arts and childcare. Patriots of every stripe were calling for Americanization programs. And agrarian publicists were pressing for a new sort of training for country life' (Cremin, 1962: 116-117).

Local communities and parents were also contending for their rights to define the priorities of public education. 'Ethnic and religious heterogeneity and racial and class divisions often made schools the focus of sharp political conflict... Although parents wanted their children to attend school, they did not expect to abdicate responsibility for what took place there, and many believed that the school should express their own particular values' (Lazerson et al, 1985: 5).

Addressing the need to promote a common citizenship, some educators of the period stressed the importance of lessons in US history and government (Krug, 1964: 168–70). Others called for an education that would foster 'social likemindedness' through the study of didactic literature and socialization in morals and manners (Robbins, 1920: 13). In the minority, social reformer Jane Addams argued that the children of the newer immigrants would be more fully integrated within US public life if the value of their own cultural traditions were acknowledged and represented in the curriculum (Addams, 1910: 172–73).

Within this context, John Dewey proposed that the schools counter social fragmentation by becoming embryonic democratic communities. Invoking the historic rationales of Jefferson and Mann, but attempting to provide a model that would address what he saw as the interdependent nature of political, social and vocational components of citizenship, he maintained that 'nothing counts as much as the school' in mediating the relationship between individual and society (Dewey, 1900: 7). However, Dewey rejected the idea that the goal of education in a democracy was to preserve and reproduce an existing social order. Affirming a faith in the transformative powers of the school, he wrote, 'When the school introduces and trains each child of society into membership within such a little community, saturating him with the spirit of social service, and providing him with the instruments of effective self-direction, we shall have the deepest and best guarantee of a larger society which is worthy, lovely, and harmonious' (Dewey, 1900: 29).

Dewey was critical of the view that public schools in a democratic state exist merely to educate an electorate. 'A democracy', he argued, 'is more than a form of government; it is primarily a mode of associated living, of conjoint communicated experience' in which a diversity of interests interact and barriers of status and culture are overcome in common cooperative activity (Dewey, 1916: 101–02). Democracy and democratic schools, he argued, allow progressive social reconstruction and improvement. The Laboratory School that Dewey founded at the University of Chicago in 1896 was intended to demonstrate how these principles might work in practice. For Dewey, democratic dispositions would be formed by engaging all students in interdisciplinary group problem solving that focused on the history of human culture, industry and science (Tanner, 1997: 163–68).

In part, Dewey was attempting to reclaim and reconstruct the ideal for schools as nurseries of citizenship. But his work was also an attempt to redefine the nature of democratic citizenship. In his view, effective participation in a democracy involved more than adjustment and accommodation; it required inculcating both 'the spirit of service' and 'effective self direction' in the interests of individual growth and positive social change. According to Dewey, these goals could only be achieved through a radical reconstruction of the school curriculum and the introduction of a more child-centred and activity-based pedagogy. Dewey's ideas were taken up by members of the Progressive Education Association and had some impact on elementary teacher training programmes but they had little direct effect on public school classroom practices (Cremin, 1962: 140–42). The idea that education could change and improve society as well as unify it was accepted and became a governing assumption within 20th-century educational discourse. However, Dewey's conceptualization of an inclusive democratic citizenship failed to take hold. Social change and improvement through schooling began to be seen as providing students with different curricula rather than a common educational experience.

Framing 'the one best system' for civic education

A search for what the historian David Tyack termed 'the one best system' during the first half of the 20th century involved professional educators in reforms that standardized curricula in the elementary schools and introduced differentiated courses of study within the secondary schools. On the issue of citizenship, professional education associations and regional teachers organizations continued to debate whether academic studies, vocational training or character formation should be given the greatest weight within the school's curriculum and considered lobbying for the adoption of a required course in 'basic civics' for all students.

In 1916 the American Political Science Association recommended that 'community civics', the study of responsible participation in family, work and local community life, become compulsory in the elementary schools. Community civics would meet the needs of the vast majority of students for training in 'ordinary citizenship' while reserving the study of state and national history and the principles of US government for the minority of students who would attend secondary schools. In concert with the American Political Science Association's proposal, and drawing on Dewey's model for interdisciplinary studies, the National Education Association (NEA) advocated a new curricular organization for elementary schools in which the traditional subjects of history, geography, economics and government would be integrated within a course in 'social studies'. Civic education in the social studies would concentrate on fostering the values of 'family, vocation, good character, good health, profitable use of leisure time, and cognitive skills' (Butts, 1978: 194). A distinction was made between an 'old civics' and a 'new civics':

> The old civics, almost exclusively a study of government machinery, must give way to the new civics, a study of all manner of social efforts to improve mankind. It is not so important that the pupil know how the President is elected as that he shall understand the duties of the health officer in his community. Time formerly spent in the effort to understand the process of passing a law over the President's veto is now to be more profitably used in the observation of the vocational resources of the community. (Butts, 1978: 195)

In the absence of any federal authority in education or any government agency to direct system-wide educational practices, the NEA – which included a majority of the country's teachers and school administrators – exerted considerable influence in the policies of the nation's public schools during this period (Tyack and Cuban, 1995: 17–19). Throughout the United States, courses in social studies and a 'new civics' approach were adopted by elementary schools and courses in US government became required in the upper levels of the secondary schools.

Between 1900 and 1930, secondary public school enrolment of 14–17-year-old students grew from almost 8 per cent to over 44 per cent (Lazerson et al,

1985: 19). As school administrators turned to industrial models and scientific management strategies to organize the diverse population of students now going on to public high schools, standardized assessments of ability and vocational guidance programmes were used to select students for placement in academic or vocational tracks.

> The moral and political terms that had dominated nineteenth-century discussions of education gave way to technical and economic terms... As the rationale for public schooling shifted, the political ends of schooling were subordinated to the economic ones. Equality in education was redefined as equality of opportunity in an economically inegalitarian society. In preparation for their different roles as adults, high school students were exposed to different curricula, thus providing the justification for the comprehensive curriculum of twentieth-century schools. Equality under this doctrine no longer meant equal exposure to a common curriculum. (Lazerson *et al*, 1985: 52–53)

Distinctions between academic and vocational courses of study, like the distinctions between the old and new civics, indicated a shift away from the goal of providing the common curriculum for citizenship that had been envisioned in earlier rationales for public education. The schools now moved toward a curricular model tied to the goals of economic and social efficiency that would predominate throughout the century. Tiers of citizenship, derived from expectations about students' future roles in the workforce, were consistently articulated within this model.

Reconfigurations of educational participation and control

The structure of control in US public education remained decentralized at mid-century, with the states assuming responsibilities for the creation and regulation of standards for curricula, instruction, graduation, teacher education and school accreditation, and the municipalities of the states assuming the major responsibilities for the implementation of policy and the appropriation of taxes to fund local school districts. While this structure prevented the creation of a true 'system' of public education in the United States, the country's public schools nevertheless became more systematic in organizational form and curricular content during the 1930s, and more systematic in extent after the Second World War.

Following the war, educational policy makers were preoccupied with meeting demands for expansion and improving instruction in curricular areas thought to be most important to the readjustments of the economy. Civic education received less attention. The organization of curricula in social studies and US history and government that had emerged before the war remained virtually unchanged as the need to strengthen mathematics, science and technology became a primary focus of cold war policies (Spring, 1986: 281–84). During the 1950s the federal government began to intervene in state systems by providing funds for targeted educational improvements. In 1950 the United States Congress passed the National Science Foundation Act (NSF), which allocated grants to the states for teacher training, curriculum development, and vocational and health programmes. After the Soviet Union succeeded in launching Sputnik in 1957, NSF appropriations were increased and Congress approved the National Defense Education Act (NDEA), which initiated programmes to modernize curricula, promote patriotism and introduce state-wide achievement testing in foreign languages as well as in mathematics and science.

Although the federal government's interventions under NSF and NDEA marked the beginnings of a change in the structure of control in US public education, these interventions were relatively uncontroversial. State systems welcomed financial support during an era in which their budgets were being stretched to accommodate an unprecedented growth in school enrolments. More controversial was the federal government's involvement in state policy following the 1954 Supreme Court decision in *Brown* v *Board of Education*. This decision established that the racially segregated schools of the southern states had denied black children their constitutional rights as future citizens to equality of educational opportunity. It also, coupled with the civil rights legislation that followed it in the early 1960s, gave the federal government the authority to overturn discriminatory educational policies within the states and to enforce civil rights law in the nation's public schools. As a result, equality of educational opportunity was extended and federal legislation throughout the 1960s and 1970s expanded its scope to prevent or compensate for other forms of educational discrimination. Federal funds were used to establish compensatory and entitlement programmes that would address the needs of low-income, handicapped, female and bilingual students.

Federal government intervention during this period effectively democratized the parameters of educational participation, but there were few corresponding efforts to alter the existing inequities in internal school structures that had arisen in past decades. 'The most important advance was enlarging access to public education for those previously disenfranchised, but inclusion was not matched by improvements in the quality of education provided to new entrants... Structurally, compensatory programs have established yet another basis for tracking, labelling, and lowered expectations' (Bastian *et al*, 1986: 44–45).

There were some changes in the schools' curricula during the 1960s and early 1970s. Federal grants encouraged innovations in advanced placement courses for students of high ability in science and mathematics (Lazerson *et al*, 1985: 23–46), and there were significant efforts to integrate materials on minorities and women within literature and history courses (Frazier and Sadker, 1977). However, most observers noted few changes in the schools' approach to civic education. Looking back over courses of study in the social studies, Fred Newmann found, for example, 'a lack of consensus on goals', 'no thorough conceptual base' and 'an absence of systematic rationales' for citizenship even when citizenship was articulated as an explicit curricular goal (Newmann, 1977: 16–18). Thus, while educational reforms had addressed the question of who might claim the citizen's right to an education, there was less clarity on what education for citizenship should entail.

Following Newmann's and others' work there was a revival of interest in civic education within academic circles. Mirroring discussions of the past, scholars began to reassess the school's role in 'forming a public' (Hill, 1982; Raywid, Tesconi and Warren, 1984). Initiating the discussion, R Freeman Butts called for a return to a Deweyian tradition of social reconstruction (Butts, 1980). Butts noted that school civics had lost its focus and coherence amid an era of 'segmented pluralisms' and urged instruction in a uniform core of democratic principles and values for all students. As if in illustration of Butts's contentions, scholars advanced a series of conflicting proposals for reform. Some, like Butts, advocated identifying a core set of democratic principles and values but disagreed on what should comprise the core (Stanley, 1983; Adler, 1983; Pratte, 1988). Some stressed the need for a representation of diverse cultural perspectives and maintained that agreement on a core was untenable and could only lead to the repression of minority group values (Gordon, 1988; Wood, 1988). Others turned from a consideration of curricular content to propose new participatory and student-centred teaching methods designed to foster the skills of critical thinking and decision making (Torney-Purta and Schwille, 1986). These pedagogical proposals were countered by writers on the left who claimed that they encouraged 'mastery of procedural tasks devoid of any political commitment regarding what is democratically just or morally defensible' (Giroux, 1987), as well as writers on the right who charged that participatory models would promote relativistic thinking and prevent students from achieving a common standard of cultural literacy (Finn, 1988). While these debates received considerable attention at professional conferences and in academic journals during the early 1980s, they were eclipsed as a new agenda for public education was advanced by the federal government. Often characterized as a conservative restoration, the Reagan–Bush agenda defined the primary role of public schooling as 'meeting the needs of a new global economy'. Within this context, citizenship education was understood chiefly as preparation for participation in the workforce.

The 'crisis' of public education in the 1980s

As Peter Cookson observes, 'One of the ironies of the 1980s was that the federal government became so deeply involved in educational reform while at the same time arguing against federal involvement in social policy' (Cookson,

1994: 24). During the presidential administration of Ronald Reagan, as the country was experiencing the strains of an economic recession, the federal government's stance on public education shifted from a liberal consensus concerned with extending equality of educational opportunity toward a conservative interest in decentralization, cost management and improved effectiveness. Early on, the Reagan administration announced an agenda for a 'new federalism' that would decrease the central government's regulatory powers and 'restore' control to the individual states. Members of the administration charged that 'excessive egalitarianism and oppressive public sector intervention' in education during the 1960s and 1970s had compromised the states' local authority and led to an over-bureaucratized system unable to meet the labour force, scientific and technological needs of the nation. 'For the past twenty years', stated one presidential advisory group, 'federal mandates have favoured "disadvantaged" pupils at the expense of those who have the highest potential to contribute to society' (Bastian *et al*, 1986: 14).

The schools were characterized by the Reagan administration as failing to set high standards for teaching and learning or counter an erosion of morality in youth. As the administration saw it, a new federalism applied to public education would encourage the states' own initiatives to improve their schools. In reality, the new federalism meant reductions in federal expenditures for special education, bilingual education and educational equity programmes, student loan programmes in higher education, and technical assistance and development grants (Bastian *et al*, 1986: 46–47) as well as the development of a powerful rhetoric of privatization and competition. Dramatically departing from a traditional commitment to public education and the common school ideals of the past, the government's arguments for national improvement also included calls for support of schools in the private sector through tuition vouchers that would allow for parental choice and foster market-driven competition between schools (Cookson, 1994: 488). Acceding to the lobbying of religious fundamentalists, proposals for school choice, by allowing the choice of a religious school, posed a serious threat to the separation of church and state that had been established under the United States constitution.

Responding to declines identified in cross-national studies of student achievement, the dissatisfactions of influential members of the business community and taxpayer demands for accountability, the United States Department of Education began to issue a series of commissioned reports that were highly critical of the nation's public schools. The most well-known, the 1983 US Department of Education, US National Commission on Excellence in Education's *A Nation at Risk*, emerged from within this context and proved to be a foundation for policy on public education throughout the decade. Warning that the country's 'once unchallenged pre-eminence in industry, science, and technological innovation is being taken over by competitors throughout the world', *A Nation at Risk* called for higher performance criteria, a more streamlined and rigorous curriculum, national academic standards, regularized as-

sessments of students and teachers, and closer ties between the education and
business communities (p 3).

In the five years following the release of *A Nation at Risk*, over 30 other national reports on education were published. Most reiterated what were seen
as the failures of the public school system and framed their recommendations
for school improvement in terms of perceived economic, national defence and
technological needs (Cremin, 1990: 6–8). When citizenship was mentioned it
was defined largely in terms of the individual's potential to contribute to the
country's economic development and growth. In David Berliner's and Bruce
Biddle's summary of federal recommendations advanced during the period,
for example, they note the stress placed on 'achievement, individual initiative,
free enterprise, and other values thought to help students become informa-
tion-age leaders' and the virtual absence of attention to the goals of informed
political participation, personal development or educational equity (Berliner
and Biddle, 1997: 142). Further, educational equity was implicitly conceptualized as being in opposition to the achievement of educational excellence.

While the accuracy and political intent of many of the 1980s reports were
challenged – and are still being challenged – their findings were nevertheless
reported regularly in the media and helped to erode public confidence in the
nation's schools (Lazerson *et al*, 1985: 13–18). The administration's characterization of the condition of public education 'shift[ed] the blame for unemployment and underemployment, for the loss of economic competitiveness, and
the supposed breakdown of 'traditional' values… from the economic, cultural, and social policies and effects of dominant groups to the schools' (Apple,
1993: 28). It also had the effect of changing the nature and distribution of federally sponsored grants, which in turn influenced school policies and the direction of curricular reform at the state level. Although university-based
scholars continued to address the need for a rethinking of civic education and
pointed out that the school's curriculum for citizenship should involve more
than preparation for employment, these issues were all but ignored by state
departments of education as they concentrated on devising accountability
measures for student achievement and teacher competency.

Against a backdrop of governmental critique and public dissatisfaction, interpretative studies of the schools also emerged during the 1980s. The most influential, Ernest Boyer's *High School: A report on secondary education in America*
(1983), John Goodlad's *A Place Called School: Prospects for the future* (1983) and
Theodore Sizer's *Horace's Compromise: The dilemma of the American high school*
(1984), departed from the federally commissioned reports and pointed to de-
personalized school cultures, authoritarian organizational structures, routin-
ized approaches to curricula and classroom management, and
disempowered, overworked teachers, rather than the erosion of standards
and falling student achievement scores, as public education's chief problems.
According to these authors, the focus for educational reform should be on improving the conditions for teaching and learning. What was needed, they ar-

gued, was strategies to foster student and teacher engagement and rebuild a sense of community within schools.

Boyer's, Goodlad's and Siser's studies helped to initiate a variety of intentional school reform networks that, in line with the federal government's recommendations for privatization and increased competition, were funded primarily through grants from private foundations. Researchers, teachers, administrators, parents, community members and representatives from professional and civic organizations began to form coalitions – including the Effective Schools Movement, the Coalition for Essential Schools, the National Network for Educational Renewal and the National Center for Restructuring Education, Schools, and Teaching – that worked to create nationally linked community-based efforts to restructure the schools. Providing an alternative to government-directed reforms, these networks recruited membership schools throughout the 1980s and began to design collaborative models for educational improvement. Other more conservative groups, representing proponents of school choice, voucher systems and character education adopted these organizational strategies and formed single-issue reform networks. However, by the end of the decade these efforts had not yet received very much national attention. Rather, the focus remained on the federal government's evolving agenda for addressing what were now seen as the failures of the public schools.

In 1989, newly elected President George Bush responded to what he termed the 'crisis of American education' and convened an education summit of the country's state governors to identify educational goals for the nation. Drawing on the governors' recommendations, the Bush administration's educational agenda was published in *America 2000* (United States Department of Education, 1991). Funds for a National Education Goals Panel, charged with establishing goals and monitoring progress toward their attainment, were approved by the United States Congress. In 1991, the Goals Panel issued *Goals 2000*, which listed six national goals to be achieved by the turn of the century (National Educational Goals Panel, 1991: vi):

- All children will start school ready to learn.
- The high school graduation rate will increase to at least 90 per cent.
- All students will become competent in challenging subject matter.
- US students will be first in the world in mathematics and science achievement.
- Every adult American will be literate.
- Schools will be safe and disciplined.

In keeping with constitutional provisions for state control of public education, state adoption of *Goals 2000* was voluntary and, if adopted, each state was encouraged to pursue the federal government's goals agenda in its own way. Federal funds were provided as an incentive to states that agreed to develop strategies for improvement and to implement national assessment of educational progress (NAEP) assessment and reporting mechanisms. In 1991, base-line data for each state was collected and the National Assessment Governing Board established student achievement levels for NAEP (National Educational Goals Panel, 1992). In 1994, during the Clinton administration, Congress reauthorized appropriations for *Goals 2000* programmes and approved the following two additional national goals (National Educational Goals Panel, 1994: 1):

- Teachers will have the knowledge and skills that they need.
- Schools will promote parental involvement and participation.

Although there was some initial resistance from a minority of states in which legislators and school board members expressed anxiety about federal intervention in local curricular matters, by 1995 all 50 states had applied for *Goals 2000* funds to support improvement toward one or more of the national goals. A nominal decentralization of the educational system was thus maintained by keeping adoption voluntary and delegating responsibilities for development and implementation to the states, while at the same time centralizing the federal government's authority to define, monitor and assess the attainment of common national goals.

Emerging patterns of reform: prospects for citizenship education

Evolving from President Reagan's new federalism, the government strategy for educational reform throughout the last decade, and throughout both Republican and Democratic presidential administrations, has been to offer initial support and technical assistance for nationally targeted goals with the expectations that state and local authorities will implement change and that private foundations, professional associations and businesses, acting as partners to the schools, will provide funds to sustain school improvement projects as federal funds are withdrawn.

Directed at different goals and receiving their initial funding from private rather than public sources, intentional educational reform networks have tended to mirror a number of components of the federal government's reform strategy. For example, since its inception in 1984, the Coalition of Essential Schools – which grew from a membership of nine schools in four states to a membership of over a thousand schools in 38 states – has developed supporting partnerships with both private and public organizations and worked in collaboration with local and state boards of education to advance its agenda. Member schools adopt the Coalition's 'nine common principles' and agree to redesign their structures and practices in accord with them. The Coalition's efforts have been directed at creating communities of learning that, like the Deweyian Laboratory School earlier in the century, provide models for democratic participation and engagement. However: 'The Coalition offers no specific "model" or program for schools to adopt... Each school develops its own programs, suited to its particular students, faculty, and community' (Coalition of Essential Schools, 1997: 2).

The same organizational pattern dominates within intentional reform networks formed by more conservative groups. In the case of the Center for the Advancement of Ethics and Character, grants from private foundations and corporate sector partnerships have supported curriculum development and teacher training in local schools as well as the Center's lobbying of state departments of education. The objective of the Center is to counter the 'sentimentalism' and 'cultural relativism of the 1960s and 1970s' by restoring the 19th-century ideal for character formation as 'an uncontested educational priority'. The Center has developed a framework, 'The school assessment checklist', and guidelines, 'The 100 ways educators can help students acquire good character', to stimulate local implementation but notes 'that they are not intended to be flatly prescriptive. The applicability depends on... opportunities and problems now confronting the school, and the skills and interests of the faculty' (Wynne and Ryan, 1997: xix).

Thus since the mid-1980s, a range of educational reforms have been initiated by privately funded networks as well as the federal government, adapted to local needs and circumstances, and sustained (if sustained) by gaining the approval of state educational authorities and winning the support of local and regional constituencies. In many cases this organizational pattern has given educators and parents, as well as special interest groups, a more direct role in determining state and local implementation policies and practices. However, it has not facilitated a national dialogue on the central purposes of public education nor has it provided a framework in which conflicting publics might reach consensus on a common curriculum for a modern citizenship. In fact, as Michael Apple has pointed out, the delegation of responsibility to local communities has tended to remove 'fundamental questions... about the basis of community, the conditions of citizenship, and the achievement of human dignity' from public debate (Apple, 1993: 113). Within this context, intentional reform networks have pursued their conflicting local agendas leaving the federal government to provide direction for large-scale comprehensive educational change at the national level through *Goals 2000*.

Since 1992, the National Educational Goals Panel has issued annual progress reports on *Goals 2000* that provide summaries of nationwide improvement and state-by-state comparisons. The report of 1999, *Building a Nation of Learners*, indicates that there have been significant gains in pre-school children's health and preparation for school, 8th grade reading competency, 4th, 8th and 12th grade mathematics proficiency, and increases in the number of post-secondary degrees awarded in mathematics and the sciences. Areas of national decline include school safety, student drug use and the subject matter preparation of teachers (National Educational Goals Panel, 1999: 10–11). The report stresses, however, that the most important achievements under

Goals 2000 have been the setting of national academic performance levels and the creation of a system to monitor and report state progress. These achievements are understood by the Goals Panel as the necessary foundation for 'standards-based educational reforms' throughout the states. The 1999 report includes a description of the process (p 4):

> The US Department of Education, other federal agencies, and private foundations awarded grants to private professional organisations to begin a multi-year effort to develop voluntary national standards in key subject areas... The Goals Panel convened an advisory group of experts to suggest specific guidelines that might be used to review the quality of proposed standards developed by these national professional organisations or by the states [and] joined forces with numerous professional organisations, states, and school districts to advance standard-based reforms. Voluntary national standards have been created in the academic subjects specified in Goal 3, and have served as models or resources for the development of state and local standards. (National Educational Goals Panel, 1999: 4)

The report notes that all but one of the states have now adopted some of the national standards in core subjects and all but two states have implemented state-wide assessment programmes. 'Though much work remains to be done,' write the report's authors, 'there is widespread agreement that the longevity and success of the academic standards movement to date have been extraordinary' (National Educational Goals Panel, 1999: 4).

Goals 2000 assessments have provided very few specifics on curricular standards that might be related to the practice of democratic citizenship. The only explicit reference to academic subject matter dealing with political participation is the specification of 'civics and government' under Goal 3:

> By the year 2000, all students will leave grades 4, 8, and 12, having demonstrated competency over challenging subject matter including English, mathematics, science, foreign languages, civics and government, economics, arts, history, and geography, and every school in America will ensure that all students learn to use their minds well, so that they may be prepared for responsible citizenship, further learning, and productive employment in our Nation's modern economy. (National Educational Goals Panel, 1999: v)

The components of 'responsible citizenship' are not clearly delineated. Indicators of progress toward Goal 3 are confined to improvement on standardized NAEP assessment tests. Yet, assessment of student proficiency in civics and government has not been a priority under *Goals 2000*. Nor has there been much success in encouraging the implementation of standards for civics and government within the states.

During the mid-1990s, national standards and curriculum frameworks in civics and government were developed by NAEP in collaboration with the Center for Civic Education, a private foundation that developed from the work of R Freeman Butts during the 1980s (Butts, 1989). NAEP assessments of student proficiency in civics and government were conducted for the first time in 1998. Although not included in the most recent *Goals 2000* report, the results released by NAEP indicate that only 25 per cent of the nation's students scored at the proficient or advanced level on the assessment (National Assessment Governing Board, 1999). Despite these low scores, the development of standards in civics and government within the states has received considerably less federal funding than similar efforts in mathematics, science, reading and writing and, in contrast to the yearly assessments conducted in these areas, the Goals Panel plans to administer civics and government assessments at five-year intervals (Branson, 1999: 4). Progress on standards-based educational reforms in civics has been unimpressive with only three states having adopted NAEP standards (Quigley, 2000: 2). This situation may change as the next NAEP assessment draws near. However, at present, it seems clear that academic experiences in civics are not valued very highly in *Goals 2000* standards-based reforms.

While curricular reforms initiated under *Goals 2000* have seemed to undervalue academic courses traditionally concerned with fostering informed political participation, *Goals 2000* programmes nevertheless reveal a powerful government consensus on the school's role in the production of a national citizenry. That consensus reflects the persistence of a belief in the social and economic efficacy of meritocratic public school structures to produce citizens who will contribute to the country's economic growth, technological development and ability to compete globally. Within this framework, standards-based reforms in curricula associated with workforce preparation, basic literacy, advanced achievement in mathematics and the sciences, school choice demonstration projects and school-to-work initiatives have received the most sustained financial support. With the exception of pre-school intervention and adult literacy programmes, the expansion of equality of educational opportunity has received virtually no attention. Throughout, precedence has been given to the construction of highly bureaucratized national and state systems to measure and monitor student achievement and normalize existing school structures.

Echoing historic rationales for US public education, Benjamin Barber maintains that, 'Schools are the public nurseries of our future... Whether schools produce merely literate private individuals and competent workers or truly democratic citizens will condition our global destiny' (Barber, 1992: 263). Clearly, the education initiatives of the federal government during the last two decades have favoured the production of 'merely literate private individuals and competent workers'. They have also fostered the growth of free-market patterns of decentralization, competition and privatization in educational reform, inhibiting national dialogue on the nature of democratic citizenship. The growth of an 'assessment culture' may have the effect of moving the country closer to an acceptance of a national curriculum as the achievement of particular forms of knowledge and skill are legitimated through testing. However, in the absence of any attempt to address widespread disparities in school funding, discriminatory tracking practices, and student and teacher disengagement, national testing will do little to counter educational inequalities or to create democratic communities within the public schools.

References

Addams, J (1910) *Twenty Years at Hull House*, Macmillan, New York

Adler, M (1983) Understanding the USA, *Journal of Teacher Education*, **34** (6)

Apple, M (1993) *Official Knowledge: Democratic education in a conservative age*, Routledge, London

Barber, B (1992) *An Aristocracy of Everyone: The politics of education and the future of America*, Oxford University Press, New York

Bastian, A et al (1986) *Choosing Equality: The case for democratic schooling*, Temple University Press, Philadelphia

Berliner, D C and Biddle, B J (1997) *The Manufactured Crisis: Myths, frauds, and the attack on America's public schools*, Longman Publishers, White Plains, NY

Boyer, E (1983) *High School: A report on secondary education in America*, Carnegie Foundation for the Advancement of Teaching, New York

Branson, M (1999) *Making the Case for Civic Education: Where we stand at the end of the 20th century*, Center for Civic Education, Caslabas, CA

Butts, R F (1978) *Public Education in the United States: From revolution to reform*, Holt, Rhinehart and Winston, New York

Butts, R F (1980) *The Revival of Civic Learning: A rationale for citizenship education in American schools*, Phi Delta Kappa Educational Foundation, Bloomington, IN

Butts, R F (1989) *The Morality of Democratic Citizenship: Goals for civic education in the Republic's third century*, Center for Civic Education, Caslabas, CA

Coalition of Essential Schools (1997) Description, *Horace*, **3** (4)

Cookson, P (1994) *School Choice: The struggle for the soul of American education*, Yale University Press, New Haven, CT

Cremin, L (1962) *The Transformation of the School: Progressivism in American education, 1876–1957*, Alfred Knopf, New York

Cremin, L (1990) *Popular Education and its Discontents*, Harper Collins, New York

Dewey, J (1900) *The School and Society*, University of Chicago Press, Chicago, IL

Dewey, J (1916) *Democracy and Education*, Macmillan, New York

Finn, C (1988) Among the educationaloids: the social studies debacle, *American Spectator*, **21** (5), pp 35–36

Frazier, N and Sadker, M (1977) *Sexism in School and Society*, Harper and Row, New York

Giroux, H (1987) Citizenship, public philosophy, and the retreat from democracy in the United States, in *In the Nation's Image: Civic education in Japan, the Soviet Union, the United States, France, and Britain*, ed E B Gumber, pp 61–84, University of Georgia Press, Atlanta, GA

Goodlad, J (1983) *A Place Called School: Prospects for the future*, McGraw-Hill, New York

Gordon, B (1988) The use of cultural knowledge in the civic education of teachers, in *Civic Education: Its limits and conditions*, ed S D Franzosa, pp 68–98, Prakken Publications, Ann Arbor, MI

Hill, B A (ed) (1982) The civic purposes of education, *Liberal Education*, Special issue, Winter

Jefferson, T (1779) A bill for the more general diffusion of knowledge, in *Crusade Against Ignorance: Thomas Jefferson on education*, ed G Lee (1961), Teachers College Press, New York

Krug, E (1964) *The Shaping of the American High School*, vol 1, University of Wisconsin Press, Madison, WI

Lazerson, M et al (1985) *An Education of Value: The purposes and practices of schools*, Cambridge University Press, Cambridge, UK

Mann, H (1957) *The Republic and the School: Horace Mann on the education of free men*, ed L Cremin, Teachers College Press, New York

National Assessment Governing Board (1999) *Report Card in Civics*, National Assessment Governing Board, Washington, DC

National Commission on Excellence in Education (1983) *A Nation at Risk: The imperative for educational reform*, United States Department of Education, Washington, DC

National Educational Goals Panel (1991) *Goals 2000*, US Government Printing Office, Washington, DC

National Educational Goals Panel (1992) *National Educational Goals Report*, US Government Printing Office, Washington, DC

National Educational Goals Panel (1994) *National Educational Goals Report*, US Government Printing Office, Washington, DC

National Educational Goals Panel (1999) *National Educational Goals Report: Building a nation of learners*, US Government Printing Office, Washington, DC

Newmann, F M (1977) *Building a Rationale for Civic Education*, National Council for the Social Studies, Arlington, VA

Pratte, R (1988) *The Civic Imperative: Examining the need for civic education*, Teachers College Press, New York

Quigley, C N (2000) *Response to Findings of the NAEP 1998 Civics Report Card for the Nation*, Center for Civic Education, Caslabas, CA

Raywid, M A, Tesconi, C A and Warren, D R (1984) *Pride and Promise: Schools of excellence for all the people*, American Educational Studies Association, Westbury, NY

Robbins, C (1920) *The Socialised Recitation*, Henry Holt, New York

Sizer, T (1984) *Horace's Compromise: The dilemma of the American high school*, Houghton Mifflin, Boston

Spring, J (1986) *The American School, 1642–1985: Varieties of historical interpretation of the foundations and development of American education*, Longman, New York

Stanley, M (1983) How to think anew about civic education, *Journal of Teacher Education*, **34** (6)

Tanner, L (1997) *Dewey's Laboratory School: Lessons for today*, Teachers College Press, New York

Torney-Purta, J and Schwille, J (1986) Civic values learned in school: policy and practice in industrialised nations, *Comparative Education Review*, **30** (1), pp 30–49

Tyack, D (1974) *The One Best System: A history of American urban education*, Harvard University Press, Cambridge, MA

Tyack, D and Cuban, L (1995) *Tinkering Toward Utopia: A century of public school reform*, Harvard University Press, Cambridge, MA

US Department of Education (1991) *America 2000*, US Government Printing Office, Washington, DC

US Department of Education, US National Commission on Excellence in Education (1983) *A Nation at Risk: The imperative for educational reform – a report to the nation and the secretary of education*, US Government Printing Office, Washington, DC

Wood, G (1988) Civic education for participatory democracy, in *Civic Education: Its limits and conditions*, ed S D Franzosa, pp 68–98, Prakken Publications, Ann Arbor, MI

Wynne, E A and Ryan, K (1997) *Reclaiming Our Schools: Teaching character, academics and discipline*, Prentice Hall, Upper Saddle River, NJ

Conclusion

Denis Lawton

The structural intention of this *Yearbook* was to look at education, culture and values in a two-dimensional way. The first dimension was the obvious one of place: to what extent can we review in a meaningful way education, values and culture in a number of very different countries? The other dimension slices reality in another way by asking a number of specialists to look at this general area from the point of view of their own discipline or special interest. In addition, most contributors have referred to a third dimension – change over time. In addition we asked Andreas Kazamias to begin the volume with a general overview. Finally, I have the task of discussing, very briefly, the volume as a whole. I will not attempt to summarize each of the chapters but rather to make a few general observations based on what our specialists have discussed.

Although the new century, and the new millennium, was our obvious starting-point, many of our contributors referred back to the Enlightenment as the most significant set of educational ideas in the history of education over the last few hundred years. Why? According to Bierstedt's classic analysis (1979), the Enlightenment was concerned with at least four massive shifts in Western values and value systems: from the supernatural to the natural (or from religion to science); the exaltation of reason, which together with human experience was expected to solve all problems; the belief in the perfectibility of humankind and society and therefore in progress; and finally a humanitarian regard for rights. All that might be seen as the basis of our 'modern' world, but it was far from the end of the story. The reaction against Enlightenment ideas came early in the 19th century with the proliferation of repressive governments after 1815 attempting the restoration of the *ancien régime* as well as a host of conservative publications that criticized Enlightenment thinkers for exaggerating the power of human reason and underestimating the value of traditions that somehow express the wisdom of countless previous generations in ways difficult to analyse. Needless to say, the conservative writers were strongly opposed to such abstract ideas as equality and universal rights. Some, like Burke, were also particularly concerned with the legislative aspects of the French Revolution – including the provision and control of education.

The debate about pre-Enlightenment and post-Enlightenment values has continued ever since, even to the end of the 20th century, with the ongoing disputes about late modernism and postmodernism. The debate is essentially between those who wish to retain or revive a stable social order and those who wish to journey further along the path to a better society –more egalitarian, with greater freedom and happiness. A major difference exists between those who look back to the past as a model of society and those who are optimistic about the possibility of future progress. There were, of course, other strands in the post-Enlightenment history of ideas. Part of the disagreement about late modernity concerns the capitalist Industrial Revolution and the extent to which we can now sensibly talk of post-industrial society, post-Fordism and even post-capitalism. The answer may well be that such terminology is useful – if at all – only when we are careful to specify time and place.

How do these changes in values and ideas relate to developments in education? One clear difference is between those who wish to educate the young to admire the past, not just as cultural heritage but as a model to be strived for, and those who want to use education to enable the young to adjust to future scenarios. Another persisting tension is between collectivism and individualism – but, as Cowen and I outlined in Chapter 1, this is a more complex matter than might be assumed. It is not surprising, then, that we find in our selected countries very different stages of development in the debate about values, culture and education. Some societies are more secularized than others and most (but not all) are more secularized than they used to be. But it seems that there is no such thing as a totally secular society. And at some point on the secularizing route strong anti-materialist tendencies begin to develop within the culture. It seems that there is a need in the human psyche for religious or spiritual values or something like them. Modernity seems so full of paradoxes, tensions and cultural contradictions that human beings seek some kind of meaning – but not necessarily religious meaning. Jo Cairns, in her chapter, quotes the poet Seamus Heaney on the need for 'a search for images and symbols adequate to our predicament'.

I am reluctant to generalize about such complex multi-dimensional trends concerning values and culture, but some kind of coherent statement is usually expected at the end of a volume of this kind. My suggestion is, therefore, that as far as education is concerned there is a tendency for all modern or modernizing countries to be moving in roughly the same general direction (albeit with significant local variations). We can also establish significant milestones, some that have been almost universally accepted, others that are still some distance from the achievement – or even the aspiration – of most countries. I will comment briefly on five of these milestones, starting with the most general and proceeding eventually to the comparatively rare. Examples of all five will be found discussed in more detail in earlier chapters.

The first milestone is that a country will aspire to and perhaps achieve education for all. This will begin with primary education for all, then secondary and eventually higher education or even lifelong education for all. The scope of education at these stages tends to be defined in an unspecific way. At some point compulsion tends to be replaced by 'entitlement'. For example, in most of our case studies there is compulsory education for about 10 years, with few politicians advocating extending the period of compulsion, preferring to use the terminology of rights or entitlement.

The second milestone is the point at which specific curriculum areas are singled out for some degree of priority. Several of our contributors have mentioned education for citizenship and the school responsibility for teaching moral values. At this stage many central authorities begin to be concerned about the ethos of the school. It becomes clear that real education for morality and citizenship can only be acquired by experience, but in many countries schools are repressive and authoritarian institutions allowing little active participation by pupils. Franzosa, in her chapter, reminds us that Dewey alerted us to this problem long ago. At this stage there are embryonic discussions of effectiveness and social ethos or culture, without much progress being made towards improved institutions.

The third stage is where governments begin to talk of the education of the whole person, providing a richer definition than either stage one or stage two, perhaps specifying a list of moral, social, cultural, physical, intellectual, aesthetic and spiritual development as a set of aims. At first, this list of aspects of human development may be unaccompanied by any more specific guidance but that will tend to follow a little later. Once again the problem of the ethos of the school tends to conflict with this aspiration.

The fourth stage is where authorities begin to talk in terms of 'self-directed learning' and the empowerment of students to take responsibility for their own education. This implies a different kind of role for the teacher as well as the achievement of, rather than just an expressed aspiration for, a more educative school environment and ethos. Progress is likely to be slow because to convert aspiration to achievement would involve more in-service education for teachers than most countries want to afford.

A fifth stage may occur that attempts to provide some kind of meaning for life, which was referred to above. Here again the role of the teacher is crucial. Jo Cairns quoted Stewart Sutherland on this topic: 'the problem facing teachers is a very serious one. Unless the society in which they live and work gives some coherent account of what it considers important in human life then teachers have no real framework in which to operate.' Few societies, if any, have yet solved that problem, although there is evidence to suggest that some kinds of school have made considerable progress in that direction when they develop a vision of education that goes beyond the teaching of subjects and preparing the young for the world of work.

It would, of course, be a mistake to envisage these five stages as some kind of inevitable progression. I have already mentioned the importance of local cultural differences, which may accelerate or impede any stage. In addition, there may be 'false gods' that appear from time to time, interrupting the sequence above – if indeed it is a sequence. For example, one kind of false god that has been widespread is the idea of abandoning educational planning and leaving everything to market forces. John Mace in his chapter demonstrated the folly of that belief. Another has been the extreme kind of moral and cultural relativism that has sometimes come close to paralysing the ideals and values on which education depends. A third false god may occur when countries become obsessed with international economic comparisons and believe that education should make them more competitive. This view is frequently accompanied by exaggerated vocationalization of the curriculum resulting in loss of balance: maths and science tend to be prioritized with art, music and literature being neglected. This false god may be reinforced by heightened 'accountability' in which children and teachers are tested and given standards or targets that are assumed to correlate with enhanced efficiency. Even if this assumption were correct, which is extremely unlikely, it would have a distorting effect on the learning processes and the quality of education in the schools. It is no coincidence that those countries that appear to be the most efficient on international comparisons of achievement in maths and science now appear to want to see education in a much broader – less materialistic – way.

Reference

Bierstedt, R (1979) Sociological thought in the 18th century, in *A History of Sociological Analysis*, ed T Bottomore and R Nisbet, Heinemann, London

Burke, E (1910) *(1729–1797), Reflections on the Revolution in France* (with an introduction by AJ Grieve), Dent, London

Index